Self-organised learning

Self-organised learning

Foundations of a conversational
science for psychology

Laurie F. Thomas and E. Sheila Harri-Augstein

Centre for the Study of Human Learning, Brunel University

ROUTLEDGE & KEGAN PAUL

London, Boston, Melbourne and Henley

First published in 1985
by Routledge & Kegan Paul plc

39 Store Street, London WC1E 7DD, England

9 Park Street, Boston, Mass. 02108, USA

464 St Kilda Road, Melbourne,
Victoria 3004, Australia and

Broadway House, Newtown Road,
Henley-on-Thames, Oxon RG9 1EN, England

Set in IBM Press Roman 10 on 12 pt
by Columns of Reading
and printed in Great Britain
by St Edmundsbury Press Ltd
Bury St Edmunds, Suffolk

Library of Congress Cataloging in Publication Data

Thomas, Laurie F.

Self-organised learning.
Bibliography: p.
Includes index.
1. Learning, Psychology of.   2. Helping behavior.
3. Repertory grid technique.   4. Meaning (Psychology).
5. Self-perception.   I. Harri-Augstein, E. Sheila.
II. Title.   [DNLM: 1. Learning.   2. Programmed instruction
—Methods.   3. Psychology, Educational.   LB 1051 T458s]
BF318.T49   1985   153.1'5   85-6791

British Library CIP data also available

ISBN 0 7100 9990 8

In the spirit of George Kelly this book is dedicated to:

All students of the Centre for the Study of Human Learning who have learnt from us and with us and who have challenged and inspired us over the last two decades to create a conversational repertory-grid based technology for self-organised learning.

All those C-Indis, individuals, pairs, groups and institutions who strive for greater awareness of their learning processes and so to construct and reconstruct their destinies,

and

all those practitioners, teachers, trainers, therapists, tutors, counsellors, coaches, custodians and consultants who see their task as enabling others to enhance their capacity to learn, and so to take better control of the direction, quality and content of their living.

Contents

Foreword by Don Bannister   xix

Acknowledgments   xxi

General introduction: the self-organised learner and the repertory grid xxii
   Prospects for learning: strategies for survival   xxii
   Personal meaning and self-organised learning   xxiii
   Who the book is for   xxiv
   The need for a conversational methodology   xxv
   Conversations for self-organised learning   xxvii
   The scope of the book   xxix

1 The personal nature of self-organised learning   1
   What is learning? that we may reflect upon it   1
   T-C as the management of self-organised learning   4
   Experience as a resource for learning   5
   Personal myths of learning   10
   The disabled learner and impersonal learning   14
   The universal need for self-organised learning   16

2 Introducing the repertory grid: elements and constructs   18
   A prelude to the repertory grid   18
   On the meaning of meaning   19
   A technology of the psyche   20
   Content-free procedures   23
   Bill Shard's view of learning   25
   Adam Stewart's view of learning   27
   The 'introducing a topic' technique   28

3 **The construction of personal meaning**   38
  The power of a conversational technology   38
  To represent a system of personal constructs   39
  Eliciting a repertory grid   42
  Identifying the meaning hidden in the grid   49

4 **FOCUSing: the emergent pattern**   57
  Introduction   57
  The hand-FOCUSing technique   58
    FOCUSing the elements: (a) Identifying similarities
    FOCUSing the elements: (b) Element re-ordering
  FOCUSing the constructs: identifying similarities and re-ordering
    the constructs   62
  The FOCUSed grid   66
  The SPACEd FOCUSed grid   68
  Dimensions of personal judgment: using a FOCUSed grid
    to raise awareness in staff appraisal   70

5 **Talkback through a FOCUSed grid**   77
  The FOCUSed repertory grid as a mirror of constructions of
    experience   77
  Understanding the pattern of meaning in a FOCUSed grid   79
  An outline guide to interpreting a FOCUSed grid   81
  The major steps in a 'talkback conversation'   81
  Extracts from 'real' talkback conversations   82
    Introduction   82
    Conversation 1: An Open University student   84
    Conversation 2: A production manager   86

6 **Grid conversations for achieving self-awareness**   92
  On the nature of conversation   92
  On the dangers of offering elements and/or constructs   93
  Stage 1: need negotiation and purpose definition   96
  Stage 2: the topic: deciding upon the nature of the elements   98
  Reflecting stage 2 back on to stage 1   99
  Stage 3: eliciting a repertory grid   101
    (a) Selecting specific elements   101
    (bi) Eliciting constructs: on the nature of construing   102
    (bii) Eliciting constructs: conversational methods   104
    (c) Assigning the elements to the constructs   107
  Reflecting stage 3 back on to stage 2 and stage 1   110
  Stage 4: analysing the grid   112
  Stage 5: talkback through an analysed grid   113
  Stage 6: revising the grid, the topic and/or the purpose   113
  Stage 7: beyond the grid   116

7 **The space within which personal meaning may be represented**   117
The limitations of the FOCUSed display   117
Learning to read the TRIGRID display   123
FOCUSing a grid containing rated (or ranked) responses   127
   Calculating the matrix of difference scores   132
   Clustering the elements   132
   Clustering the constructs   133
SPACE-ing a FOCUSed grid containing ratings or rankings   135
The TRIGRID display showing difference matrices   136
Alternative methods for analysing a grid   139
   Principal component analysis   139
   POLE-MAPS: how construct poles relate to each other   142
'Spaces for meaning': beyond the scope of the grid   145
   The use or mis-use of 'Not Applicables' (NAs)   146
   Sub-grids and super-grids: an alternative to laddering   147
   Sets, networks, hierarchies and heterarchies   148

8 **A PCP approach to perception**   156
Part 1 Perception, skill and learning   156
An apology   156
Perception — a new idea?   156
The perceptual components of all human activity   158
Perception   160
Perception and competance   163
Conversational elicitation of a perceptual grid   164
Skilled and unskilled perceptions: a T-C problem   168
Conclusions   170
   The Indian miniature   170
The authors' construing of skill, competence and creativity   173
Part 2 Perceptual grids   174
Learning to perceive: perceiving to learn   174
Levels in perceptual experience: robots and hierarchical
   organisation   176
A partial taxonomy of perceptual processes   177
The perceptual grid: three grids in one   179
The sense-datum grid   180
The public perception grid   181
The inferential grid   182
The mythologies of skill   183
Using the three perceptual grids   185
PAIRS: a method for re-combining the perceptual grids   185

9 The critical self: conversational self-assessment   187
  Perceiving from within   187
  The critical self   188
    Referents and comment from the outside world   189
    The knotted ones: human components of self-evaluation   191
    The identification of feedback   192
    Self-assessment as a perceptual process   193
    Self-evaluation of the reading process   195
    Moving from the private to the public world of evaluation   199
  Extending the use of the PAIRS technique   200
  DIFF. and CORE   201
  The CHANGE grid: a conversational heuristic for self-
    development   213
  The CHANGE grid conversation   218
    Conversational examples   219
  Conversation: the mind's construction of the mind   224
    Self-assessment: additional grid techniques   226
  Critical selves   236

10 Grid conversations for the sharing of meaning   237
  Part 1 EXCHANGE grids and the process of conversation   237
  Articulating a conversation both as content and process   237
  Agreement, understanding and judgment as exchange of
    meaning   243
  EXCHANGE grids: a basic tool for enabling conversation   246
    The detailed procedure   247
    Introspective reports   253
    Refinements in the EXCHANGE grid technique   253
    General comment   254
  A systematic approach to the creative encounter   260
  *Part 2 Assessment and examinations: a peculiar form of
    conversation*   264
  Examinations and assessment   264
  Examination performance and the examiner's and the learner's
    grids   266
  On the meaning of the mathematics exam questions   270
  The monitoring of tutor-marked assignments   275
  The implications of EXCHANGE of meaning   277

11 Groups and institutions as personal learning systems   282
  The construction, exchange and negotiation of meaning in a
    group   282
  SOCIO-GRIDS: in which elements are shared and constructs
    are personal   283
    The structure of the individual feedback session   288
    Results and conclusions   289
    Follow-up   290
  Negotiating shared elements and shared constructs for a
    group topic   290
  POOL, REFINE and CONSENSUS FRAME   292
    Personal interpretations of the shared language: individual
    CONSENSUS FRAME grids   293
  Exploring and comparing the views of the management group   295
    Comparing two managers' usage of the shared language   295
  SOCIO-NETS in which elements and constructs are shared   298
  The individual as a community of selves   302

**12 The theory and practice of conversational science: tools for
the T-C practitioner**   307
  Learning as an inference from behaviour and experience   307
  Appreciative perspectives on learning   308
  The teaching/learning contract   315
  The seven faces of teaching and learning   318
  Increasing the human capacity for learning   322
  Beyond the grid   325
  STRUCTURES OF MEANING   326
  Conducting LEARNING CONVERSATIONS   328
    Challenging the robot   329
    The need for three related dialogues   329
    The management of learning   331
    Learning managers   332

**Grid tricks: an accessing system to the CSHL reflective learning
technology**   333
  Introduction   333
  Section I On the nature of construing systems   333
  Section II The grid as a conversational tool   335
  Section IIA Conversational grids for self-awareness   335
  Section IIB Grids for conviviality   338
  Section III Beyond the grid   340
  Section IV The CSHL computer programs   341

xii   Contents

Appendix A Applications of the repertory grid   344
  A1.1 A classification of items of personal experience   344
  A1.2 Purposes for which grids have been elicited   350

Appendix B The Centre for the Study of Human Learning   353
  The Centre   353
  Aims   353
  The CSHL reflective learning technology and methodology   354
  Research projects and applications   356
  Workshops and courses   357
  CSHL publications   358

Glossary: The personal structure of meaning of the authors   359
  Glossary   359
  Major Themes   364

Bibliography   372

Index   385

Figures

Figure 2.1	Categorisation of all contents used by members of the man-management course	30
Figure 2.2	Introducing a topic: a procedural guide	36
Figure 3.1	A two-dimensional representation of a simple construct system	41
Figure 3.2	Assigning elements to construct poles	46
Figure 3.3	Bill Shard's raw grid	48
Figure 3.4	Eliciting a repertory grid: an algorithm	50
Figure 3.5	Similar construing of two learning experiences	51
Figure 3.6	Mick's raw grid	55
Figure 3.7	Ben's raw mathematical grid	55
Figure 3.8	Sybil's raw grid	56
Figure 4.1	Identifying element similarities	59
Figure 4.2	Element similarity matrix	59
Figure 4.3	Element resorting sequence	60
Figure 4.4	Identifying construct similarities	63
Figure 4.5	Construct similarity matrix	63
Figure 4.6	Construct resorting sequence	64
Figure 4.7	Bill Shard's SPACEd FOCUSed grid	67
Figure 4.8	Mr Donaldson's grid — layout form	71
Figure 4.9	Mr Donaldson's raw grid	72
Figure 4.10	Mr Donaldson's SPACEd FOCUSed grid	73
Figure 4.11	FOCUSing a repertory grid: an algorithm	74
Figure 4.12	SPACE-ing a FOCUSed grid: an algorithm	75
Figure 5.1	Mick's SPACEd FOCUSed grid	80
Figure 5.2	Talkback through a FOCUSed grid: an algorithm	83
Figure 5.3	Gwen's purposes-for-reading grid	85
Figure 6.1	Simple version of the grid conversation: an algorithm	94
Figure 6.2	Iterative grid conversation: an algorithm	115
Figure 7.1	The triangle of difference diagram superimposed on Bill Shard's FOCUSed grid	128

Figure 7.2	Adam Stewart's FOCUSed grid	129
Figure 7.3	Dr Tisch's bosses grid	130
Figure 7.4	Dr Tisch's jobs grid	131
Figure 7.5	A FOCUSed grid (with rated responses)	135
Figure 7.6	A SPACEd FOCUSed grid	136
Figure 7.7	SPACEd FOCUSed grid showing all relationships	140
Figure 7.8	TRIGRID: an algorithm	141
Figure 7.9	POLE-MAP matrix	143
Figure 7.10	Ms Shop assistant's grid with 'Not Applicables'	147
Figure 7.11	Categorisation of constructs from maths exam questions	150
Figure 7.12	Table of categories	155
Figure 8.1	Table A	160
Figure 8.2	Table B	160
Figure 8.3	Twelve postcards	166
Figure 8.4	An Indian miniature	171
Figure 8.5	Perceptual grids: an algorithm	184
Figure 9.1	Evaluative grid: an algorithm	195
Figure 9.2	Sentence-reading patterns for a 'good' reader	197
Figure 9.3	Fred D'Arcy's FOCUSed grid with verbal labels	198
Figure 9.4	Simple PAIRS: an algorithm	201
Figure 9.5	Construct-by-construct PAIRS: an algorithm	202
Figure 9.6	The double grid: ratings on two successive grids	203
Figure 9.7	The difference matrix	203
Figure 9.8A	Revealing the CORE grid: step one	205
Figure 9.8B	Revealing the CORE grid: step two	205
Figure 9.8C	Revealing the CORE grid: step three	206
Figure 9.8D	Revealing the CORE grid: step four	206
Figure 9.8E	Revealing the CORE grid: step five	207
Figure 9.8F	Revealing the CORE grid: step six	207
Figure 9.8G	Revealing the CORE grid: step seven	208
Figure 9.8H	Revealing the CORE grid: step eight	208
Figure 9.8I	Revealing the CORE grid: step nine	209
Figure 9.8J	Revealing the CORE grid: step ten	209
Figure 9.8K	The CORE grid	210
Figure 9.9	DIFF. – the difference grid: an algorithm	211
Figure 9.10	CORE grid: an algorithm	212
Figure 9.11	A CHANGE grid for a manager	214
Figure 9.12	The CHANGE grid conversation: an algorithm	215
Figure 9.13	Calculating the CHANGE grid: an algorithm	216
Figure 9.14	Talkback through the CHANGE grid: an algorithm	217
Figure 9.15	Gwen's CHANGE grid on purposes for reading	220
Figure 9.16	Awareness-raising heuristic for personal learning	225
Figure 9.17	Kenny's dyadic grid	229
Figure 9.18	Two verbally similar grids	230

Figure 9.19   Matching all Cs with all Cs   231
Figure 9.20   The double grid, Cs constant, Es changeable   231
Figure 9.21(i)   Jane's acquaintance grid   233
Figure 9.21(ii)   Dave's acquaintance grid   234
Figure 9.21(iii)   Jane and Dave's PAIRS grid   235
Figure 10.1   Conversation as content and process   241
Figure 10.2   Observational analysis of conversation   242
Figure 10.3(i)   A's completed grid   248
Figure 10.3(ii)   A's empty grid to be completed by B   249
Figure 10.3(iii)   B's version of A's grid   250
Figure 10.3(iv)   The difference grid   251
Figure 10.3(v)   The re-organised difference grid   252
Figure 10.4(i)   Mick's FOCUSed grid   255
Figure 10.4(ii)   Father's FOCUSed grid   255
Figure 10.4(iii)   Auntie Ada's FOCUSed grid   256
Figure 10.4(iv)   Father's version of Mick's grid   256
Figure 10.4(v)   Difference grid: Father on Mick   257
Figure 10.5   Summary of EXCHANGE   257
Figure 10.6   The EXCHANGE grid: an algorithm   259
Figure 10.7   The creative encounter: an algorithm   263
Figure 10.8   Raw grids to be PAIRed   266
Figure 10.9   The clustering of constructs in two PAIRed grids   267
Figure 10.10   The marking and construing of 'O' level essays   268
Figure 10.11   The marking and construing of laboratory reports   269
Figure 10.12   Preferences for mathematics command words   271
Figure 10.13   'Fred's' grid of command words   271
Figure 10.14   Cluster hierarchy of constructs   272
Figure 10.15   Construct weightings   273
Figure 10.16   'Fred's' grid showing weighted construct responses   273
Figure 10.17   'Fred's' rankings of command words compared with
                   the results from the weighted grid   274
Figure 10.18   Distribution of Spearman's Rho for 18 students   274
Figure 10.19   Network of three grids   280
Figure 10.20   POOL and EXCHANGE: an algorithm   281
Figure 11.1   Example of a second appraisal grid   284
Figure 11.2   Simplified MODE grid showing which managers
                   contributed which constructs   286
Figure 11.3   SOCIO-NETS   287
Figure 11.4   Constructs categorised by appraisal form criteria   291
Figure 11.5   Mr Production's CONSENSUS FRAME grid   294
Figure 11.6   Agreement and disagreement on Es   296
Figure 11.7   Agreement and disagreement on Cs   297
Figure 11.8   SOCIO-NET display of 'quality'   299
Figure 11.9   Community of selves   302
Figure 11.10   The CSHL repertory grid communication technology   306

Figure 12.1   Two perspectives of learning   310
Figure 12.2   The four perspectives of teaching/learning   311
Figure 12.3   The eight perspectives of teaching/learning   311
Figure 12.4   The work perspective of teaching/learning   312
Figure 12.5(i)   Perspectives on learning   314
Figure 12.5(ii)   315
Figure 12.6   The teacher interpreting the resource   318
Figure 12.7   The teacher interpreting the resource and the
                   learner questioning   319
Figure 12.8   The teacher as resource   319
Figure 12.9   The teacher as resource organiser/designer/minder   320
Figure 12.10   The teacher helping the learner to reflect on self
                   as person   320
Figure 12.11   The teacher helping the learner to reflect using
                   personal experience as resource   321
Figure 12.12   The teacher helping the learner to explore and
                   experiment   321
Figure 12.13   Learning-to-learn reflecting on the learning
                   process   322
Figure 12.14   The capacity for learning   323
Figure 12.15   The learning trough   330

Activities

Activity 1.1	Reflecting on how topics influence learning	7
Activity 1.2	Reflecting on how clients influence learning	8
Activity 1.3	Reflecting on how institutions influence learning	8
Activity 1.4	Reflecting on how methods influence learning	9
Activity 1.5	Reflecting on how pedagogic authorities influence learning	9
Activity 1.6	Identifying your personal myths about your capacity for learning	12
Activity 2.1	Eliciting personal constructs	21
Activity 2.2	Constructing personally significant learning events	23
Activity 2.3	Elements and constructs	37
Activity 3.1	Completing a repertory grid	53
Activity 4.1	Hand-FOCUSing a grid	76
Activity 4.2	SPACE-ing a FOCUSed grid	76
Activity 4.3	Eliciting a grid of your own	76
Activity 4.4	Hand-FOCUSing with some talkback	76
Activity 5.1	Talkback through a FOCUSed grid	90
Activity 6.1	Negotiating needs and defining a topic and a purpose	98
Activity 6.2	Selecting the element type and revising the topic and purpose if necessary	100
Activity 6.3	Eliciting specific elements	102
Activity 6.4	Eliciting constructs	109
Activity 6.5	Reviewing the raw grid	111
Activity 6.6	Talking back through the analysed grid	113
Activity 6.7	A grid conversation	116
Activity 7.1	Add TRIGRID matrices to a FOCUSed grid	139
Activity 7.2 to 7.x	Explore the patterns revealed by TRIGRID matrices	139
Activity 8.1	Exploring perception	158
Activity 8.2	Eliciting perceptual constructs – auditory	162
Activity 8.3	Eliciting perceptual constructs – tactile	162
Activity 8.4	Exercising non-verbal constructs	162

Activity 8.5	FOCUSing non-verbal constructs	163
Activity 8.6	Talkback through a non-verbal grid	163
Activity 8.7	Exploring the descriptive and control functions of perception	164
Activity 8.8	Identifying a system of perceptual constructs	168
Activity 8.9	A taste panel	169
Activity 8.10	An Indian miniature grid	170
Activity 10.1	Conceptual analysis of conversations	241
Activity 10.2	Observational analysis of conversations	242
Activity 10.3	Carl Rogers's conditions of learning	246
Activity 10.4	Revealing an 'examiners' construct system	276
Activity 10.5	Comparing assessors	277
Activity 10.6	Exchanging evaluative systems	277
Activity 10.7	Improving performance by knowing how to evaluate it	277
Activity 11.1	Exploring the different selves within	304
Activity 11.2	Exploring topics from different points of view	305

Foreword

This book performs a kindly, necessary and powerful act: it rehabilitates the concept of *learning*.

The long decades of Behaviourism in psychology promoted 'learning' to the status of a dominant concept but defined it in a way which made it repressive when applied to education and unfruitful when used in psychological theorising and research. The idea of learning as consisting of essentially mechanical changes in task performance, brought about by practice, is characterised by that most fatal of flaws in an idea: it is uninteresting. Trying to give life to this central notion of learning by attaching to it half-defined bits and pieces — ideational learning, incidental learning, selective learning, learning set, discriminative learning and so forth — helped keep boredom at bay but failed to provide us with a pathway for exploring and understanding human experience in terms of 'learning'. The human subject remained a pale and shadowy figure, lost between the stimulus (as defined by the psychologist) and the response (as defined by the psychologist); an 'organism' without self-possessed point or purpose.

Thomas and Harri-Augstein would acknowledge forebears in offering a dynamic vision of learning, Fred Bartlett for one, but their particular contribution, in this book, is vividly to redefine learning in terms of the way we elaborate structures of meaning and to offer rich tools to aid that elaboration. The tools which they offer are not only brilliant techniques but represent operational definitives of creative learning. Many of them are imaginative developments of repertory grid method, as originally offered by George Kelly, and in developing it they have substantially extended our understanding of what can be done with the computer, by way of using it not simply as a galloping abacus but as a reflective companion.

The book's central model of learning is the conversation — perhaps our oldest, richest and most particularly human way of learning. In using this model, they cast light on much of the everyday, yet somehow mysterious, experience we have of conversation, including its dual nature. We reflect to ourselves as well as exchanging with others, so that two conversations, one internal and one external, seem always to be taking place.

The book integrates and sings a harmonious song about areas that have traditionally been treated as separate and barely communicating segments. Thus, the way in which the authors discuss, explore and experiment with learning, cannot meaningfully be filed in the pigeon holes of 'cognition' or 'motivation' or 'emotion', though no doubt the book will be duly categorised in such ways because historically we have splintered our image of the whole person.

A further set of distinctions over which the authors ride rough shod, on their way to larger goals, are the distinctions between teaching, training and therapy. These are now old and entrenched distinctions to which we have attached different psychologies, different professions and different languages. Thomas and Harri-Augstein argue that when we teach a child to read, or train someone to operate a capstan lathe, or work as a psychotherapist with the psychologically distressed, we are (or ought to be) enabling them to become self-organised learners and that self-organised learning is both the pathway to particular 'skills' and is also that very self-mastery which lies at the heart of creative change.

Not only do the authors elaborate Kelly's methods, they give life to many of the ideas of personal construct theory. The book seems to begin its journey from the old boundaries of 'learning experiments' as described by Kelly in *The Psychology of Personal Constructs* (p. 77): 'the problem of learning is not merely one of determining how many or what kinds of reinforcements fix a response, or how many nonreinforcements extinguish it, but rather, how does the subject phrase the experience, what recurrent themes does he hear, what movements does he define, and what validations of his predictions does he reap? When a subject fails to meet the experimenter's expectations, it may be inappropriate to say that "he has not learned"; rather, one might say that what the subject learned was not what the experimenter expected him to learn'.

The book is necessarily reflexive. Its writing and the twenty years of experiment and exploration upon which it is based, is a monumental demonstration of self-organised learning.

D. Bannister

Acknowledgments

The authors are especially indebted to Don Bannister for advising, cajolling and supporting us to finish this volume. It was begun during Laurie's sabbatical in 1973. In the intervening years much time has been given to supervise post-graduate students and to carry out our many action research projects in education, industry, defence, and government. The manuscript has gone through a chequered history; it has been lost, stolen, plagiarised, split into two volumes, re-written, revised and finally pruned into the current volume. Without Don it would have remained as a series of CSHL papers, and as the guts of the published works of others, mainly postgraduates of the Centre.

The individual contributions of our students are acknowledged in the Bibliography. In particular we are indebted to Frazer Reid and Steven Mendoza for their outstanding contributions to the original development of FOCUS, the DEMON-PEGASUS interactive grid elicitation computer program and the EXCHANGE grid procedures developed in the late 1960s. A special thanks to them and to David Pendleton, Len Chapman, Roger Beard, Nigel Hastings, Don McLeod, Ranulph Glanville, Alan Radley, Ken Eason, Norman Chell and Graham Crosby, for their loyalty, dedication to the Centre's ideals and friendship.

Finally, we wish to thank all students and members of the CSHL who have participated in the Centre seminars and assisted us in testing out our techniques, kits and computer programs in the Centre's action research projects and in their own studies. Thank you also to John and Tara for their loyalty and invaluable assistance in preparing the manuscript.

General introduction: the self-organised learner and the repertory grid

Prospects for learning: strategies for survival

From birth each person strives for understanding — grows and develops — reaches for greater awareness — constructs personal worlds — achieves at least some needs and purposes — invents new patterns of thoughts and feelings — acts to validate these — builds new personal-worlds — habituates into stable routines — survives — declines — lives through personal and social crises — adapts — struggles to be reborn — and repeats variations upon these themes. Pairs, families, informal groups, private enterprises and public institutions go through analogous cycles. This process of action, experience, setbacks, growth, death and re-birth is learning.

The ubiquity of learning is taken for granted as a characteristic of our species. But what we learn, and how we learn it, is the question. What becomes of us need not be merely the result of Darwinian chance and happenstance. Some individuals, groups and institutions construct their experience, reflect upon their constructions and converse with others to influence their own destinies. It is 'learning' which has earned us our place on top of the evolutionary tree and it is freedom-to-learn which enables us to rise above the constraints of the gene pool. How freedom is built into the human condition recurs as an issue in every area and node of life. Examples can be endlessly multiplied: from the unemployed to the boardroom, from the home to the hospital, from the sportsfield to the battlefield, from centres for research to the shopfloor, from weapon guidance to marriage guidance. Every form of human endeavour is another opportunity for learning.

Living is always an opportunity for learning; but how people use it depends upon what they bring to each event and what they make of each experience. The capacity to learn from experience and to take control of the direction, quality and content of one's learning is central both to mental health and to making the best use of educational, job and life opportunities.

Learning may be self-organised or it may be organised by others. Learning how to learn is not the same as successfully submitting to being taught. Self-organised learners are purposive and can bring their thoughts, feelings and actions into consciousness; creating an awareness in which learning is alive, relevant and viable. Other organised learning inevitably leads to de-personalised knowing, which if this continues will eventually accumulate into boredom and dissociation from the topic.

In a society which is reviewing its deepest social attitudes and institutions, and is facing an accelerating rate of change in its economic and industrial structures, the ability to participate in these changes, influencing them and adapting to them, depends upon a capacity for self-organised learning. We have created a society which demands greater skill in manipulating symbols, sophisticated machines, bio-engineering technologies and complex financial and legal systems; more and more has to be learned to a higher level of precision and performance. Today's technology has extended space and time to hitherto unimaginable limits and amplified our sensory capacities. Accurate and permanent records in visual, auditory and tactile forms have been evolved. The products of our learning have changed our way of life. The artifacts which we ourselves create feed back into the evolving mindpool creating an expanding process of cultural change. The exponential rate of change in today's world is making ever-increasing demands on human learning and today's thoughts will become the chains of tomorrow's mind unless we face the problems of re-learning and continuing to learn throughout our lives. Freedom to construct our personal destinies by creatively adapting to change requires an ever-increasing capacity for learning. To achieve this, learning has to become a consciously growing process rather than a ubiquitous part of life.

Personal meaning and self-organised learning

Many commentators have observed that young children have a natural capacity for learning, but that in the majority of the population this is stifled by their experiences in formal education. The pessimistic assumptions about human potential held by teachers and others contribute to the gradual extinction of this spontaneous self-organised capacity to learn. Their pessimistic models of how learning takes place leads them to act in ways which disrupt and inhibit spontaneously creative learning. The aptitude, personality and intelligence tests of the psychologist add a pseudo-scientific respectability to this formal, authoritarian and essentially product-oriented approach.

It has often been suggested that schools need only to encourage personal learning for them to automatically produce self-organised learners. But a non-interventionist policy is not enough, as demonstrated by the demise of the discovery-based curriculum. Most educational institutions offer only restricted opportunities for generating adequate learning conversations which facilitate the growth of self-organised learning. Human beings of all ages readily habituate into stable but sub-optimal strategies of learning. In the past these have allowed them to get by, but as demands for learning increase, many find they are unable to cope. Failure leads to negative attitudes which combine with inadequate skills to produce the all-too-familiar experience of educational inadequacy. On the other hand, optimistic assumptions about human learning combined with a reflective awareness-raising methodology can enable teachers, trainers and others to support and guide the development of self-organised learners. Learning naturally and spontaneously from experience derives from the creation of personal meaning. We have found it useful to define learning as:

> The construction, reconstruction, negotiation and exchange of personally significant, relevant and viable meaning.

If learning is to be an enriching experience, the meanings that emerge must be personally significant in some part of the person's life. The viability of these meanings depends on how richly the individual incorporates them into personal experience. They must prove useful and effective in mediating future trans-actions. The process of learning how to learn provides individuals with skills for conversing with the cultural mindpool in active, personally meaningful terms. In becoming more aware of this process people can increase their capacity for learning.

Who the book is for

This book is aimed at three groups of reader. Firstly, *a lay group* composed of people who feel, no matter how fuzzily, that they could do and be more than they are. It is for those of all ages, nationalities, positions and pursuits in life who wish to increase their capacity for learning. We are each ultimately respon-sible for what we become. We may construct ourselves in many ways: stupidly and dogmatically if we remain the blind and dependent prisoners of our past assumptions; or joyously and creatively if we can find the freedom within ourselves so to do. Anybody can, by putting aside time and making the effort, begin to explore how they think and feel about their existance and endeavours. The techniques offered and explained throughout the book are content-free procedures which will aid this process; they work equally well in all areas of human experience.

Whilst the book is designed to be used by pairs and small groups, readers can use two-thirds of it on their own. The last four chapters require more than one person since they introduce techniques which are designed to increase our capacity to share personal experience as a basis for learning. This tech-nology can be used by any self-help group to enable its members to increase their individual and their shared capacity for learning.

The second group of readers for whom the book is intended is that com-prising those who have entered a career, job or profession, the purpose of which is to help others learn. *Teachers* from primary school to university, who are interested not only in presenting their subjects but also with how it is learned, will find that these techniques can transform their teaching. *Industrial and commercial trainers* who are concerned with learning processes which can change attitudes and increase skill and competence can use the ideas to design more effective training methods. *Tutors* who are not quite sure how to set about tutoring someone sensitively and creatively will find guidelines in these pages. *Therapists* are offered a flexible conversational technology which will enable them to systematically explore issues which are otherwise difficult to probe. *Counsellors* will find techniques for quickly and effectively getting to the heart of a client's problem. *Coaches* will find here methods for exploring those questions of personal perception and judgment which are crucial to the success of their clients but with which they often find it difficult to get to grips. *Custodians* who are concerned for their charges' future will find techniques here for initiating and sustaining a conversation which can lead to fruitful change. Finally *Consultants* who feel that they are helping individuals, groups and institutions to grow will find these techniques rapidly becoming some of the tools of their trade. All these, and any other profession such as doctors, lawyers or architects who might also conceive of their purpose as 'enabling others to increase their personal awareness' will find this book useful.

A final specialist group of intended readers are *psychologists* who are interested in a repertory grid-based technology presented within a 'conversational science' paradigm. This is not only useful as a systematic method for making personal meaning explicit, but also points in a direction for the development of 'hard tools for soft psychologists'. Psychological tool-making need no longer be restricted to the laboratory and to the measurement of 'individual differences', but can contribute to the growing science of humanistic psychology.

The need for a conversational methodology

At first, one of the most puzzling features of psychological research is that things are not what they are claimed to be. Nine times out of ten what is designated a theory of learning is concerned to show how a teacher's (or experimenter's) actions appear to bring about changes in a learner's (or animal's) behaviour. Such explanations are theories of instruction. They are theories about how to produce impersonal learning in others. For us, a theory of learning must be concerned with how learners self-organise their own behaviour and experience to produce changes, which they themselves value. This definition of a theory of person-centred learning allows us to look again at theories of teaching and/or instruction. The chief advocate of trainer-organised learning has for the past forty years been B. F. Skinner. Others such as R. Mager have developed training by objectives. C. Rogers, the originator of client-centred therapy, studied the conditions which a therapist, teacher, tutor, trainer, counsellor, coach, custodian or consultant must create, if they are to enable self-organised learning in others. Rogers identifies 'unconditional positive regard', 'empathy' and 'congruence' as necessary conditions for therapeutic conversation. This approach is nearer to the spirit of this book than that of Skinner and

Mager but it still falls short of addressing the learner directly. Rogers's concepts of 'flowering' and 'growth' reveal a belief that when the facilitator can produce the right conditions each and any of us will learn. But the enhancement of the capacity to learn requires more than this. It requires techniques for making explicit the person's own constructions of the world, so that they may reflect upon them.

Skinner's position is based on the assumption that psychology and training will best be served by recruiting the methods of the traditional sciences into our pursuit of an understanding of human beings. Let us designate this position the 'physical science' paradigm. It assumes that the scientist theorises about other people and systematically tests, improves and develops his or her theory by carrying out experiments on them. The scientist may converse with the subject to obtain her or his good will. But the subject remains the uncomprehending object of the scientist's theories and experiments. All responsibility for explanations lies with the scientist. The subjects' explanations are merely 'verbal data'.

Rogers's position is rather different. He believes that the only valid or useful explanation of the client's experience and behaviour is that offered by the client. This is not to say that the client's initial explanations are true, but merely acknowledges them as the only valid starting point for an exploration by the client into their own process. Let us designate this a 'personal science' paradigm. This paradigm is based on the belief that people must understand and thus explain themselves and that the role of the practitioner is to create the conditions in which this may happen.

A third theoretical and methodological paradigm is more suited to human beings' search for a better understanding of the human condition. This 'conversational science' paradigm is based on the belief that no one can know themselves unaided; nor can they exploit their infinite potential by merely being facilitated by a non-directive practitioner. The unique attribute of people is that they can converse. They can pool their experience and even store it in some externally recorded form. They can identify individual needs. They can form into groups to formulate and pursue mutually relevant purposes. They can even invent more flexible forms of institution within which to work, play or live together.

If co-operation within pairs, groups and institutions is to form the basis for learning, for self-organised learning and for enabling people to increase their capacity for learning, then the process must be truly conversational. Conversation implies that whilst meaning is shared, each participant remains free to accept, reject and/or reconstruct the shared meanings. They can invent new meanings. All these are added to the potential for conversation.

Thus the 'conversational science' paradigm recognises that each person is a separate node of personal meaning; but that people can communicate and therefore influence each other. Such influence is not one of direct 'cause and effect' since each person has the potential for self-organisation. A conversational technology accepts people as full participants using their unique position as observer of their own experience. The repertory grid is purpose built for use within this paradigm. It was invented by George Kelly.

Kelly's original statement offers elegant form to a model of man which embodies this conversational, people-centred approach in psychology. His Personal Construct Psychology identifies individual constructions of experience as the source of a person's behaviour and then reconstrued behaviour as the test-bed for a person's constructions. Kelly fashioned his own experience including that as psychotherapist and teacher into a statement which is specific, coherent and comprehensive. He summarised his position in a fundamental postulate and ten corollaries. These warrant the description of 'scientific theory' as that term is used by the more rigorous exponents of the philosophy of science. This is uncommon in psychology where the term 'theory' is applied to almost any attempt at explanation and where the expression 'scientific theory' has for too long been associated with physical instrumentation and with a non-pheno-menological or anti-experiential interpretation of repeatability.

The form given by Kelly to his model of man is by its very nature content-free. It may be inhabited by any system of constructions which would constitute 'a person'. Indeed, we would argue that it may be animated by any system of constructions which would constitute a living organism. The potency of Kelly's construct system is that it offers not only a theory but also the beginnings of an integral and systematic methodology. To claim that Kelly's theory and repertory grid technique mark a watershed in social science comparable to Copernicus and the telescope in natural science, may not appear historically so outrageous as it now does to many contemporary psychologists. Together the theory and method contain an embryo of a new breed of aids for navigating the psyche, and for exploring and charting personal, inter-personal and social space. New content-free psychological tools are being invented and basic design principles are beginning to emerge. Cyberneticians and computer engineers developing expert systems and knowledge engineering are inventing ways of representing, storing and transmitting knowledge. Our approach is concerned with developing a technology which can represent personal meaning in ways which enable reflection, review and effective transformation of the quality of human experience and performance. A major purpose of this book is to introduce and explain that part of our technology which has grown out of the repertory grid.

Conversations for self-organised learning

Learning-to-learn in a free and creative way is an intellectually challenging but emotionally difficult enterprise. It involves clear-sightedly using the widest range of learning resources. Most people are almost totally unaware of how they attribute personal meaning to the events, objects, activities and people in their personal worlds. Self-organisation consists in the ability to converse with oneself about one's own learning processes and to observe, search, analyse, formulate, review, judge, decide and act on the basis of such creative encounters. This involves as much feeling as thought. Unaided, most people are not able to generate effective learning conversations with themselves or with others.

Experimental psychologists constructing theories in their meaning-isolated laboratories have largely ignored the simple truth that it is the meaning attributed to each event, not the event itself, which influences a person's reactions to it. It is the personal meaning which becomes the personal cause. Actions and subsequent events represent the 'effects' of this meaning, as it plays out in a given situation. The construction of *personal experience* is prior. This process is essentially conversational. An awareness of this process demands an awareness of a meta-conversation about learning.

An individual, a pair, a group or an institution can each become the focus of a learning conversation. Such 'conversational individuals' (C-indis) are each and all capable of self-organised learning.

A series of tools for reflecting on our own experience and sharing in the experience of others is systematically offered and explained. These techniques can be seen to build together into the solid base of an attractive conversational technology. This can only be properly appreciated through using it. Activities offered in each chapter offer the reader a guide for obtaining this experience. The potential of these tools has already inspired a few to steal some of them unacknowledged. The authors invite the reader to acknowledge their true sources and to join them in the more rewarding enterprise of openly developing, elaborating, refining and transforming this technology into an ever more effective means for increasing our capacity to learn. This technology can enable any individual or group to self-help themselves towards achieving a greater capacity for self-organised learning. It is also flexible, adaptable and powerful enough to offer a whole new vista of opportunities to any profession or enterprise whose purpose it is to help others to learn.

Despite many strident new claims, and despite much clamouring and protestation to the contrary, most of the approaches which use terms like 'independent learning', 'self-paced learning', 'independent study skills', 'autonomous learning' and so on . . . misrepresent what they are about. Most of them are about successfully submitting to be taught. They are about how to accept instruction at a distance or how to rote learn some of the tricks and short-cuts which those who have already been through the system have developed for themselves. These methods may work as stop gaps in the short term, but they have little or nothing to do with effectively taking control of your own learning destiny. These imitative techniques do not confront the issues involved in 'learning from experience', nor in continuing to learn 'on the job' or 'in life' once the stimulus and guidance of the teacher, the trainer or the therapist has disappeared.

Self-organised learners have the inner freedom and the skills to realistically identify the learning resources available to them, to define their own learning purposes in relation to these resources, be they naturally occurring or organised by institutions offering education, training or therapy. It is the self-organised learner who can selectively best make use of the tips and potted experience, the tricks and occasional insights which are often so initially attractive and so rapidly disappointing to the disabled or dependent learner. Self-organisation enables them to escape the dangers of:

(a) the outraged rebellion which is merely the reverse side of an over-dependence;
(b) of going it alone with all the brutality and dour results of the fictional self-made man or woman;
(c) the dependent internally alienated existence awaiting all those who really do merely submit to being taught.

The scope of the book

Constructing personal meaning in a clear-sighted and a positive way and creatively negotiating shared meaning with others in the habitats of home, work, education and society is a very different enterprise to coping with and struggling through a dogmatic system of public knowledge. The ability to take better control of the direction, quality and content of our lives is central to mental health and to making the best use of educational, life and job opportunities. At a superficial level this is widely acknowledged, but as yet education is only fumbling toward an effective methodology by which this can be achieved. Diminishing educational resources, open learning systems, youth training schemes and retraining are challenging educators to reconsider their myths about educational aims and teaching practice. Learning creatively through personal experience has to be formally recognised, systematically studied, valued, and expertly managed.

This book attempts to trace out three basic principles and seven themes concerned with enabling personal learning and the sharing of personal meaning.

The three principles are:

1. Real personal learning depends upon an ability to use oneself as a test-bed for personal validity and viability. The construction of internal referents is primary. External criteria, normative standards, and assessment by others are secondary. Thus the quality of learning becomes defined within the person's own evaluative systems rather than judged against the criteria arrived at by 'experts'.
2. The dynamics of self-organised learning depends upon an ability to monitor the construction and reconstruction of personal meaning over time. The development, expansion, modification and refinement of our personal models of the world can thus be systematically regulated and appreciated. Inadequate monitoring leads to inappropriate models and this can be viewed as disruptions to personal growth.
3. Shared meaning as against public knowledge must be truly negotiated. Individuals, pairs, groups and institutions can each become conversational entities

capable of adaptive, organised learning. Such conversational networks construct their own viability and validity and thus exhibit a capacity for creative and flexible growth.

The themes may be outlined as follows:

1. In an ideal world the primary purpose of teachers, trainers and therapists would be to enable clients to learn more effectively and to increase their capacity for learning.
2. This ideal purpose is often not appreciated and may be in direct contradiction to the ways in which the practitioners see their job. The more explicit and practitioner-controlled the instruction or the treatment, the easier it is for the client whilst the practitioner is present, but the more difficult it is for such clients when the practitioner is no longer there, since they are inevitably unprepared for the need to continue learning on their own.
3. Special awareness-raising techniques are required to help people to become more effective and self-organised learners. These techniques are designed to enable people to reflect on their expressed or unexpressed thoughts, feelings and actions as these form part of, or contribute to, learning.
4. As they become more aware of themselves as learners people can begin to take control of their own learning. Conversational techniques are required to enable this to happen and to support and guide the learner through the processes of change.
5. The process of becoming self-organised is the development of an ability to conduct such learning conversations with oneself.
6. An important resource for learning is other people. Special awareness-raising techniques may be necessary to help people learn how to exchange experience. Networks of such creative conversations for learning can convert a pair, a group or an institution into an effective learning system. If it can reflect on its own process, it can conduct a learning conversation with itself and the system becomes self-organised.
7. By analogy to the creatively communicating network of self-organised learners we come round full circle to illuminate how any individual may become more fully functioning by recognising that each of us is a 'community of selves'. When released and free to converse with one another these selves all add to the quality of our inner life and to the effectiveness of our outer activities.

The contents of each chapter may be summarised as follows:

Chapter 1 Attempts to get at the core issues of personal meaning and explores how this relates to public knowledge, artifacts of human culture, experience and endeavour. Art, science, technology, religion and social systems have produced artifacts which represent a store-house of the most enduring systems of public meaning, the mindpool of human cultures. It defines personal learning by contrasting it with impersonal, public or alienated learning. It explores

the idea that it is the process of self-organisation, of taking effective responsibility for one's own learning, which makes knowledge, skills and attitudes
truly personal. Self-organised learning is seen as the process of constructing
personally relevant and viable meanings.

Chapter 2 Explores how, by reflecting upon significant items in our own experience, we may gradually become aware of how we learn. The process of elicitation of items of experience is itself part of reflective learning.

Chapters 3, 4 and 5 Explain and demonstrate how the repertory grid technique
may be used first to elicit personal meanings and then to reflect upon patterns
of meaning which have been unappreciated before they were externally
represented. The process of eliciting a grid is explained, and a simple method
('FOCUS') for revealing the patterns of meaning hidden within the raw grid is
explained step by step. Then, the process of talking someone back through the
implications of their FOCUSed grid is explained and illustrated. The reflective
process starts with the elicitation of elements and constructs and moves on to
feedback the FOCUSed grid, offering reflection at a deeper structure of personal
meaning.

Chapter 6 Summarises the reflective use of single grids and reveals the need for
a conversational approach. This illustrates the fundamental difference between
self-organised learning and the current practice of much teaching, training and
therapy. The conversational method is explained with the FOCUSed grid as
the tool for purposeful learning activities. The 'learning conversation' in its
embryonic form is developed here. Having established the idea that the construction of personal meaning is the essential ingredient of effective learning,
alternate methods for representing systems of meaning in space and time need
to be considered.

Chapter 7 Expands and elaborates on how such meaning may be represented
and how such representations enable or inhibit reflection. Other dimensions
of reflection are considered and the TRIGRID technique is introduced as a
more precise and flexible reflective learning tool.

Chapter 8 Suggests that the process of perception, the means by which we attribute meaning to the stuff of our senses, should be of much more central concern
in education, training and therapy. One mechanism that produces the robot-
learner is the unquestionableness of perception which gives the illusion of
objective knowledge. This chapter takes perception apart so that one may reflect
upon it as part of the process of construction of personal meaning. The PERCEP-
TUAL grid is introduced, explained and demonstrated. Procedures for conducting learning conversations about perceptual and judgmental organisations are
introduced. Some of perception is not descriptive. Its contributions control
information and this can be enhanced in the development of skilled behaviour.

Chapter 9 Leads on to the idea of the EVALUATE grid which allows us to explore the processes of subjective judgment. Methods for comparing one grid with another are explained and illustrated. The idea of self-assessment is explored and methods for reflecting upon this process are illustrated. The CHANGE grid uses these techniques to examine and reflect upon how our thoughts and feelings change with time. The CHANGE grid enables the learner to examine learning in personal terms without recourse to the intentions of the teacher, trainer or therapist.

Chapter 10 Returns to the idea that all learning is conversational. It puts forward a model of the conversational exchange process and shows how a series of techniques under the general heading of EXCHANGE grids can be used to enhance the quality and effectiveness of interpersonal communication. Whilst Chapter 6 uses conversational methods for eliciting and reflecting on individual grids, Chapter 10 uses grids for reflecting upon the quality of conversational exchange. It also examines the notion of how the choice of referents is an important component of an effective learning conversation. This leads on to a discussion of examinations and assessment as a process of exchange between teachers and learners.

Chapter 11 Shows how the THESAURUS, POOL and REFINE, and CON-SENSUS FRAME grids can be used by a group to elicit, pool and refine all the significant meanings contributed by any member into a self-generated two-level language. This can be used to systematically explore areas of real agreement and disagreement in the group as part of the conversational process. The idea of the group or institution as a learning system is consolidated around the SOCIO-GRID technique. By analogy to a learning conversation within a group, this technique can be used to illuminate the person as a 'community of selves'. Awareness of this internal community is part of the process of self-organised learning.

In Chapters 1-11 the grid is recruited as a feedback device to bring into greater awareness the structure of personal systems for modelling the world, so that individuals, groups and institutions can become more effective as learners, people and as social enterprises. This CSHL grid-based technology has trans-formed the use of the grid into a precise, sensitive and flexible instrument that allows individuals, pairs and groups to explicitly construct their meaning systems about any topic. Such uniquely individual systems of meaning are created as indicators of how they experience the topic, acting, as Kelly suggests, like a pair of spectacles focusing and colouring their personal worlds. We have tried to grind the lens more finely and to extend the repertory grid displays to any facet of human learning and experience. Individual, two-person, group and institutional grids have been used to enhance the quality of personal mean-ing generated by reflection and review of a chosen topic. But there is nothing sacrosanct about the two-dimensional matrix of the grid. Kelly saw construct systems as fragmented, partially permeable hierarchical structures. From the early 1970s onwards we have expanded our technology to include the suite of 'structures of meaning' techniques capable of expressing personal systems of meaning more flexibly, and also more recently three-dimensional computer graphic displays capable of running outside real time and of representing multi-causal systems. There is an infinite scope for processing and displaying constructions of experience and for using these to generate powerful learning conversations in education, training and therapy.

Chapter 12 Reconfronts the basic message throughout the book, namely that reflective learning is essentially conversational and that this requires a systematic methodology. This book has taken the FOCUSed repertory grid in all its manifestations and applications as the primary tool for enhancing learning competence. This reflective grid methodology forms part of the meta-theoretical framework of a more fully articulated theory of 'learning conversations'. Chapter 12 reviews the role of systematic awareness-raising techniques in the practice of learning conversations and points forward to a wider class of 'beyond the grid techniques' capable of representing meaning more fully and dynamically.

A *'grid tricks'* section pulls together the different aspects of the Repertory Grid Reflective Learning Technology so that readers can easily identify how these relate to each chapter and to the pattern of the book as a whole. Associated with the technology is an integrated system of computer programs. A brief description of these and their functions within our self-organised approach to learning is presented in this section. Areas and examples of grid application are described in *Appendix A*. A brief outline of the aims, functions, methodology and publications of the CSHL is presented in *Appendix B*.

Throughout this book our approach has been practical. The manual aspect of the book enables readers to work through activities and examples so that they gain sufficient familiarity to apply the techniques and ideas. Each chapter gives sufficient information in the form of flow charts, step-by-step descriptions and activities to enable readers to work and re-work through the techniques. Cases and examples have been selected from the wide range of CSHL research projects in industry, education, government and commerce. These include management training, quality control, team work in research, manufacturing and production, self-organised learning at a distance and in higher education, learning-to-learn in junior schools, course evaluation, appraisal, job selection, youth training, teaching and learning subject matter, e.g. chemistry, maths, art, statistics or architecture, as well as reading-to-learn, staff development, social work, counselling and therapy.

Through practical experience, our aim has been to communicate the philosophy, basic concepts, techniques and also the excitement of our approach to self-organised learning, rooted in a mass of research work at the Centre for the Study of Human Learning over the past twenty years. The repertory grid has been recruited as part of a radical technology. This reflective learning technology has allowed us to tackle the complexity of human learning as it occurs in the habitats of work, education and society. It has thus been thoroughly tested and validated in many applied areas of human learning. It can be recruited by the individual, pairs, small and large groups as well as whole organisations to change our whole way of thinking about and developing our learning.

A Flow Diagram representation of the book Self-Organised Learning

Chapters	Links and referencing systems	Main theme — The Conversational Science	Qualifications — Repertory Grid techniques	Elaborations — Activities	Elaborations — Algorithms (figs)
	Contents				
	Foreword by Don Bannister				
	Acknowledgments				
	General Introduction — The self-organised learner and the repertory grid				
1		The personal nature of self-organised learning		1.1–1.6	
2		Introducing the repertory grid, elements and constructs		2.1–2.3	Fig. 2.2
3			The construction of personal meaning	3.1	Fig. 3.4
4			FOCUSing: the emergent pattern	4.1–4.4	Figs 4.11, 4.12
5			Talkback through a FOCUSed grid	5.1	Fig. 5.2
6		Grid conversations for achieving self-awareness		6.1–6.7	Figs 6.1, 6.2

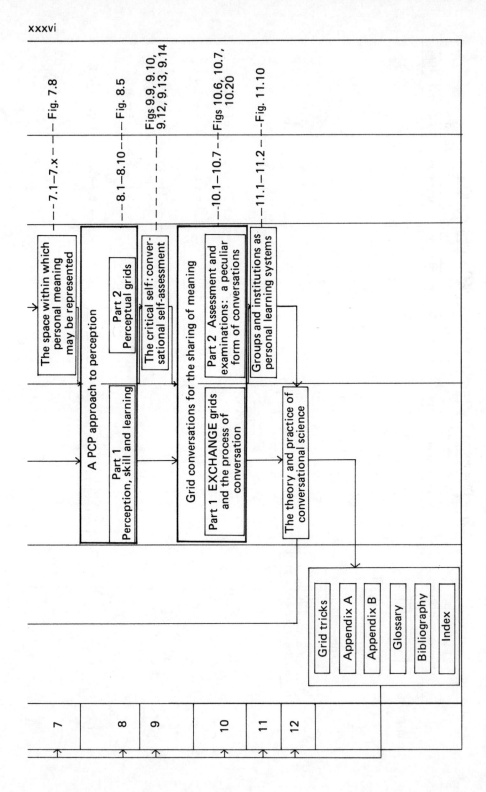

Chapter 1

The personal nature of self-organised learning

What is learning? that we may reflect upon it

In some fuzzily defined sense everybody knows what is meant by 'learning'. Most people in our society have been to school. Many have spent some time in continuing education. All learned from these experiences. Many, also, even learned some of what was intended by their teachers and by those who designed the curricular events. Those able to work for a living may have been exposed to training programmes in industry, commerce, government service or elsewhere; those not able to obtain work may have been introduced to community enterprise activities or other programmes designed to help them. A significant proportion of the population has enjoyed or suffered the 'emotional' or 'whole person' learning associated with some form of psychotherapy or counselling. There are, in contemporary society, more organised opportunities for learning than at any other time in history. But, it is this very universality of institutionally authorised learning which can mislead people into believing that everybody's ideas about learning are much the same. Paradoxically, this assumption, that we know exactly how it is for others, co-exists with the deep-seated conviction that our own significant learning experiences are unique. Indeed, many people feel that most of their 'real learning' has taken place outside the realms of organised education, training and counselling.

'This book is about learning' is a statement which, at first sight, appears both lucid and straightforward. But, it will not arouse the same ideas in each reader. Nor will the 'pattern of meaning' attributed to it by any reader, either now or after reading this chapter, be the same as that in the minds of the authors as they write it. Reading is just one example of the process of learning.

But what is learning?

Many practitioners would define it as:

The acquisition of appropriate knowledge, skills and attitudes to be measured according to publicly acknowledged standards.
Or as:

> The achievement of valued changes in behaviour or experience, to be assessed according to some predetermined norm.

However, learning can always be viewed from several perspectives.

> Who is to decide what is appropriate?

> Who is to value the changes?

New insights gained by the student of thermodynamics, when designing a heat pump for the central heating system of her Thames-side barge, may not guarantee that the chemistry tutor awards her a 'B' grade in an essay on that topic. Changes viewed by the trainer, teacher or the therapist as desirable may not appear so to the manager of the trainee, to the parent of the schoolchild or to the family of the patient.

Here the view is taken that the learner's own evaluation should have priority. Hence the 'personal' nature of self-organised learning. The trainees, the students and the clients will themselves have their own views which influence what and how they learn.

Earlier (page xxii) we suggested that learning is best defined as:

> The construction and reconstruction, exchange and negotiation of significant, relevant and viable meanings.

This results in personally valued changes in thoughts, feelings and actions. New patterns of meaning are expressed as knowledge, attitudes and skills unique to each individual. Changes in meaning contribute to changes in both experience and behaviour.

This book is about 'personal learning'. It is about how each of us can make better use of public knowledge, of other people and of the day-to-day events of our own life. It indicates how each individual may become more aware of these universally available but individually unique, personal resources for learning i.e. personal experience. It is, therefore, about enabling people to develop and grow in ways and directions that are best suited to each person's own needs and purposes in their own place and time.

Here it is argued that teaching, training and therapy are at their best when construed as the encouragement and management of self-organised learning. The following chapters provide a scheme and techniques for transforming the essentially derivative activities of being instructed, trained or treated into more autonomous and self-appreciating processes. Tools are offered with which individuals and groups can achieve a personal revolution without feeling that this necessarily requires other people, institutions, political systems or society as a whole to change.

The outcomes of personal, self-organised learning are different for each individual. The saint, the sinner, the artist, the scientist, the musician, the technician and the candlestick-maker can each be enabled,

(1) to identify their practical, intellectual and emotional needs;
(2) to define their purposes more clearly;
(3) to achieve them more effectively.

They can learn-how-to-learn.

People often need to learn from some systematic presentation of public information. It may be a television programme, a lecture, a speech at a conference or a public meeting. People attending such an event may all behave in much the same way. They will wander in and sit down facing the speaker; they will appear to be attending to what is being said, they may or may not ask questions and when the event finishes they will leave. But what goes on inside each of them is very different. Most of the audience will attempt to understand what the speaker intends to convey. Some will feel that, in their own terms, they have succeeded. Others may feel they have failed. Some may believe that they have succeeded but later discover that they remember very little, or they will discover that what they 'remember' is very different from what others recollect. Some will be convinced by each word of the speaker, others will find themselves in hot dispute. A few of the audience may not be trying to follow the lecture very closely. They are more interested in appreciating an entertaining public performance; or they may be happily daydreaming. Just occasionally a self-organised learner will be constructing a personal experience which will stay with him or her for the rest of his or her life. The ways in which each individual member of the audience listens — how they relate what the lecturer is saying and displaying, to their own experience — how they create a private conversation with the speaker in their heads — will largely determine what they learn and therefore what they will later be able to think, feel, say and do about it.

One person being made redundant may use the experience to begin a whole new line of productive achievement; whereas another faced with the 'same' event experiences it as an unmitigated disaster. Two people fortunate enough to be starting in similar jobs at the same time can make very different use of their opportunities. Circumstances do differ, times can be harder or easier, but, much more than is usually recognised, people differ in their ability to learn from experience. They differ in how they select, construct and reflect upon their experience so that they may learn from it.

Each of us can learn to be more sensitive to relevant events. We can take more care in attributing meaning to them, and we can all spend more time reflecting upon our experiences. We can also learn to create experiences from which to learn.

This is equally true for most realms of human existence in: marriage — work — art — sport — play — entertainment — friendships — rivalries — societies — institutions — and between nations. We could and should all learn to create and use our experience more effectively.

T-C as the management of self-organised learning

All those who are responsible for producing the systematically organised events from which others are intended to learn will find that the ideas and conversational procedures here on offer could radically change their thinking, feelings and practice. The following chapters contain a new approach to the task of enabling others to learn more effectively. Teachers, trainers, tutors, therapists, coaches, counsellors, custodians and consultants (T-C) may all value a set of new tools which can enable them to identify, and thus to start from, where the learner truly is, experientially, in his or her own terms. It is as important, if not more important, for such practitioners to appreciate the learner's (student's, client's, patient's, pupil's,) personal constructions of experience, as it is for them to observe the learner's behaviour.

This book is also intended to be of direct use to learners. Learners of all ages may value methods with which they can become more aware of their own perceptions, thoughts and feelings. Learners from many different walks of life may appreciate a methodology through which they can systematically learn how to learn more competently, by and for themselves. They may value techniques with which they can more effectively enter into the perceptions, thoughts and feelings of others; and they may value tools with which they can construct, negotiate and share meanings more fully and effectively with a wider range of fellows.

This message is, therefore, intended for a wide audience. The repertory grid, and the philosophy of personal learning which the authors here associate with it, cuts across many traditional boundaries. The reason for this diversity of appeal is that these techniques are 'content-free'. They focus on the processes of reflective learning, recruiting the specific contents of each person's experience as their own unique and necessary resources for personal growth and development.

Readers who have a vested interest in their professed topic may, at first, find this approach strange. The methods are essentially independent of the topic being learned, but this does not mean that the material and/or previous training and experience is ignored or degraded. On the contrary these methods are used to enable and manage the process of learning so that any topic becomes more alive in terms that are different but personally relevant for each participant. Thus, these techniques can routinely bring about what only the outstanding practitioner achieves intuitively. They can also help to break down the barriers which usually prevent any combination of teachers, trainers, tutors and therapists, coaches, counsellors, custodians and consultants from learning about the management of learning through an exchange of experience.

The terms 'training', 'teaching', 'tutoring', 'therapy', 'coaching', 'counselling', 'custody' and 'consulting' define some of the professional activities which are, or should be, concerned with the encouragement of personal learning. To avoid lengthy repetition and to encourage the reader to place their own interests at the centre of attention this whole apparent kaleidoscope of professions will be referred to as T-C. The term will be used as both noun (e.g. teacher, consultant) and as a verb (e.g. to teach and to consult). Thus it is hoped that, amongst others, the football coach, the primary school teacher, the management consultant, the apprentice supervisor, the psychiatrist, the prison officer and the don will find these variations on, and developments of, the repertory grid personally and professionally useful.

Experience as a resource for learning

T-C is not usually treated as one coherent set of related activities. The idea that a practitioner in any of these professional areas could gain by construing what they do as 'encouraging and managing self-organised learning' may seem naïve. But it identifies a purpose which could become the shared aim of all of them. It is a theme which may allow practitioners to transcend their own investment in one particular area of expertise. However, before considering the implications of this idea more fully, readers are asked to contemplate their own thoughts and feelings about the categorisations which normally separate and divide them.

T-Cs are often grouped according to:

1 the topic they profess;
2 the clients whom they serve;
3 the institutions for which they work;
4 the personal style and methods of the practitioner;
5 the clinical, pedagogic or academic authority to whom they offer allegiance.

These diversive categorisations are accepted and often reinforced by the practitioners themselves.

Mathematics teachers feel that they have little in common with language experts. The instructor chef does not feel that he has much to learn from the nursing tutor. At tertiary level this topic division can become so strong that, for example, the staff of a physics department may want to teach its own mathematics because the maths department 'does not seem able to understand what we need'. Such divisions multiply where topic knowledge is seen to be the prime and only expertise. The army instructor, the teacher in the finishing school for young ladies, the training manager in a multi-national company, the consultant psychiatrist in a teaching hospital and the polytechnic professor may each feel that they are defined (and inevitably divided) by their institutional allegiance. The coach of young Olympics swimming hopefuls, the staff in a school for the blind and the custodians of a remand home for teenage delinquents gain much of their confidence from their specialist experience and understanding of their clients. The well-prepared 'factual' lecturer depreciates equally the skills of the eratic inspirational teacher and the hypersensitive encounter group leader. The effective tutor may have little time for Computer-Aided Instruction. The followers of Montessori have fought with those that owed allegiance to Froebel, and Coverdale differs from M. Argyle. The Skinnerian behaviour therapist can hardly talk to the more Rogerian client-centred counsellor and they may both appear to hate the psychoanalyst.

But these divisions all contain successful and less successful practitioners. It is our contention that much of the basis of success lies in the individual's attitudes towards personal learning. It lies in their appreciation of self-organisation both in themselves and in others.

The reader is invited to take a further step towards understanding what the authors intend, by reflecting upon their own thoughts and feelings about practitioners who are so categorised. Consider your construing of the implications of some 'typical' topic divisions. How do people — employed to help others learn the following topics — teach, train, tutor, treat, coach, consult with, constrain and/or counsel their clients?

LIST 1 - TOPICS

cost accounting	computer programming	work study
tennis	social work	theology
sheet metal work	sales technique	sex therapy
local government	English literature	ballet
Ikebana	boxing	Russian
omelette-making	knife throwing	feeding a baby

(The reader is invited to add topics from their own experience to this list.)

Contemplate the 'images of learning' evoked in you by each topic in turn. The process of reflecting upon experience is the nub of the methodology advocated throughout this book. Each personal image is, in the jargon of the repertory grid, called an 'element' or 'item of experience'. The grid is designed to help people explore such 'items of experience'. Deeply personal thoughts and feelings about any issue are both our greatest resource and a major barrier to our learning. The repertory grid is a key to unlocking the barrier and accessing the resource. It is a systematic procedure for constructively recruiting these resources into our learning. It can also help us to reflect upon and thus begin to dissolve the internal barricades of prejudice, disruptive feelings and wilful misunderstanding which so often prevent us from learning. Conversational use of the grid can free us to review our personal resources and rebuild our ideas, skills and attitudes into more personally constructive patterns of meaning and action.

The authors' purpose in writing this book is to challenge all those concerned with the giving or receiving of T-C to reconsider the basic nature of these activities. You, the reader, are invited to recruit your own personal experience into this enterprise. You are asked to consider and 'stay with' the possibility that you may have some ways of thinking and feeling which are prejudicial to effective personal learning. This is equally likely (or unlikely) whether you believe in 'permissive' or 'autocratic', 'structured' or 'unstructured', 'participative' or 'distanced' methods of T-C. You are invited now to contemplate your own immediate experience. How do you perceive, think and feel about what you are reading? The answer to this question may reveal how habitual thoughts, feelings and reactions are enabling you to, or preventing you from, really trying to fully understand the authors' point of view. You do not necessarily have to agree, merely to allow yourself to appreciate what may be being offered.

Contrary to our experience in face-to-face courses, we, the authors, have been advised, and, having reflected upon our own experiences of others' books, have reluctantly concluded that for many readers a challenging first-person form of presentation is felt to be unprofessional and can therefore be rather off-putting and counter-productive. We therefore propose to decently submerge ourselves again into the content and to hide within a third person form, only occasionally re-emerging to re-affirm the essentially personal nature of what we are proposing.

Throughout the text there are exercises and procedures, and there are suggestions for projects. Together these illustrate some of the repertory grid components of the CSHL personal learning technology. Readers who are considering using these techniques with their clients or on themselves are very strongly recommended to work through these activities. Enabling personal learning with the repertory grid is rather like learning to swim, to manipulate the calculus or to speak a foreign language. A certain amount of initial briefing can save a lot of wasted time. But no amount of study, reading or talking about the topic can substitute for trying out the skills for oneself. The meaning of much of what is presented here will be transformed for those who elicit, reflect upon, exchange and negotiate their own personal values, perceptions, thoughts and feelings as they proceed through the text.

Activity 1.1 Reflecting on how topics influence learning

Consider the topics in List 1 (page 6). Add others to represent the types of T-C with which you are most familiar, either as practitioner or client. If the idea of thinking about any specific topic in the list puts you off the whole exercise, cross it out (but remain aware that you have done so). Now for each topic in your list put yourself in the position of a learner, and think and feel yourself into what is for you a 'true-to-life' reconstruction of an event which you feel typically occurs in the organised learning of that topic. Accept and briefly explore whatever your own assumptions reveal. For example, think about tennis, put yourself into what you feel would be a typical tennis coaching situation. Make only sufficient notes to act as a personal reminder of the event you have associated with each topic. Now reconsider each event and, still from the position of learner, imagine how you could make the best use of it. Again make only sufficient notes to remind you of what a good learning experience would have been. When you have finished this for all the topics in your list consider how each might have (been) turned into a bad learning experience.

For example, how would you expect a Zen master to teach you Ikebana. How could you make the best use of the experience of being with him whilst he makes a flower arrangement? and how might you have reacted to turn it into a negative learning experience? Similarly for learning Russian, sheet metal work, boxing or ballet.

Now, put yourself into the position of a T-C practitioner. What is your own topic? Could you enrich your skills by reflecting upon some of the events which you have felt were typical of other topics? Could you increase the range of events which you usually create (or have seen created) for clients learning your topic? How would you manage these events to enable your clients/learners to maximise their learning? How could you help them to avoid turning such events into negative learning experiences?

Note: This is a tentative first step in the direction of using your own experience as a resource for learning. As the guidance becomes more specific and systematic the reconstruction of the personal experience becomes more thorough and detailed, and the process of reflection becomes more focused and penetrating.

Activities 1.2 - 1.5

You may find it illuminating, now or later, to repeat Activity 1.1 using the following lists to trigger off other aspects of your thoughts and feelings (pre-judices and understanding) about learning.

Activity 1.2 Reflecting on how clients influence learning

List 2 — Clients

Six-year-olds in primary school	School-leavers
Suburban housewives	Postgraduate clinicians
Engineering undergraduates	Homosexuals in their middle twenties
Asian immigrants	The Olympic rowing squad
Gas fitter apprentices	Dolphins

A group of senior managers from multi-national companies

Activity 1.3 Reflecting on how institutions influence learning

List 3 — Institutions

Summerhill	Technical college
Nursery school	Staff college

The Marriage Guidance Council
The Open University
A prison workshop
Oxbridge university
The central training dept of a large
  company

A co-counselling group
An apprentice training school
The army catering school
Greyfriars

Activity 1.4 Reflecting on how methods influence learning

List 4 - Methods

Lecture
Look and say
Project work
Simulator
Language laboratory
Experiental workshop
Training within industry
Micro-computer
Repertory grid

Action learning
Business game
Tutorial
Discussion group
Change agency
Laboratory experiment
Reading
Seminar

Activity 1.5 Reflecting on how pedagogic authorities influence learning

List 5 - Pedagogic authorities

Montessori
Socrates
B.F. Skinner
Ivan Illich
Douglas Seymour
Vygotsky

Mahatma Gandhi
Alf Garnett
Jerome Bruner
Coverdale
Piaget
Froebel

Carl Rogers
Pavlov
Janet and John
Arnold of Rugby
Idries Shah

It is possible that the ideas about learning revitalised by Activities 1.1 to 1.5 have revealed some personal assumptions of which the reader was not initially fully aware or willing to consciously admit. Sharing the experience of these exercises with others who have also tried them may heighten this awareness. The similarities and contrasts between people's assumptions can create a context in which each person becomes more aware of the limitations of his or her own view.

Personal myths of learning

Topics, clients, institutions, techniques, authorities (clinical, pedagogic or academic) and personal style are not necessarily the most useful categorisations within which to explore the relationships between the processes of learning and the practices of T-C. It is hidden assumptions made by both clients and practitioners about how learning takes place which directly influence how T-C events are created and how such learning opportunities are exploited or missed.

There is a superficial layer of apparently shared understanding about the nature of learning. From this, tokens are moulded for use in the typically frozen conversations of everyday exchange. These derive from, and help to perpetuate, a belief in the commonality of experience of people in our society. Beneath this ritualistic layer of agreement, even those involved in the 'same' opportunities construct very dissimilar personal explanations of their own learning processes. They also develop very disparate feelings towards the activity of learning. This can be equally true among (say):

1 Young 'high-flyer' managers from a multi-national company who are, say, supporting each other in carrying out action learning projects.
2 Twelve-year-olds in a secondary modern school who are learning, lesson by lesson, how more successfully to disrupt their arithmetic class.
3 A disparate group of people aged 23 to 56 re-training as watch and clock repairers in a government skill centre.
4 Lively middle-class suburbanites who are all, for a variety of reasons, studying Russian at an evening class.
5 Potential marriage guidance counsellors taking part in a residential experiential 'social skills' course.
6 School-leavers 'sitting by Nellie' to learn to wire printed circuit boards for inclusion in colour television sets.
7 Teenagers informally studying at the modern equivalent of Fagin's school for pickpockets.

The attitudes and assumptions which the members of any one of these groups bring to their learning situation, and therefore their capacity to learn in it, are influenced by the cumulative impact of what they intuitively take to be their relevant past. One has only to see a group of foundry foremen, helicopter pilots or nursery school teachers taking their seats for, say, a 'safety' lecture in a space laid out like a traditional classroom to realise how quickly all the old associations come crowding back. Such associations cannot easily be expressed even to oneself, but they influence one's capacity to learn in each new situation.

One of the first studies in which the authors collaborated revealed the wide variety of personal myths which guide undergraduates in their learning activities. The most easily related myths were usually about what students felt to be the necessary physical or social conditions of learning. Many described how they must have coffee or snacks to hand all the time, but others saw even regular meals as interruptions which disturbed their efforts to learn. Some students knew that they had to sit up 'properly' at a desk if they were to read something and really remember it, whilst others were equally convinced that they could only really concentrate if they were comfortably stretched out on the carpet. There were those who had to have complete silence if they were studying. Others 'knew' that they could not work without a background of radio or recorded music. Alistair Cooke, Tony Blackburn, the Beatles, Beethoven, Richard Baker, Michael Parkinson and the Who were all known to be personally helpful to certain processes of learning. For some 'serious learning' was always and only achieved privately on their own, whilst others only thoroughly understood a topic after talking it over with other students. Personal beliefs about being 'a morning person' or only being able to work effectively between 10 p.m. and 3 a.m. at night were held equally strongly by different learners; so were ideas about the optimal length of personal study sessions. Preferences varied from 20 to 30 minutes to 6 or 8 hours. Thus, even at the most superficial level of personal myth, the token agreement soon disperses to reveal a welter of conflicting personal assumptions.

Towards the end of the third session in a series of four interviews to explore the impact of exams on his study habits, one psychology honours student found himself revealing the following view of his own learning. Thinking himself to be mature (26 years old) he was convinced that his memory had reached its limits. He had, therefore, to be very careful not to learn anything which was not crucially important because whenever he now learned anything he inevitably forgot something else. This deep-seated belief about his own processes was unaffected by his 'carefully filtered' public knowledge of various psychologists' approach to learning; he was familiar, for example, with the work of B.F. Skinner, J. Piaget, C. Rogers, J. Bruner and S. Freud. Another interviewee harboured the personal myth that his Cockney accent prevented him from ever learning a foreign language. Discussion revealed that during his first few weeks of modern languages at school he had been instructed to stand on a stool in front of his class and was then ridiculed for his attempts to pronounce simple French words. Similar studies among other, publicly less successful, groups of learners have revealed a veritable Aladdin's cave of seemingly bizarre personal models of the learning process. But who is to say that each of these do not influence their possessor's capacity for learning? Indeed, since such myths exist and each exerts its own unique influence, can they really be thought bizarre?

Deeper, implicit myths are about the learners' views of their own 'innate' capacities. They have come to a firm belief about their talents for maths or dancing, for writing, athletics, chess, house repairs or embroidery. Everybody into or beyond their teens already 'seem to know' that they lack a whole range of special aptitudes or talents.

Another hidden source of personal myths about learning is the habitual mode in which an individual imagines or remembers events. People who think largely in visual terms believe this to be a universal human characteristic. Little do these visualisers know that some of us have never experienced a coloured visual image in our life, that we do not see words as we are wondering what to say, and do not experience number patterns as we do arithmetic. People who habitually sub-vocalise, have auditory imagery, or 'feel' themselves doing things with their muscle sense, are often equally convinced that everybody else remembers or imagines as they do. The increased learning potential that lies in achieving consciously controlled multiple imagery is in itself sufficient justification for the encouragement of greater awareness of one's own processes. What is true for the blind, deaf and dumb in the external world is true for the internally disabled in the world of imagination. Self-organisation is partly a matter of being able to exercise more choice over the mode of one's own memory, thoughts and imagination.

People have negative myths about their body, their inability to think logically, the bluntness of their aesthetic sensibilities, their lack of inventiveness or their incapacity to empathise with others. Many of these disabling myths are hidden within what are construed as positive personal attributes. These are expressed, for example, as toughness, femininity, common sense, academic purity, hard-headed business nous etc., etc. In themselves all and each of these characteristics can be operationally positive when they are taken as indicating active potential for certain types of human experience. But many individuals stifle their own personal learning by implicitly formulating a supposedly positive characteristic as the avoidance or suppression of certain areas of experience in oneself or in others.

Deeper still are the personal myths constructed to 'excuse' habitual operational incompetence. These are expressed as objective knowledge about intelligence, personality, health and creativity. Such assumptions about 'my ability to learn' are often only dimly recognised by the person possessing them. Indeed, sometimes the surface or easily verbalised beliefs of the individual run counter to the deeper patterns of meaning which are the springs of action. The deep patterns, those implicit assumptions, the personal myths and insights, play out as feelings, thoughts and actions in the classroom, the boardroom, the workshop, the lecture theatre or the surgery; in the consulting room, on the sportsfield, in prisons, on the job or with one's children in the home. 'Objective' records (e.g. video tapes) of the detailed behaviour taking place in these situations can be used to help participants raise their implicit assumptions into awareness by talking themselves back through such events. This allows them to attempt to reconstruct the original experience and thus systematically explore the non-conscious decision-making which shapes their behaviours. The patterns in this spontaneous decision-making reveal the values and the meanings which are contained in their deeply held but hidden personal myths about their own learning capacities.

Activity 1.6 Identifying your personal myths about your capacity for learning

These unacknowledged feelings and implicit assumptions about learning can be explored using the repertory grid. The techniques, examples and exercises in the following chapters explain how this may be done.

1 Identify an area or topic of learning which is currently important to you, e.g. 'O' level maths, getting on with people at a cocktail party, digging a hole in hard ground, playing the piano, being more political (with a small p) at work, etc., etc.

2 Think about the conditions, physical and social, in which you are trying to learn.

   (a) List all the possible physical conditions in which you might try to learn. Rate them on a seven-point scale from:

       7 perfect for me to learn in
       6 good for me to learn in
       5 fairly good for me to learn in
       4 average for me to learn in
       3 not easy for me to learn in
       2 difficult for me to learn in
       1 impossible for me to learn in

   (b) List all the social conditions in which you might try to learn. Rate these on the same seven-point scale.

3 Think about all the resources available to you for learning in your selected area or topic, e.g. lessons, books, outside lecturers, practicals, visits, teachers, skilled practitioners or experts on the topic, other learners, audio tapes, video recordings, equipment, mock-ups, feasibility studies, sitting by Nellie, etc., etc. List all those resources. Rate them on the seven-point scale.

4 Think about your learning skills, e.g. listening, talking, reading, writing, thinking, feeling, tasting, problem-solving, empathising with others, etc., etc. List all those relevant to your learning. Rate them on the seven-point scale.

5 Think about what you believe to be your own talents, learning capacities, personality traits, character, etc., etc. Rate them on a seven-point scale from:

       7 Make it very easy for me to learn
       6 Make it easy for me to learn
       5 Make it relatively easy for me to learn
       4 Make it average for me to learn
       3 Make it relatively difficult for me to learn
       2 Make it difficult for me to learn
       1 Make it very difficult for me to learn

6 Explore your personal myths about your learning capacity in different topic areas.

7 Compare your myths with those of your peers or colleagues in the same topic areas.

The disabled learner and impersonal learning

Together, the authors share over fifty years of widely varying experience in training, teaching, tutoring, therapy, coaching, custody, counselling and consulting. They also, together, represent nearly a hundred years of learning. This experience, practice and research, reinforced by observation and conversation with, over the years, thousands of other practitioners has for the most part been profoundly depressing. It has convinced us that many of the implicit assumptions about the nature of learning which permeate organised T-C are incompatible with the encouragement of personally significant learning. As such anti-personal-learning assumptions play themselves out in practice they produce boredom, anxiety, alienation, fear, apathy and humiliation. They produce in the learners a loss of belief in themselves and an active dislike of 'learning' which is all too typical of the clients in many T-C institutions. These anti-personal-learning assumptions of practitioners produce complementary assumptions in the clients. Most people practising T-C do have their clients' interests at heart most of the time, but at some level in their perceptions, thoughts and feelings are beliefs about, for example, intelligence, physical prowess, personality, special talents, age, race, religion, sex, politics and the effectiveness of certain methods which seriously interfere with the personal learning of their clients. This is true in psychiatry and in primary schools, in swimming pools and machine shops, in TOPS* courses and master classes. This vicious circle of self-perpetuating myths re-fertilises itself from generation to generation.

If learning is to be felt as a positive experience, then the products of learning must be effectively integrated into a wide and flexible array of subsequent thoughts, feelings and actions. The learning must become personally significant. Individuals achieve personal learning by reflecting upon their own experience to incorporate it into their developing understanding. For those who achieve the happy habit or knack of personal learning, each T-C event becomes an opportunity for growth and development. For those who do not learn to bring this relatively simple mechanism into operation, each event adds to their intellectual burden and reinforces the barriers within them that interfere with creative understanding. This is why one person learns enormously from an opportunity in which another finds nothing significant. For example, a first job, a school trip abroad, a conference, a pay negotiation, a love affair or an accident.

Much organised education, training and therapy does not encourage personal learning. Short-term, personally irrelevant public-knowledge-laden outcomes of T-C are valued (and evaluated) at the expense of sustained, personally valued learning achievements. Even among the 'successful' most people learn how to be

*TOPS — Manpower Services Commission Retraining Courses.

taught, not how to learn. They become dependent upon being instructed; and then at work and in life, in the absence of organised T-C, they are unable to continue learning.

Thus many people leave school (or further and tertiary education) believing that effective learning consists of receiving established systems of objective knowledge in well-organised pre-digested forms. Such impersonal knowledge is either rejected or it remains separated from real-life experience and can only be used for limited pre-determined purposes in limited pre-determined situations. Such people may have learned how to be taught but they have not learned how to learn. For them the knowledge acquired by instruction never gets fully incorporated into their imagination, perceptions, feelings and thoughts. For others, more disastrously, the instructed knowledge replaces the central system of living meaning and, at worst, they become the impossible T-Cs of the next generation. Just occasionally each of us becomes free enough to recognise some fragment of this process in ourselves; and the horrifying thought breaks through that most of us are in this condition most of the time. We are so programmed by our up-bringing, education, training and the media to think, feel and then act in the ways acceptable to the dogma of society that we do not even know this to be so.

The impersonal learner and the personal learner may both either fail or succeed when measured against criteria invented by institutionalised T-Cs. This is also true for the learners' own evaluation of themselves. The impersonal and the personal learner can both feel that they have not done too well, or that they have done brilliantly. The difference is that whilst personal learners are aware of the social assessment, they will ultimately judge themselves by their own personally constructed standards. The poor impersonal learners have nothing but the standards of their referent society within which to define themselves. But because these assessments are not based on their own tried values they remain ultimately uneasy with them. Because they have not created standards out of their own raw experience, they remain basically insecure in their assessments of themselves.

Personal learning, reflecting in context upon one's own experience, integrates the results of education, therapy and training into the developing life experience of the individual. The cumulative pool of experience available for reflection is enriched when a person allows the curiosity which arises naturally out of their wishes, needs, thoughts and feelings, to drive their actions. Experience is enriched by exploration and experiment. It is also enriched by entering more fully into the experience of others. Empathising as completely as possible with another's reconstruction of personal events and exploring these with them in detail and in depth does in some true, if limited, sense add to one's own personal experience. Hence the value of literature.

The CSHL personal learning technology adds a new dimension to the practice of T-C. It enables it to develop as the management of personal self-organised learning. It converts one important dimension of the 'unteachable' art of teaching into a series of flexible procedures and methods which most practitioners can learn to use.

The universal need for self-organised learning

Central to the philosophy of personal learning constructed by the authors is the fact that the same T-C event will be experienced differently by each person involved in it.

Each lecture, discussion, test, laboratory experiment, lesson, book, project, seminar, field trip, business game, list of examples, tutorial, or spelling quiz, each hour at work or play is a unique experience for each person taking part in it. The art of teaching (T-C) involves full acceptance of this fact. Assumptions antithetical to personal learning will often contain a component assumption that what is going on in each individual is best seen as a regrettable deviation from how it should ideally be. The uniqueness of the individual experience is devalued into a merely incomplete, unauthentic, or unnecessarily elaborated version of the one best and correct experience. Hence the feelings of inadequacy experienced by most learners. The art of teaching requires full acknowledgment that only the individual learners know what their learning experiences have been and what they have meant to them. The inference made by the practitioners of T-C from the behaviour of the learner is at best a pale distorted image of the learner's personal experience. At worst, and far too often, it completely misrepresents it.

These misrepresentations, communicated back with authority, diminish the learners' confidence in their ability to reflect upon their own experience, often to the point where they cease to reflect constructively at all. They abdicate responsibility for control over their own processes. Their thoughts, perceptions and feelings are accepted as events which happen to them. The disabled personal learner becomes self-defined within organised T-C as naughty, unable to concentrate, stupid, bloodyminded, pathological, daydreaming, bored, distracted or as always interested in the irrelevant. In one socially acceptable adjustment to this the successful impersonal learner emerges. Other socially less acceptable adjustments are rebellion, creativity, delinquency and the cessation of belief in the systematic acquisition of understanding. The cost of impersonal T-C is an increasing army of alienated and/or disabled personal learners who will eventually achieve the disintegration of society.

The irony lies in the paradox that whilst there is a universe of misunderstanding between the personal and the impersonal learner, once this experiential chasm is bridged much existing practice falls into place. Once the primacy of personal learning is acknowledged, much of the fabric of T-C can be re-justified.

The two ingredients of personal effectiveness, of becoming more fully functioning and thus appreciating the tough wholesome fun of being alive are:

(1) to be able to move from a reliance on impersonal meaning to the construction of personal meanings, i.e. to personal learning;
(2) to move from the external manipulation of being instructed to the disciplined freedom of self-organised learning.

Most learners are almost totally unaware of how they attribute meaning to people, things and events, to organised resources or the happenstance experiences of living, working and playing. Reading, listening, talking, writing, thinking and feeling, judging, deciding and doing have become long-established habits that are so fixed and unavailable to conscious review that the learner is the unwitting prisoner of his or her own competencies and disabilities. Hence the prevailing tendency to deal in the descriptive constancies of personality assessments and intelligence tests, with problems which inherently arise from unbalanced or inadequate personal learning competencies.

Self-organisation in learning arises out of the ability to converse with oneself and others about the processes of learning; and to observe, search, analyse, formulate, reflect and review on the basis of such encounters. Conversation is not just chit-chat nor is it an exchange of instruction, prescription or cajoling. Unaided, most people are not able to generate effective learning conversations with themselves. This book explains and demonstrates how the repertory grid can be used as a major tool in effective learning conversations. It can be used to move the disabled learner towards personal self-organised activities.

The self-organised learner can learn effectively from the dedicated topic specialist. People fully aware of their own needs and purposes can use institutionalised evaluation as one referent, among many, of what may be valuable. Self-organised learners can listen and participate as effectively as they can reject and rebel. They can build on the past as well as they can innovate. Impersonal learners are the unwitting prisoners of the value system and pattern of social meanings within which they exist. The personal learner is as free to enter social systems as she or he is to leave them. This is the advantage of the personal revolution.

This contrasting of personal with impersonal learning is 'content-free'. It is equally applicable to learning in all its forms. It applies to operating a lathe and to writing a novel, to running a business and to translating Octavio Paz; to identifying dry soldered joints, to making bread, to playing the trombone, to programming a computer. Hence the diversity of the audience who may find this book useful.

Chapter 2

Introducing the repertory grid: elements and constructs

A prelude to the repertory grid

The repertory grid was invented as a therapeutic technique. It was designed to enable clients to explore the pattern of their deepest thoughts and feelings about the people closest to them. It allows each individual client to express significant personal meaning in the terms which are most natural to them. They are not forced to dilute their meanings by dissolving them into the terminology of the teacher, trainer or therapist. Other psychological methods may also appear to offer a similar freedom of expression, but this is mostly illusory. When using other 'free response' techniques practitioners either have to interpret and summarise the results in their own terms, or the material remains voluminous and fragmented, rather disorganised and therefore difficult for the client to use and for the T-Cs to compare with their other materials.

For example, the open-ended (or depth) interview is designed to leave clients free to express themselves fully in their own terms. But many problems arise when the interviewer comes to selectively code, sum-up and/or interpret the results of the interview. The report is either exceedingly tedious and discursive or the interviewer's interpretation inevitably distorts and selectively biases the interviewee's meanings. This is equally true when the interview is called a conversation, discussion or frank exchange of views. The grid avoids this by offering a systematic two-level space in which the personal meaning of the client can be collected, unadulterated by any need to simplify or translate it into a common or standardised language. Thus the repertory grid differs from almost every other psychological method in being formally structured whilst remaining content-free.

Other methods pre-empt not only the language but also the experience of the client. A questionnaire already defines its content in the questions it contains. An attitude scale or a personality test already contains pre-selected content items for the client to react to. The grid does not. It starts content-free, ready for clients to contribute meaning in the terms which they feel best express their undistorted thoughts and feelings.

The personal learning technology developed at the Centre for the Study of

Human Learning (CSHL) makes use of this capability of the grid. It enables learners to express their own meanings in their own terms. It offers therefore a uniquely apposite set of tools for encouraging personal learning. The key move in recruiting the grid as a tool for personal learning was the recognition that the topics to be explored with the grid need not be restricted to those originally envisaged as appropriate to its clinical use, i.e. 'people'. Since 1964 members of CSHL have used the grid to explore an ever-widening range of topics. They have used it to explore the personal meanings of:

art objects, architectural drawings, the blending of whisky, staff comments on students essays, soldered joints, purposes for reading, mathematical examination questions, company research policy, events in a language class, man-management events . . . and the 249 other topics mentioned in the technical publications of the Centre (see Appendix A).

Gradually this idea has diffused through a network of users of the grid who have come to accept that it can be employed to explore personal meaning on any topic. The versatility of the grid is restricted only by the ingenuity and experience of practitioners and clients in finding the appropriate forms in which to construe the selected topic.

On the meaning of meaning

The word 'meaning' itself has a surprisingly wide range of meanings. Experience shows that for many scientifically practising people the term has rather negative connotations of subjectivity and unreliability. For them 'the meaning' of something can change with the whims and fancies of the individual moment, but behind such wavering the 'reality', as known to true scientists, remains firm and constant. Here the word 'meaning' is used in a less trivial sense. Centuries of careful negotiation both with the external world and with each other, have enabled scientists to construct areas of shared subjectivity, of carefully checked and articulated meaning which enable them to achieve feats which those who do not share their meaning (models of the external world) find amazing or even magical. But anthropologists have found many other groups of people with equally long-lasting and painstakingly constructed meanings (models of the external world) who have also been convinced that their realities allow them to produce amazing and repeatable results. Thus for us the 'meaning' of something is not an attribute of the thing itself, nor is it some arbitrary pattern of thoughts and feelings that exist solely in an individual free-floating imagination.

Meaning is a relationship between a person and the 'something' to which reality is attributed. Meaning can never be either true or false in any absolute sense: but it can be:

(a) agreed, among a group, a nation, or a civilisation; for the life-time of a project, for a generation or for centuries;

(b) viable, i.e. it can so model reality that it allows people to pursue and sometimes achieve purposes which they might not even conceive in the absence of that pattern of meaning (e.g. fall in love, fly to the moon, cast out the mote in their own eye, polish a diamond, experience the peace of Nirvana, add seven to eleven, change the structure of a DNA molecule or paint the Mona Lisa).

The repertory grid allows us to recognise (i.e. construct a meaning of) human beings as meaning, constructing, negotiating and attributing organisms. This will allow us to pursue and sometimes achieve results of personal learning which may from other perspectives be magic, i.e. impossible to conceive.

A technology of the psyche

The already popular repertory grid technique attracts people's attention for many differing, and sometimes dubious, reasons. Some see it as a fashionable psychological test, some as a new market research tool or as an alternate approach to attitude surveys. There are numerous ways in which 'a technique resembling the repertory grid' has been used. Many of these abuse the essential properties of the repertory grid by offering either items of public experience or a public descriptive system to the clients, rather than eliciting items of personal experience and personal systems of meaning from them. Unfortunately most of these widely unquestioned methodological heresies add nothing new to psychological technology. They merely reflect the users' fascination with an apparently popular new technique whilst revealing their inability to appreciate its truly innovative nature. People who operate 'a technique resembling the repertory grid' in a content-bound form thereby equate it with the semantic differential, or degrade it back into the undistinguished mass of traditional psycho-metrics. This is comparable to, say, moving in the fashionable society of the period in which the convex lens was invented and finding pieces of glass resembling lenses being used for purposes of decoration (or for burning holes in paper). Very few users of the grid seem to realise that a whole new technology of the 'psyche' (analogous to that of the 'visual technology' embodied in telescopes, microscopes, binoculars, spectacles, spectroscopes, image intensifiers, lasers and all the other optical instruments which depend upon, or have developed from, the original uses of the lens) is waiting to be invented. The CSHL personal learning technology builds from the basic character of the grid to extend, elaborate and refine the personal processes of understanding it can evoke and encourage to develop.

There are certain recurrent but unnecessary difficulties that arise in teaching, training, tutoring, treating, coaching, counselling, constraining and consulting with people about the repertory grid. (Some of these relate directly to the questions of personal perspectives introduced later in chapter 12.) The grid is a content-free technique, but for most new users preoccupation with their own favourite 'subject matter' can distract from a dispassionate appreciation of the subtleties of the technique itself. The choice of topic with which to introduce the process of eliciting a grid is, therefore, quite important. The teacher who intends to prepare her pupils for examinations using a system of mathematical command words as her topic may never come to appreciate the power and versatility of the grid if all she ever considers is the use of such 'items of experience' as — calculate — solve — hence or otherwise — evaluate — explain — show — and — prove. But she may be made rather over-anxious if her first grid challenges her to reflect upon her relationships with her mother, father, husband, lover, sons, daughters (and optionally the judge who sentenced her). On the other hand the example should not be too trivial, since someone who intends to use the grid to enhance their tutoring and counselling skills may become a little restless if their first introduction to the grid requires them to contemplate the similarities and differences between a roll of sellotape, a pencil and a paper clip.

In running face-to-face courses it is the authors' practice to invite their clients to identify the variety of purposes for which they will be using the grid once they have acquired sufficient skill. These can then be examined and discussed to find appropriate illustrative examples which whet the clients' appetites before they get down to the detailed business of eliciting a first grid. In some ways these first two chapters should be seen as a substitute for this discussion about the relevance of the grid to the reader's own particular purposes.

The elicitation of a repertory grid is a skilled activity. The term 'repertory' derives from the idea that each individual has their own repertoire of personal constructions of experience. To adequately explore this repertoire requires the humility and sensitivity to actually listen and faithfully record the client's own descriptions in their own terms. In addition it requires an understanding of the formal structure of the grid. And it requires a comprehending appreciation of the purpose of the grid interview. If grid-learners appreciate this, then it is best to start with a simple topic for the first grid. If they do not, it is best to do some introductory exercise on a significant topic to demonstrate the power and relevance of the technique. This second approach is here adopted.

Activity 2.1 Eliciting personal constructs

The reader is asked to participate in the following exercise:
Think of six people whom you have recently taught, trained, tutored, treated, coached, consulted with, constrained or counselled (or if you are not a T-C practitioner, think of six people in your life who have significantly taught, trained, tutored, coached, consulted with, constrained or counselled you). Cut a thin card (or tear up a sheet of scrap paper) into pieces about $3'' \times 2''$ (8cm $\times$ 5cm).

Write one of your learners' (or practitioners') names on each of your six cards. Shuffle them and number the cards E1-E6. Deal out cards E1, E2, E3 in front of you and think about each of these three people in turn. Try to imagine yourself back in a situation with each of them in turn to revive your memory of them. Now think about them as learners (or as T-C practitioners). Think and feel about them deeply and (if appropriate) seriously. Which two of the three are most alike as learners (or T-C) and which one is most different as a learner, from the other two? Put the two 'similar learners' cards together and separate the 'different kind of learner' card from this pair.

Tear up another piece of card or scrap paper, preferably of a different colour, into 5" X 3" (12cm X 8cm) pieces. Label the first piece C1P1 and write on it a brief description of what it is about the pair which leads you to put them together. When you have done that label a second 5" X 3" piece of card C1P2 and write on it a brief description of what it is about the third person that makes him or her different as a learner.

Put the C1P2 and C1P1 descriptions aside and pick up cards E1, E2 and E3. Deal out cards E4, E5 and E6 and repeat the procedure. Which two are most alike as learners (or as practitioners) and which one is different from the other two? Write a description of the similarity between the new pair on a piece of coloured card labelled C2P1 and a description of what separates the singleton from them on another coloured card C2P2. Put C2P1 and C2P2 aside. Pick up E4, E5 and E6 and deal out E1 and E3 and E5. Repeat the procedure, filling in coloured cards C3P1 and C3P2. Finally deal out E2, E4 and E6 and repeat, completing the C4P1 and C4P2 cards.

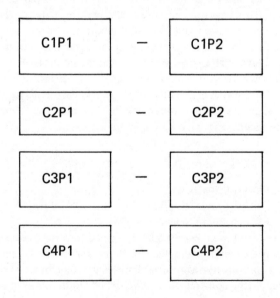

These 'construct cards' begin to display something. Something not necessarily about the people you have named on your 'element cards' (E1 to E6), but about yourself. They display some of the ways in which you think and feel about learners. What they contain will be as significant or as trivial as you were in your approach to the exercise. Did you know that you thought and felt about learners in these ways? If all the thoughts and feelings re-vitalised by this activity were already familiar to you, it is suggested that you sit and think again for a while about each of your six people in turn. Try to recall them in a learning situation. Now repeat the activity seeking more significant similarities and differences.

Content-free procedures

Activity 2.1 demonstrates what is meant by a content-free procedure. We, the authors, have no idea who you the reader were thinking about or in what ways you saw similarities and differences between them as learners. But our experience with similar exercises carried out face-to-face (individually or with large groups) is that when more E cards are used and more C P cards elicited, people quite often find out something significant about their attitudes to learners and hence to learning. This is even more likely to happen if you can persuade one or more friends or colleagues to do the same exercise independently and then join you in comparing the descriptions on the C P cards. Are you surprised by the pattern of similarities and differences between their ways of thinking and feeling about learners and your own?

Note: Those of the readers who have some familiarity with the repertory grid will recognise that cards E1 to E6 represent the elements (Es) and C P cards represent the constructs (Cs): C1P1 and C1P2 represent the two poles (Ps) of construct 1. For those who have yet to meet the grid for the first time an explanation of the terms element, pole and construct will be given later in this chapter (or you can find them in the glossary).

For the reader who finds the isolation of a content-free procedure a little frustrating and for clients in face-to-face courses it is often useful to exchange or exhibit results. But to emphasise the content-free-ness (and optionally private nature) of this technique, the results offered below are taken from an exercise in which the topic has been changed. So, unless you encourage others to do Activity 2.1 you may never know how similarly or differently you and other people think and feel about learners (or T-C practitioners).

Activity 2.2 Constructing personally significant learning events

Think back over your life and make some entirely private notes about any event from which you feel you learned something really significant. Sketch in as many 'significant learning events' as you can. At this stage note down everything without evaluation or comment, until you begin to feel that you have adequate notes to begin a sketch for your 'learning biography'. Variations on this exercise are to restrict the scope of the biography by:

1 Specifying a time period
   e.g. over the past three months.
2 Specifying a 'content' or 'topic' area
   e.g. (a) significant events in my learning of French as a foreign language;
         (b) significant learning events at work, or during my marriage.
3 Specifying a location.
   e.g. (a) at school;
         (b) whilst I was in the army.
4 Specifying the type of learning
   e.g. (a) that really taught me to think;
         (b) that really taught me to stand on my own two feet;
         (c) that increased my creativity;
         (d) that made me more ruthless;
         (e) that really got me interested in computers.

Now, having made the biographical notes, sort out what in retrospect appear as the most significant events. Note each of these on a separate (E) card.
   Now sort out your E cards into three piles:

(1) Very important to my learning and development.
(2) Quite important to my learning and development.
(3) Less important to my learning and development.

Starting with the 'very important' sort out nine cards which are most representative of the significant learning events in your life (or that aspect of it upon which you have chosen to concentrate).
   Now, using the content-free procedure of Activity 2.1, discover what are, for you, crucial similarities and differences between these events as learning experiences. Discover the terms in which you think and feel about your own significant learning experiences. The nine cards can be dealt out in the following sets of three without repeating any pair of cards in a triad. Each card is used four times.

        1,2,3   2,5,8   3,4,8

        4,5,6   3,6,9   3,5,7

        7,8,9   1,5,9   2,4,9

1,4,7   2,6,7   1,6,8

You may find yourself hard pushed to discover what are for you twelve naturally occurring but entirely different ways of thinking and feeling about learning experiences. In chapters 6-11 a number of grid tricks are suggested for extending the range of constructs explored.

Bill Shard's view of learning

The following example of 'significant learning events' is reported from one interview of a grid study with technical college students. These students were taking part in a course on 'learning to learn-by-reading' run by members of CSHL. During the first three half-days of the course it became increasingly apparent that the students had problems, not only with learning-to-learn, but more insistently with not wanting to learn from the technical college courses. After lively discussion it was decided to use the repertory grid to help each of them become more aware of what they meant by 'learning' and what parts of it they valued. This was viewed as a first step towards educational counselling. The *purpose* of the grid conversation determines the range of elements which are included. Again, discussion with the students revealed a general feeling that organised school and academic experiences were about being taught/instructed in some dry-as-dust topics; and that they did not thereby learn much of personal significance. It was therefore agreed that 'events over the past two years from which I learned something really useful' would be the best general definition of the relevant range of elements.

The early part of the grid conversation is designed to elicit these elements. When Bill Shard reflected on his last two years' experience, he produced the following set of events:

E1 Being near death in a dinghy
E2 Competition with a clever girl
E3 Thinking, after a family argument, that divorce was really a good idea
E4 Reading the lesson in church from the Bible
E5 Splitting up with girlfriend
E6 Meeting Marc Bolan (a pop star, now deceased)
E7 Being hit by woodwork teacher
E8 Failing my RAF medical
E9 A month's visit to Finland

In fact the real Bill Shard found twenty-nine such elements but for clarity this example offers only nine. The elicitation of these elements was already in itself a learning experience for Bill. He had never systematically reflected upon his idea of significant learning before.

Bill considered the first three elements. He was asked to try to recall and relive each of them as a learning experience. When he had done this he was asked which two experiences were most alike. After some consideration, he decided that: E2 — Competition with a clever girl', and 'E1 — Being near death in a dinghy' were most alike, and that 'E3 — Thinking, after a family argument, that divorce was really a good idea', was a different type of learning experience from the other two. When asked to describe what it was about E1 and E2 that made them similar, he replied: 'Finding out about my own character'; and when asked what made E3 different, he replied: 'Finding out about other people's true character'.

The complete set of CPs elicited from Bill Shard were as follows:

C1P1 Finding out about my own character	v.	C1P2 Finding out about other people's true character
C2P1 Spontaneous activity	v.	C2P2 Considered activity
C3P1 Affected my attitude to life negatively	v.	C3P2 Affected my attitude positively
C4P1 Grudge against a person	v.	C4P2 No grudge
C5P1 Same generation	v.	C5P2 Older generation
C6P1 External events (no control), impinging on emotions	v.	C6P2 Emotions internally generated (control)
C7P1 Take notice of and learn	v.	C7P2 Ignore and not remember
C8P1 Open; free to talk about what I like	v.	C8P2 On guard; not free to say what I like

The reader is for now asked merely to keep this example in mind as it will be used in chapter 3 to illustrate the elicitation of a complete grid.

The following example is offered to demonstrate how the 'same' content-free procedure evoked a very different reflection upon experience from another person.

Adam Stewart's view of learning

Adam Stewart was a senior local government administrator. He offered the following 'significant learning experience':

Writing poetry	First painting house
Reading two books at 17 years old	Building bedroom units
Professional course	Minutes of first committee
Unsatisfactory statistics class	Reconstituting the union
Lectures on handling groups	Chairing student council
Interpersonal skills course	Learning London
Russian evening classes	Picking up job in the first year at work
Relearning the trombone	New information strategy
Social sciences experience	Glass works
Chairing working party	How to delegate
Preparing session	Remembering things now

He identified the following similarities and differences in his thoughts and feelings about these events:

Learning on my own	v.	Tutoring by person or aid
Learning was a by-product	v.	Learning became the main outcome
Outside reasons for learning	v.	Attracted by subject matter itself
About facts	v.	Learning fundamental concepts
Learned very little	v.	Learned most from (after reflection)
Not very enjoyable	v.	Most enjoyable activity
Not deeply involved	v.	Highly involved
Thinking	v.	Doing things
I wanted to	v.	I had to

It is only to be expected that an 18-year-old and a 48-year-old will have rather different ranges of experience. But it may be slightly less obvious to some technical college teachers that 'meeting Marc Bolan' or 'nearly drowning in a dinghy' are relevant starting points for generating a personally relevant discussion with a student about the significance of learning. It also might not occur to them that having 'a grudge against somebody' was a motivating factor in learning from experience.

But identifying the *elements* (significant items of experience evoked by learning events) and the *personal constructs* (ways of thinking and feeling about these events) which a person uses in defining a topic is only part of the procedure for eliciting a repertory grid. The complete procedure is offered in chapter 3.

This 'elements' and 'constructs' procedure does, however, offer an introduction to the first set of techniques which may prove of use to the reader as a T-C practitioner.

The 'Introducing a Topic' technique

The process of eliciting 'items of experience' and then getting people to exchange and explore the terms in which they 'think and feel' about these is an example of a content-free conversational procedure. If it is used with a group who then share the results, it becomes a very powerful technique for 'Introducing a Topic' in a way that is personally relevant to them. It gets each participant thinking about it firstly in their own terms, and then in the context of those of their fellow participants.

It will be useful to consider three rather different types of example to exhibit the content-free nature of the procedure and to illustrate certain important variations.

Example 1: Social skills

A group of middle-level managers is meeting for a two-week course on 'The Management of People'. (They might have been a group of teachers reflecting upon their classroom experiences; or research and development engineers on their project work experiences; therapists reflecting on treating someone; or salesmen on selling experiences.) They were middle managers who were offered the following list of situations in which 'I might be called upon to exert man-management skills'. Each member of the course was asked to recall events from their own experiences, which were evoked by each of the 'situation descriptions'. They were asked to write brief private notes on each specific event. These were to be sufficient to remind themselves of what they had in mind: i.e. time, place, people involved, etc.

The list of 'element types' from which each was invited to identify items of personal man-management experience were:

- Informal comments on performance
- A non-productive event in a department meeting
- Describing a problem for a group
- Handling a problem arising out of work
- Socialising
- Planning ahead
- Giving instructions how to do something
- Seeking advice and suggestions
- Innovating – producing change
- Dealing with a tense situation
- Keeping an event going (wheel turning)
- A formal appraisal
- Finding the solution to a problem
- A departmental meeting that went well
- Working with colleagues

The notes about each event were written on separate cards. They were then asked to sort the cards into three piles:

(a) very important 'man-management event';
(b) fairly important 'man-management event';
(c) not so important 'man-management event';

and then to order the cards to identify what were for them the twelve most important ones.

They were then asked to shuffle these twelve and to number them E1 to E12. Thus a group of eighteen managers has each separately explored their own experience for examples of 'Me managing someone'. They are each introducing their own personal content into the procedure. The guide-list of 'element types' is used merely to ensure that all eighteen managers are exploring the 'same' topic. If anyone identified a particularly important 'man-management' event which did not fit the guide-list they were encouraged to include it. They were then talked through the three-card procedure to reveal the terms in which each personally identified similarities and differences in how they think and feel about their own man-management experiences. By construing a series of triads (sets of three cards), each participant identified his own repertoire of personal constructs about man-management events.

Now the eighteen participants are asked to re-group into six groups of three. Each group of three share their constructs and discuss similarities and differences in their repertoires of constructs. Specifically each construct consists of two poles (i.e. the similarity between the pair and the difference of the singleton (see Activity 2.1). Each pole of each construct has been written on a separate card. The three managers pool their cards and sort them into a classification system which they invent as they share their construing. If other members of the group have difficulty in understanding one participant's construct he or she may choose to explain it by using the original items of man-management experience from which it arose. But if a participant feels that the original experience was too personal to be discussed they are perfectly free to keep it private and explain their construct in more public terms. Each group of three people produce a set of categories (types of man-management experience) into which all their construct poles can be placed.

The six groups now pair up to form three groups of six. These share their category systems with each other. Each original group of three explains how they arrived at their categories, and the two groups combine to produce an expanded system of categories that can contain all the original constructs. This may be a fairly simple process of identifying the common categories and adding or combining those remaining; or it may involve a certain amount of renegotiation to invent a new category system which superordinates the two earlier ones. Finally, the three groups of six come back together and the whole group shares and discusses the types of construct (i.e. ways of thinking and feeling about man-management events) which are represented among all eighteen managers.

It should be emphasised that the personal learning provoked by this procedure comes from identifying one's own construing and then having to expand one's repertoire to include other people's constructions of their experience. The primary result is thus the raising of personal awareness by enriching the system of alternatives within which one can attribute personal meaning to events.

The choice of man-management events as the 'items of experience' to be construed only evolved after less appropriate elements (e.g. managers and management styles) had been piloted with earlier courses and discarded because they did not evoke quite the most relevant and useful areas of understanding. The category system which emerged from sixteen managers who used 'managers that I know well' as elements in one of these earlier exercises is as shown in Figure 2.1.

---

1 *Performance*

Effectual	v.	Cannot put theory into practise
Functionaly competent	v.	Incompetent
Obtains maximum performance from subordinates	v.	Does not obtain maximum performance from subordinates
Good administrator	v.	Hopeless at paperwork
Cost conscious	v.	Not cost conscious
Generates a good working environment	v.	Does not generate a good working environment
Uses training courses	v.	Little use for training
Good at personnel skills	v.	Poor at personnel skills
Represents the people under him	v.	Does not represent the people under him
Spends time with subordinates	v.	Does not spend time with subordinates

2 *Verbal Communication*

Good communicator	v.	Poor communicator
Speaks well	v.	Speaks hesitantly, uncertainly
Makes points clearly	v.	Repetitive
At ease in talking	v.	Uneasy in talking
Speaks softly	v.	Speaks loudly

3 *Delegation*

Accepts responsibility	v.	Avoids responsibility
Delegates	v.	Does not delegate
Gives responsibility	v.	Retains responsibility
Allows freedom	v.	Interferes
Allows subordinates responsibility for detail	v.	Gets too involved in detail

4 *Decision-making*

Decisive	v.	Indecisive
Makes own decisions	v.	Awaits instructions
Poor	v.	Good
Finds easy	v.	Finds difficult
Quick	v.	Slow
Sets objectives	v.	No policy
Long-term planner	v.	Short-term
Considers repercussions	v.	Short-sighted
Considers parallel repercussions	v.	Ignores parallel repercussions
Multi-option	v.	Single option
Acts without full knowledge or all facts	v.	Requires full knowledge and all facts

5 *Time-keeping*

Is seldom late	v.	Often late
Expects good time-keeping by subordinates	v.	Does not expect good time-keeping by subordinates
Willing to work long hours if necessary	v.	Unwilling to work long hours if necessary

6 *Methods of working with people*
Involves others in setting objectives
by – discussing
   listening
   explaining
   sharing information
   seeking suggestions and advice

Involves others in solving problems
by – discussing
   listening
   explaining
   sharing information
   seeking suggestions and advice

Involves others in making decisions
by – discussing
   listening
   explaining
   sharing information
   seeking suggestions and advice

7 *Innovation*

Innovative	v.	Conservative

Open minded	v.	Closed mind
Imaginative	v.	Unimaginative
Flexible	v.	Inflexible
Not afraid of new ideas	v.	Fearful
Looking for alternatives	v.	Status quo

8 *Thinking and doing*

Thinker	v.	Doer
Clear thinker	v.	Muddled, fuzzy
Logical	v.	Not logical
Precise	v.	Vague

9 *Personal attributes*

Managerial bearing	v.	Does not convey authority
Confident	v.	Lacks confidence
Independent	v.	Needs to be recognised
Independent	v.	Needs to be liked
Straight	v.	Devious
Consistent	v.	Inconsistent
Fair	v.	Unfair
Helpful	v.	Unhelpful
Approachable	v.	Remote/Aloof
Cheerful	v.	Worried and miserable
Friendly	v.	Unfriendly
Considerate	v.	Inconsiderate
Generous	v.	Selfish
Weak personality	v.	Strong personality
Introvert	v.	Extrovert

10 *Attitudes to subordinates about work*

Democratic	v.	Autocratic
Participative	v.	Authoritarian
Works together with sub-ordinates	v.	Works on his own
Supports subordinates	v.	Does not support subordinates
Encourages subordinates	v.	Does not encourage sub-ordinates
Rarely provokes	v.	Arrogant, abrasive, aggressive
Self effacing	v.	Arrogant, abrasive, aggressive
Keeps cool	v.	Loses temper
Respected by sub's.	v.	Not respected by sub's.
Prepared to admit wrong decisions	v.	Not prepared to admit wrong decisions
Acknowledges good work	v.	Casual about acknowledging good work

Rigidly applies company rules	v.	Flexes company rules
Political	v.	Rarely considers politics

11 *Attitudes to subordinates about personal and outside activities*

Person oriented	v.	Task oriented
Concern for people	v.	Little concern for people
Interested in personal problems	v.	Not interested in personal problems
Interest in family and outside activities	v.	No interest in family and outside activities
Usually takes part in social functions	v.	Hardly ever takes part in social functions

Figure 2.1 Categorisation of all constructs used by members of the man-management course

This specific category system was extremely useful to the members of the course from whom it had been elicited, but it would be less useful to other similar courses and of almost no use to managers operating in very different commercial, technical, geographic and social circumstances. The emergent list is virtually only a by-product of the active personal learning process which went on in this specific group. The man-management events were especially suited to evoking thoughts and feelings most appropriate to the purpose for which these people had come together. The 'significant learning events' (see Activity 2.1) have been used very successfully with a group of student counsellors, with teachers and with industrial trainers and 'events occurring during a sales transaction' proved very productive with a group of young sales managers. Other 'social skills' events with which this procedure has been used include 'appraisal interviews', 'managing a hotel dining room' and 'conducting a learning conversation'. Any area of social skill, i.e. any activity in which one person pursues his or her purpose with others, may be illuminated using this technique.

The reader is challenged to evolve a set of 'element types' uniquely appropriate to a topic in their own area of T-C. The choice of elements which will lead to the most fruitful exchanges within any group is worth careful consideration and some detailed investigatory pilot work.

Note: This example was introduced to show how a variation of the grid technique can be used with a large group without diluting the direct involvement of each participant.

Example 2: Objects in the here and now

A class of first-year sculpture students in a college of art used an analogous content-free conversational procedure for exploring their personal systems of aesthetic appreciation. Each student was asked to bring three objects to the session. They were asked to select objects which they felt had some value as 'items of sculpture'. The class was again divided into groups of three who thus each had nine 'items of sculpture' between them. These served as the elements to be construed. The exercise proceeded in a similar way to that with the man-management group, but there were some key differences. Firstly, the 'items of sculpture' had to be very thoroughly explored, examined and appreciated by each of the participants. Only then did these objects to be construed become 'items of personal experience' for each of the participants. The students often had some difficulty in putting their aesthetic constructs into words. There was a danger that they would trivialise or debase their true construing in order to use constructs which were easily verbalised and exchanged. This was avoided by insisting that constructs were illustrated by continual reference back to the pieces of sculpture. This became even more important when groups were exchanging and negotiating category systems. The most interesting result of this exercise was the number of times that students obviously experienced a radical reorganisation of their perceptions of a piece of sculpture whilst trying to appreciate how someone else construed it. Over and over again they made comments such as: 'I had never looked at it like that before', or 'I really am seeing something quite different now'. The importance of the non-verbal components in conveying the personal perceptions which were exchanged is illustrated by the obscurity of some of the constructs e.g.:

Break away	v. Accepted way of working
No aim	v. Projected aim
Questioning	v. Answering
Inclusion of incidental effects	v. Tight control over materials
Sensual effect	v. Non-sensual
Organic	v. Mechanical

Again the choice of 'elements' or 'items of experience' is quite crucial to the degree of personal learning that is likely to be provoked by this exercise. A T-C's choice of items might have little appeal to their clients unless they take the trouble to explore and negotiate with them. Other variations on this 'construing of physical objects' are:

(1) A set of 'identical' products offered to trainee industrial inspectors early in their period of training. It is important that they should be allowed to identify their own 'similarities' and 'differences' and not be guided too quickly into seeing only 'faults and defects' as defined by more experienced people.

(2) A 'wine-tasting' event organised according to this content-free conversational procedure proved very successful. But in retrospect it might have produced more personal learning (though perhaps less enjoyment) if the pro-

fessional habit of 'tasting not drinking' had been more rigorously adhered to. More seriously, this procedure has been used for establishing a base of shared experience out of which a 'taste panel' can begin to define its standards.

(3) Specimens found during a field trip by a class of botany or geology students or photographs from a museum can also be used as 'items of experience'.

(4) Examiners faced with answer scripts to the same question from twenty different candidates very quickly discovered, by using this procedure, some of the reasons for their unreliability in marking.

(5) Eight-year-olds construing items in a story achieved a much richer and more informed view of what the story was about than any individual child could have produced before the exercise.

Example 3: Apparently abstruse topics

A group of engineering consultants met for a workshop/seminar on 'The skills of consulting'. They were asked individually to prepare for the workshop by listing 'projects in which I have been involved'. They were also briefed how to elicit the constructs which they felt were most relevant to identifying the crucial 'similarities and differences' between projects. The sharing, categorising and pooling of personal constructs about consultancy proved to be quite a good method of starting off the workshop. Subsequently another similar group were asked to identify not 'whole projects' but 'significant phases in particular projects' as the elements or 'items of experience' to be construed. This increase in the specificity of the referents to personal experience led to far richer repertoires of personal constructs and a much more decisive start to the workshop.

Other examples analogous to these are:

(1) English literature students construing 'Poems I know well'.

(2) Maintenance staff listing 'equipment problems' and sharing their construing.

(3) It was suggested to a group of industrial and commercial trainers that they might construe 'training techniques', 'management activities', or 'members of the Industrial Training Board' (privately). Working in three separate groups these participants become very deeply involved in exchanging and clarifying their experiences.

(4) Physicists construing some of the basic concepts of their subject, e.g. 'mass', 'entropy', 'time', 'length', 'quanta', 'electron', 'laser', etc. rapidly arrived at some new (for them) insights.

(5) Directors of a company discussing qualities expected of a 'high flyer'.

These examples illustrate the meaning of a content-free conversational procedure. The procedure remains substantially the same whether inspectors are sharing their understanding of faults on a razor blade, students are pooling their

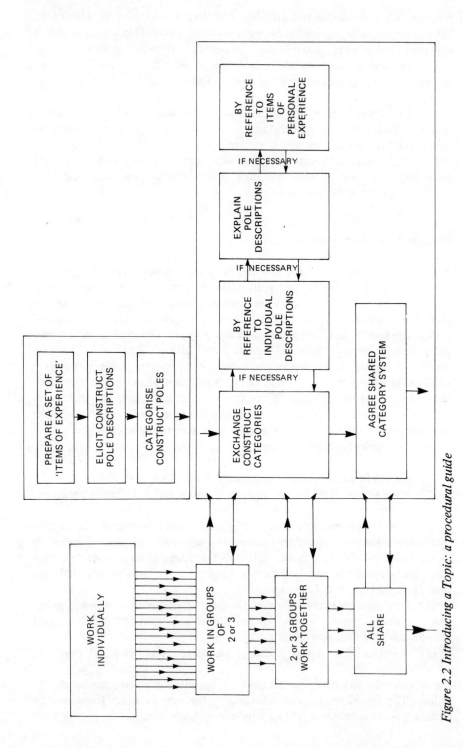

Figure 2.2 Introducing a Topic: a procedural guide

appreciation of Shakespeare's plays, 8-year-olds are exchanging views about what parts of their body are exercised by different pieces of PE equipment or the directors of the research division of a company are exploring how they construe their research and development plans for possible new products.

An outline *algorithm* for this 'Introducing a topic' procedure is summarised in Figure 2.2.

The examples of 'items of significant personal learning' given earlier in this chapter under the pen-names of Bill Shard and Adam Stewart could have been elicited as part of such 'Introducing a Topic' procedures but in fact they were not. They were partly completed descriptions of how one elicits a repertory grid. The next chapter describes how this is done.

Activity 2.3 Elements and constructs

The reader could now select a topic of interest to her or him. Choose a set of elements which seem to define a topic. Elicit a series of constructs using triads of elements. Record any difficulties which may be experienced. Bear these in mind as you proceed to chapter 3.

Chapter 3

The construction of personal meaning

The power of a conversational technology

It has been noted that at any given time there are more people engaged in organised learning (T-C) than in the whole of manufacturing industry. Techniques which can make the subject matter (topic being learnt) more personally relevant would increase the effectiveness of this army of people many times over.

In chapter 1 it was suggested that certain of the constructions which we impose upon our experience develop into personal myths and models about our own intelligence, talents and potential. These mostly pessimistic assumptions about our own learning processes are often the major influence on our capacity to learn. It was also suggested that many people experience much organised T-C as irrelevant, boring and tedious or as difficult and frustrating. This observation was not made lightly. It is one of those ephemeral facts which are universally acknowledged, informally in conversation, but almost as universally ignored or publicly denied by the relevant professions and institutions. Many of the problems of individuals, groups, institutions and society can be squarely laid at the feet of the T-C professions. They have failed to produce a theory or practice with which to enable people to question and then to increase their capacity for learning. Thus, most practitioners are still so bound up in their beliefs about personality traits, natural aptitudes, endowed abilities, etc., that they cannot conduct a truly liberating learning conversation with their clients.

In chapter 2 methods were introduced for helping each individual in a group to explore their own understanding and assumptions about a topic in their own terms in the context of others. Suggestions were also made for how the groups could use the 'Introducing a Topic' procedure to sample the experience of every individual. The full repertory grid technique allows T-C to develop such personal learning activities much further.

For example, most arts-based social scientists find statistics a notoriously difficult subject to learn. After attending lectures on the topic for two years some students still have qualms about calculating a mean and standard deviation and many are scared silly by the idea of estimating the significance of the difference between the means of two related samples. The cumulative effect of their 'attempts at learning' has been to alienate them completely from the subject matter. Some of them will tell you that because of their inborn mathematical ineptitude they have never understood more than a consecutive sentence or two from any of the lecturers. Some readers may have had similar experiences with other subjects (for example, languages, book-keeping, music or woodwork) at school. Such attitudes to a topic are much more likely to arise from bad early learning experiences than from innate inability. The authors have used the repertory grid with social science statistics students to great effect. Words like 'risk', 'utility', 'deviation', 'chance', 'probability', 'mean', 'range', 'frequency', are used in statistics as specialist terms. To some students they remain completely meaningless in the context of statistics lectures. At best the topic remains totally impersonal and unrelated to the experience of such learners. At worst it is positively repelling. In one instance, nine students, who had all badly failed their mock statistics examination came to one of the authors for tutorial advice. He got them each to do a conversational repertory grid using statistical terms as elements (see Chapter 2). The exercise took each student an average of two hours. They then spent another session exchanging and discussing their new understandings. This experience was a watershed in the learning of these students. Within six weeks they had all gone on to pass their statistics exam. The grid did not teach them statistics. What it did was to relate statistical concepts to the learners' personal experience thus releasing them to begin to make personal sense of the topic.

The repertory grid is a technique for enabling a person to explore their thoughts and feelings about a topic in their own terms. This is a crucial move towards making the topic personally relevant, positively interesting, and therefore more available to be learned. On this occasion the 'statistics grid' experience enabled the students to completely change the trajectory of their learning. Similar exercises involving various repertory grid techniques have been used by members of the CSHL to help people explore the personal relevance of many different topics from 'biological specimens' to events during 'an education student's first teaching practice' and from 'faults in breakfast cereals' to the nature of 'the training/learning relationship'.

To represent a system of personal constructs

Despite the title of the previous chapter, it did not describe a repertory grid, nor did it describe how to elicit one. What it did was to introduce the ideas of 'element', 'construct' and 'construct pole'.

The elements in a grid are not pieces of sculpture, man-management events, products to be inspected, statistical concepts, books... etc. The elements in the grid are *the client's experience of* pieces of sculpture, events, products, concepts, books, etc. The elements in the grid are always 'items of personal experience'. This being so, any set of such items can be used to elicit a grid.

The relevance of the grid to the *purpose* for which it is being used will depend entirely upon the type of elements which it contains. The choice of elements is crucially important but, in the last analysis, pragmatic. The correct set of elements are those that enable the client to more fully explore their own pattern of personal meaning, to become more usefully aware of his or her pattern of thoughts and feelings, as they relate to his or her purposes.

A personal construct can be envisaged as a dimension of personal meaning. The system of personal constructs is the person's psychological space, the structure of personal meaning within which the items of experience ('elements') acquire their significance, one in relation to another. Thus if two items of experience are thought and felt to be similar, they will lie close to each other in the personal construct system. If two elements are construed differently they will lie in separate areas of the construct system. Words such as 'space', 'structure', 'lie close' and 'separate areas' reveal that the basic model or analogy that is here being used to introduce the idea of a system of personal constructs is that of physical space. This idea can be very useful in providing some sort of image around which to start thinking about the nature of construing, but it can very rapidly become misleading unless it clearly remains only a model or analogy. It will become an impediment to further progress unless it can be discarded or modified and replaced when it ceases to add to our understanding. If a personal construct is defined as 'a dimension of the psychological space within which items of experience acquire meaning' then the poles of a construct define the ends or the opposite directions of such a dimension.

'Green v. Red' might be the poles of a personal construct in the authors' system of meaning concerned with fruit and vegetables. 'Hard v. Soft' might be poles of another construct in the same system of meaning.

Thus tomato, cucumber, carrot and avocado might be construed so:

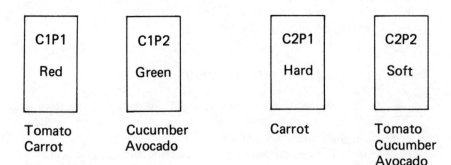

C1P1	C1P2		C2P1	C2P2
Red	Green		Hard	Soft

Tomato   Cucumber   Carrot   Tomato
Carrot   Avocado   Cucumber
                                      Avocado

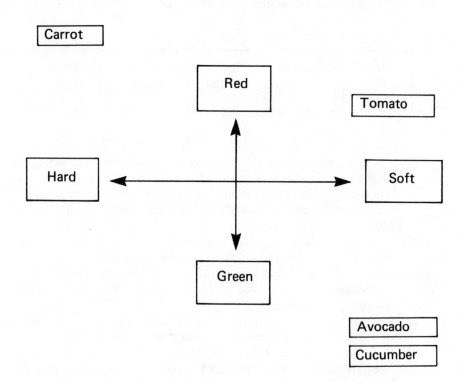

Figure 3.1 A two-dimensional representation of a simple construct system

Thus, when placed in this two-dimensional space, 'carrot', 'tomato', 'cucumber' and 'avocado' would distribute as shown in Fig. 3.1. The fact that you, the reader, may feel that most tomatoes are green or that cucumbers are hard only demonstrates that meaning is a relationship between a person and his or her experience. Meaning lies within a personal construct system. Here the elements in this system are 'items of the author's experience', not some generalised public concept of 'tomato' or 'cucumber'. This simple example reveals some of the questions of grid technique which will be explored, analysed and answered throughout the remainder of this book.

(1) How hard is 'hard' and how soft is 'soft'? This raises a variety of issues, including:
    (a) How does one person construe the construct system of another?
    (b) Is a personal construct to be construed as a bi-polar? i.e. either red

or green, or as a continuous dimension, i.e.

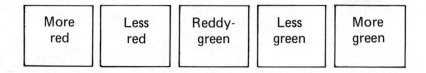

(2) What happens to 'potato'? Can there be an element that cannot be assigned to a personal construct? Can there be a construct that does not accept certain elements although they lie within the topic definition (i.e. fruit and vegetables)? Is 'fruit and vegetables' one topic or two?

(3) If we, the authors, introduce another construct, 'I like it' v. 'I never eat it' what does that do to the positions shown in Fig. 3.1?

Do descriptions such as red, soft, etc. go into the same structure of meaning as feelings such as 'I like it'? Are descriptions 'objective' and feelings 'subjective'?

(4) Is my red your red? Does 'red' carry the same meaning for everybody? How does one personal construct system 'map' on to another?

(5) How do you know an avocado is not a pear? How do people with different personal construct systems negotiate a public system of agreed meanings?

(6) What if we elicit four or more (say 15) constructs?
   (a) Can we imagine a four- (or15-) dimensional space? What alternate analogies or models are available for helping us construe a complex construct system?
   (b) Are all constructs to be seen as operating at the same level or could 'squashy v. firm' be a sub-construct of 'soft'?

(7) Is 'red' v. 'green' totally separate from 'hard' v. 'soft'? If not, should the two dimensions in Fig. 3.1 be shown at right angles?

Eliciting a repertory grid

Before exploring these questions it will be useful to understand the repertory grid more fully. More important than the formal procedure for eliciting the grid is the spirit in which this elicitation is carried out. The reason that it has taken two and a half chapters to reach this point is that in the authors' experience this spirit is not easily communicated. The clients/learners descriptions of their own experiences must be respected. They must be encouraged to explore them fully and then to express them in personally significant terms. The purpose for using the grid should, ideally, come from the learners. If it does not, then they must fully understand why the grid is being elicited and how it is to be used. This enables them to explore and interrogate their own experience within the most useful frame of reference.

The elicitation should be conversational, guided by both the learner and the T-C. This is true even when the self-organised learner, being his or her own mentor, conducts the conversation within him or herself.

The example of Bill Shard's personal learning experiences which was offered in chapter 2 is here used to illustrate the steps in the complete elicitation procedure.

Step 1: Decide upon the purpose of the grid

The purpose for eliciting the grid is to help 'Bill Shard' explore his understanding of personal learning (see chapter 2). Issues arising out of the negotiation of purpose are discussed in more detail in chapter 6. A list of purposes for which grids have been elicited by the authors is presented in appendix A1.2. This is offered only as an illustrative guide, as Bill Shard's need to explore his assumptions about learning arose directly out of the situation in his technical college.

Step 2: Identify the type of 'elements' which will best allow the purpose to be achieved

This has been one of the most under-developed parts of repertory grid technology. It is often not even mentioned. Inappropriate elements provoke inadequate constructs. It is for this reason that the results of many students using 'a technique resembling the repertory grid' are suspect. The 'elements' in a grid are always items of personal experience. If the experience is shallow, merely verbal or second-hand, the grid will contain shallow, merely verbal or second-hand meaning.

The elements in Bill Shard's grid are 'events in my life from which I learned something significant'. This definition was not just invented. It arose out of the situation in the technical college and from Bill Shard's rejection of academic learning.

Step 3: Elicit the elements

The discussion during which Bill identified those 'events in my life from which I learned something significant' was discursive. He was encouraged to digress and explore as wide an area of his experience as he wished. The discussion was, eventually, by mutual agreement, restricted to 'the past two years'. He was cued to explore various periods during those two years as thoroughly as he could (e.g. what were you doing last summer before you started college? etc.) but the interviewer offered no suggestions about events. Time and place were used merely as aids to recall. Each item of experience was noted by the interviewer but the flow of conversation was not interrupted. The purpose of the interviewer was to ensure that Bill tapped as rich and wide a range of his personally significant learning experiences as possible. At convenient intervals Bill was asked how he would describe the events which had already been noted so that he would have no doubt or trouble later in identifying the particular event.

For example: 'I was out in the sailing dinghy and we were racing along when we realised that the tack we were on would not clear the head, I swung the tiller over and the jib caught my friend a blow on the shoulder. I dived to save him going overboard and the dinghy capsized. He was thrown clear but I got caught up in a line and for a minute or two had a lot of trouble freeing myself and getting away and up to the surface. I swallowed a lot of water. I really thought my time had come. It disturbed me very much and afterwards I thought a lot about dying and how I was living my life.' Bill decided to call this: 'Being near death in a dinghy'.

Bill's conversational elicitor identified 48 'items of experience' during this exploratory part of the conversation. From these Bill eliminated many as trivial or 'not really a learning experience'. This left 29 items in a selected list of 'personal shorthand' element descriptions. These were:

* 1   Being near death in a dinghy.
  2   Short eyesight made me give up playing football for my team.
  3   Learning how to avoid trouble when in my early teens.
  4   Determined to endure educational system to obtain ambition in electronics.
* 5   Competition with a clever girl.
  6   Musical outlook broadened by 'Deep Purple'.
* 7   A month's visit to Finland.
* 8   Thinking, after a family argument, that divorce was really a good idea.
* 9   Being hit by woodwork teacher.
  10   A change of school.
  11   Grandmother came to live with us.
*12   Reading the lesson in church from the Bible.
  13   Dinner party in Paris.
  14   Reading *Lord of the Rings*.
*15   Failing my RAF medical.
  16   Guys watching us who crashed.
  17   Seeing *The Devils*.
*18   Splitting up with girlfriend.
  19   Learning to play the guitar.
  20   Chemical warfare — knowledge of dangers.
*21   Meeting Marc Bolan.
  22   Sister being overweight.
  23   Interest in electronics inspired by father.

24   Coming to college gave me a surprising freedom.
25   Talking to master outside school.
26   A poetry evening.
27   A highly condensed history course with an enthusiastic young teacher.
28   Having to cope with a man possibly drunk.
29   Moving house — different kind of business.

For clarity of presentation these were edited to nine elements in chapter 2 and this useful explanatory fiction is maintained both in this example and in chapter 4.

* Items used in the illustrative example running through chapters 2, 3 and 4.

Step 4: Eliciting a personal construct

When Bill had consolidated his element descriptions, the elicitation of personal constructs commenced.

'Now I want you to think and feel yourself back into these events and really consider them deeply as personal learning experiences.
Here are the first three:
    E1   Being near death in a dinghy.
    E2   Competition with a clever girl.
    E3   Thinking, after a family argument, that divorce was really a good idea.
Now take your time, which two of these were most alike as learning experiences and which one was most different from the other two?' Bill tried to recall and re-live each event. After some time he decided that:
    E2   Competition with a clever girl.
and E1   Being near death in a dinghy.
were most alike; and that:
    E3   Thinking, after a family argument, that divorce was really a good idea.
was a very different learning experience from the other two. When asked what it was about E2 and E1 that made them similar, he replied:
    'I don't really know. In each of them I was finding out something about myself. How I react to challenge or crises. I suppose I was getting to know myself better, discovering bits of me I didn't know were there. The family thing was very different. I saw my mother and my sister in a completely different light. I didn't know — well I mean — I had never thought they could feel so strongly or so badly about my father. I suppose I was finding out things about them.'
When asked to describe these two 'construct poles' in a personal shorthand which would remind him of exactly what he had in mind he decided:
E2 and E1 were about:
    C1P1   'Finding out about my own character.'
and E 3 was:

C1P2 'Finding out about another person's true character'.
(The reader will have realised that this narrative description is a rather more complete version of the construct elicitation described in chapter 2, pages (25-6). It is offered to remind the reader once again of the wealth of detailed personal meaning that is encapsulated in the rather bald 'verbal labels' of grid elements and constructs.)

When the purpose of the grid is that of raising personal awareness the short-hand verbal labels serve as adequate reminders which trigger the individual back into this rich resource of personal meaning. As we shall see later when the purpose is to communicate personal meaning to another, verbal labels are not sufficient. What is required is a common pool of shared experience and a carefully controlled referencing to and from such experience. Only thus can the meaning of the shared labels be established. This is not achieved by more and more detailed one-way verbal descriptions, but through carefully controlled two-way illustrated conversations.

Step 5: Assign the elements to the construct

When the poles of the first construct had been elicited Bill was asked to assign each of the other elements to one or other poles of the construct.

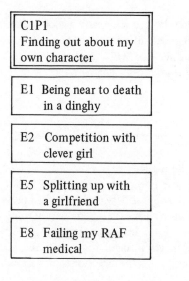

Figure 3.2 Assigning elements to construct poles

This he did by sorting the element cards into two groups. Those similar to the pair in one group and those similar to the singleton in the other. These results are shown entered onto a raw grid form in Fig. 3.3. All the elements grouped under C1P1 (i.e. E1, E2, E5 and E8) are indicated by ticks ($\sqrt{}$) in the appropriate columns on the form. All the elements grouped under C1P2 (i.e. E3, E4, E6, E7 and E9) are indicated by crosses (X) in their columns.

Step 6: Elicit further constructs and assign the elements to them

In chapter 2 the repertoire of constructs elicited from Bill were listed. Although not mentioned in chapter 2, after each construct was elicited the elements were assigned to the construct poles. The results were entered on the raw grid form. Fig. 3.3 shows Bill's completed raw grid.

The triads (sets of three elements) used to elicit the constructs may, as will be discussed later, be selected to insist that the client makes particular comparisons which are especially relevant to the purpose for which the grid is being used. In the absence of any reason to emphasise particular comparisons, triads should be selected so that:

(a) All elements are used as often as each other.
(b) No pair of elements recurs until all pairs have been used once. It is useful to remember that each triad contains three pairs,
e.g. Triad 'E1, E2 & E3' contains E1 & E2; E2 & E3; and E3 & E1.

The method for assigning elements to constructs described in step 5 involved physically sorting the element cards into two columns defined by the two poles of the construct. Laying out the element cards in this way offers the client/learner an opportunity to review all his assignings together when he has finished sorting the cards. He can then make any revisions which seem necessary. Whilst this method requires the preparation of element cards and construct pole cards, the extra work and time involved is more than compensated for by the improved quality of the results: and the additional reflection induced by the process of holistic comparison.

In making the judgments required in assigning the elements to the construct poles, the client's thoughts and feelings about a pole may change slightly (or even radically). They should be encouraged to re-write on the raw grid form descriptions which for them truly capture the basis on which elements were eventually assigned to the construct poles even when these differ from the descriptions on their CP cards.

The elicitation of constructs continues until the client/learner feels that he or she is only repeating, and can only repeat, earlier pole names. Sometimes a client will feel that a triad can be split in more than one meaningful way and it is then good practice to allow them to identify two constructs from the same triad. The interviewer can either enter both successively on the raw grid

CONSTRUCT POLE RATED - ✓ -

CONSTRUCT POLE RATED - X -

ELEMENTS

```
                                    E E E E E E E E E
                                    0 0 0 0 0 0 0 0 0
                                    1 2 3 4 5 6 7 8 9
                                   *************************
FINDING OUT ABOUT MY OWN CHARACTER  C1 * ✓ ✓ X X ✓ X ✓ X * C1   FINDING OUT ABOUT OTHER'S CHARACTER
              ABOUT PEOPLE          C2 * ✓ X ✓ X X ✓ ✓ * C2    ABOUT LIFE
        FROM OTHERS' INSIGHT        C3 * ✓ ✓ ✓ X X ✓ X * C3    FROM OWN INSIGHT
  GROWING UP MORE AUTHORITY         C4 * ✓ ✓ ✓ X ✓ X X * C4    GROWING UP EMBARRASSMENT
            OWN CONDITIONS          C5 * ✓ X X ✓ X X X * C5    IMPOSED BY PARENTS AND OTHERS
             SELF-RELIANT           C6 * X X ✓ ✓ X X X * C6    GROUP ACTIVITY
                  TENSE             C7 * ✓ ✓ ✓ ✓ ✓ X ✓ * C7   RELAXED
          SAME GENERATION           C8 * ✓ ✓ X X ✓ ✓ ✓ * C8   OLDER GENERATION
         MADE ME CAUTIOUS           C9 * ✓ ✓ X X ✓ X ✓ * C9   GUIDING EFFECT
                                   *************************
                          * * * * * * * * * E9   A MONTH'S VISIT TO FINLAND
                          * * * * * * * * E8   FAILING MY R.A.F MEDICAL
                          * * * * * * * E7   BEING HIT BY MY WOODWORK TEACHER
                          * * * * * * E6   MEETING MARC BOLAN
                          * * * * * E5   SPLITTING UP WITH GIRLFRIEND
                          * * * * E4   READING THE LESSON IN CHURCH FROM THE BIBLE
                          * * * E3   THINKING AFTER A FAMILY ARGUMENT THAT DIVORCE IS REALLY A GOOD IDEA
                          * * E2   COMPETITION WITH A CLEVER GIRL
                          * E1   BEING NEAR DEATH IN A DINGHY
```

Figure 3.3 Bill Shard's raw grid

or simply note down the second for later reference. Any comments about constructs or poles should also be noted. When the clients feel that they have exhausted their repertoire of constructs, these notes should be used to jog their memory and to elicit any further similarities and differences which occur to them. Another method for fully exhausting the repertoire is to finally lay out all the E cards for inspection. Successive grouping of one with another may provoke further constructs. (This is known as the open field method.) When clients mention another construct and then begin to express doubts about whether it is really very different from an earlier one, they should be encouraged to include it unless the verbal labels of both poles are exactly similar to those of an earlier construct.

It is important that the element descriptions and the construct pole descriptions should be expressed in exactly those words which the client feels are most suitable. It is all too easy for interviewers to believe that they can help the client to express their thoughts and feelings more clearly by offering them words and terminology which would not spontaneously spring into their minds. This should almost always be avoided. It leads to the verbal labels becoming the interviewer's construing of the client's construing. This can defeat the whole object of the grid exercise.

Since the aim of the grid exercise is to exhaust the relevant repertoire of the client's constructs, any variation of the procedure which enriches the conversational process and thus taps more 'relevant items of experience' or more significant 'ways of thinking and feeling about those items' is not only legitimate but should be encouraged. Any procedural pre-occupations with pseudo-scientifc considerations such as treating each client in exactly the same way, or with the timing of the interview, are actually anti-scientific since the similarity to be pursued is the similarly adequate exploration of each client's unique, personal experience and not a superficial similarity of outward forms. The latter deflates the technique into one resembling the repertory grid only in appearance and not in spirit. An outline algorithm for this 'eliciting a repertory grid' procedure is shown in Fig. 3.4.

Identifying the meaning hidden in the grid

Whilst the raw grid shows the client's repertoire of personal constructs and it also shows how each element is assigned to the poles of each construct, it does not display the total pattern of personal meaning that lies hidden within it.

For example, examination of Bill Shard's raw grid will reveal that E2 and E5 are assigned to the poles of each construct in the same way. Thus Bill Shard thinks and feels that:

        E5 Competition with a clever girl,
and   E2 Splitting up with a girlfriend

were very similar personal learning experiences.

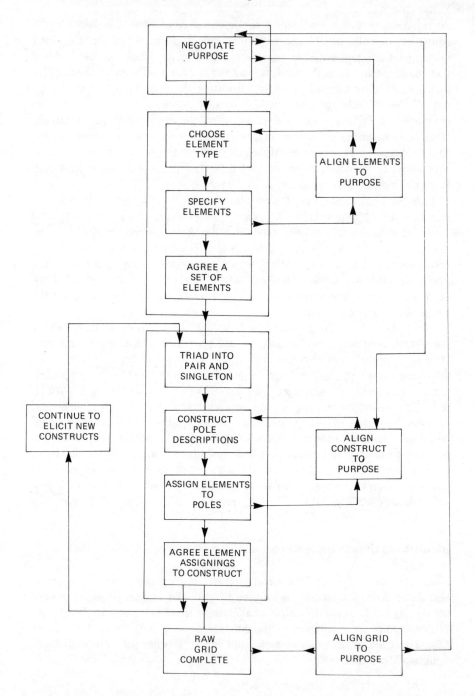

Figure 3.4 Eliciting a repertory grid: an algorithm

Extracting these two elements from the raw grid reveals that he experienced both as:

Pole 1		E5	E2		Pole 2
Finding out about my own character	C1	√	√		
		X	X	C2	About life
From others' insight	C3	√	√		
Growing up – more authority	C4	√	√		
Own conditions	C5	√	√		
		X	X	C6	Group activity
Tense	C7	√	√		
Same generation	C8	√	√		
		X	X	C9	Guiding effect
		E5	E2		
		*	*		
		*	*		
		*			Competition with a clever girl E2
		*			

Splitting up with girlfriend E5

Figure 3.5 Similar construing of two learning experiences

When the rows of √s and Xs in the grid are inspected, C5 and C8 are revealed as having the elements assigned to their poles in very nearly the same way, i.e.:

		E1	E2	E3	E4	E5	E6	E7	E8	E9		
C5	Own condi-itions	√	√	X	X	√	√	X	X	X	C5	Imposed by parents and others
C8	Same gene-ration	√	√	X	X	√	√	X	X	√	C8	Older generation

E9 is the only element which is assigned differently to C5 and C8. Thus 8 times out of 9 when Bill thinks and feels about a personal learning experience as being concerned with the 'same generation' as himself, he also feels that he is able to deal with it on his 'own conditions' but when he feels that the experience involved the 'older generation', it was also 'imposed by parents and others'.

Thus, as we identify the similarity in patterns of response between elements and between constructs, some of the personal meaning hidden in the grid emerges.

Further inspection reveals that:

C2 and C3 have the elements assigned to their poles in exactly the opposite ways, i.e.:

		E1	E2	E3	E4	E5	E6	E7	E8	E9		
C2	About people	X	X	√	√	X	√	X	X	√	C2	About life
C3	From others' insight	√	√	X	X	√	X	√	√	X	C3	From own insight

Every 'X' on C2 is a '√' on C3 and every '√' on C2 is an 'X' on C3. But the left and right locations of the poles of the construct are, in some sense, arbitrary, being merely the result of a pair of elements having one property and the single-ton having another.*

So there is no reason why C2 should not be re-written with 'About Life' on the left and 'About people' on the right. If this is done, then to preserve the positional convention for '√s' and 'Xs' all the old 'Xs' become '√s' and all the '√s' becomes 'Xs'.
Thus:

	E1	E2	E3	E4	E5	E6	E7	E8	E9		
C2 (R) About life	√	√	X	X	√	X	√	√	X	C2 (R) About people

This reversal of C2 has not changed the meaning in the grid.

E1 E2 E5 E7 E8   remain assigned to 'About life'.

E3 E4 E6 E9   remain assigned to 'About people'.

But now this part of the grid display becomes easier to interpret.

	E1	E2	E3	E4	E5	E6	E7	E8	E9		
About life (R) C2	√	√	X	X	√	X	√	√	X	C2 (R) About people
From others' insight C3	√	√	X	X	√	X	√	√	X	C3 From own insight

All the elements assigned to: 'About life' are also assigned to 'From others' insight'. Again, what is revealed by analysis of the grid is something about how the client is thinking and feeling about the topic. A strong correlation between two elements suggests that the client does not feel or think that there is much difference between the two. But this inference must be fed back to him or her

* As we shall see later the difference between the emergent pole (as defined by the similarity between the paired elements), and the submerged pole (as defined by the difference of the single element) may be important for some purposes. When reversing pole descriptions care should be taken to identify the originally emergent pole.

since clients are the final arbiters of how they think and feel about things. Similarly the idea that Bill learns 'about life' from 'others' insight' and 'about people' from his 'own insight' is not a fact, it is an inference to be offered back to him for his observation and comment.

These two processes of: (a) identifying 'clusters' of elements which are assigned to the poles of the construct in much the same way, and (b) identifying 'clusters' of constructs which (with reversals if necessary) have elements assigned to them in the same way, are the basic operations by which the 'raw' repertory grid is FOCUSed to display the pattern of personal meanings which lies hidden in the responses. The complete process of FOCUSing a grid is described in the next chapter.

Three other raw grids are offered at the end of this chapter (Figs.3.6, 3.7 and 3.8). They are intended to extend the range of examples both of elements and of constructs. They are also intended to illustrate the difficulty and dangers of misinterpretation which lie in any attempt to construe another's construing directly from the verbal labels in the grid without referring back and negotiating a shared system of meaning with the client.

Activity 3.1 Completing a repertory grid

It is suggested that readers use the elements and constructs which they elicited in one of the exercises in chapter 2 to complete a repertory grid.

You will need a raw grid form (empty) which is easily drawn up using Fig. 3.3 as a guide.

The construct pole cards are then used to define the 'verbal labels' which may be entered into the left and right construct pole boxes. But before entering the verbal labels sort your element cards into two piles, most like C1P1 and most like C1P2. Now look through the C1P1 pile and decide whether the verbal label on card C1P1 adequately describes why you have put them together. If it does not, change the description as you enter it on to the raw grid form. Similarly decide whether you wish to change the verbal label of C1P2 which is entered into the right-hand 'construct pole box'. Now enter a '√' under those element columns on the grid form, the element numbers of which (e.g. E3) correspond to those in the C1P1 pile of element cards. Similarly enter an 'X' in the column of each element number which occurs in the C1P2 pile. All your columns should now contain a '√' or an 'X' unless you have assigned some cards to a 'don't know' or 'not applicable' pile, in which case for the purpose of this exercise force yourself to assign the queried elements into either the C1P1 '√' category or into the C1P2 'X' category. This will enable you to carry out the initial exercises in chapter 4 more easily.

Activity 3.2 Eliciting a repertory grid on a topic of your own choice

Negotiate with some friend or colleague (not a T-C client at this stage) a topic on which they would like to do a grid. Discuss the topic with them and identify some significant 'items of experience' which are for them associated with it. Try to formulate a 'class of appropriate elements' from these. Continue the discussion until you have identified 12 significant, comparable but different items of experience which represent the topic to you and to your friend or colleague.

Now elicit 9-12 constructs, using the procedure and hints about conversational methodology which you remember from these first three chapters. (Try to do this without referring back to the book.) Now use the E cards to assign each of the elements to one or other of the poles of each of your constructs. Enter the results on a raw grid form. Talk with your friend or colleague about their experience of your elicitation procedure. Listen carefully to what they say: particularly note any criticism or difficulties which they identify.

Now scan through appendix A to see whether it contains ideas about other types of topic which may be of interest to you. When you have identified such a topic consider the nature of the 'items of personal experience' which might be appropriate as elements to be used in an 'awareness-raising' grid on the topic.

Try another grid with another friend or colleague using a very different type of topic and elements from those used in the first one. Good Luck!

```
                              RAW GRID

CONSTRUCT POLE RATED - √ -        ELEMENTS        CONSTRUCT POLE RATED - X -

                        E E E E E E E E E
                        0 0 0 0 0 0 0 0 0
                        1 2 3 4 5 6 7 8 9
                        *********************
        WITH IT   C1 *  X √ √ X √ X √ √ √  * C1   OLD AND BORING
OKAY WITH FATHER   C2 *  √ X √ √ X X X X √  * C2   LIKELY TO UPSET FATHER
         CHATTY   C3 *  √ X √ √ X √ X X √  * C3   REAL
   DOWN TO EARTH   C4 *  X √ √ X √ X √ √ √  * C4   TOO CLEVER
     GOOD FOR ME   C5 *  √ X √ √ X X √ √ X  * C5   I ENJOY BUT FEEL GUILTY
       ONE THING   C6 *  √ X √ √ X X √ √ X  * C6   LIVELY AND CHANGING
                        *********************
                        * * * * * * * * *SPORTS DESK
                        * * * * * * * *A BOOK AT BEDTIME
                        * * * * * * *STUDY ON 3
                        * * * * *WOMAN'S HOUR
                        * * * *THE ARCHERS
                        * * *ANY QUESTIONS
                        * *LIGHTEN OUR DARKNESS
                        * *DOUBLE TOP TEN SHOW
                        *TALKING ABOUT ANTIQUES
```

Figure 3.6 Mick's raw grid

```
                              RAW GRID

CONSTRUCT POLE RATED - √ -        ELEMENTS        CONSTRUCT POLE RATED - X -

                        E E E E E E
                        1 2 3 4 5 6
                        ***************
          LINGUISTIC   C1 *  √ X X √ √ X  * C1   VERBAL
UNIQUE ANSWER DESIRED   C2 *  X √ √ X X √  * C2   VARIABLE ANSWER DESIRED
    GLOBAL (ABSOLUTE)   C3 *  √ √ X X √ X  * C3   LOCAL
             LOGICAL   C4 *  √ X X √ √ X  * C4   MECHANICAL
         THEORETICAL   C5 *  √ √ X √ √ X  * C5   PRACTICAL
                        ***************
                        * * * * * * E6 CALCULATE
                        * * * * * E5 EXPLAIN
                        * * * * E4 SHOW
                        * * * E3 FIND
                        * * E2 DEFINE
                        * E1 PROVE
```

Figure 3.7 Ben's raw mathematical grid

CONSTRUCT POLE RATED – √ –

CONSTRUCT POLE RATED – X –

RAW GRID

ELEMENTS

```
                 E E E E E E E E E E
                 0 0 0 0 0 0 0 0 0 1
                 1 2 3 4 5 6 7 8 9 0
                 * * * * * * * * * * *
OWN INTEREST INDEPENDENT OF SET WORK    C1 *  √ √ √ X √ √ X √ √ √ *  C1  SPECIFIC SET WORK
                            NO AIM      C2 *  X X √ √ X X √ √ X √ *  C2  SET WORK WITH REASON AND PURPOSE
CURIOSITY FROM OWN DESIRE FOR KNOWLEDGE C3 *  √ √ X X √ √ X √ √ √ *  C3  CURIOSITY INDUCED BY OTHERS' IDEAS
PLEASURE FOR KNOWLEDGE AND SATISFACTION C4 *  X √ √ √ X X √ X X √ *  C4  ANXIETY
INFLUENCED BY OTHERS IDEAS, BY CHOICE   C5 *  X X √ √ X X √ √ √ √ *  C5  SET WORK UNDER PRESSURE
CHOICE BUT NOT NECESSARILY PLEASURE     C6 *  √ √ √ X √ √ X X √ √ *  C6  SET WORK
                            NO AIM      C7 *  X √ X X √ X X √ X √ *  C7  AIM AND PURPOSE TO GAIN KNOWLEDGE
                 * * * * * * * * * * *
                 * * * * * * * * * * E10  PLEASURE
                 * * * * * * * * * E9  ESSAY FOR SEMINAR
                 * * * * * * * * E8  BECAUSE RECOMMENDED
                 * * * * * * * E7  SET FOR DISCUSSION
                 * * * * * * E6  KNOWLEDGE OF SUBJECT
                 * * * * * E5  OUGHT BUT DONT FEEL LIKE
                 * * * * E4  REFERENCE
                 * * * E3  EXAM REVISION
                 * * E2  PASS THE TIME
                 * E1  INTEREST AND CURIOSITY
```

Figure 3.8 Sybil's raw grid

Chapter 4

FOCUSing: the emergent pattern

Introduction

Bill Shard's raw grid was shown, in chapter 3 (Fig. 3.3), to have some interesting aspects of personal meaning hidden within it. Comparison of how each element was construed revealed that for him the learning from 'Competition with a clever girl' (E2) and that from 'Splitting up with a girlfriend' (E5) were very similar experiences.

Comparison of how each construct ordered the elements showed that most of the time when he felt a learning experience involved the 'same generation' (C8) he also felt that he was learning on his 'own conditions' (C5). Whereas experiences involving the 'older generation' (C8) were felt to be 'imposed by parents and others' (C5). It also appeared that he learned 'about life' (C2) from 'others' insight' (C3) and 'about people' (C2) from his 'own insight' (C3).

But these relationships were rather arbitrarily extracted from Bill's grid merely to illustrate that a deeper pattern of meaning lay hidden within it.

There are various methods for analysing a grid, some of which will be discussed later in chapters 6 and 7, but here the purpose is to preserve the individual responses as they appear in the raw grid, merely reorganising the layout of these responses to highlight the pattern. Analysis of the similarities between elements and between constructs can be used to systematically reorganise the display to emphasise the pattern of personal meaning within it. This is achieved by re-ordering the elements and the constructs on the basis of two-way cluster analysis. This can be done painlessly with a personal computer containing the FOCUS suite of programs; but here a 'paper and pencil' hand-FOCUSing technique is described. It is most easily executed if the raw grid is drawn on thin card. The card is then cut up into vertical strips which are used to FOCUS the elements. The partly FOCUSed grid (elements) is then entered on to another card which is cut into horizontal strips. These are used to FOCUS the constructs (additional strips are required when reversing constructs). When the elements and the constructs have been FOCUSed, the grid can be re-drawn to give the SPACEd FOCUSed display in which the spacing between columns and between rows reflects the degree of similarity between adjacent elements and constructs. It is especially designed for easy talkback to the client.

The hand-FOCUSing technique

FOCUSing the elements (a) Identifying similarities

The searching out of clusters of similar elements can be achieved by eye, but to carry out the FOCUSing procedure effectively it is more economical in the long run to systematically record how each element compares with every other element. Cutting the grid into element strips makes such comparison relatively simple.

In Bill Shard's grid strip E1 can be compared with strip E2 to reveal that they differ only in their assigning to the poles of construct C9. This difference is illustrated in the first sketch of Fig. 4.1 and is recorded in the similarity matrix shown in Fig. 4.2 as a '1' in row 1 (E1) – column 2 (E2). (The significance of the circle around the '1' will emerge later.) The first two sketches in Fig. 4.1 show how strip E1 can be moved across the grid to compare E1 successively with E2 (illustrated) -E3-E4-E5-E6-E7-E8 (illustrated) and E9. These comparisons are systematically recorded in the E row of the matrix in Fig. 4.2. Strip E1 is then replaced. Strip E2 has already been compared with E1 so comparisons with E3-E9 are systematically recorded. For example, the third sketch in Fig. 4.1 shows that E2 and E5 have identical assignings to every construct. Therefore the matrix in Fig. 4.2 shows a '0' (zero) difference in row 2 (E2) and column 5 (E5). Thus by systematically comparing each element strip with its higher numbered companions the triangular table of differences shown in Fig. 4.2 can be assembled. The fourth, fifth and sixth sketches show E3 and E4, E6 and E9, E7 and E8, being compared. Once this has been done the clustering of elements (i.e. the systematic re-ordering of the E strips) can proceed. The new sequence re-arranges elements so that 'like' is associated with 'like'. This ensures that there is a minimum cumulative difference between adjacent columns. Fig. 4.3 shows this procedure.

FOCUSing the elements (b) Re-ordering the elements

The triangular table of comparisons in Fig. 4.2 reveals that the only '0' (zero) difference between elements is:
    E5 with E2.

In the first sketch sequence of Fig. 4.3 these two element strips are shown being removed from the original raw grid on the left and clustered in the beginnings of the element-FOCUSed grid on the right.

The pairs of elements 'E1 & E2', 'E1 & E5' and 'E3 & E4' are identified from Fig. 4.2 as differing on only one construct out of nine. Strip E2 is already FOCUSed with E5, therefore E1 joins their cluster, and since it cannot be

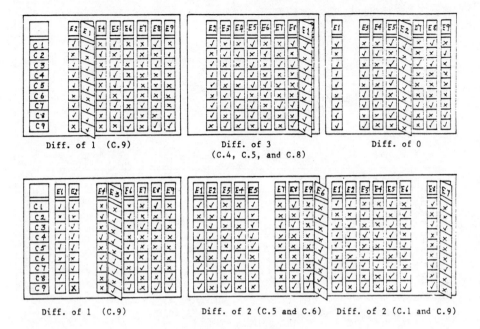

Figure 4.1 Identifying element similarities

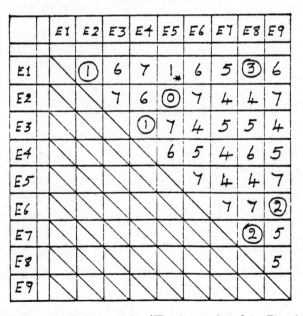

Figure 4.2 Element similarity matrix. (The items ringed in Fig. 4.2 are those illustrated in the six sketches of Fig. 4.1)

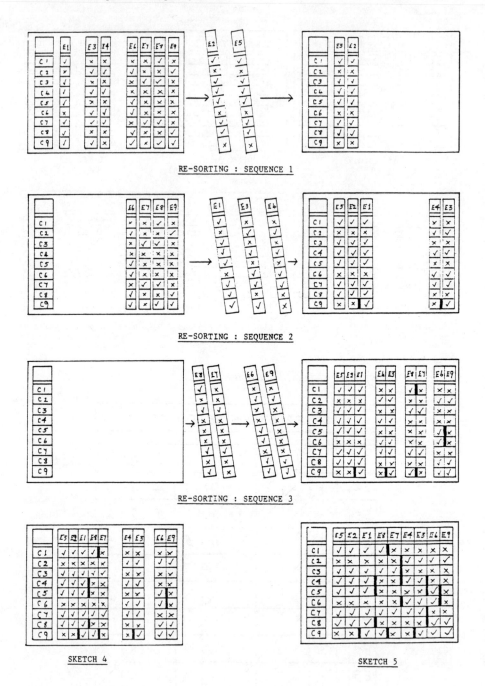

Figure 4.3 Element resorting sequence

placed simultaneously alongside both E2 and E5 without splitting the 'E2-E5' '0' (zero) difference cluster, it is arbitrarily placed alongside E2 (rather than E5). E3 and E4 starts a new '1' difference cluster.

E5–E2–E1   E4–E3

The exact locations of the differences are indicated by the thickened black lines in Fig. 4.3. The reader will find that if they use two constrastingly coloured pens or pencils (e.g. blue and red) for entering the ticks ($\sqrt{}$) and the crosses (X) on the original raw grid card the location of these differences between element strips is automatically highlighted. When all the differences of '1' in Fig. 4.2 have been accounted for, differences of '2' are noted. These are located as follows – 'E7 with E8' and 'E6 with E9'. Since E6, E7, E8 and E9 are not already members of existing clusters they are free to form two new clusters each having differences of '2'.

E5–E1–E1   E4–E3   E8-E7   E6–E9

These are shown in the third sketch sequence in Fig. 4.3. It will also be seen that all element strips have now been moved from the raw grid to the element-clustered grid. However, the element-FOCUSed grid is not yet complete. Whilst it consists of all nine elements in four separate clusters 'E5-E2-E1', 'E4-E3', 'E8-E7' and 'E6-E9', these clusters are not yet ordered in such a way as to produce the minimum differences between all adjacent columns in the grid. The bottom two sketches in Fig. 4.3 show how this is achieved. Inspection of Fig. 4.2 reveals only one pair of element strips 'E1 and E8' having a difference of '3'. Since this is now the minimum difference between columns remaining unused in the clustering, strips E1 and E8 can be placed adjacent to each other by re-ordering the clusters so:

E5–E2–E1–E8–E7   E4–E3   E6–E9

Finally, inspection of Fig. 4.2 shows that the following pairs display a difference of '4' 'E2-E7', 'E2-E8', 'E3-E6', 'E3-E9', 'E4-E7', 'E5-E7' and 'E5-E8'. However E2, E1 and E8 are unavailable being already contained within the major cluster, therefore: 'E3-E6', 'E3-E9', E4-E7' and 'E5-E7' are the only pairings which allow the elements to continue to be FOCUSed with the minimum differences between columns. Arbitrarily E7 and E4 are brought together and E3 is located alongside E6. This gives

E5–E2–E1–E8–E7–E4–E3–E6–E9

as the final 'FOCUSed' ordering of elements. The thickened lines in Fig. 4.3 show where the differences between columns lie in the element-FOCUSed grid. The significance of the 'ringing' of certain numbers in Fig. 4.2 is now revealed. It indicates the pairings which were used to FOCUS the elements.

Focusing the constructs: identifying similarities and re-ordering the constructs

The element-FOCUSed grid is now re-written on to another grid card and cut up into horizontal construct strips as shown in Fig. 4.4. Now by analogy to the element comparisons every construct can be compared with every other construct.

The first sketch in Fig. 4.4 shows how strip C1 can be moved down to be compared with C2-C3-C4-C5-C6-C7-C8 and C9 in turn. For example, comparison of C1 with C3 reveals a difference of '1' on Element E7 (which as the element columns have already been re-ordered in the element-FOCUSed grid now lies in the fifth column). The first row of the matrix shown in Fig. 4.5 records the differences revealed by these eight comparisons. As with the elements, construct strip C1 can be returned to its place and strip C2 compared with all its higher numbered companions. However, the second sketch in Fig. 4.4 shows how comparison of strip C2 and strip C3 reveals a difference of '9', i.e. a complete mismatch. As was explained towards the end of chapter 3 this is identical with a difference of '0' (zero) between C3 and a hypothetical construct C2R in which the pole descriptions (not shown in Fig. 4.4) and the assignings of ticks (√) and crosses (X) has been reversed from those in C2. The bottom sketch in Fig. 4.4 illustrates this. The matrix of comparisons for every construct with every other construct shown in Fig. 4.5 therefore consists in two triangular sections.

The top right-hand triangular section above the diagonal line shows the differences between each construct and every other. The lower left-hand triangular section under the diagonal line shows a similar set of comparisons when each construct in turn is reversed and compared with the rest. Thus for example the column (C1) shows C1R compared with all other constructs, and so on. It will be observed, that the cell C1/C2 and cell C2/C1 are complementary, the difference of '1' becoming a difference of '8' when one of the constructs is reversed. Whilst the apparent repetition in the bottom triangle of Fig. 4.5 may appear tedious, readers new to the analysis of grids will find that the few moments required to 'reverse' the difference scores (i.e. subtract them from '9') will make the clustering of constructs much more straightforward. Fig. 4.6 shows how this clustering proceeds.

Inspection of Fig. 4.5 reveals only one pair of constructs

C3 – C2R

with a '0' (zero) difference. The first sketch sequence in Fig. 4.6 shows strip C2 re-written as RC2 and clustered with strip C3 on the construct-clustered grid. Next 'C1-C3', 'C2-C8', 'RC1-C2' and 'RC3-C6' are revealed in Fig. 4.5 as showing differences of '1'. The second sketch in Fig. 4.6 shows C1 joining the 'C-RC2' cluster and 'C5-C8' forming a new cluster.

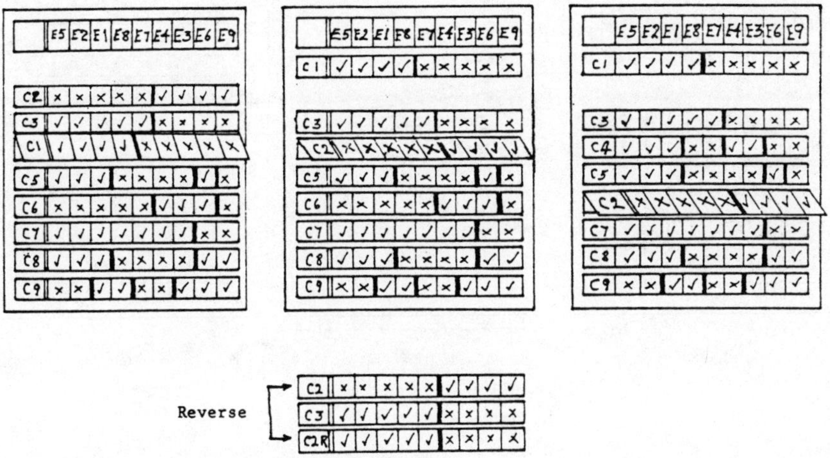

Figure 4.4 Identifying construct similarities

	C1	C2	C3	C4	C5	C6	C7	C8	C9
C1		8	(1)	3	(2)*	7	3	3	5
C2	1		(9)	5	6	(1)	7	5	3
C3	8	(0)		4	3	8	2	4	6
C4	6	4	5		3	4	(2)*	4	6
C5	7	3	6	6		5	5	(1)*	5
C6	2	8	1	5	4		6	6	4
C7	6	2	7	7	4	3		6	6
C8	6	4	5	5	8	3	3		4
C9	4	6	3	(3)*	4	5	3	5	

Figure 4.5 Construct similarity matrix

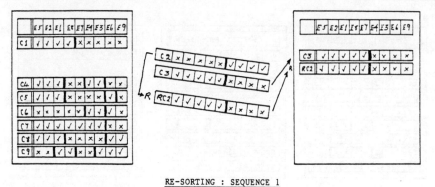

RE-SORTING : SEQUENCE 1

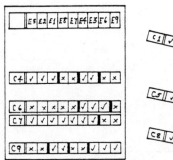

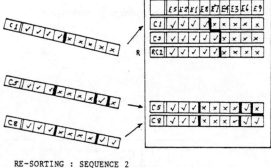

RE-SORTING : SEQUENCE 2

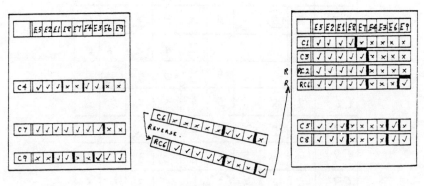

RE-SORTING : SEQUENCE 3

Cont. . . . .

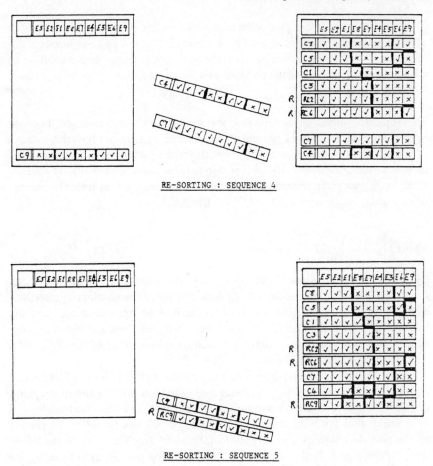

RE-SORTING : SEQUENCE 4

RE-SORTING : SEQUENCE 5

Figure 4.6 Construct resorting sequence

C1—C3—RC2   C5—C8

The third sketch sequence shows C6 being reversed and RC6 joining the 'C1-C3-RC2' cluster.

C1—C3—RC2—RC6   C5—C8

This takes care of all the construct pairs with a difference of '1'. Next Fig. 4.5 shows 'C1-C5', 'C3-C7', 'C4-C7', 'RC1-C6', 'RC2-C7' as having differences of '2'. Thus in Fig. 4.6 the fourth sketch sequence shows C5 joining C1 to form the major cluster and C4 joining C7 to form a new cluster.

C8—C5—C1—C3—RC2—RC6   C7—C4

The other pairings are precluded because of earlier clustering of one or both of their members. Inspection of Fig. 4.5 reveals thirteen pairings having a difference of '3'. The final sketch sequence in Fig. 4.6 shows one resolution of these into the final construct-FOCUSed grid.

C8–C5–C1–C3–RC2–RC6–C7–C4–RC9

The thickened black lines depicting the positions of the differences between rows and between columns (or the colour pattern if the reader has contrastingly coloured ticks ($\sqrt{}$) and crosses (X) show that: 'the pattern of personal meaning hidden within the complexity of language may be more simple than it appears' (even in the raw grid). (Again the ringed numbers in Fig. 4.5 indicate the pairings of constructs which were used to FOCUS the grid.)

The FOCUSed grid

By re-ordering the elements and re-ordering the constructs according to rules for FOCUSing, the grid becomes an optimal display of the relationships between elements and constructs. The verbal labels can now be replaced to complete Bill Shard's fully FOCUSed grid. Care must be taken to reverse the verbal descriptions of the poles of those constructs which have been reversed, i.e. RC2, RC6 and RC9 in Bill Shard's grid Fig. 4.7.

In Fig. 4.7 the similarity between 'splitting up with girlfriend' E5 and 'competition with a clever girl' E2 which was first noted towards the end of chapter 3 is highlighted as two identical columns of ticks ($\sqrt{}$). The observant reader will have noted that reversing constructs C2, C6 and C9 has the effect of placing all the pole descriptions which apply to E2 and E5 (see Fig. 3.4) on the left of the FOCUSed grid. It also shows that Bill sees 'being near death in a dinghy' E1 as very much like this pair, differing only in having 'made me cautious' rather than having a 'guiding effect'. The FOCUSing also shows that Bill feels that 'reading the lesson in church from the Bible' was a similar learning experience to 'thinking after a family argument that divorce was really a good idea' and that this pair of learning experiences differ from the earlier three on the first six constructs, by having the attributes of the six pole descriptions on the right side of the grid. 'Failing my RAF medical' and 'Being hit by my woodwork teacher' are similarly assigned to seven out of nine constructs. Reading the left-hand descriptions for the ticks ($\sqrt{}$) and the right-hand ones for the crosses (X) explains a little of how Bill thought and felt about these events. Thus the FOCUSed grid reveals some of the pattern of Bill's thoughts and feelings about personal learning events by indicating how his 'items of experience' cluster on to the pole descriptions of his constructs. But this is only half the story.

At the end of chapter 3 the construct pole 'about life' was shown to be similar to 'from others' insight' and the pole 'about people' was like 'from own insight'. The FOCUSing shows that 'finding out about my own character' and 'group activity' join the former and that 'finding out about other people's

CONSTRUCT POLE RATED - / -   ELEMENTS   CONSTRUCT POLE RATED - X -

		E5 E2 E1 E8 E7 E3 E4 E6 E9		
SAME GENERATION	C8		C8	OLDER GENERATION
OWN CONDITIONS	C5		C5	IMPOSED BY PARENTS AND OTHERS
FINDING OUT ABOUT MY OWN CHARACTER	C1		C1	FINDING OUT ABOUT OTHER PEOPLE'S TRUE CHARACTER
FROM OTHERS' INSIGHT	C3		C3	FROM OWN INSIGHT
ABOUT LIFE	RC2		RC2	ABOUT PEOPLE
GROUP ACTIVITY	RC6		RC6	SELF-RELIANCE
TENSE	C7		C7	RELAXED
GROWING UP, MORE AUTHORITY	C4		C4	GROWING UP, EMBARRASSMENT
A GUIDING EFFECT	RC9		RC9	MADE ME CAUTIOUS

E9 A MONTH'S VISIT TO FINLAND
E6 MEETING MARC BOLAN
E3 THINKING AFTER A FAMILY ARGUMENT THAT DIVORCE WAS REALLY A GOOD IDEA
E4 READING THE LESSON IN CHURCH FROM THE BIBLE
E7 BEING HIT BY MY WOODWORK TEACHER
E8 FAILING MY RAF MEDICAL
E1 BEING NEAR DEATH IN A DINGHY
E2 COMPETITION WITH A CLEVER GIRL
E5 SPLITTING UP WITH GIRLFRIEND

Figure 4.7 Bill Shard's SPACEd FOCUSed grid

true character' and 'self-reliance' join the latter. These four constructs (C1, C3, RC2 and RC6) seem to form a significant cluster in Bill's ways of thinking and feeling about learning experiences. 'Tense' v. 'Relaxed' and 'Growing-up, more authority' v. Growing up, embarrassment' go together seven times out of nine.

Thus by exploring the clustering of elements and how they have been assigned to the pole descriptions of clusters of constructs, and by studying the clusterings of constructs which have separated out clusters of those elements which are assigned in much the same way, it is possible to reflect the unappreciated patterning in a client's feelings and thoughts about the topic back to them for more serious consideration.

For example, the nursery school teacher who finds that all the children he construes as 'clean and tidy' he thinks of as 'bright' and all those who appear 'scruffy' are also 'dim' might feel the need to examine certain of his basic assumptions rather carefully.

The SPACEd FOCUSed grid

The process of FOCUSing aims to highlight the pattern of personal meaning in the grid for display and talkback to the client. The layout of Bill Shard's FOCUSed grid shown in Fig. 4.7 enhances the visual display by using spacing (and colour) to emphasise the pattern of responses. All √s can be coloured blue and all Xs red. The distance between rows (and the distance between columns) increases as the mismatch between adjacent rows or between adjacent columns increases, see opposite).

Now the distance between element columns was made proportional to the difference between the elements they represent. Likewise the vertical spacing between rows was made proportional to the difference between the constructs which they represent. The SPACEd FOCUSed grid layout is obtained by combining these horizontal and vertical spacings.

Finally, in passing, it is probably worth noting that if the strips of card used for FOCUSing have the 'verbal labels' of the elements and constructs written on them, then the client can participate in the process. This conversational re-sorting of the grid, in which the clients can discover the hidden pattern for themselves is probably one of the most effective simple awareness-raising tools available to the T-C.

Again this technique is content-free. Any grid can be analysed by using the same step-by-step process. It is therefore easily carried out with a whole group of clients each of whom is analysing their own unique set of elements and constructs.

The authors have a particularly happy memory of a group of Mexican university staff. They spent a day eliciting grids in which the elements were 'items of teaching experience' designed to encourage the development of different types of 'comprehension'. Many of the participants spoke very little English

Thus for the ELEMENTS:
the differences between adjacent columns are as follows:

0	1	3	2	4	1	4	2	
E5	E2	E1	E8	E7	E4	E3	E6	E9

and for the CONSTRUCTS:

the differences between adjacent rows are:

C8
    1
C5
    2
C1
    1
C3
    0
RC2
    1
RC6
    3
C7
    2
C4
    3
RC9

but even so, had sufficient knowledge to understand the procedural instructions. The step-by-step instructions for eliciting and then FOCUSing the grid were issued by the authors. They were truly content-free since the thirty participants each completed their own grids in Spanish. We could see and check whether the procedures were being carried out successfully but we knew nothing of the content. All we could understand were the appreciative noises, the high level of involvement and feeling in the exchange conversations and the very gratifying ah-ha experiences which seemed to be going on almost continuously. Later our interpreter provided us with detailed content descriptions in English.

At the end of this chapter Figs. 4.11 and 4.12 (algorithms for FOCUSing and SPACE-ing a FOCUSed grid) illustrate step-by-step procedures for displaying the elements and constructs in an optimal form for feedback.

Dimensions of personal judgment: using a FOCUSed grid to raise awareness in staff appraisal

The repertory grid can be used to elicit systematic information about individual dimensions of judgment; it can reveal the personal structure of values which form the basis of a manager's appraisal of the people working for him. These may be very different, both in quality and the importance attached to them, from the pre-defined 'rating scales' embodied in the formal structure of the appraisal scheme. The unappreciated mismatch between these formal public dimensions of appraisal and each manager's own personal constructs may seriously undermine the working of the scheme.

The following case was constructed from a study carried out with a large company. It illustrates one use of the FOCUSing technique.

The purposes of this particular study were:

(1) To help each manager become more aware of his own personal dimensions for judging subordinates.
(2) To produce material which would allow a more complete description of the pattern of judgments within the group.
(3) To use (1) and (2) as the basis for discussions about the similarity and differences that exist in the group; and thus generate:
   (a) A more explicit consensus about the bases of appraisal within the department.
   (b) A more refined understanding of how and where each manager was placed within the total pattern of group judgment.

Mr Donaldson's grid

In the following example Mr Donaldson and his subordinates are invented, but his constructs are a small sample of those most widely shared by the managers who took part in this study. In this study the elements are the people to be appraised; or to be more precise each element was Mr Donaldson's experience of one of his subordinates. Mr Donaldson has subordinates Mr Smith, Miss Jones, Mr Brown, Mrs Green, Mr Black and Miss White.

To begin to elicit a repertory grid from Mr Donaldson three elements are selected (say Mr Smith, Miss Jones and Mr Brown). He is asked to consider them as people working for him. 'Now if you consider each of them as people that you know well and who work for you, which two seem most alike and which one seems most different from the other two?' Mr Donaldson thinks about this for some time and then he replies, 'Mr Smith and Miss Jones are similar and Mr Brown is different.' He is then asked what it is about these two which make them similar and he replies, 'They are poor at planning and analysing problems.' Mr Donaldson is then asked what it is about Mr Brown that makes him different. He says, 'Oh, Brown has good planning and creative ability.' Mr Donaldson has now revealed his first bi-polar construct.

Poor at planning and analysing problems	v.	Good planning and creative ability

The person eliciting the grid faithfully records Mr Donaldson's terminology. The repertory grid and each construct in it are taken to be samples of how Mr Donaldson thinks and feels about his subordinates in his own terms. He is now asked to assign the three remaining elements, Mrs Green, Mr Black and Miss White to one or another pole of the construct. He places:

Miss White with Mr Smith and and Miss Jones	—and—	Mrs Green and Mr Black with Mr Brown

The repertory grid form is usually filled in as in Fig. 4.8.

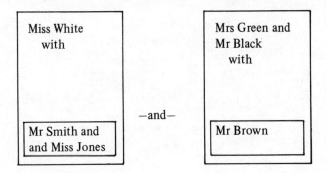

	.✓. Pole 1 .✓.	E1 E2 E3 E4 E5 E6	.✗. Pole 2 .✗.	
C1	Poor at planning and analysing problems	☑ ☑ ☒ x x	Good planning and creative ability	C1

```
                    *  *  *  *  *  *
                    *  *  *  *  *  *
                    *  *  *  *  *  Miss White
                    *  *  *  *  *
                    *  *  *  *  Mr Black
                    *  *  *  *
                    *  *  *  Mrs Green
                    *  *  *
                    *  *  Mr Brown
                    *  *
                    *  Miss Jones
                    *
                    Mr Smith
```

Figure 4.8 Mr Donaldson's grid – layout form

Assignment to Pole 1 is represented as '√' and assignment to Pole 2 is represented as 'X'. The original three elements which were used to elicit the construct (Mr Smith, Miss Jones and Mr Brown) are known in repertory grid jargon as 'the triad'. In this form the responses assigned to the triad are shown by boxes in the raw grid.

The second construct is elicited in the same way. Mrs Green, Mr Black and Miss White are used as the second triad. Mr Donaldson puts Miss White and Mrs Green together as 'followers' and calls Mr Black a 'leader'.

Four more constructs are elicited and each time all the elements are assigned to one or other pole. The complete raw grid is shown in Fig. 4.9. (It will be noted that each subordinate has been equally represented in the triads.)

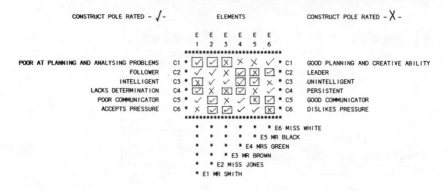

Figure 4.9 Mr Donaldson's raw grid

In its raw form the repertory grid presents the elements in the order in which they were originally named and the constructs in the order in which they were elicited. But this is not the best form of presentation from which to abstract the full meaning of the responses. Visual inspection of the elements reveals that Mr Smith and Miss White have been similarly assigned to the constructs. Mr Black and Mr Brown have also been assigned similar responses. The elements can be FOCUSed:

Now visual inspection reveals that constructs C2 and C5 contain a similar pattern of responses and that C3 and C6 are also the same.

Finally, since constructs are bi-polar, the pole description and the associated '√' and 'X' codings can be reversed without changing the underlying meanings in the responses. Thus, in the example, constructs 3 and 6 can be reversed showing E6 and E1 as having all '√'s and E3 and E5 as having all 'X's.

The fully 'SPACEd' 'FOCUSed' grid can be presented so that the meaning hidden in the responses recorded in the raw grid is made explicit (Fig. 4.10).

The FOCUSed grid shows that Mr Donaldson sees Mr Black and Mr Brown as intelligent, creative, persistent leaders, good at planning and communicating and who are well able to accept pressure. On the other hand, he sees Miss White

CONSTRUCT POLE RATED - ✓ -   ELEMENTS   CONSTRUCT POLE RATED - X -

```
                                          EE  E E  EE
                                          61  4 2  35
                                       *****************
                FOLLOWER     C2 *  √√ √√ XX  * C2    LEADER
         POOR COMMUNICATOR   C5 *  √√ √√ XX  * C5    GOOD COMMUNICATOR

         LACKS DETERMINATION C4 *  √√ √X XX  * C4    PERSISTENT

POOR AT PLANNING AND ANALYSING PROBLEMS  C1 *  √√ X √ XX  * C1    GOOD PLANNING AND CREATIVE ABILITY

              UNINTELLIGENT  RC3 *  √√ XX XX  * RC3   INTELLIGENT
           DISLIKES PRESSURE C6 *  √√ XX XX  * C6    ACCEPTS PRESSURE
                                       *****************
                                          **  * *  ** E5 MR BLACK
                                          **  * *  *  E3 MR BROWN
                                          **  * *
                                          **  * *  * E2 MISS JONES
                                          **  *
                                          **  *  E4 MRS GREEN
                                          **
                                          ** E1 MR SMITH
                                          * E6 MISS WHITE
```

Figure 4.10 Mr Donaldson's SPACEd FOCUSed grid

and Mr Smith as unintelligent followers, lacking in determination, who dislike pressure, are poor at planning, analysing problems and communicating. He sees Mrs Green and Miss Jones as having some good and some bad characteristics. But the grid reveals as much about Mr Donaldson as it does about his subordinates. It shows the terms in which he thinks and feels about subordinates. (The actual grids elicited in this study contained twelve elements and from ten to fifteen constructs.) It shows how his different thoughts and feelings relate to each other. On the evidence of these six elements, Mr Donaldson feels that:

(a) Followers are poor communicators and leaders are good communicators.
(b) Intelligent people can accept pressure and unintelligent ones dislike it.

These meanings in Mr Donaldson's grid can be discussed with him. Talking people back through their FOCUSed grids raises their awareness of the structure of thoughts and feelings that lie implicit in their more intuitive judgments and decision-making.

PEGASUS: A computer-aided repertory grid technique

This project was based upon the on-line interactive computer program PEGASUS which elicits a repertory grid from the user; it uses real-time analysis of the structure of the developing grid to provide feedback to the user during the elicitation. This encourages the user to explore, clarify and elaborate his or

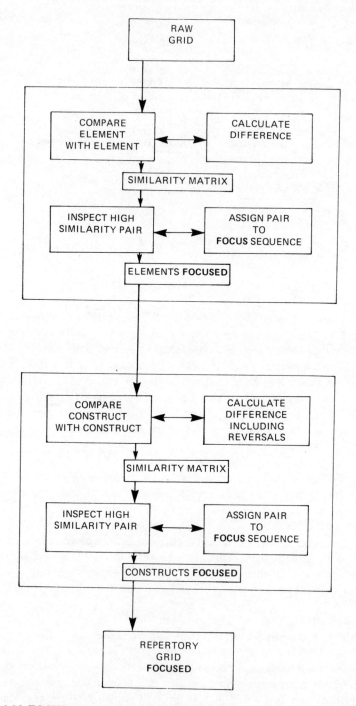

Figure 4.11 FOCUSing a repertory grid: an algorithm

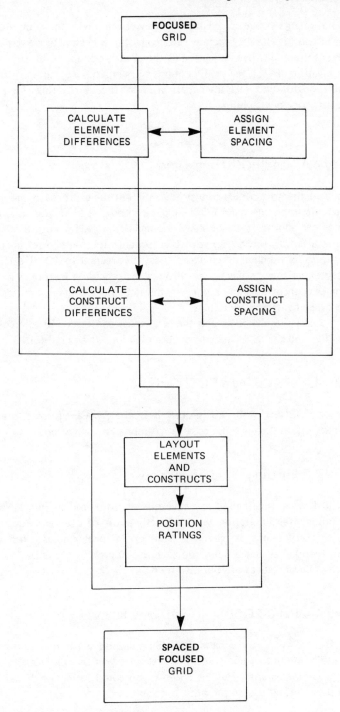

Figure 4.12 SPACE-ing a FOCUSed grid: an algorithm

her own thoughts and feelings whilst 'in conversation with the computer'. In this version of the PEGASUS program each construct is elicited as a five-point scale. This gives a more sensitive indication of the client's opinion of his subordinates.

The resulting 'FOCUSed grid' contains a systematic description of the dimension of thoughts and feelings experienced by the user during this computer-aided conversation with himself.

Activity 4.1 Hand-FOCUSing a grid

Take one of the grids which you produced from the exercises in chapters 2 and 3. 'Focus' it using the hand-FOCUSing technique, even if you usually have a computer (or another type of slave) available to do it for you. (Preferably for your first attempt, use a grid with a reasonably low number of elements and about the same number of constructs, say between 6 to 10 of each.) It is a necessary experience to have gone through the process at least once and to have seen the pattern of meaning hidden in the raw grid emerge as you identify the clusters of elements and constructs.

Use a colour for the CP1s and the $\sqrt{}$s which contrasts with the colour used for the CP2s and the 'X's. The authors use blue for $\sqrt{}$s and red for Xs.

Activity 4.2 SPACE-ing a FOCUSed grid

Take your FOCUSed grid and re-draw it in the SPACEd format to emphasise the pattern within it. Again use colours to emphasise the pattern.

Activity 4.3 Eliciting a grid of your own

When you feel confident that you have mastered the grid elicitation techniques try a content-free elicitation with a small group of friends. 'Food', 'drink', 'plays', 'football teams or players', 'radio or TV programmes', 'funny experiences' or 'people' all make good topics, but you probably have better, i.e. more personally relevant, ideas of your own by now.

Activity 4.4 Hand-FOCUSing with some talkback

If you feel up to it, try a hand-FOCUSing session with friends. Be prepared for a certain amount of confusion the first time you try this. Keep a record of where the problems arise. Reflect on how you could anticipate them and act to prevent these difficulties on subsequent occasions.

Have fun!

Chapter 5

Talkback through a FOCUSed grid

The FOCUSed repertory grid as a mirror of constructions of experience

The client's initially tacit thoughts and feelings are made explicit in the raw grid. This displays the elements and constructs as they are elicited. When the grid is FOCUSed, a pattern emerges. When it is SPACEd, the pattern is emphasised. The translation of the pattern into the client's heightened awareness is achieved by 'talking them back through their FOCUSed grid'. During this 'talkback conversation' they are encouraged to systematically explore how their elements and their constructs relate one to another; and they are encouraged to seek personally satisfying explanations of this patterning of their thoughts and feelings about the topic.

Confronted with the FOCUSed image of his or her responses, a learner's first reaction is to take it away quietly into a corner and peruse it. Reactions vary from 'Ah-ha' to incomprehension, from 'so what' to disbelief and occasionally to the acknowledgment of a significant new insight. Beyond this immediate response, the inexperienced grid user finds it difficult to fully interpret the implications of the reflections offered in this mirror. By sensitively engaging the learner in talking himself or herself back into the original meaning of the elements as they were construed in the raw grid, the personal significance of the components of the image is re-established. Detailed consideration of the emergent patterns often produces a need for the client to change some responses, to add new elements and constructs, or to refine others. It also leads the client to want to drop what have, in the light of reflection, become less relevant elements and constructs. The authors' teaching and research experience using this talkback technique with, for example, mechanical engineering students on 'great engineers', psychology students on 'creative acts', industrial inspection managers on 'alternative suppliers of raw materials', young offenders on 'figures of authority', social workers on 'my cases', magistrates on 'court sentences', English literature students on their 'attempts to answer exam questions', university students on their 'lecturers', and football players on 'situations in the field of play', has shown that the majority of these clients immediately became deeply involved. A thorough exploration of their personal understandings of the topic usually ensued.

But for the conversation to be effective, talkback through the FOCUSed grid must be as collaborative, accepting and purposeful as the elicitation conversation itself. The elements originally introduced into the grid may not be representative of all those items which the person later feels warrant consideration. Either through lapse in memory or more conscious suppression, certain relevant elements may not appear in the original set. The 10-20 elements usually found in a grid represent a pool of much larger dimensions. As elicitation proceeds, the search for constructs jogs the memory and releases other elements into consciousness, as if a small hand mirror had been used to examine the face and only a certain number of features can come into attention at any one time. The assumptions in the learner's head influence the elements and constructs that emerge. Such assumptions may relate to the client's views of the repertory grid technique itself, they may relate to their purposes for doing the grid, they may be assumptions about the personality and purpose of the grid interviewer or they may relate to the situation and role relationship between interviewer and client. Participants are often conscious of various inhibitions about using constructs which would not be 'acceptable' or 'respectable' in the context of the elicitation conversation. In our development of conversational technique much attention has been given to how to help learners recognise and value the intricacies and richness of texture in the network of their own thoughts and feelings. One important condition for achieving this is confidentiality. If the image in the mirror is in danger of becoming a 'dirty postcard' to be passed from hand to hand, the learner suppresses his thoughts and emotions and holds his tongue. Often it is necessary to agree that the learner may go through the whole elicitation and mirroring process and then destroy all the grid information without anyone else ever seeing it.

Much of the power of the grid as a reflector depends upon the relevance of the elicited elements and constructs to a person's living experience. The verbal descriptions ascribed to an element cannot adequately embody the personal meaning of that item of experience. The verbal descriptions of the poles of a construct do not necessarily explain the learner's construing to any third person. But this is irrelevant so long as clients acknowledge the descriptions simply as tokens for use in conversations with themselves. Each construct should represent an important dimension of the learner's construing. Those constructs depicting feelings are as important as those depicting thoughts if the reflective learning is to be effective. The ways in which feelings cluster with the more descriptive constructs help to reveal prejudices, attitudes, intuitive understanding and implicit values to the viewer. The experience of reflecting on one's own grid always seems to become very involving and usually initiates a process of further and deeper exploration. Such explorations can themselves be systematised by encouraging the learner to re-FOCUS his or her own subsequently enriched grid and to watch the pattern changing. Guidance can be given in his or her own terms about how to extend, differentiate, and/or elaborate the grid by selecting additional elements to meet a chosen set of construct ratings or by adding constructs that bring new order to the earlier element responses. This is analogous to enlarging and polishing the hand mirror to get an enhanced view of one's whole face. Such extensions of the FOCUSing tool will be discussed in more detail later in chapter 7.

Understanding the pattern of meaning in a FOCUSed grid

The repertory grid on 'radio programmes' offered at the end of chapter 3 was a simplified version of a grid elicited during work with a family of three: 'Dad', 'Aunt Ada' and 'Mick'. These three were experiencing serious problems in living together and they chose 'radio programmes' as an endurable 'topic' around which to discuss how their relationships played out in day-to-day living. One example of their continual bickering was prolonged and unnecessary emotional quarrels over when to have the radio on, and which programmes to listen to. Here only Mick's grid is discussed.

The SPACEd FOCUSed grid enabled Mick to more easily understand the structure of personal meaning which was latent in his raw grid. The Xs in this reorganised form of his grid responses mostly represented what were for him positive characteristics of radio programmes and the $\sqrt{}$s mostly represented what were for him more negative characteristics. (This positive and negative valuing of the Xs and $\sqrt{}$s is not in any way necessarily true for other grids, nor is it in any way a consequence of FOCUSing.) However, Mick was surprised to discover that for most elements what was:

> 'down to earth', 'with it', 'real', and 'lively and changing' was also 'I enjoy but feel guilty' and 'likely to upset father'.

This made explicit something which Mick obviously felt, but which he found difficult to face when so clearly presented. It was only through a fairly exhausting discussion of how the elements (i.e. specific radio programmes) distributed themselves on his positively valued and negatively valued construct poles that he was able to explore in depth and thus face some of the underlying implications of this pattern of thoughts and feelings for the problems of still continuing to live at home.

A detailed inspection of his grid (Fig. 5.1) reveals three pairs of identical elements in his grid.

      E2   *The Double Top Ten Show*
and E5   *The Archers*

are both assigned Xs on all his constructs.

      E4   *Any Questions*
and E1   *Talking About Antiques*

are both assigned $\sqrt{}$s on all his constructs whilst

E7 *Study on Three*
and E8 *Book at Bedtime*
have four Xs and two √s.

Detailed talkback through the implications of this clustering revealed that for *Study on Three* and *Book at Bedtime* being assigned to the 'Good for me' and 'One thing' construct poles meant 'one enjoyable coherent continuous story from which I feel I will learn', whereas for *Lighten our Darkness*, *Any Questions* and *Talking about Antiques* it meant 'I suffer it whilst it goes on and on because I suppose it is good for me.'

This was one of the constructs which had caused him some difficulty as it was elicited. During the talkback he divided it into two separate constructs.

Woman's Hour was ambiguous, partly because the 'I enjoy but feel guilty' construct was interpreted differently when it was applied to this programme. Mick felt that he shouldn't listen to *Woman's Hour* because it was unmanly whereas with *The Double Top Ten Show*, *The Archers* and *Sports Desk* he felt that he was enjoying wasting his time. *Woman's Hour* was also ambiguous because it had a fluctuating meaning. He liked some of the items and not others. This led him to differentiate three separate elements.

```
                                SPACED FOCUSED GRID

   CONSTRUCT POLE RATED - √ -          ELEMENTS          CONSTRUCT POLE RATED - X -

                               E  EE E  E  E E  E E
                               6  14 3  9  2 5  7 8
                             **************************
            TOO CLEVER   RC4 * √  √√ X  X  X X  X X * RC4  DOWN TO EARTH
       OLD AND BORING    RC1 * √  √√ √  X  X X  X X * RC1  WITH IT
                CHATTY    C3 * √  √√ √  √  X X  X X * C3   REAL
     OKAY WITH FATHER     C2 * X  √√ √  √  X X  X X * C2   LIKELY TO UPSET FATHER

           GOOD FOR ME    C5 * X  √√ √  X  X X  √ √ * C5   I ENJOY BUT FEEL GUILTY
             ONE THING    C6 * X  √√ √  X  X X  √ √ * C6   LIVELY AND CHANGING
                             **************************
                               *  ** *  *  * *  * * E8 A BOOK AT BEDTIME
                               *  ** *  *  * *  * E7 STUDY ON 3
                               *  ** *  *  * *
                               *  ** *  *  * * E5 THE ARCHERS
                               *  ** *  *  * E2 DOUBLE TOP TEN SHOW
                               *  ** *  *
                               *  ** *  * E9 SPORTS DESK
                               *  ** *
                               *  ** * E3 LIGHTEN OUR DARKNESS
                               *  ** E4 ANY QUESTIONS
                               *  * E1 TALKING ABOUT ANTIQUES
                               *
                               * E6 WOMAN'S HOUR
```

Figure 5.1 Mick's SPACEd FOCUSed grid

The 'talkback conversation' enabled Mick to clarify his ideas about the problems of living at home by elaborating and clarifying his grid. He replaced ambiguous or mixed poles by purified or clarified descriptions which made the pattern of meaning more lucid. He separated the general descriptions of 'radio programmes' into specific events which enabled him more fully to get to grips with his own personally meaningful 'items of experience'.

An outline guide to interpreting a FOCUSed grid

Having examined the talkback through one (artificially simplified) grid in a little detail, it is possible to begin to trace out a general approach to the exploration of a FOCUSed grid. The following notes should be seen only as an introduction towards the personal researching of grids. This guide, outlined in nine steps, will be improved, changed, elaborated and discarded as the reader becomes familiar with the process of talkback. Fig. 5.2 shows a simplified algorithm based on the REFLECT computer program which takes the user through the essentials of a talkback conversation.

The major steps in a 'talkback conversation'

Step 1

Encourage the client to read the element descriptions slowly and carefully. Check whether the elements were elicited or offered. If they were offered take special care to encourage clients into re-constructing just what the 'element description' had meant to them during the grid elicitation conversation. Either way, use any additional information that you have about the elements, the elicitation conversation and the participants to talk the client back into as full a re-construction of each 'item of experience' as he or she can achieve.

Step 2

Encourage the client to read the construct pole descriptions slowly and carefully. Read the two pole descriptions of each construct and consider them as one bi-polar dimension. Interpret each in the context of what else you know of the elicitation conditions and conversation. Try to encourage the client to recall exactly what he or she had in mind when original similarities and differences were identified and encourage them to explore how this changed or consolidated as the elements were assigned to one or other pole.

Step 3

Note the nature of the responses in the cells of the grid. Do they simply form a dichotomous $\sqrt{}$ and X response system? Was the client using a rating scale or ranking elements from one pole to the other. Or was the response system something more complex, e.g. the use of Not Applicables (NAs) or measures of doubt? Was the client consistent in their use of the response system?

Step 4

Look at the major areas of similar responses. Read off the elements and the pole descriptions which define each major grouping. Is there a balancing group of elements on the contrast poles of the same group of constructs?

Encourage the client to consider each of the 'cluster of elements' and discuss whether all the elements in any one cluster might be subsumed under one and the same 'verbal label'. Do the same for constructs and their clusters of pole names.

Step 5

Work through the grid identifying the areas of similar responses, and then work down to the smaller and smaller groupings until all responses have been surveyed. Repeat the talkback process described in Step 4 for each grouping in turn.

Step 6

Explore the elements looking first at the tight clusters of similar elements and then at looser clusters until all elements have been inspected. Read each cluster as one unit and look for unifying principles. Note any additional 'items of experience' which come to mind during this part of the conversation.

Step 7

Explore the constructs looking first at the tight clusters and then at the looser clusters. Read all the pole 1 descriptions and then all the pole 2 descriptions in a cluster. Look for unifying principles. Note any additional 'construct poles' which come to mind during this part of the conversation.

Step 8

Recognise each element and each construct as a separate entity and scan the grid for emerging structure.

Step 9

Recognise that unless you are a client interpreting your own grid, you are construing another's constructions of their own unique experiences. Do not too easily believe that you fully understand (in thought and feeling) what they mean.

Extracts from 'real' talkback conversations

Introduction

The following edited extracts are taken from two talkback conversations. The

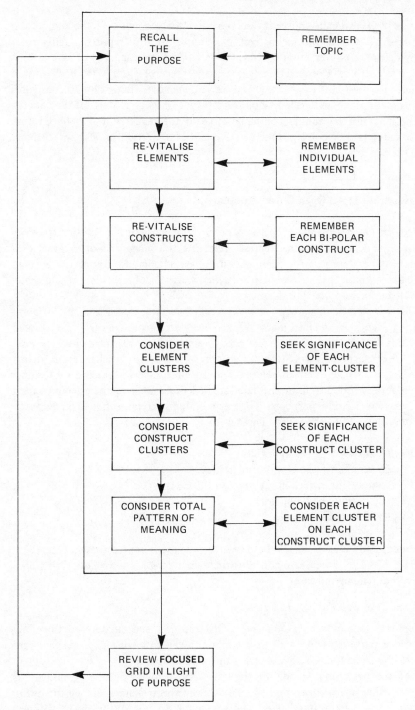

Figure 5.2 Talkback through a FOCUSed grid: an algorithm

first is with an Open University student and the second with the production manager of a food processing factory. Conversation 1 reports a fairly brief snippet from a conversation based on a FOCUSed grid made up of 14 elements and 9 constructs. Conversation 2 is a longer excerpt from a talkback session which took two hours and was based on a 50 elements (faults) by 30 constructs (ways of thinking and feeling about faults) FOCUSed grid. Many of the detailed terms may not be totally comprehensible to the reader but it is hoped that these extracts may convey some of the qualities of a 'real live talkback' through a FOCUSed grid.

Conversation 1: An Open University student

Gwen, an Open University post-experience student taking a Reading Development Course, was concerned about improving the range and operational efficiency of her 'purpose for reading'. An individual elicitation interview enabled Gwen to explore reading experiences which were personally relevant and representative of her approach to learning.

She was helped to relive the past 3 weeks and so to recall as many different reading events as possible. Each of these was used to discuss *why* she entered into this reading opportunity. *The emerging reason was expressed as a purpose*. The list of purposes was reduced to 9 items by a successive dichotomous sorting on the basis of her view of relevance and significance in learning by reading. Gwen revised this list until she felt satisfied that the 9 items best represented her view of reading purposes. To these 9 items, 5 more based on Barrett's *Taxonomy* (1968) were added. These were:

10   To answer a factual question
11   To summarise the author's main ideas
12   To draw inferences about issues in the text
13   To evaluate the argument
14   To appreciate the style

She identified items of personal experience which represented these ideas.

The SPACEd FOCUSed grid illustrated in Fig. 5.3 shows how Gwen construed her reading purposes.

Talkback through the FOCUSed grid

Gwen was talked-back through her FOCUSed grid and encouraged to reflect upon the pattern of meaning this exhibited. The following explanations were offered by her during successive stages of the talkback:

'At the beginning I couldn't think of any reading purposes. Gradually as you talked me through my life as a student and teacher I realised that intuitively I was expecting myself and my pupils to use text in many different ways.'

```
                                    SPACED FOCUSED GRID

CONSTRUCT POLE RATED - 1 -                  ELEMENTS              CONSTRUCT POLE RATED - 3 -

                        E   E EE E  E E   E EEEE E  E
                        0   0 01 1  1 1   0 0100 0  0
                        7   4 54 2  3 1   9 1083 6  2
                        *************************************************
             PRACTICAL  C2 * 3   3 33 1  1 1   2 1111 1  2 * C2  IMAGERY
                  WORK  C5 * 3   3 33 1  1 1   2 1111 1  2 * C5  ENJOYMENT

       EVERYDAY REALITY  C6 * 3   3 33 3  3 1   1 1111 1  1 * C6  UNUSUAL EXPERIENCE
TO ANSWER FACTUAL QUESTION  C1 * 3   3 33 3  3 3   1 1112 2  1 * C1  TO ELUCIDATE OWN VIEW
   TO INSTRUCT MYSELF HOW  C3 * 1   3 33 3  3 3   1 1111 1  1 * C3  TO REFLECT ON SOMETHING

TO GIVE MYSELF OVER TO AUTHOR  C7 * 1   3 33 3  3 1   2 1111 3  3 * C7  TO CLARIFY OWN THOUGHTS
                USEFUL  C8 * 1   3 33 3  1 1   2 2111 3  3 * C8  CREATIVE

             I DISLIKE  C9 * 3   3 33 3  1 1   1 1112 2  3 * C9  I LIKE

    TO APPRECIATE LOGIC  C4 * 3   1 33 3  1 1   1 2211 1  3 * C4  TO FANTASISE
                        *************************************************
                        *   * ** *  * *   * * ** *  * E2 TO LEARN THE PHOTOSYNTHESIS EQUATION
                        *   * ** *  * *   * * ** *
                        *   * ** *  * *   * * ** * E6 TO CHECK ON MATHEMATICAL PROOF
                        *   * ** *  * *   * * ** E3 TO FIND OUT HOW TO DO AN EXPERIMENT
                        *   * ** *  * *   * * * E8 TO CHECK A REFERENCE FOR AN ESSAY
                        *   * ** *  * *   * * E10 TO ANSWER A FACTUAL QUESTION
                        *   * ** *  * *   * E1 TO FIND OUT WHAT MATERIALS ARE NEEDED FOR PHOTOSYNTHESIS
                        *   * ** *  * *   E9 TO LEARN THE NAMES OF GERMAN RIVERS AND TOWNS
                        *   * ** *  * *
                        *   * ** *  * * E11 TO SUMMARISE AUTHOR'S MAIN IDEAS
                        *   * ** *  * E13 TO EVALUATE AUTHOR'S ARGUEMENT
                        *   * ** *
                        *   * ** * E12 TO DRAW INFERENCES ABOUT ISSUES RAISED BY THE AUTHOR
                        *   * ** E14 TO APPRECIATE THE STYLE OF A STORY
                        *   * * E5 TO FEEL HOW DYLAN THOMAS EXPERIENCED XMAS AS A CHILD
                        *   * E4 TO LEARN WHAT BURTON MAKES OF KING LEAR
                        *
                        * E7 TO LEARN ABOUT THE SOCIAL HABITS OF RABBITS
```

Figure 5.3 Gwen's purposes-for-reading grid

'I think my constructs tell me a lot about how I value reading in relation to my work overall. I hadn't realised the extent to which I associate "WORK" with "practical", "everyday reality" and "to instruct myself how to do something" and "ENJOYMENT" with "imagery" "unusual experience of entering someone else's world" and "reflecting on something" . . . and also how little I seemed to use "reflection" in my approach to reading purposes.'

'I think "clarifying my own feelings" and "being creative" are important in reading and yet my grid shows me how little I seem to use this approach in my reading purposes. It's also true I do "dislike" the academic type purposes I describe and there appear to be many of these listed in my elements. I think it's largely because I don't really know how to implement these purposes in ways which are satisfying. Certainly from my own tutor's comments I don't seem to be able to "evaluate" and "summarise" adequately nor keep to factual descriptions as a result of my own reading. . . .'

Further reflection of Gwen's overall grid indicates that although she offered 9 of her own elements and 9 of her own constructs, the pattern of responses shows how undifferentiated these are. The majority of her responses indicate that 'reading purposes' to do with her own studies and her work as a teacher are covered by many 'practical' aspects of learning. Responses to 'elucidate my own view' were somewhat of an anomaly and since these correlate closely with responses to 'enjoyment' Gwen considered this to be an important area for further reflection and review.

Conversation 2: A production manager

This is part of a conversation with the production manager about a grid on the topic of 'Quality of Products'. The grid is not shown.

CONSULTANT: If we look at how 'the ways in which you thought and felt about quality' cluster the 'faults', we see that:

    Uneven colour   (E1)
and   Spotted   (E4)

are both rated in almost the same way. The colour and shape pattern in the grid emphasises this.

They are both seen as:

    Appearance   (C2) i.e. rated 1
    Frequent and process faults (C3) i.e. rated 1
    Fairly 'tolerable (to me)'   (C1) i.e. rated 4
and   'To do with oven'   (C4) i.e. rated 5

although they are both:

    To do with flour   (C6)

'Spotted' is rated more extremely, i.e. (5) than 'Uneven colour' (4).

The way in which you see them as slightly differing is that you see 'Spotted' as being a 'Maintenance' problem (C5) (i.e. rated 5) whereas 'Uneven colour' can be either 'Maintenance' or an 'Operator control' problem (C5) (i.e. rated 3).

MR PRODUCTION: Yes, well, 'Uneven colour' can be produced in a number of ways but 'Spotting' always results from the same cause.

CONSULTANT: You also view:

    'Married berries'   (E5)
    'Gluten lumps'   (E6)
and   'Poor flour coating'   (E3)

all in much the same way. They are:

    'Process faults'   (C3)
    'Intolerable'   (C1)
    'Operator control problems'   (C5)

and to do with:

'Flour and rice'   (C6)

You see 'Married berries' and 'Gluten lumps' as:

'Appearance faults'   (C2)

but 'Poor flour coating' you view as:

'A process fault'   (C2)

MR PRODUCTION: Yes. We have had a lot of trouble with flour coating recently. I consider that to be a 'process fault' which does cause low protein. The QA Inspectors have held off a number of tanks for reclaiming due to this fault.

CONSULTANT: Now 'Metal' (E7) is very different . . . .

Discussion of Mr Production's views of how faults relate one to another in terms of his ways of thinking and feeling about quality continues . . . .

CONSULTANT: Now if we look at the first two rows in the FOCUSed grid it seems that when a fault is an 'Appearance' fault (C2) it is almost always also a 'Frequent process' fault (C3) and when it is rated as 'Contamination' (C2), it is also rated as 'Intermittent' (C3).

MR PRODUCTION: Yes, that's right. That's why it is so important for everybody to keep their eyes open and pick up the early signs. Not just QA but Production people also.

CONSULTANT: And it looks as if you feel that most 'Operator control problems' (C5) are 'Intolerable (to me)' (C1).

MR PRODUCTION: They are my responsibility and operators should be experienced enough not to let it happen. Maintenance problems or oven characteristics may be inherent in the process, but even within those limitations we should be able to produce at least a reasonably consistent product.

CONSULTANT: This diagram shows how your elements map together in the FOCUSed grid . . . . Let's now systematically examine these element/fault clusters . . . .

— 'Dirty fines' and 'Dark brown fines' are almost identical. Both to do with oven — over toasted.

— 'Small berries', 'Size variation' and 'Wrong size' are highly related. Do you see these as the same thing or are they slightly different but related?

MR PRODUCTION: Basically they are the same thing ... a raw material fault, breakage in the rice .... so it's a raw material or could be bumping rolls. ...

CONSULTANT: 'Dusty' and 'fines'.

MR PRODUCTION: These have an appearance similarity ... dustiness could be the flour falling off and dirty fines could be fracturing of the berries, but not necessarily the same cause. ... coating faults ... singed in the oven. ...

CONSULTANT: Now we've got —'Low protein', 'Iron below claim', and 'Low vitamins'.

MR PRODUCTION: Yes that's a problem of flour adhesion but. .. the iron really gets in at the cooker so they're not really causally related, I've made a mistake in my grid. ...

CONSULTANT: No, the clusters are not necessarily causally related. What they show is the relationships with your own construing... they come together. ... if I can interpret back to you my guess is they're to do with claims.

MR PRODUCTION: Yes, they are legal claims and they've got to be right ... but I really think it was inaccurate remembering of the process... the iron goes in with the rice, people don't really know, could be to do with B(ii) on the flow diagram. Basically, I saw the three together as coating faults, but iron could be B(ii), add flavour... add iron... could be in the flour coating, could be in the cooker...
This is a real example of incomplete knowledge and people have different views on how it could be ... we've had several instances recently. ...

... Toasting oven... Toasting fault... Cooked rice drier. ...

The more you personally look at the implications one sees that everything is interrelated... the business of the real causality is much more complex. This is what I find interesting — as one moves into the fine analysis of the clusters of faults you get more detailed disagreement between people... explaining the relationships within clusters brings out different explanations from different people... Roll fault... Bumping roll fault... Oven. ...

CONSULTANT: So — if you take an overall view of the cluster descriptions they are largely causal and very much related to your own responsibilities, is that really how you see the process? ... If you forget about causes are the clusters related in any other way? To some extent, as a consumer, I see some clusters as more to do with appearance or taste, but basically they are causal. ... Let's re-direct this feedback conversation at this point. ... To what extent do you think about the faults in sensory terms?

MR PRODUCTION: Well, visual and flavour. . . we had problems with rice flavour but we can usually deduce what a product will be like from its appearance. . . if it's too light it tastes raw, i.e. floury. Then smell, when I open a packet, sniff it and check if it's musty – as you open it out on a tray you lose this. . . . a raw material is bumping roll fault. . . .

CONSULTANT: Now, one would say, anyone experiencing the product for the first time might concentrate on the physical attributes or say as consumer begin to associate them with the senses in various ways and also with causes which are entirely unrelated to the manufacturing process.

MR PRODUCTION: This might be important in training – to actually raise awareness of physical attributes, gradually clarify the sensory attributes and then move into an exploration of causalities. . . as you gain experience, you refine your own causal model.

CONSULTANT: How does consumer preference get interpreted back into acceptability/unacceptability?

MR PRODUCTION: It isn't – hence the need to develop the project. . . .

CONSULTANT: Where does the reference come from then?

MR PRODUCTION: It's the ideal that's held in top management. . . .

CONSULTANT: It's a mythology, then, to have an absolute consumer ideal of quality. . . .

MR PRODUCTION: Yes, and if a product is successful, they will let it go – even if it's seen as 'rubbish'.

CONSULTANT: Let's take you now through the construct clusters. The tightest cluster is: 'Relates to advertising image', 'Product acceptability to consumer', 'Important to customer'.

MR PRODUCTION: Yes, if you can satisfy their needs, you get fewer complaints and therefore a more successful product and . . .
– 'Important for cost', 'Very important'.
Again these relate to this. I see cost and quality acceptability as very important.

CONSULTANT: 'Legal requirements', 'Nutritional problem', 'Manufacturing problem', 'To do with storage', 'Influences product appearance', does this make a sensible cluster?

MR PRODUCTION: Basically this is a manufacturing/customer-care supra-construct which I see as very important.

Together both major clusters so far are the most important and cover manufacturing and the customer.

CONSULTANT: — 'Predictable fault', 'Related to colour variation', 'Operator control problem'.

MR PRODUCTION: Well, you can predict, for instance you can get under- or over-toasted because the plant is run by people and this aspect is under their control.

CONSULTANT: So, you are thinking about the capacity of the system?

MR PRODUCTION: Yes, and also the operators. . . one shift produces higher protein and another low protein and this is predictable to a greater or lesser extent.

CONSULTANT: — 'Poor ingredient control', 'Flour fault', 'Flour coating', 'Drying problem'.

MR PRODUCTION: Well, here one is going into the realms of the unknown, everyone has their pet views. . . .

CONSULTANT: So, now that gives us your view of most of the construct clusters. You are thinking in terms of 'Importance for cost', 'Consumer acceptability' and 'Manufacturing predictability and control' — these are major ways in which you have differentiated the faults. . . one way of thinking about them does not exclude the other. . . .

Activity 5.1 Talkback through a FOCUSed grid

The reader could at this stage usefully try to elicit, FOCUS and feedback a repertory grid. Choose a topic which is very different from any you have previously explored but which is of mutual interest to yourself and a friend or colleague. Select the type of elements which will awaken 'items of experience' relevant to your 'shared personal understanding' of the chosen topic. Proceed to elicit a grid using the techniques described in chapters 2 and 3. When the raw grid is completed (and after a convenient pause for recovery and sustenance) use the hand sorting technique described in chapter 4, collaborating to reveal both the patterns of meaning and to pace the talkback conversation. As each element cluster is identified and FOCUSed its significance can be examined and discussed. The hand-FOCUSing technique makes it particularly easy to introduce new elements into the conversational grid as and when these arise. Ambiguous elements can be split and redefined adding clarity and precision to the content of the grid. Elements which become trivial or redundant as the conversation proceeds can be discarded.

Similarly with the constructs. Extra ones can be added, mixed poles can be separated and more clearly defined, ideas can be elaborated and trivial or redundant construing can be discarded and replaced by that which is more relevant.

This conversational use of the hand-FOCUSing technique by two people provides a forerunner to the grid conversations which are introduced in the next chapter.

Chapter 6

Grid conversations for achieving self-awareness

On the nature of conversation

Throughout this book the term 'conversation' is being used as a specialist technical term. Negotiating the purpose, eliciting the raw grid, FOCUSing the grid, and talking the client back through the emergent pattern of meaning should all together constitute a conversational event. Conversation is not chit-chat, nor is it a pre-planned formal exchange totally determined by the intentions of one participant. Conversation, in this technical sense, implies some degree of creative encounter, which neither participant could have predicted. People do not emerge from this type of conversation feeling manipulated, but they do feel as if hard effective collaborate work has been done.

Another technical term which may at first sight be misleading is the word 'control'. It is here used in the sense of steering, encouraging, guiding and enabling and should not be taken to imply any hint of inhibition or restriction.

The essence of conversation, as the term is here used, is that there is more than one 'autonomous node of control' within it, and these nodes harmonise or synchronise so that the passing of control back and forth between them achieves an enterprise that neither could have created separately. What is contributed by each is not predictable by the other. Indeed what will be contributed is not predictable by the contributor himself or herself since it is dependent upon what will be contributed by the other. Thus without a totally preconceived notion of the path which the conversation will take, nor of the content which will be covered, the conversants enter upon a collaborative interactive enterprise for which they have significant expectations.

In later chapters we discuss the possibility that a conversation may take place between two 'nodes of control' within one head, or between two groups of people. Here the 'autonomous node of control' is equated with one person, either a T-C practitioner or a client.

However, even between people, there are symmetrical conversations and asymmetrical conversations. The grid conversation as offered up to this point (i.e. in chapters 2, 3, 4 and 5) has been asymmetrical. Whilst practitioner and client are both, clearly, separate nodes of control within the conversation, the nature of the control operated by each is different. At the first level of approximation (e.g. in a grid conversation between a grid-skilled practitioner and a grid-naive client) the practitioner controls the *process* or *form* of the conversation and the client controls the *content*. But to describe the distribution of their contributions as exclusively one or the other is only an approximation to what actually happens.

The stages in such an asymmetrically controlled grid conversation as specified in the first half of the book (i.e. chapters 2-8) are:

Stage 1   Negotiating the purpose.

Stage 2   Deciding upon the nature of the elements which will best contribute to achieving this purpose.

Stage 3   Using this definition of element type as the basis for eliciting a grid by:
(a) Eliciting a representative set of personally significant items of experience for use as elements in:-
(b) Eliciting an appropriate repertoire of constructs and then eventually:-
(c) Assigning all elements to all constructs, so completing the grid (see Chapters 2, 3, 8, 9).

Stage 4   Analysing the grid and constructing a method of displaying its structure which enables the client to identify the pattern of meaning initially concealed and hidden within the raw grid.
(e.g. FOCUS, SPACE and/or TRIGRID). See chapters 4 and 7.

Stage 5   Talking the client back through the content and structure of the grid leads to increased awareness of the topic in the context of the purpose. This is achieved by exploring the implications of the emergent pattern of meaning revealed by the analysis of the grid (see examples of talkback in chapters 5 and 8).

Stage 6   Creating a 'new improved' version of the grid more representative of the client's reviewed state of intention and personal knowing. This will be better aligned on any newly emerging perspective on the topic and towards achieving the, perhaps, now revised purpose of the client.

Stage 7   Moving away from the grid carrying new patterns of meaning and increased awareness of personal intentions in the topic area back into everyday life.

A simplified algorithm of how these seven stages relate one to the other is shown in Fig. 6.1.

On the dangers of offering elements and/or constructs

There are occasions when the purpose for eliciting a grid derives from the

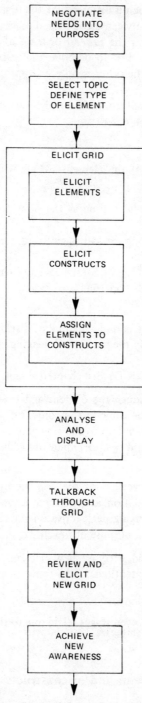

Figure 6.1 Simple version of the grid conversation: an algorithm

objectives of a group of people rather than from the needs of any one individual. Under these circumstances, sometimes, there would appear to be good reasons for asking all the members of the group to use the same elements in their grids. When this is so it is tempting for T-Cs to assume that they can save a lot of time and seemingly pointless discussion by selecting suitable elements for the group to use. Among users of 'a technique resembling the repertory grid' this practice is very common. They happily select elements for use by people they have never met. If 'shared elements' are to lead to successful grid conversations great care must be taken to ensure that each element is full of personal meaning to each individual client. Each element must also represent a very similar 'item of experience' to each of them. If these conditions are not met then not only is the reason for using shared elements no longer valid but there is a real danger that the grid will become merely a container for recording impersonal or second-hand construing.

There is also, for some T-Cs, a great temptation to 'get everybody to use the same constructs'. This is particularly so when a practitioner wishes to use the grid as a sort of survey technique, i.e. when they want to be able to easily compare one person's grid with another. This practice of using 'offered constructs' is beset by the same dangers as threaten the use of offered elements. The often only apparent comparability is traded against the probability that the grid experience and any 'grid results' will be trivialised.

Towards the end of this book various techniques are introduced which are designed to deal with these problems. Here it suffices to indicate the dangers.

A shared language is not merely a question of people using the same words. T-Cs have to help their groups to develop a shared in-group language which retains the capacity to express the personal meanings of each individual but is based on sufficient shared or common experience for each item to mean much the same thing to everybody.

Some readers and colleagues of the authors will feel that the English language is capable of expressing anything that any group may want to say. In one sense this is not in dispute. What is in dispute is the assumption that the words used in the everyday jargon or group shorthand, which are familiar to everybody, carry exactly the same meaning for everybody. What is in dispute is that the everyday use of the English language is sufficient for the negotiation of the types of personal learning which T-Cs, theoretically at least, aim to achieve.

In practice this problem means that any group aiming to arrive at a common set of elements must have some preliminary discussion. The group should agree what their shared purpose is and should decide together upon the most useful type of element to use. They are then in a position to agree a series of specific elements which appear to be the 'same kind of experience' for each member of the group. Similarly, if there are to be any 'offered constructs', they should come from the group and be agreed and understood in the same way by each member.

It is only the widespread use of offered elements and offered constructs which has led us to digress into a preliminary discussion of group construing here. It is further discussed along with the introduction of techniques for achieving it in later chapters (see chapters 9-11). Here the emphasis is on how to heighten the awareness of one person in a topic area of personal concern to them.

Stage 1: need negotiation and purpose definition

One basis for a conversation intended to define the purpose for which the grid is to be elicited is a sound knowledge of the types of purpose which might be achieved using these techniques. Appendix A1.2 offers some examples.

Applying our view of conversation to the negotiation of an appropriate purpose for eliciting the grid reveals why the extreme asymmetric form can only ever be a first approximation to the truly effective versions of this joint enterprise. Who sets the purpose? Our asymmetric description would suggest that the practitioner should control the process by which the purpose is identified but the client should actually identify and define it.

In theory this distribution of effort sounds ideal.

How does it fit with the views of the teachers, trainers, tutors, therapists, coaches, counsellors, custodians and consultants among our readers? How does it fit with the views of those readers who see themselves (also) as learners?

In practice, inexpert attempts to produce such a pure strain of asymmetric conversation will end in less than complete success, since each participant is artificially restricted from making the full contribution of which he or she is capable.

Need negotiation and purpose definition form an important component of the work of all T-C practitioners. Many practitioners may not have explicitly formulated the process to themselves in this way. Some may nearly always assume that both they and their clients know exactly why they have come together. But the majority realise that there is a need to:

  (i) gain the interest of the client;
  (ii) demonstrate that there is something potentially useful to be learned;
or (iii) understand the client's problem.

Only rarely do practitioners offer their clients complete freedom to determine their own purposes. Perhaps such freedom should be offered more often than it is. Certainly on occasions it is the only acceptable condition on which effective collaboration can proceed. But more usually the practitioner has perfectly respectable purposes of his or her own, which are formally legitimised and apparently accepted within the larger context of the client/practitioner enterprise. (Chapters 9 and 12 elaborate on these issues.)

Thus in certain contexts practitioners may alone feel able to decide the purpose of the grid conversation and will merely negotiate the client's acceptance of it. In other contexts the problem as presented by the client may be unacceptable to practitioners. This may be because, whilst they accept it as a problem, they do not believe it can be dealt with at this stage of the relationship, or the problem as presented may be felt to be inappropriate to the formal context of their collaborative enterprise. But it is more likely to be unacceptable because practitioners, from their experience of previous 'similar' instances, believe that the presenting problem is not the central, real or crucial issue which further negotiation will reveal. This can be equally true in the primary school classroom and in the boardroom, in the consulting room, in the prison or on the practice ground. There is a delicate balance for the T-C between continually denying the fruits of one's experience or for ever being in the position of having to avoid the 'I told you so'. This dilemma must be familiar to everyone who has not long ago opted permanently to embrace one horn and closed their eyes to the other. It will certainly be well known to most clients. Some T-Cs seem continually to tantalise clients with leading questions when they all too obviously believe that they already have the answer; others are all too prone to offer the answer before they have allowed the client to identify the question. The truly conversational encounter in which certain asymmetric responsibilities are explicitly agreed is the only really viable answer to this problem. The interactive computer programs DEMON, PEGASUS and ICARUS contain purpose and topic sub-routines. The 'beyond the grid' programs introduced in chapter 12 develop this conversational paradigm further.

Given the varying nature of possible contracts between practitioner and client, the purpose negotiation phase of the grid conversation may require the practitioner to contribute to the content of the purpose:

(1) directly, i.e. by defining it;
(2) circumferencially, i.e. by defining the limits or boundaries within which it may lie;
(3) indirectly, i.e. by accepting the responsibility for judging when a 'real' or viable purpose has emerged, but leaving the content of successive clarifications and formulations to the client;
(4) not at all, i.e. by merely encouraging and guiding the process by which the client identifies, explores and acknowledges his or her own true needs and defines a purpose appropriate to them.

Similarly, and reciprocally, the client may usefully and necessarily contribute to the process by which the purpose is defined. For T-Cs to prevent this is to deny the client access to the nature of the enterprise, and to deny themselves some of the most stimulating and rewarding experiences of their job.

Creative conversation occurs when both practitioner and client transcend the formal constraints of the extreme asymmetric conversation. They are then free to negotiate how the nodes of control might be passed and distributed between them. They can negotiate this without falling into an unworkably 'fair' relationship in which both, having quite differently relevant knowledge and skill, try to take 'equal' control of everything.

Creative learning conversations result from a negotiated recognition of the unequal but necessary contributions that each participant can most effectively make. In conversations which are part of a longer-term attempt to encourage the growth of self-organisation, the practitioners may progressively try to hand more and more of the conversational control over to the learner. But they will always be prepared to offer the minimum support and intervention necessary to sustain the process of development.

Activity 6.1 Negotiating needs and defining a topic and a purpose

It is suggested that the reader work with some friend or colleague who has a problem in a topic area in which you feel competent to work. If in doubt choose to keep the issues relatively simple.

If you have access to a tape recorder it will prove useful to record the exercise and listen through it carefully afterwards to identify the 'control' contributions.

Now discuss your 'client's' needs in the topic area and work with them to define their purpose for doing the grid. Write out a short 'topic description' and 'purpose definition'.

Try to generate the pure asymmetric conversation in which you control the process and the 'client' controls the content. If your colleague or friend is also learning about grids then reverse roles. If not, negotiate with yourself a purpose for doing a grid.

Stage 2: the topic: deciding upon the nature of the elements

If a valid purpose has been negotiated, the success of the grid conversation in achieving this purpose will largely depend upon the choice of an appropriate 'type of element'. Most readers will find that perusal of appendix A1.1 will expand their view of the types of 'items of experience' that can be used as elements in a grid. Again the location of the locus of control for process and for content is better negotiated than pre-empted on a priori grounds.

If the client has no experience of grids, it is probably, at first, more pro-ductive to leave the choice of 'type of element' completely to the practitioner. But after a pilot run with some elements of this initially chosen type each of them may have useful suggestions for changes: and each or either may have identified some criteria which they feel their new 'element type' should meet.

For example, in chapter 1 readers were asked to reflect upon what they construed as 'good' or 'bad' learning/teaching events which might occur in the T-Cing of different topics. In chapter 2 'Man-management events' in the client's recent experience were found to be elements better suited than 'Managers I have known' for developing awareness of social skills in technically experienced staff. In chapter 3 'Events from which I learned something significant' were found to help a technical college student become more aware of how he thought and felt about learning.

The most useful guidelines which the authors can offer about the choice of elements are:

(1) Elements are 'items of experience'.

These may have referents in the immediate 'real' world, e.g. pieces of sculpture or classroom activities.

They may have referents in the 'real' world but these may not be available during the elicitation of the grid, e.g. people or tombstones.

They may have had referents in the 'real' world which are now no more e.g. past theatrical events, past sporting achievements or well-remembered dinners.

Or they may have no referent in the 'real' world, being realities in the life of the mind, e.g. ideas, dreams, concepts, fantasies, theories, affections, purposes, sympathies or antipathies.

Whether the referents are present or absent, existent or non-existent does not change the personal reality of the 'items of personal experience' which form the elements in the grid.

Maintaining this distinction between the real 'item of experience' in the mind of the client and its alleged referent in the shifting sands of external reality defines one major responsibility to be shouldered in the grid conversation.

(2) Elements should span the topic; given that the distinction made in (1) is kept centrally in mind, the choice of an appropriate type of element becomes easier.

One is looking for a representative sample of those items of experience which when configured in their constructional space will adequately delineate the client's pattern of perceptions, thoughts and feelings about the topic.

(3) The choice of each element should be made with the purpose of the grid conversation clearly in mind.

Whilst clarification of purpose in relation to the topic, contemplation of immediate experience and reflection upon past experience can all reduce the probability of gross error in choosing the type of element most appropriate to the client's purpose, the decision is in the final analysis pragmatic. The best type of element for use in any given situation is what works best for that client in that time and place.

Reflecting stage 2 back on to stage 1

Familiarity with the conversational use of repertory grids and with the types of element which work best in the grid conversation has implications for the types of purpose which may appropriately be pursued using this method. Since the grid deals in items of experience, the purposes which are best pursued using this technique will be changes in the construction of personal experience, i.e. purposes which involve personal learning, such as getting one's perceptions, thoughts and feelings about a topic sorted out, and becoming more aware of oneself and one's position on a topic.

This may take the form of changes in the ways in which the client perceives certain aspects of his world, i.e. a selective interpretation of the meaning of a chosen sub-set of the available sensory data (see chapter 8 for a discussion of perception and the grid). These changed perceptions will embody certain intentionalities of the client and if viable will enable him or her to better achieve certain patterns of skilled competent performance or of aesthetic appreciation, i.e. listening to jazz, tuning a motor bike, pouring molten metal into moulds, or the performances which the bodily perceptions of a ballet dancer, yogi or prize fighter enable them to achieve.

It may require changes in what are often called attitudes, i.e. changes in the client's stable patterns of thoughts and feeling about certain self-defined categories of people, things or events, e.g. blacks or whites, colonels or sergeant-majors, whips or micro-processors, American football, a royal wedding's music or the Argentinian navy.

It may require changes in what is often called understanding, knowledge or insight, i.e. those representations of causality − of how things work − which are agreed by the relevant people in our society and for which we have established semi-independent means of verification. For example, an electron flow explanation of how a hair-dryer works, a business model of the dynamics of the market, a cabinet-maker's appreciation of the woodworking properties of different timbers, a meteorologist's understanding of how temperature and air dynamics produce weather, a priest's understanding of God, an engraver's understanding of the effects of acid on glass or a salesman's understanding of how to talk people into deciding to buy one of his Gilibuck Rotoknockers.

From the viewpoint of personal learning, one man's perceptions, attitudes and understanding may become another man's illusions, prejudices and misconceptions. A proper recognition of this offers the opportunity for a giant step forward in the art of negotiating personally viable and relevant meaning. The practitioner's sensitivity and judgment in translating these considerations into effective control of the grid elicitation conversation largely determines its success.

Activity 6.2 Selecting the element type and revising the topic and purpose if necessary

Work with your colleague or friend (see Activity 6.1) to decide on the type of element which would best allow him or her to pursue the purpose in the chosen topic area. Consider carefully the 'topic description' and 'purpose definition' arrived at in Activity 6.1. Does either need revision in the light of your choice of element type? Again use the tape recorder. Listen to the recording to identify exactly who contributed what to the control of the conversation.

Stage 3: eliciting a repertory grid

(a) Selecting specific elements

Start by selecting elements which are 'appropriate', 'natural entities' for the client and which therefore maintain their identity when compared and contrasted with 'similar' or different items of experience. Thus the radio programme *Woman's Hour*, which has been a different sixty-minute event on each weekday for the past twenty years or so, is a more ambiguous element than a specific radio play which Mick had only heard once (see chapter 5).

On the other hand, since Mick had helped select the radio topic as a vehicle for examining his problems of living with Dad and Aunt Ada, it was probably appropriate for him to start with these programmes which were recurrent themes in the bickering at home (see chapter 10 for the development of this example). Thus specificity and appropriateness must be balanced against each other in selecting the type of element to include in the grid.

The conversation in which the specific items of experience chosen as elements are identified should have the following properties:

(1) It should centre around the 'purpose' but should at least initially be allowed to range fairly widely. Items personally relevant to the client should not be prematurely excluded by the practitioner's (inadvertently) misjudged control of the pace and the direction in the conversation.

(2) It should be allowed to gather momentum and flow freely, being gently ushered from one issue to another as the links become apparent.

(3) Possible items of experience should be noted during the conversation without disrupting its flow. Only at appropriate 'natural breaks' should these be reviewed and better defined in a personal shorthand which will serve the client in later stages of the process.

(4) The conversation should be allowed to take a spiral course going over the same ground more than once from different perspectives, with different selectivities and recall mechanisms operating.

(5) Selection of the final elements to be used in the grid from the larger pool of 'items of experience' identified in the earlier part of the conversation should ensure that all relevant parts and aspects of the topic (universe of discourse) are represented. Where there is a choice between competing items from the same realm, those chosen should be those salient to the client's purpose and his or her mental and emotional world.

(6) Where the grid conversation is to serve the purposes of more than one

client, the negotiation of a shared set of elements should conform to the guidelines expressed in items (1) to (5) expressed as a function of the shared experience of that group of clients.

To be truly shared each element must be an item of experience which has an unambiguous referent that is equally a part of the experience of all those taking part, e.g. people well known to all the participants, faults occurring on a product well known to all the managers in its manufacturing company, events in which all have participated.

The reader should be alert to the danger of believing that an element is shared merely because clients verbally agree that they all know it. Their experiences may each have been very different.

Activity 6.3 Eliciting specific elements

Conduct a conversation with your colleague or friend, going over the topic and purpose issues to identify 'items of experience' which fit your definition of the type of element to be used in the grid.

Conduct the conversation as a voyage through the 'client's' relevant experience. Make notes of possible elements, using the 'client's' language, without interrupting the flow. Use natural breaks in the conversation for your 'client' to define possible elements in their own terms. Enter each item on a separate card.

When together you feel the topic has been fully covered, ask your 'client' to sort out 15 to 18 items which would properly span the topic. Shuffle the selected cards. Make sure that your 'client' knows exactly what 'item of experience' the words on each card indicate. Number the cards E1 to En.

Again use the tape recorder to become more aware of the conversational process.

Are your definitions of element type an adequate description of your sample of elements?

Are your type and purpose definitions still adequate?

(bi) Eliciting constructs: on the nature of construing

Perhaps, as yet (i.e. in chapters 1-4), too little has here been said about the art of eliciting constructs. This is partly because subsequent chapters contribute substantially to this topic. Therefore much of what is written here should be seen in reverse time perspective as notes which might have been made to summarise your future reading. They are included at this point because this chapter is intended for subsequent use as a reference.

A construct system can be envisaged in a variety of ways using various forms of representation. Some of these have been discussed in chapters 3, 4, and others. All are selectively inadequate. Psychologists, physiologists, psychiatrists, theologians, witches, anthropologists, linguists, philosophers and demonologists all have, and all have many, models of the psyche. The Buddhist's Upanishads probably embody the results of man's most sustained effort to explore and map the life of the mind as it dwells in the world of the body.

The repertory grid can in its present forms only capture one small cross-section of this maelstrom at a time. In referring to a pattern of personal meaning we have avoided any extensive discussion of the meaning of meaning, in what forms it might be thought to exist and how these forms might be represented. The form of the repertory grid pre-empts many of these issues, so we shall here postpone more general observation for the final chapter. But even within the constraints of the grid form many issues still remain.

The first is to do with what meaning is or can be constructed as being. For the authors, meaning is a relationship between the construer (the attributer of meaning) and the construed (the referent to which meaning is attributed). But meaning cannot exist in isolation. For a referent to acquire meaning the item of experience associated with it must always have both a context and a structure. Each item of meaning is composed of patterns of smaller items and always forms part of a larger pattern. Except at the upper and lower (undefinable) limits it is, therefore, useful to think of meaning as being structured not only into networks at any one level but also into hierarchies or heterarchies of connections between levels. A few analogies may be helpful. Language, which some psycho-linguists mistakenly believe completely mirrors the structure of mental activity, can be viewed as one illustration of the structure of a system for representing meaning. Individual hieroglyphics on a page have little meaning except in as much as they are construed as letters, i.e. as members of an alphabet. An alphabet can be construed as one consolidated attempt to map the fundamental sound elements of the verbal language. A phonetic alphabet carries this process towards its practical limits. When viewed in relation to each other, the phonemes combine to form syllables, but the syllable alone carries little meaning for those of its users not familiar with its antecedents. It is only as the letters combine into syllables, the syllables into words, and the words structure into sentences that even a rudimentary representation of items of meaning as we experience them emerges. It is only as sentences are sequenced into paragraphs, paragraphs combine into sections, sections pattern into chapters and chapters run into books that patterns of meaning as we experience them are in anyway adequately represented.

It is this multi-level organisation of the structure of language that gives it its power in representing meaning. But powerful as it is, written language suffers from a number of major difficulties as a means of exploring personal meaning, personal knowing and personal learning.

(1) It is by definition a social construction, carrying in some not entirely credible way the cumulative experience of all its users. This social, public

function of language makes it suspect as a conveyor of personal meaning. The publicly agreed consensus over-rides the privately intended meaning. Even for the initiators of a written object, concern with publicly acceptable forms constrains their personal expression. Hence the need for every generation to break the forms of previous generations, to express fresh meanings which will have personal viability, e.g. Euclid, Chaucer, Henry James, Newton, James Joyce, Picasso, Brecht, Beckett, etc.

(2) Over-familiarity with public language pre-packages the forms of the thoughts and feelings which can be expressed. As the work of Joyce or Beckett indicates, it may be a life's work to shed the iron constraints within which our early indoctrination with public usage imprisons our meanings.

(3) Much personal meaning is contained in non-verbal structures of the mind. In sensory images, in the 'feelings' of the kinaesthetic muscle sense, in music, in art, in mathematics and in the facial expressions and gestures of what has become popularly known as sub-verbal language.

The strength of the repertory grid is that it is, and will remain for the foreseeable future, an unfamiliar but highly structured form within which fresh personal meaning may be expressed. Every decision in the grid conversation is necessarily forced into the centre of consciousness.

(bii) Eliciting constructs: conversational methods

Returning from this necessary diversion into a discussion of the nature of meaning, what has been gained for our consideration of the elicitation of constructs? First and foremost is the lesson that the verbal labels attached to the elements and construct pole descriptions should not be viewed as descriptions in a public language, but merely as the short-hand labels or symbols with which the client can generate an effective language for conversing with him or herself. The verbal labels are the temporary coinage in which the full richness of the personal experience can be negotiated and exchanged with oneself. But for most people the coinage of their verbal representations of viable and relevant personal meaning loses much of its value when traded in the foreign markets of public communication.

The bi-polar form of a construct, i.e. the fact that it has two poles, embodies a minimal assumption about meaning. This is that any one item of experience only acquires meaning when seen in a relationship of similarity and contrast to two other items. Similarity in itself confers no meaning. If everything were the same we could know nothing. Contrast in itself cannot reveal the nature of the contrast. Only similarity and contrast together assign minimal meaning. But the potential for meaning expands rapidly as the possibilities for similarity and contrast are increased. Three items offer three possibilities for meaning, i.e.:

SIMILAR	DIFFERENT
1 + 2 (hard)	3 (soft)
1 + 3 (green)	2 (red)
2 + 3 (I like)	1 (I dislike)

Four items offer twelve (12) possibilities.

Five items offer thirty (30) possibilities.

Six items offer sixty (60) possibilities.

Seven items offer one-hundred-and-five (105) possibilities.

Eight items offer one-hundred-and-sixty-eight (168) possibilities.

Nine items offer two-hundred-and-fifty-two (252) possibilities.

It is an interesting commentary on the nature of man's meaning-attribution system that whilst this potential for generating separate dimensions of meaning defined merely by similarity and difference rapidly becomes enormous, the number of dimensions which we can hold in mind at any one time is rapidly spent. Man has both the need and capacity to organise meaning in a nesting system of levels of categorisation which may be expressed as a hierarchical system of bi-polar constructs.

This immediately exposes the first major defect in the repertory grid as a form for representing meaning. It contains only a two-level descriptive capacity. The elements are assigned to each construct. It has no capacity to define or represent construing at different levels in the system.

This being so the grid conversation should take this into account. If the constructs which are elicited can be applied (with the same meaning) to a much wider-ranging set of items of experience than those represented by the elements then the grid will appear undifferentiated, i.e. the constructs are too high in the hierarchy of bi-polarities. If many of the elements cannot be assigned to the poles of the elicited constructs then the constructs are too restricted or too low in the hierarchy of bi-polars.

This can be summarised by suggesting that a grid should contain only those constructs which have a range of convenience approximating to that represented by the total set of selected elements. This is in current (bad) practice very rarely the case and it is yet one more reason why we have introduced the idea of 'a technique resembling the repertory grid'. The superficial resemblance is misleading, even though the verbal label is the same.

Thus in the grid conversation both the practitioner and the client must contribute to the controlling of the level of the construct being elicited. Skilled practitioners can guide the client into comparisons and contrasts of the right order by bringing into the conversation the idea of both the larger context and the structure of each element.

A rough and ready tool for achieving this is the technique of laddering. Questions which ask why the difference posed by the poles of a construct is important to you will provoke comments which can lead to the identification of a superordinate construct. For example, our nursery school teacher who construes children as:

neat and tidy   v.   scruffy

might be asked which kind of child he prefers. Given that he opts for the 'scruffy' ones, he would be asked why he feels the difference to be important. 'Because they are more lively and natural,' he replies. 'What would a child who was the opposite of lively and natural be?' he is asked. 'Oh, the others are guarded and over-polite.' So

lively and natural   v.   guarded and over-polite

is his superordinate construct.

Alternatively the 'same' laddering conversation might have proceeded thus:
'I like neat and tidy ones and really loathe the others although I never show it.' 'Why is the difference so important to you?' 'Because I can work well with the tidy ones. They are bright and intelligent, and they always pay attention.' 'What would the opposite kind of child be like?' 'Rowdy, noisy and stupid.'
This is a rather different superordinate construct which as a context to:

neat and tidy   v.   scruffy

gives it a rather different meaning.

Sometimes the construct originally offered is too general or superordinate for the purpose for which the grid is being used. Then the grid conversation should be laddered downwards. For example: 'You have said "scruffy" is a way in which you would describe some of the children who you teach. Could you give me an example of what you mean.' 'Well you know, buttons undone, T-shirts, dirty finger-nails, tangled hair.' 'What would the opposite kind of child be like?' 'Oh, clothes clean and pressed, a tie, proper shoes, hair brushed and combed.' By asking for examples one encourages the construing to become more specific or descriptive.

Practice in eliciting repertory grids soon leads to the laddering type of question becoming an almost non-conscious ploy for moving the level of construing up or down until it becomes appropriately pitched to the purpose of the conversation.

The skilled construct elicitation conversation will sound structured but informal, well organised but flexible. Triads (the three-card trick) will often be used initially to get the conversation moving but on occasions two elements are sufficient to elicit bi-polar construct descriptions. On the other hand, sometimes, particularly if the client is having difficulty finding additional constructs, more (or even all) of the elements may be offered so that a new similarity or difference can be more easily noticed and pulled out. Later it can be refined into acceptable bi-polar descriptions.

The meta-purpose of a grid conversation is to enable clients to explore their constructions of experience, their perceptions, thoughts and feelings about the topic in ways that are relevant to the purpose; and to enable them to do this as fully and as precisely as possible. The cards, the triads and the elicitation procedures are 'tricks', tools or knowhow which help to keep the quality of the exchange up when the ordinary unplanned exchange of words is not sufficient.

But flexibility and informality should not be equated with lack of rigour or care. The elements must be explored sufficiently to ensure that the perceptions, thoughts and feelings (the construing system) relevant to the purpose is made explicit and is fully represented in the grid.

In its pure form this construct elicitation activity should guide the client to the appropriate level of construing and should ensure that all relevant experience is re-visited, but the content of the constructs should remain entirely the responsibility of the client. The definition of what is relevant should be kept wide open so that nothing is missed. In the later parts of the conversation the client can be asked to tighten the definition of relevance, and previous construing which then appears redundant or off-centre can be re-aligned, refined or pruned away.

The relative success or failure of the grid conversation (given an adequately defined purpose and a well-chosen set of elements) depends upon the quality of the construct elicitation conversation and the extent to which it has enabled clients to explore and make explicit the essential nature of their construing. The grid is only a 'repertory' grid if the complete repertoire of constructs is revealed. Where the conversation is inadequate or some public set of constructs is assembled from other people's repertoires, the resulting verbal labels and set of assignings is merely a record of an inadequate conversation. This record only resembles the repertory grid as a forgery (or a painting done by numbers) resembles an original. Such exercises may be very useful and may have a contribution to make in a complete reflective learning technology, but this contribution can only be exploited when it is recognised for what it is.

(c) Assigning the elements to the constructs

The construct elicitation phase of the conversation was treated separately so that the descriptions of methods for assigning elements to constructs would not interfere with the central message of that previous section. However, in practice, this division is artificial. For example in chapter 3 it was seen that the process of assigning elements to constructs often leads clients to revise and refine the construct pole descriptions.

The process of assigning elements to constructs can serve three basically different functions:

(1) It may merely record how personally well-defined elements map on to the poles of personally well-defined constructs. In this form every element is assigned to every construct.

(2) It can be used more conversationally to explore and define the topic.

A client may feel that elements do not fit comfortably on to either pole of a construct. The use of a non-applicable (NA) response to record this unease reveals discontinuities and gaps in the client's operational definition of the topic. The pattern of Not-Applicables (NAS) can be used to trace out the boundaries of the client's pattern of personal meaning relating to that topic. This may lead client and practitioner together to redefine:

(a) the topic verbally to fit the selected sample of elements;
(b) the topic operationally by changing the sample of elements;
(c) the purpose of the conversation and thus change the criteria for selecting the elements and constructs.

or

(3) It can be used (again more conversationally) to help the client dredge up, retrieve and better define constructs which, whilst they feel as if they are appropriate and useful in construing the topic, appear in terms of their original verbal labels not to span the topic-defining elements. The elicitation conversation can encourage an iterative process of giving tentative verbal labels to the poles, roughly sorting the elements on to those poles, then redefining the poles to capture the communality of the elements assigned to them. The revised pole descriptions are then used to re-assign elements and the cycle repeated until the client feels happy that:

(a) the elements are partitioned in a personally significant way;
(b) the pole descriptions carry the essential nature of this partitioning at least in a personally stable short-hand which will be recognised, and can continue to be used in later phases of the conversation.

The skilled user of the grid (practitioner or client) is aware of these variations on the elicitation process and can use them to control the development of the grid conversation, moving through phases of provisionality and decisiveness to produce a creative encounter of the client with himself or herself. In combination, and carefully iterated to allow the client the psychic space and time in which to achieve increasing self-awareness, the successive approximations to an adequate representation of clients' construing of the topic are felt and usually acknowledged by them to have been encounters of the humanly creative kind. Taken more procedurally, some of the issues in scaling, in the assigning of elements to constructs, are:

(1) To use *Not Applicable* or NA (refer to Fig. 7.7 at the end of chapter 7 for an example grid – Ms Shop Assistant).
(2) To use a purely bi-polar (two-response) scale or some more flexible response scheme.
(3) (a) A nominal scale,
          i.e. a – b – c – d – e.
     and

very x, fairly x, x and y, fairly y, very y

or

(b) a numerical scale,

i.e. $1 - 2 - 3 - 4 - 5$

(4) If bi-polar, is the distribution of responses to be restricted or is a free distribution of responses to be allowed?

(5) If more than a two-response scale is to be used, how many responses points on the scale should be allowed?

   (a) An odd number of points on the scale leaves a point of indecision at the centre (i.e. 3 point, 5 point, 7 point, or 127 point);

   (b) A ranking scale in which the number of points on the scale is equal to the number of elements in the grid.

(6) If a numerical scale is chosen should it be treated as: an ordinal scale, one in which:

1 is merely less than 2 is less than 3 is merely less than 4 is merely less than 5

or as:

an interval scale, in which:

1 + diff = 2, 2 + diff = 3, 3 + diff = 4, and 4 + diff = 5, and in which the value of 'diff' may or may not be known?

or as:

a ratio scale, in which the numbers operate like 'real' numbers:

e.g. 1 is a half of 2, 2 is a fifth of 10, 2 multiplied by 3 equals 6, and 0 equals nothing?

(7) Do the statistical methods which you use (or which unbeknown to you, are used in your favourite computer analysis programs) fit your choice of scale?

Some of these issues are discussed in a little more detail in chapter 7.

Activity 6.4 Eliciting constructs

Use the elements identified in Activity 6.3 to elicit constructs. Assign elements to each construct as it is elicited. Deliberately ladder constructs up and down to get a feel for the appropriate level. Try out the TRIAD method, the PAIR method and the FULLER CONTEXT methods to get a feel for how you can encourage and enable the search for a full range of relevant constructs. Use a two-point scale (i.e. bi-polar).

Continue using the tape recorder. Check that your topic and purpose definitions still fit.

Reflecting stage 3 back on to stage 2 and stage 1

In the pure asymmetric form of the grid conversation the client always has final and complete control over the content, i.e. clients originate and select the items of experience which become elements; they produce and refine the differentiations and descriptions which become bi-polar constructs; they also decide upon the assignings of the elements to the poles of each construct. Together elements, constructs and assignings define the content and structure of the grid. When the client has fully participated in defining the purpose of the grid conversation and when the client also understands the nature of the grid sufficiently to fully control and exploit his or her psychological resources in pursuit of that purpose, then the ideal conversation may produce the pure form of repertory grid.

Only when practitioners are skilled enough to: (i) produce such pure repertory grids from themselves, and (ii) conduct such a pure grid conversation with a close and sympathetically inclined colleague on a slightly 'sticky' topic, only then are they becoming grid-skilled conversationalists. Only when they achieve such skill should they be tempted then to begin to use the offered or publicly constrained versions of elements and/or constructs.

Not all clients are yet fully self-organised learners and not all clients are familiar enough with the power and subtlety of the grid to explore fully their inner resources and thus represent their potential to themselves. Not everybody can reach self-awareness through the grid with purely process assistance. Un-self-organised naive grid users may need help from the grid-skilled practitioners in eliciting the constructs. The T-C must offer the conversational controls which the clients are unable to provide for themselves. Clinical readers will recognise that questions similar to those raised by, say, Ronnie Laing or Carl Rogers with his client-centred therapy and Fritz Perls, Albert Ellis or Eric Berne with their more interventionist approaches, may be related to those of strategy and tactics in the grid conversation. Readers not familiar with the clinical literature will have no trouble identifying friends, colleagues and relations who differ in their conversational style. Again it is revealing to consider such differences as varying competencies in conversation, as differences in the assumptions, strategy and tactics brought to the conversation rather than as the inevitable consequence of some inborn fundamental personality characteristics.

In subsequent chapters many suggestions are offered about how certain construing of constructs can be used to refine the controls exerted during the grid elicitation process. Without further explanation the reader is guided towards chapters 8 and 9 and towards the repertory grid section of the glossary, and towards the 'grid tricks' and list of activities sections. In these the reader will find suggestions for how perceptual grids, value grids, non-verbal grids, descriptive and evaluative grids, etc. can be elicited.

The nature of a grid conversation is now beginning to emerge. It is a conversation which uses the repertory grid as a vehicle for a journey into inner space. An analogy might be drawn between a grid and a rocket. In the 1940s

rockets had already been around for a long time. They had been used for entertainment and for war, for carrying mail and as signals of distress, but in other
than certain specialist areas the rocket was treated as a rather intriguing toy.
Balloons and aeroplanes were seen as the ways to get off the ground. So now
with the grid. It has its specialist uses but it is seen in the main as a intriguing
way of playing with individual opinions and ideas but there are other more
widely used and better developed methods for doing the real work of T-C.
The 1960s saw Sputnik take off into outer space. The treasured belief (some
said obsession) of such a von Braun was vindicated. Jet propulsion had been
shown as the way to escape the earth's gravity. The technology of the rocket
had achieved take-off.

People have long felt that the human race is capable of transforming itself.
The way has been sought in religions, in philosophies and in the psychologies
of such as Freud and Skinner.

The authors believe that a 'science of learning conversations' may provide
more fruitful access to an inner universe of human growth and development
than has yet proved possible with more popular but essentially inappropriate
techniques. These ideas again reinforce the general movement in social science
away from attempts to open the methods of the physical sciences through a
re-emergent sense of personal science to a newly fledged paradigm of conversational science with all that this phrase implies.

T-Cs all know that sometimes, for some reason, talking with a client can
produce startling results. There are more conflicting theories or beliefs about
how and why this happens than there are inspired practitioners who can occasionally bring it to pass. Here an attempt is being made to identify the seeds of
a theory and a symbiotic technology which may eventually generate the experiential power to achieve take-off out to inner space (see chapter 10).

This power will come from its capacity to enable non-trivial conversation.
One reason it is non-trivial is that it does not conceive of problem-identifying,
formulating and solving as a linear process. For social scientists the progression
from the 'physical science' paradigm, to 'personal science' to the 'conversational science' paradigm is producing a more coherent understanding of how
our knowledge of the human condition may better be developed.

Activity 6.5 Reviewing the raw grid

Discuss with your 'client' how thoroughly they feel the raw grid obtained in
Activities 6.3 and 6.4 really meets the needs with which he or she started. Where
there are any doubts:

1 Try to add more constructs to see whether that helps. Use open conversation to identify constructs which seem to have been missed by
   the elicitation techniques.

2 Add any additional elements which now seem relevant. Assign them to each of the constructs you have elicited so far. Add any additional constructs which are brought to mind by the new elements. Use any or all of the elicitation procedures to get at these.

3 If the raw grid still does not seem to fit the original needs then either:

(a) renegotiate a new set of items of experience better suited to the purpose; or

(b) go to the next (grid analysis) activity to discover whether the personal pattern of meaning in the grid revealed by the analysis meets the needs originally expressed. Realise that in one sense you cannot get more out of a grid than has been put in.

Continue to use the tape recorder.

Stage 4: analysing the grid

Chapter 4 has shown how the FOCUSing technique of analysing a grid can be carried out by hand, and how the SPACE procedure can be used to visually highlight the results of FOCUSing. Chapter 7 introduces the TRIGRID display technique and discusses various other methods of analysis which can be used on the raw grid.

The main purposes for analysing a grid are to reveal:

(i)   how the elements relate one to another in the client's construing;

(ii) how the bi-polar constructs relate one to another;

(iii) how the pattern of elements and the pattern of constructs each give meaning one to the other to produce a uniquely personal structure of meaning in the topic area.

Additional ways in which a grid can be analysed either offer alternate (mathematical) models for identifying and displaying the same basic relationships or they offer:

(i)   verbal analyses of element and/or construct pole labels;

(ii) displays which reveal the context and structure of the items in the grid by showing how three levels of construing relate one to the other;

(iii) the client's view of what goes with what; an analysis of pole relatedness or from the implications grid.

In later chapters methods for analysing how the construing represented in one grid may be compared with that in another grid are described and discussed. These techniques require a different type of grid conversation (see chapter 9).

Stage 5: talkback through an analysed grid

Chapter 5 has described in some detail the process of talking some one back through a FOCUSed grid. Here the emphasis is on the general nature of the talk-back conversation rather than on the details revealed by FOCUSing. The purpose of the talkback through an analysed grid is two-fold.

(i) The specific nature of the analysis will highlight certain relationships between items in the context of the grid which were not apparent in the raw grid. The client is encouraged to explore such relationships step by step until they have fully understood the implications as insights into the nature of their own construing.

(ii) The process of synthesis by which the client is enabled step by step to move out of the specifics of the grid. They are encouraged to re-construct their experience of the topic back into one coherent pattern of meaning. This pattern of meaning is probably more elaborated, comprehensive and differen-tiated than that with which they started. They are also much more aware of the context and structure of their own construing.

Activity 6.6 Talking back through the analysed grid

Choose the method which you wish to use to analyse and display the meaning in the grid. Chapter 4 introduced hand-FOCUSing and the SPACE display. Chapter 7 adds other methods.

Analyse the grid and carefully prepare yourself to talk your 'client' back through it. Make any simple visual aids you feel will be useful. Talk your 'client' back through his or her analysed grid. Take care to re-activate their awareness of the personal meaning of the elements and the construct poles.

Stage 6: revising the grid, the topic and/or the purpose

The analysis of the grid can be used to suggest ways in which the client can be encouraged to develop his or her construing. Ideas and details of various 'grid tricks' will be found throughout the book. Here only a brief outline is offered.

(a) Groups of tightly clustered or undifferentiated elements can be used to encourage the client to retrieve or invent constructs which will split up the elements. For example, your grid shows that Israel, Uganda and El Salvador appear to be very similar as countries in which to work. Can you think of any significant ways related to your purpose in which they differ?

(b) Where elements remain undifferentiated, items of experience can be combined or selectively pruned to better represent the client's construing of the topic.

(c) Clusters of tightly related constructs can be used to enable clients to retrieve or construct items of experience which will split the constructs. For example, your grid shows that whenever you say that they are 'creative' you say they are 'scruffy' and whenever you say 'neat and tidy' you say they are 'conventional'. Can you think of a 'conventional, scruffy' child — or of a 'creative, neat and tidy' one?

(d) Again if clustered constructs cannot be split then they may be combined or selectively pruned.

(e) Phantom or missing elements can also be derived from analysis of a grid. A sequence of assignings different from that of any element in the grid can be identified. The client can then be asked whether he or she can identify an 'item in their experience' which would lie on the construct poles in that way. E.g. Bill Shard might be asked to identify a personal learning experience which is:

Either

Older generation	X
Own conditions	√
Finding out about my own character	√
From own insight	X
About life	√
Self-reliance	X
Tense	√
Growing up — embarrassment	X
Guiding effect	√

Or

Same generation	√
Imposed by parents and others	X
Finding out about other people's true character	X
From others' insight	√
About people	X
Group activity	√
Relaxed	X
Growing up — more authority	√
Made me cautious	X

The reader is referred to Fig. 4.7 to see that these are phantom elements. Bill might have been given the freedom to change one, or at the most two, assignings to enable him to really explore his experience.

(f) Similarly phantom constructs can be invented as a pattern of assignings of elements, e.g. Gwen might have been asked to identify a construct with:

To learn the photosynthesis equation
To find out how to do an experiment
To answer a factual question
To learn the names of German rivers and towns

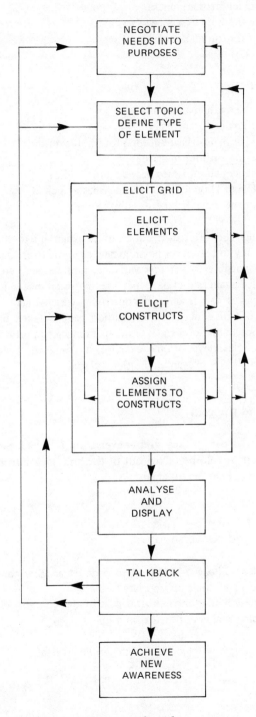

Figure 6.2 Iterative grid conversation: an algorithm

>To evaluate an author's argument
>To appreciate the style of a story
>To learn what Burton makes of King Lear.

on one pole

and on the other:

>To check on the mathematical proof
>To check a reference for an essay
>To find out what materials are needed for photosynthesis
>To summarise the author's main ideas
>To draw inferences about issues raised by the author
>To feel how Dylan Thomas experienced Xmas as a child
>To learn about the social habits of rabbits

Again Gwen could be offered freedom to re-assign up to three elements to encourage her really to search for possible new personal constructs (Fig. 5.3).

(g) It is also possible to use low variance, lopsidedness, etc. as cues to the encouragement for changes that have increased personal meaning.

These grid games can lead to re-construing which makes the whole grid experience feel out of date. The conversation can be taken back to Stages 4 and 3 to incorporate these changes. It may even be appropriate on occasions to repeat the whole conversational exercise, building on the previous experience to construct a more relevant and insightful grid.

Stage 7: beyond the grid

Finally, an essential part of any grid conversation is to link Stage 6 back into Stage 1. The client should be talked out of the grid back into its relevance for his needs and purposes in the topic area.

Activity 6.7 A grid conversation

Work with another colleague or friend to conduct another complete grid conversation. Choose a new topic appropriate to them.

Use the hand-FOCUSing technique as part of the conversation. Thus involve them in the ongoing analysis of their own grid.

Fig. 6.2 shows an iteractive algorithm of the grid conversation.

Chapter 7

The space within which personal meaning may be represented

The limitations of the FOCUSed display

In chapter 3 the 'fruit and vegetables' example was used to introduce the analogy of space in the physical world to the space in the world of the psyche. It was suggested that displays in physical space could be used to represent a system of personal constructs. In chapter 4 the SPACE procedure was explained. This illustrated how the organisation and layout of the FOCUSed grid can be used to emphasise the similarities between elements, and the relationships between constructs. It also showed how the elements are organised by the constructs, and how the constructs acquire their meaning by the ways in which they group the elements. The SPACEd, FOCUSed grid was claimed to be the 'optimal' layout for talkback. Whilst this is true within the constraints of an analysis to be fully displayed on the two-dimensional page, this layout still conceals some of the less-dominant relationships. In the FOCUSed grid on a sheet of paper the elements occupy one spatial dimension and the constructs the other. The need to express all similarities between elements within a one-dimensional (linear) ordering means that certain clusters are emphasised at the expense of other less-predominant but still significant relationships. To illustrate this, and to introduce a discussion of alternative methods for analysing a grid, Bill Shard's FOCUSed grid is further examined (see Fig. 4.7).

In chapter 4, Fig. 4.2 showed how the difference scores between each pair of elements could be collected into a matrix of similarities. A difference of zero '0' indicated total similarity and increasing differences of '1', '2', '3', etc. indicated decreasing similarity. The procedure for FOCUSing was then explained step by step. The implications of this process can be made more transparent by re-ordering the columns and rows of this similarity matrix into the FOCUS cluster sequence.

Now the relationship between adjacent resorted elements is represented by the difference scores displayed along the diagonal. E.g. E5 and E2 are assigned in the same way to all constructs and therefore show a difference of zero '0'. These were used to SPACE the FOCUSed grid (Fig. 4.7).

```
        E5   E2   E1   E8   E7   E4   E3   E6   E9

  E5    -    0    1    4    4    6    7    7    7

  E2         -    1    4    4    6    7    7    7

  E1              -    3    5    7    6    6    6

  E8                   -    2    6    5    7    5

  E7                        -    4    5    7    5

  E4                             -    1    5    5

  E3                                  -    4    4

  E6                                       -    2

  E9                                            -
```

This is perhaps easier to recognise if the triangular portion of the similarity matrix is rotated until the diagonal set of differences becomes horizontal. So:

```
                           E9      E5
                    E6      7       E2
             E3      7      7       E1
      E4      7      7      6       E8
E7    6      7      6      5        E7
E8    4      6      6      7      5    E4
E1    4      4      7      5      7   5   E3
E2   1   4      5      6      5      5   4   E6
E5   0   1   3      2      4      1      4   2   E9
 E    E    E    E    E    E    E    E    E
 5    2    1    8    7    4    3    6    9
```

Now the differences in the bottom row are those used to determine the SPACE layout. All the other differences in the matrix were ignored, even though they are relevant to a full understanding of the hidden pattern. What more would emerge if all the differences between elements were taken into account? The analysis of this matrix of differences can be approached from a slightly different perspective from that taken to SPACE it. Accepting the FOCUSed sequence of elements as a starting point, each step from the zero ('0') differences to the maximum differences (of '7') can be re-examined. The one zero ('0') score implies that within the evidence presented by his grid Bill saw E5 and E2 as identical, i.e. assigned to all his constructs in exactly the same way. To represent the zero ('0') difference spatially on the two-dimensional page, E5 and E2 would have to be positioned in exactly the same place.

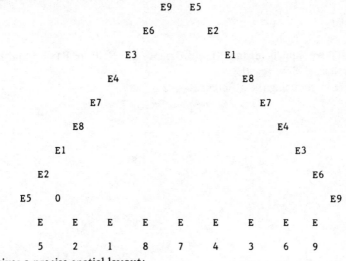

This gives a precise spatial layout:

E5 —
E2 —

So already the FOCUSed layout is seen to slightly but necessarily distort relationships by placing E5 and E2 alongside each other rather than in the same place.

Now, re-introducing the differences of one ('1'), these can be represented spatially as the two related elements being close to each other (but not in the same position) so:

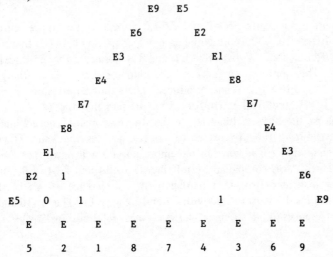

This gives a precise spatial layout:

```
E5 —
E2 — E1          E4 — E3
```

E5 and E2 are equally distant (i.e. difference of '1') from E1: E4 and E3 are similarily spaced close together.

Now, re-introducing the differences of '2':

```
                         E9   E5

                   E6          E2

               E3          E1

           E4          E8

        E7          E7

     E8          E4

  E1          E3

E2   1          E6

E5   0    1       2       1    2   E9

E    E    E    E    E    E    E    E    E

5    2    1    8    7    4    3    6    9
```

This gives a precise spatial layout:

```
E5 —
E2 — E1     E8 — — E7     E4 — E3     E6 — — E9
```

The remaining elements E8-E7 and E6-E9 appear as two more clusters, but with the difference of '2' represented as a greater spacing between them.

The difference of '3' between E1 and E8 connects the E5-E2-E1 cluster to E8-E7. This approach to revealing the hidden structure (patterning) among elements has, up to this point, produced much the same results as the hand-SPACEd FOCUSing. This is confirmed by the fact that the '0's, '1's, '2's, and '3's lie along the base of the triangle, i.e. the diagonal of the original matrix. But re-introducing the differences of '4' complicates the issue. If you refer back to chapter 4 (or if you can remember it) you will recall that the clustering of elements was completed by relating E7 to E4 and E3 to E6. This linear re-orderng discarded five other pairings with a difference of '4': i.e. E9 with E3, E5 with E7, E5 with E8, E2 with E7 and E2 with E8. The 'up to and including the differences of "4" triangle' shows all these relationships.

Introducing the difference of '3':

```
                        E9    E5
                  E6          E2
              E3              E1
          E4                      E8
       E7                          E7
   E8                              E4
   E1                                E3
  E2    1                             E6
E5    0    1    3    2        1         2    E9
   E    E    E    E    E    E    E    E    E
   5    2    1    8    7    4    3    6    9
```

This gives a precise spatial layout:

```
E5 –
E2 – E1 – – – E8 – – E7     E4 – E3     E6 – – E9
```

```
                        E9    E5
                  E6          E2
              E3              E1
          E4                      E8
       E7                          E7
   E8    4                          E4
   E1    4    4                        E3
  E2    1    4                      4    E6
E5    0    1    3    2    4    1    4    2    E9
   E    E    E    E    E    E    E    E    E
   5    2    1    8    7    4    3    6    9
```

The differences along the bottom line give the following spatial layout:

```
E5 –
E2 – E1 – – – E8 – – E7 – – – – E4 – E3 – – – – E6 – – E9
```

But this ignores the '4's in the rows above. The spatial representation of these differences poses a problem. Other than the difference of zero '0', requiring that E2 and E5 be placed in the 'same' place, the differences of '1', '2', and '3' could be represented as distances proportional to 1, 2 and 3 whilst remaining compatible with the linear SPACEd layout. However, to represent the differences of '4' as equal distances of length '4' requires more than one dimension.

The introduction of the differences of '4' means that the nine elements can no longer be SPACEd along one straight line without seriously distorting the distances between them. For example, whilst E6 and E9 are a difference of '2' apart they are each a distance of '4' from E3. The only true spatial representation of this is a (two-dimensional) triangle.

```
                    --E6
                -----  '
E3 -------- E9
```

Similarly, for E7 and E8 to be a distance of '2' apart and each also to be '4' away from E2 and E5 requires triangular representation; and E1 lies at distances of '1' from E2 and '3' from E8.

```
E5  .           --E8
E2  -  E1 -----    '
         ----      '
            ----E7
```

Thus introducing the differences of '4' requires a two-dimensional representation. The FOCUSing and SPACE-ing operations are now shown to be concealing a complexity of relationships which could not be displayed in the linear re-ordering of the elements.

Re-introducing the differences of '5' further complicates the display problem.

```
                            E9    E5

                        E6        E2

                    E3            E1

                E4            E8

            E7            5    E7

        E8     4              5    E4

    E1    4      4       5       5    E3

E2    1    4     5      5    5    4    E6

E5  0   1    3    2    4    1    4    2   E9

 E    E    E    E    E    E    E    E    E

 5    2    1    8    7    4    3    6    9
```

There is no way in which the difference of '5' between E1 and E7 can be represented without distortion of the emergent two-dimensional structure. A third and fourth dimension are required to preserve the undistorted distances. Similarly, as the differences of '5' are introduced on to the E8, E7, E4, E3, E6, E9 structure, it is no longer possible to represent all the relationships in a two-dimensional space. In re-introducing the differences of '6' and '7', the problems of spatial representation multiply. Thus a nearer and nearer approximation to the 'true' spatial representation of all the differences in the matrix of similarities calls first for a two-dimensional, and then for a three-dimensional display. But beyond this the analogy to physical space breaks down. One and two-dimensional relationships are easily drawn on a page. Even a three-dimensional representation is fairly easily visualised and represented in perspective; but when the differences (and therefore the distances) between elements require more than three dimensions to hold them all simultaneously without distortion, then some other form of representation or analogy is required.

Learning to read the TRIGRID display

It is possible to learn to 'read' a TRIGRID display without recourse to visual representations. For example, if only the bottom two rows of differences are attended to:

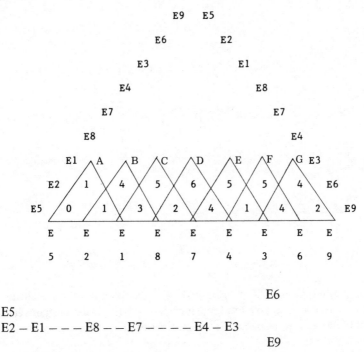

then the difference between E5 and E2 is '0' and between E2 and E1 is '1'.
Linearly this means that E5 to E1 = 0 + 1 = 1. The '1' in the second row of
TRIANGLE A indicates that so long as E5 and E2 are seen as identical they
can each be '1' different from E1. Similarly E2 is '1' different from E1, and
E1 is '3' different from E8. For a linear relationship to exist E1 to E8 should
be '1' + '3' = '4'. The '4' in the second row of TRIANGLE B shows this to be
the case. TRIANGLES C, D, E and F show that:

E1 – – – E8 – – E7 – – – – E4 – E3

can all be represented along the same one dimension. But in TRIANGLE G
E3 to E6 = '4', E6 to E9 = '2' and yet E3 to E9 = '4' rather than '6'. This indicates a clustering of E3, E6 and E9 which requires more than one dimension
to represent it. Thus when the difference scores along the base of any triangle
add up to something greater than the difference score at its apex then a clustering is indicated.

Inspecting the triangles produced by the first and the third rows reveals
whether the sum of the 'adjacent' differences along the bottom row is equal
to or greater than the spanned difference at each triangle's apex. These comparisons show that only the linearity of E5, E2, E1 and E8 is preserved. The
other triangles begin to show clustering.

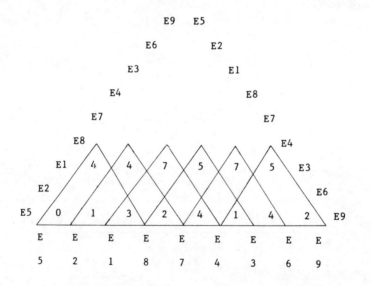

Similarly, as the span of each triangle widens so the full nature of the clustering
is revealed. The reader is asked to look at each of the following diagrams in turn
and to appreciate how inspection of each level of triangle reveals more of the
structure.

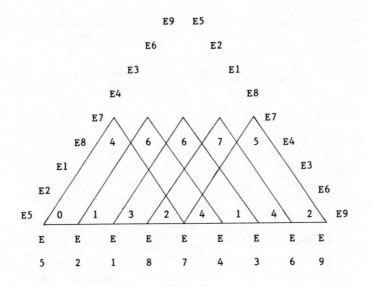

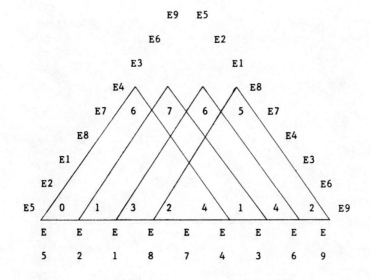

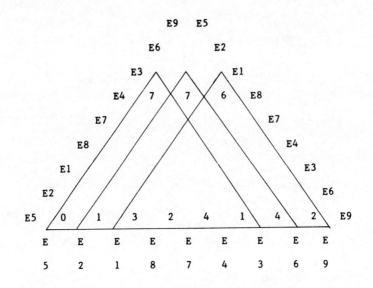

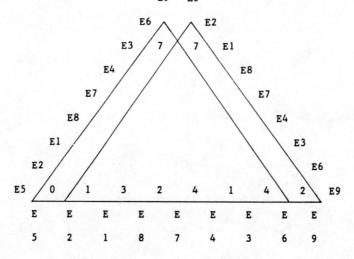

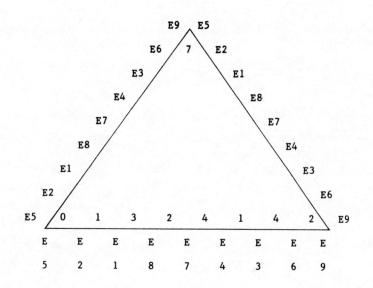

The reader should now turn to Fig. 7.1 which shows the full triangle of differences superimposed on Bill Shard's FOCUSed grid.

FOCUSing a grid containing rated (or ranked) responses

The elements and construct pole descriptions for Adam Stewart's grid were listed in chapter 3. The grid he produced was not shown. It is reproduced as Fig. 7.2. This shows that he used a 1 to 5 rating scale to assign his elements to his constructs. The use of such a rating scale makes the visual FOCUSing of a repertory grid slightly more complicated.

Two more examples of rated grids (Figs. 7.3 and 7.4) show how a more differentiated scale reveals more subtle patterns within the assigning of elements to constructs. These grids were used in deciding what jobs a senior executive in a pharmaceutical company was considering for career development and what kind of people he would most enjoy working with.

```
                              E9   E5
                          E6    7    E2
                      E3    7    7    E1
                  E4    7    7    6    E8
              E7    6    7    6    5    E7
          E8    4    6    6    7    5    E4
      E1    4    4    7    5    7    5    E3
  E2    1    4    5    6    5    5    4    E6
E5  0    1    3    2    4    1    4    2    E9

  E     E    E    E    E    E    E    E    E
  5     2    1    8    7    4    3    6    9
```

	E5	E2	E1	E8	E7	E4	E3	E6	E9
C8	/	/	/	X	X	X	X	/	/
C5	/	/	/	X	X	X	X	/	X
C1	/	/	/	/	X	X	X	X	X
C3	/	/	/	/	/	X	X	X	X
RC2	/	/	/	/	/	X	X	X	X
RC6	/	/	/	/	/	X	X	X	/
C7	/	/	/	/	/	/	/	X	X
C4	/	/	/	X	X	/	/	X	X
RC9	/	/	X	X	/	/	X	X	X

Figure 7.1 The triangle of difference diagram superimposed on Bill Shard's FOCUSed grid

RAW GRID

CONSTRUCT POLE RATED - 1 -   ELEMENTS   CONSTRUCT POLE RATED - 5 -

```
                                    E E E E E E E E E E E E E E E E E E E E E
                                    2 1 1 0 0 1 0 2 0 0 1 1 0 1 1 0 1 1 0 0 2 1
                                    1 0 1 3 7 9 6 0 8 4 3 5 5 4 8 1 6 7 2 9 2 2
                                    *********************************************
         TUTORING BY PERSON OR AID  C4 * 5 5 1 1 1 1 1 2 3 4 4 2 2 3 3 5 4 4 5 5 4 5 * C4   NOT TUTORING BY PERSON OR AID
LEARNING WAS OR BECAME THE MAIN OUTCOME C2 * 2 2 1 1 1 1 1 1 4 3 2 2 3 3 3 3 2 4 5 5 5 3 * C2   LEARNING WAS NOT THE MAIN OUTCOME
SUBJECT MATTER ACTIVELY TRIGGERED ME OFF C7 * 1 2 1 2 2 2 1 1 4 4 3 3 3 2 3 3 3 4 4 5 5 * C7   SUBJECT MATTER DID NOT ACTIVELY TRIGGER ME
   LEARNING FUNDAMENTAL CONCEPTS   C5 * 1 1 1 2 2 5 5 4 2 2 2 3 3 4 4 3 5 5 4 4 3 5 * C5   NOT LEARNING FUNDAMENTAL CONCEPTS
LEARNED MOST FROM (REFLECTING BACK) C9 * 2 1 1 5 4 4 2 2 3 3 2 1 2 1 1 2 3 3 3 4 4 5 * C9   NOT LEARNED FROM REFLECTION
      MOST ENJOYABLE ACTIVITY     C8 * 1 1 1 4 4 4 3 2 3 3 3 2 2 2 1 1 2 4 3 4 5 5 * C8   MOST UNENJOYABLE ACTIVITY
           HIGHLY INVOLVED        C1 * 3 3 3 5 5 5 4 2 2 1 2 2 2 2 1 1 3 4 4 3 4 4 * C1   NOT INVOLVED
             DOING THINGS         C3 * 4 4 4 5 4 1 5 1 2 2 1 1 1 1 2 2 3 3 2 2 5 * C3   NOT DOING THINGS
               I HAD TO           C6 * 5 5 1 1 1 3 4 5 1 2 1 2 2 1 2 1 3 2 3 3 3 1 * C6   I DID NOT HAVE TO
                                    *********************************************
```

```
· · · · · · · · · · · · · · · · · · · · · · · *REMEMBERING THINGS NOW
· · · · · · · · · · · · · · · · · · · · · *HOW TO DELEGATE
· · · · · · · · · · · · · · · · · · · · *GEC GLASS WORKS
· · · · · · · · · · · · · · · · · · · *HCITB INFORMATION STRATEGY
· · · · · · · · · · · · · · · · · · *H&C PICKING UP IN 1ST YEAR
· · · · · · · · · · · · · · · · *LEARNING LONDON
· · · · · · · · · · · · · · · *CHAIRING STUDENT COUNCIL 1949
· · · · · · · · · · · · · · *RECONSTITUTING UNION
· · · · · · · · · · · · *MINUTES OF 1ST COMMITTEE
· · · · · · · · · · · *BUILDING BEDROOM UNITS
· · · · · · · · · · *54 1ST PAINTING HOUSE
· · · · · · · · · *PREPARING SESSION
· · · · · · · · *CHAIRMAN WG PARTY I.P.M
· · · · · · · *SOCIAL SCIENCES DSIR
· · · · · · *RELEARNING THE TROMBONE
· · · · · *RUSSIAN EVENING CLASSES
· · · · · *INTERPERSONAL SKILLS COURSE
· · · · *LECTURES ON HANDLING GROUPS
· · · *STATS CLASS UNSATISFACTORY QUESTION
· · *MAN. DIP. PSYCHOLOGY ASPECTS 49
· *READING TWO BOOKS AT 17
*WRITING POETRY
```

Figure 7.2 Adam Stewart's FOCUSed grid

FOCUSed GRID

CONSTRUCT POLE RATED – 1 –   ELEMENTS   **CONSTRUCT POLE RATED – 5 –**

```
                        E E E E E E E E E
                        0 0 0 0 0 1 0 0 0 0
                        2 4 7 5 6 0 8 9 1 3
                      *************************
          CLEAR    C7  * 3 4 3 3 2 1 1 1 2 1 *  C7    CONFUSED
      ORGANISED   RC6  * 4 3 3 2 1 1 1 1 2 5 * RC6    DISORGANISED
      DEMANDING    C9  * 2 3 3 3 4 2 1 1 1 5 *  C9    EASY GOING
      DIRECTIVE    C3  * 2 2 3 3 4 4 3 3 1 5 *  C3    CONSULTATIVE
      UNHELPFUL    C8  * 1 2 3 4 5 5 3 4 3 5 *  C8    HELPFUL
      DISHONEST    C4  * 1 3 3 4 5 5 4 4 5 4 *  C4    HONEST
   NON-DESIRABLE  C10  * 1 3 3 4 4 5 3 3 5 4 * C10    DESIRABLE
 OVER-ENTHUSIASTIC  C2 * 2 1 3 5 3 3 4 3 3 4 *  C2    CAUTIOUS
        THINKER    C5  * 3 2 3 5 3 3 3 3 2 1 *  C5    PLODDER
      EXTROVERT    C1  * 1 3 5 4 3 4 4 2 1 5 *  C1    PRIVATE PERSON
                      *************************
                        * * * * * * * * * * E3  REGINALD C
                        * * * * * * * * * E1   VINCENT A
                        * * * * * * * * E9  CHARLES I
                        * * * * * * * E8  EDWARD H
                        * * * * * * E10  ARTHUR J
                        * * * * * E6  HORACE F
                        * * * * E5  JAMES E
                        * * * E7  FREDERICK G
                        * * E4  MAXWELL D
                        * E2  THOMAS B
```

Figure 7.3 Dr Tisch's bosses grid

FOCUSED GRID

CONSTRUCT POLE RATED - 1 -   ELEMENTS   CONSTRUCT POLE RATED - 5 -

```
                              E E E E E E E E E E E E E E E E E
                              0 0 1 0 1 0 0 0 1 1 1 0 1 1 1 0 1 0
                              6 2 4 4 6 7 3 5 3 2 0 8 1 5 7 9 8 1
                              ***************************************
     INTELLECTUALLY CHALLENGING  C10 * 2 4 3 2 1 2 1 2 2 2 1 1 4 3 2 2 1 1 * C10  INTELLECTUALLY NOT CHALLENGING
                    VARIABILITY  RC20 * 5 3 3 2 2 1 1 2 2 2 2 3 5 3 2 2 1 1 * RC20  ROUTINE
                 HIGH JOB CONTENT  C9 * 3 5 4 2 1 1 1 2 1 2 2 3 3 5 2 1 5 * C9  LOW JOB CONTENT
            SEARCHING FOR NOVELTY  C18 * 5 4 4 3 2 2 2 2 1 2 1 3 3 3 3 2 2 5 * C18  NON-INNOVATIVE
                 MOST CREATIVITY  C16 * 4 4 4 3 3 2 2 2 1 1 1 3 3 3 2 1 5 * C16  LEAST CREATIVITY
          HIGH ORGANISATIONAL INPUT  C15 * 5 4 4 2 3 5 1 1 1 1 1 2 3 3 4 1 1 5 * C15  LOW ORGANISATIONAL INPUT
            MOST INVOLVED WITH PEOPLE  C13 * 4 2 2 1 2 2 2 2 1 1 1 1 2 3 3 3 3 5 * C13  INVOLVED WITH PEOPLE BUT LESS SO
          MOST CONTACT WITH ACADEMICS  C17 * 5 3 2 1 3 1 1 2 2 1 1 3 5 5 5 5 3 5 * C17  LEAST CONTACT WITH ACADEMICS
                 DEALING WITH OTHERS  C14 * 5 3 3 3 4 4 1 2 2 2 1 3 4 5 5 2 3 5 * C14  SELF
          WORKING WITHIN ORGANISATION  C19 * 4 2 3 3 3 3 2 2 2 1 1 1 5 5 5 3 2 5 * C19  INDEPENDANT
IMPORTANT GOOD RELATIONSHIP WITH BOSS  C6 * 3 2 2 3 3 2 3 2 1 1 2 1 5 5 5 5 3 5 * C6  LEAST IMPORTANT TO HAVE GOOD RELATIONSHIP WITH BOSS
      REQUIRES COMPLIANCE NOT FREEDOM  C2 * 2 2 3 3 3 3 3 3 2 2 2 1 5 5 5 4 4 5 * C2  OFFER FREEDOM OF WORKING
 WORKING WITHIN JOB AND COMPANY RULES  C21 * 1 3 3 3 4 3 4 3 4 4 5 2 5 5 5 4 4 5 * C21  FREEDOM OF OPERATION
          DEPENDENT ON ORGANISATION  RC22 * 2 3 3 4 4 3 4 3 3 3 3 2 5 5 5 5 3 5 * RC22  OWN BOSS
                     STUCK IN RUT  RC23 * 3 3 5 5 5 4 4 3 3 3 3 1 5 5 5 5 5 5 * RC23  NEW AND CHALLENGING
              SAME OUTLOOK ON LIFE  RC8 * 3 3 5 5 5 4 4 2 1 1 2 1 5 5 5 5 5 5 * RC8  FRESH OUTLOOK
                WOULD NOT APPLY IF  RC25 * 2 3 5 5 5 4 4 1 1 1 2 2 3 5 5 5 5 5 * RC25  WOULD APPLY IF
                  WILL LEAST ENJOY  RC11 * 1 3 5 4 5 4 3 1 1 2 1 1 2 5 5 5 5 5 * RC11  WILL MOST ENJOY
                  LEAST WORTHWHILE  RC12 * 1 2 5 4 4 3 3 2 1 2 1 1 4 5 5 5 5 5 * RC12  MOST WORTHWHILE
                 LEAST ATTRACTIVE  RC5 * 1 2 5 4 4 3 2 2 2 1 1 1 3 5 5 5 5 5 * RC5  MOST ATTRACTIVE
                             REAL  RC3 * 1 2 5 4 3 3 4 5 4 4 1 5 4 4 5 5 5 5 * RC3  IDEALISED BUT NOT REAL
              CONFINED ENVIRONMENT  RC24 * 1 3 4 5 4 4 4 3 3 2 2 2 4 3 3 5 4 5 * RC24  PUBLIC RELATIONS
              LOW FINANCIAL REWARD  RC26 * 2 2 2 4 4 4 4 3 3 3 4 2 2 1 1 5 1 5 * RC26  HIGH FINANCIAL REWARD
                        HIGH RISK  C7 * 4 3 4 4 4 2 2 2 3 2 2 1 1 1 1 3 4 5 * C7  LOW RISK
                   LOW IN SECURITY  C1 * 5 2 3 4 4 4 3 2 2 2 3 1 1 3 2 4 5 5 * C1  HIGH IN SECURITY
                 REQUIRES COURAGE  C4 * 5 3 3 4 3 4 3 2 3 4 3 1 1 2 1 1 4 5 * C4  DOES NOT REQUIRE MUCH COURAGE
                              ***************************************
                              * * * * * * * * * * * * * * * * * E1  RETIRE WITH SECURITY
                              * * * * * * * * * * * * * * * E18  PROJECT MANAGEMENT
                              * * * * * * * * * * * * * * E9  PATENTS
                              * * * * * * * * * * * * * E17  PARIS RESEARCH JOB
                              * * * * * * * * * * * * * E15  HEAD OF CHEMISTRY
                              * * * * * * * * * * * * E11  JOIN CONSULTANCY GROUP
                              * * * * * * * * * * * E8  AUSTRALIAN REPRESENTATIVE
                              * * * * * * * * * * E10  RESEARCH TRUST
                              * * * * * * * * * E12  MARKETING JOB
                              * * * * * * * * E13  RESEARCH DIRECTOR
                              * * * * * * * E5  BOOKSHOP
                              * * * * * * E3  NATURE RESERVE
                              * * * * * E7  PRODUCT AFFAIRS
                              * * * * E16  HEAD OF RESEARCH GROUP
                              * * * E4  MY IDEAL JOB
                              * * E14  R & D BRUSSELS
                              * * E2  RUN TOP CLASS HOTEL
                              * E6  RESTAURANT
```

Figure 7.4 Dr Tisch's jobs grid

As we have demonstrated, the paper and pencil FOCUSing of a grid is not difficult. But it can become a little tedious to carry out the calculation by hand when a rating scale is used. The process of FOCUSing a grid containing ratings is therefore best illustrated by means of one containing a small number of elements and constructs.

Calculating the matrix of difference scores

The following grid has been invented to illustrate the method of FOCUSing a grid containing ratings. The strips of card method can, obviously, be used with a rated grid, particularly if coloured pencils are used to enter the ratings, e.g.

	Dark Blue	Light Blue	Grey	Light Red	Dark Red
Ratings	1	2	3	4	5

However, the fact that the degree of mismatch is now expressed in much finer gradations means that the process of visual sorting requires more discrimination. It is, therefore, even more necessary to record the complete matrix of difference scores before commencing the FOCUSing. (This method of recording the complete matrix has already been used with the earlier 'bi-polar' 'Bill Shard' grid to explain the procedure step by step: but experienced grid users can often visually sort a bi-polar grid without recourse to this intermediate step.)

Clustering the elements

The method proceeds as before. E1 is compared with E2 and the differences between the ratings on each construct are calculated and summed (ignoring the direction of the differences).

E1	E2	Diff.
1	2	1
5	5	0
3	3	0
5	4	1
1	2	1
3	3	0

TOTAL DIFF. 3

Thus E1 differs from E2 by a total difference of '3'.
E1 is then compared with E3 (Total diff.13)
E4 (Total diff.17)
E5 (Total diff.18)
and E6 (Total diff.12).

These results are entered in the first row of the matrix of element differences.

E2 has already been compared with E1 so E2 is compared successively with E3, E4, E5 and E6. Differences of 10, 14, 15 and 9 are entered under the appropriate columns in row E2.

Then E3 is compared with E4, E5 and E6
E4 is compared with   E5 and E6
E5 is compared with   E6

until all the possible difference scores have been calculated.
The table of differences allows immediate identification of the significant clusters, i.e. the smallest difference is 3:

E1 with E2
E3 with E6
E4 with E5

Then E6 goes with E2 at a total diff. of 9. Giving clusters of (E3-E6-E1-E1) and (E4-E5).
Of the possible remaining pairings which could join the two clusters:

E3 – E4 at 14 total diff.
E1 – E4 at 17 total diff.
E3 – E5 at 15 total diff.
E1 – E5 at 18 total diff.

E3 with E4 (at a total diff. of 14) is the least of these. This gives E5-E4-E3-E6-E2-E1 as the re-ordered clustering.

Clustering the constructs

For clustering the constructs we can return to the raw grid and see for example:

	E1	E2	E3	E4	E5	E6	
C1	1	2	3	4	5	3	
C2	5	5	1	2	2	1	
Diff.	4	3	2	2	3	2	Total 16

But we must also consider the reversals. On a five-point scale reversing means that

a rating of 1 becomes 5
a rating of 2 becomes 4
a rating of 3 remains 3
a rating of 4 becomes 2
a rating of 5 becomes 1

So, comparing C1 with RC2 (i.e. C2 reversed):

	E1	E2	E3	E4	E5	E6
C1	1	2	3	4	5	3
RC2	1	1	5	4	4	1
Diff.	0	1	2	0	1	2 Total 6

Unfortunately, if the client is allowed to make free responses on the rating
scale to each element on every construct there is no simple relationship between
the 'C1–C1' difference and the 'C1–RC2' difference. This is because the number (distribution) of 1, 2, 3, 4 and 5 ratings differs from construct to construct.
So the matrix has to be computed separately for positive and negative match-
ings.
   From the complete analysis (not shown) the initial clusterings are:

C3 – C6   RC1 – C4 – RC5

Note: If C4 differs from RC5 by 2,
      then it also follows that
      RC4 differs from C5 by 2.

RC5 goes with C6 at total diff. of 6
C2 goes with C4 at total diff. of 6
C2 goes with RC1 at total diff. of 6
giving clustering of:

C2 – RC1 – C4 – RC5 – C6 – C3.

Thus the FOCUSed grid will have the elements re-ordered:

E5   E4   E3   E6   E2   E2   E1

and the constructs re-ordered:

C2   RC1   C4   RC5   C6   C3

giving a FOCUSed grid as in Fig. 7.5.

	E5	E4	E3	E6	E2	E1	
C2	2	2	1	1	5	5	C2
RC1	1	2	3	3	4	5	RC1
C4	1	2	3	3	4	5	C4
C5	1	1	4	3	4	5	RC5
C6	2	1	5	4	3	3	C6
C3	1	1	5	4	3	3	C3
	E5	E4	E3	E6	E2	E1	

Figure 7.5 A FOCUSed grid (with rated responses)

SPACE-ing a FOCUSed grid containing ratings or rankings

To SPACE a FOCUSed grid containing rating or ranking, the differences between adjacent elements and adjacent constructs must be identified, i.e.:

Diff.		3		14		3		9		3	
Elements	E5		E4		E3		E6		E2		E1

Diff.		6		0		2		6		1	
Constructs	C2		RC1		C4		RC5		C6		C3

And the distances between adjacent columns and adjacent rows must then be scaled in proportion to the differences.

e.g. differences 0, 1 and 2 are represented by 1 space.

differences 3, 4 and 5 are represented by 2 spaces
differences 6, 7 and 8 are represented by 3 spaces
differences 9, 10 and 11 are represented by 4 spaces
differences 12, 13 and 14 are represented by 5 spaces

This (together with a colour scheme for the rating scale) gives the layout shown in Fig. 7.6.

As this grid was invented to illustrate the FOCUSing technique using ratings or ranking scores there are no verbal labels to assign to the construct poles.

There is, however, one more facility that may be added to enhance the interpretation of personal meaning in the FOCUS display. Readers who find the plethora of numbers rather overwhelming on a first reading may choose to skip the end of this chapter and refer back to it when they are more familiar with the interpretation of FOCUSed grids.

	E5	E4	E3	E6	E2	E1	
C2	2	2	1	1	5	5	C2
RC1	1	2	3	3	4	5	C1R
C4	1	2	3	3	4	5	C4
RC5	1	1	4	3	4	5	C5R
C6	2	1	5	4	3	3	C6
C3	1	1	5	4	3	3	C3
	E5	E4	E3	E6	E2	E1	

Figure 7.6 A SPACEd FOCUSed grid

The TRIGRID display showing difference matrices

In the example grid shown in Fig. 7.6, elements E5, E4, E3, E6, E2 and E1 have been re-sorted into this order because it gives the least cumulative difference between adjacent rows. As has been shown previously there is no other way of re-ordering these elements which would have given a smaller cumulative difference between rows. However, at various points during the sorting process, there were equally good, but mutually exclusive, choices which could have been made. Where such choices are made between significant relationships one was exhibited whilst others were excluded. This includes those clusterings where one element associated fairly closely with another is already embedded in a closer cluster. As has been discussed in the earlier part of this chapter, these distortions of the natural multi-dimensional clusterings are induced by the need to preserve the ordering of elements along one linear display. Given some understanding of the structural implications of the re-ordered matrix of differences, the following display technique allows these distortions to be quickly identified. The concealed additional patterns in the clusterings can thus be identified and introduced into the talkback through the personal meaning in the grid.

In calculating the number of spaces to be introduced between adjacent columns in the SPACEd FOCUSed grid the difference scores were shown as follows:

	3		14		3		9		3	
E5		E4		E3		E6		E2		E1

It would have been possible to indicate that the difference between E5 and E3 is 15 by showing it as follows:

        15

    E5   E4   E3   E6   E2   E1

or all the second-order differences (i.e. differences between E columns which are separated from each other by another E column) could have been shown so:

        15   11   10   12

    E5   E4   E3   E6   E2   E1

All third-order differences (i.e. differences between E columns that are separated by two other E columns) could be shown so:

            12   14   13

    E5   E4   E3   E6   E2   E1

and so on:
fourth-order differences:

            15   17

    E5   E4   E3   E6   E2   E1

Fifth-order differences:

                18

    E5   E4   E3   E6   E2   E1

Now, by combining these displays, all the difference scores can be shown in one diagram.

				18(4)					
			15(11)			17(10)			
		12(14)			14(7)			13(9)	
	15(2)			11(6)			10(2)		12(0)
	3		14		3		9		3
E5		E4		E3		E6		E2	E1

Familiarity with this type of display (which was examined in some detail at the beginning of this chapter) makes it very easy to identify 'lines of stress' induced by imposing one linear ordering on the multi-dimensional structure of the pattern of meaning in the grid.

Readers who like to pursue a systematic exposition to its logical conclusion should attend to the figures in brackets associated with each difference score. We have seen earlier that each difference score can be represented as a distance between two elements. Thus the distance between E5 and E4 is '3' and that between E4 and E3 is '14'. If all three elements could be truly represented as lying along one straight line the distance between E5 and E3 would have to be '17' i.e. 3 + 14. It is actually '15'. Thus a stress of (2) i.e. 17-15 is induced on the linearity of these relationships. Similarly the '11' between E4 and E6 implies a stress of (6) and the '10' between E3 and E2 induces a stress of (2). However the distances between E6 and E2 of '9' and between E2 and E1 of '3' are totally compatible with the '12' between E6 and E1 inducing (0) stress. At the next level the '12' between E5 and E6 could have been made up in two different ways. E5 to E3 is '15' plus E3 to E6 is '3' giving 15 + 3 = 18. Or E4 to E6 is '11' and E4 to E5 is '3' giving 11 + 3 = 14. The lesser of these would induce a stress of (2) in the '12' between E5 and E6. Similarly all the other minimal stresses can be calculated and are shown in brackets beside their associated difference scores.

Thus whilst the SPACEd FOCUSed grid shows that E5 and E4 'cleave away' (difference of 14) from E3 and E6, to a slightly lesser extent, '9' E2 and E1 also cleave away. In fact the stress of (6) associated with the difference of '11' between E4 and E6 shows that it would be worth inspecting this cluster. Similarly the stress at E4-E2 calls for reflection. Fig. 7.7 shows how all these distances and stresses can be represented.

Similar reasoning and methods of display can be used to show the relationships between constructs. Again it must be kept in mind that constructs have both direct and reversed relationships. Fig. 7.7 shows the FOCUSed grid with both element and construct split matrix displays. The TRIGRID and INTER-ACTIVE TRIGRID programs provide such displays.

This display shows that both for elements and for constructs the FOCUSing procedure has identified most of the significant relationships. But it does show that the relationships between E5 and E4 with E6 are slightly under-emphasised; and the positive construct split matrix shows that C6 and C3 might usefully have been in each other's positions so that the $5 - 7 - 7$ sequence would lie inside the $6 - 8 - 8$ sequence.

However, this would have interchanged the 12 and 13 at the apex. The dropping away of the number (i.e. $12 - 13 - 11$ and $12 - 12 - 10$) at the top of the reversed construct split diff. matrix implies that there is some spiralling of the bi-polar constructs and the C6 and C3 cluster.

Activity 7.1 Add TRIGRID matrices to a FOCUSed grid

Add the Trigrid half-matrixes to your previously FOCUSed grids.
    Use colours to emphasise the patterns.

Activities 7.2 to 7.x Explore the patterns revealed by TRIGRID matrices

If or when you have elicited a grid using rated or ranked responses FOCUS it, SPACE it and add the TRIGRID matrices.
    Now explore the patterns of personal meaning which are revealed.
    Use a system of graded colours which highlights the nature of the scaling or rankings. Fig. 7.8 outlines the procedure for putting a FOCUSed grid into TRIGRID.

NOTE: There are computer programs which can be run on PET, APPLE II, WANG and PDP II computers available from CSHL; but for those who are not able to make use of such computer facilities there is also a grid FOCUS kit including a hand-grid sorter which facilitates this process of FOCUSing, SPACE-ing and applying TRIGRIDS to the repertory grid.

Alternative methods for analysing a grid

Principal component analysis

The idea that the relationships between elements and constructs can be represented in n-dimensional space has led to the use of multi-dimensional scaling techniques of analysis. In particular the method of principal component analysis

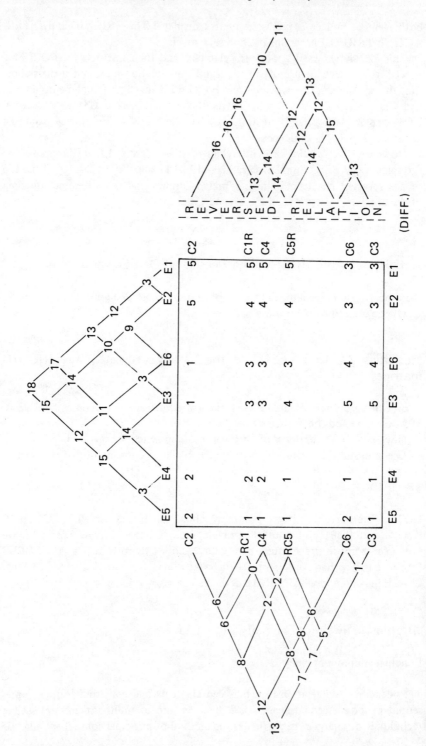

Figure 7.7 SPACEd FOCUSed grid showing all relationships

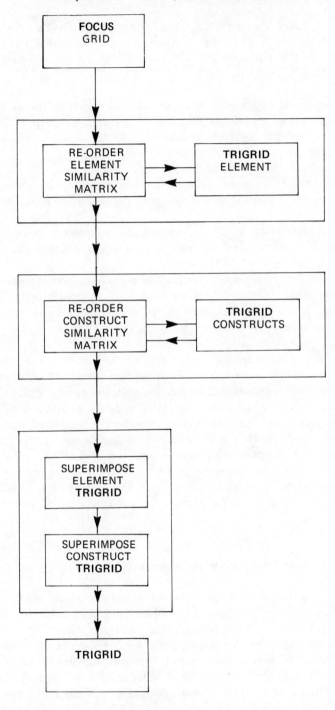

Figure 7.8 TRIGRID: an algorithm

as applied by P. Slater has been widely used for grids. This treats the constructs as a series of vectors or directions in n-dimensional space within which the elements have specific positions. This technique does give a pictorial view, but it suffers from the following drawbacks.

(a) It is impossible to get back in a commonsense way from the results of the analysis to the original grid data. There is, therefore, always a danger of mystification when the client is asked to take the computer results on trust from the T-C practitioner.

(b) The pictorial view produced by the Slater analysis uses only the first two components (dimensions) and can therefore sometimes be a very distorted representation of the true distances in the theoretical n-dimensional space.

(c) The calculations involved in computing the components assume that the assignings of elements to constructs can be represented as a numerical scale with full ratio properties. This is never true.

(d) T-C practitioners are sorely tempted to give verbal labels to principal components. This construing by a third party of the already opaque and distorted representation further distances the clients from a direct mirroring of their construing.

For these and other reasons the authors have felt compelled to develop methods which highlight the patterns of relationships in the grid whilst maintaining as direct and transparent a connection with the original grid data as possible. They began by using various cluster analysis techniques including McQuitty's various forms of cluster analysis, which they then developed into two-way cluster methods. These evolved through McQuitty into the FOCUSing procedure, first as a computer program and then as a hand sorting technique. SPACE and TRIGRID are successive attempts to increase the information in the grid display without moving away from the original data. TRIGRID succeeds in displaying all the relationships without distancing clients from their original responses.

POLE-MAPS: how construct poles relate to each other

It is possible to go beyond the pure grid to an analysis of the implications of one construct for another. A method evolved from the FOCUS procedure offers T-Cs a way of identifying how separate construct poles relate to each other. It was developed by the authors and other members of the CSHL in the early 1970s. It consists in dividing each construct into its two poles and dealing separately with how each relates to other poles in the grid. By reference to Bill Shard's SPACEd FOCUSed grid in Fig. 4.7 the reader can see for example that:

'Older generation' is always 'Imposed by parents and others' whereas:

'Imposed by parents and others' is not always 'Older generation'.
But:
'Older generation' is the right pole of C8;
'Imposed by parents and others' is the right pole of C5.

Looking at the left poles of these constructs:
'Own conditions' is always 'Same generation'.
But:
'Same generation' is not always 'Own conditions'.
When a construct pole is compared with every other pole in the grid, a pattern can be traced of 'what implies what'. We have used this POLE-MAP technique to make explicit the relationship between construct poles. A comparison between the POLE-MAP and an implications grid shows the client's awareness of 'what goes with what'.

Fig. 7.9 shows Bill Shard's construct poles analysed in this way. The '0' in the first column means that all the C5's √s map on to the √s of C8. But the '1' at the top of the second column means that one of C8's √s maps on to a X of C5.

	C8	C5	C1	C3	RC2	RC6	C7	C4	RC9
C8	–	1	2	2	2	1	2	2	3
C5	0	–	1	1	1	1	1	1	2
C1	1	1	–	0	0	0	0	1	2
C3	2	2	1	–	0	0	0	2	2
RC2	2	2	1	0	–	0	0	2	2
RC6	2	3	2	1	1	–	1	3	3
C7	4	4	3	2	2	2	–	2	3
C4	2	2	2	2	2	2	0	–	2
RC9	2	2	2	1	1	1	0	1	–

Figure 7.9 POLE-MAP matrix

The zero's ('0's) show the following pattern:

C5	──	always	──	C8

C1	──	always	──	C3
C1	──		──	RC2
C1	──		──	RC6
C1	──		──	C7

C3	──	always	──	RC2
C3	──		──	RC6
C3	──		──	C7

RC2	──	always	──	C3
RC2	──		──	RC6
RC2	──		──	C7

C4	──	always	──	C7
RC9	──		──	C7

This can be re-written as:

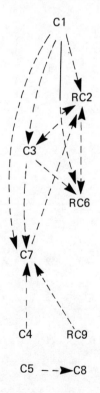

C5 ──►C8

Expressed as verbal labels this gives:

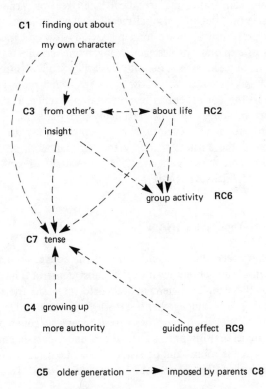

C1   finding out about
       my own character

C3   from other's   about life   RC2
       insight

                    group activity   RC6

C7   tense

C4   growing up
       more authority   guiding effect   RC9

C5   older generation – – – ▶ imposed by parents C8
                                   and others

These analyses offer another transparent device for talkback.

Whilst many methods for analysing a raw grid are available, the requirements for personal learning and for the grid conversation make the client's
understanding paramount. The client must be able to appreciate exactly how
the analysed grid derives from the results of the elicitation conversation.
FOCUSing, SPACE-ing, TRIGRID and POLE-MAPS are designed to meet
this requirement. The remaining chapters will introduce a series of similarly
transparent techniques for enabling individuals, pairs and groups to appreciate
exactly how one grid relates to another.

'Spaces for meaning': beyond the scope of the grid

A continuing effort by the authors (aided by successive generations of postgraduate students) has explored the mathematical structure of the repertory
grid towards its limits in various directions. Chapters 3 to 7 have presented the
distillation of these studies but have not referred in detail to the work that
has gone into achieving this distillation.

The result of this mathematical activity has been the exploration of other forms of geometry, algebra and other mathematical languages for more fully representing the personal structures of personal meaning. What follows can be seen from two opposite perspectives. If we look backwards towards the grid, it can be seen as a series of explorations designed to overcome grid limitations. If we look forward it can be seen as a series of 'feasibility studies' into new forms, techniques and languages which will allow more space and more appropriate space within which 'the construction, reconstruction, exchange, sharing and negotiation of personal meaning' can conversationally take place.

The advent of third to fifth generation micro-computers with their larger memories has allowed the authors to apply their earlier work on interactive computer elicitation and reflective learning in more easily flexible and transmittable forms (see Grid Tricks Appendix).

The use and mis-use of 'Not Applicables' (NAs)

In previous chapters we have seen that in eliciting a grid the conversational use of a 'up and down laddering' sub-routine ensures that most constructs have the 'range of convenience' of the sample of elements taken to represent the topic. Thus the conversation artificially guides clients into a coherence which they otherwise might not achieve. For most purposes this achieving of coherence is a step forward in the awareness-raising process. However, under certain circumstances where the incoherence is robust and persistent it may be useful to reveal it by allowing a liberal use of 'Not Applicable' responses (NAs). This was mentioned in chapter 6.

'Not Applicables' are a particularly knotty problem in the mathematical analysis of grids. They form a discontinuity in the scaling of elements. Psychologically the NA means that the element lies outside the range of convenience of the construct. The almost universal 'statistically convenient' trick of assigning the NA to the mid-point of the scale runs completely counter to the psychological reality, placing the element centrally within the range of convenience. One method which we have used to overcome such difficulties is to initially assign all NAs to one end of a two-point scale and all rated responses to the other, i.e. we create a scale:

inside the range of convenience   v.   outside the range of convenience

FOCUSing the NAs-polluted grid on this basis clusters those elements and those constructs which share similar ranges of convenience. In effect this is equivalent to creating a series of small grids which no longer occupy the same n-dimensional space. The effect is similar to a rough and ready Q-Sort, although the mathematics of that technique is much more complicated. The Ms Shop Assistant's grid shown in Fig. 7.10 is a simple example of this technique.

Each of the coherent sub-grids can now be FOCUSed separately and explored independently before it is returned to its position in the larger incoherent

NOT APPLICABLES GRID

CONSTRUCT POLE RATED - √ -   ELEMENTS   CONSTRUCT POLE RATED - X -

```
                              E E E E E E E E E E E E E E
                              0 0 0 0 0 0 0 0 0 1 1 1 1 1
                              1 2 3 4 5 6 7 8 9 0 1 2 3 4 5
                              *********************************
          CUSTOMERS    C1  *  √ √ √ √ √ √ √ √ √  X  X  X  NA NA NA NA* C1   SORTING AND ORGANISING THINGS
            SELLING    C2  *  √ √ √ √ √ √ √ √ √  X  X  X  NA NANA NA* C2   KEEPING THE SHOP STRAIGHT
            FITTING    C3  *  √ √ √ √ √ √ √ √  X  X  X  NA NA NA NA* C3   STOCK, THINGS IN THE SHOP
          CUSTOMERS    C4  *  √ √ √ √ √ √ √ √ √  X  X  X  NA NA NA NA* C4   CHECKING AND PUTTING AWAY STOCK
      MAKING A SALE    C5  *  √ √ √ √ √ √ √ √ √  X  X  X  X  X  X  X * C5   BACK UP THE SELLING
      WORKING ALONE    C6  *  √ √ √ √ √ √ √ √ √ NA √ √  X  X  X  X * C6   WORKING WITH OTHER STAFF
WORKING WITH THINGS    C7  *  X  X  X  X  X  X  X  X  √ √ √  X  X  X * C7   WORKING WITH PEOPLE
WORKING WITH OTHER STAFF C8 * NA NA NA NA NA NA NA NA NA √ √ √  X  X  X  X * C8   SOCIAL WITH OTHER STAFF
       BEING BRIEFED   C9  * NA NA NA NA NA NA NA NA X  X  X  √ √ √ √* C9   DOING WHAT I'M BRIEFED TO DO
            SOCIAL    C10  * NA NA NA  NA  NA NA NA X  X  X  √ √ √ √* C10  JOBS IN SHOP
INVOLVES ME MORE PERSONALLY C11 * X  X  X  X  X  X  X  X  NA NANA √ √ √ √* C11  WITH CUSTOMERS
WITH STAFF WORKMATES  C12  * X  X  X  X  X  X  X  X  NA NA NA √ √ √ √* C12  WITH CUSTOMERS
                              *********************************
                              * * * * * * * * * * * * * *  THE TOP MANAGER LOOKED IN AND I WARNED OUR
                              * * * * * * * * * * * * *  TALKING WITH SATURDAY GIRLS        MANAGER
                              * * * * * * * * * * * *  THE WEEKLY TRAINING SESSION
                              * * * * * * * * * * *  GOING ON COURSE TO SHOE MAKER
                              * * * * * * * * * *  BEING TOLD OFF ABOUT FORGETTING COMPUTER CARDS
                              * * * * * * * * *  PREPARING SALES STICKERS
                              * * * * * * * *  GETTING STOCK CHECKED IN
                              * * * * * * *  THE ITALIAN WHO TALKED ABOUT ROME
                              * * * * * *  ANOTHER SALES GIRL SOLD A PAIR OF SHOE TREES BY SHOUTING
                              * * * * *  SWAPPING SHOES BECAUSE HUSBAND DOES NOT LIKE STYLE
                              * * * *  SELLING A PAIR OF BADLY FITTING SHOES
                              * * *  A LADY TRIED ON EVERYTHING AND THEN WALKED OUT
                              * *  CUSTOMER FRUSTRATED WHEN WE DID NOT HAVE FITTING
                              *  A TYPICAL MOTHER AND ELEVEN-YEAR-OLD DAUGHTER YESTERDAY
                              LITTLE OLD LADY: A VERY GOOD SALE
```

Figure 7.10 Ms Shop assistant's grid with 'Not Applicables'

'Not Applicables' polluted space. This is analogous to simple form of the STRUCTURES OF MEANING technique introduced in chapter 12. Conversational talkback through this only patchily coherent pseudo-grid can help a client to face some often quite elusive problems. For example, many of the shoe shop girls involved in the study from which we have taken Fig. 7.10 were completely unable to find any connection between helping customers find the right style/fit of shoe and the tasks of reception, storage and ordering of shoes. This caused considerable problems in the orderly running of the shoe shop and clearly identified an outstanding training need.

Sub-grids and Super-grids: an alternative to laddering

Another way to approach the question of 'Not Applicables' was implied in our reference to the 'up and down laddering' sub-routine in the grid conversation. By laddering each construct up or down until it achieves the range of convenience of the elements in the grid we ensure that the constructs in the grid are all at the same level. Thus a comparison of like with like is achieved.

In exploratory grid conversations this may artificially close down the scope and definition of the topic at too early a stage in the personal learning. This may prevent important links with other relevant areas of meaning from being made. Alternatively, it may mean that sufficient discrimination and precision to significantly move the learning forward is never achieved because the ranges of convenience are always too large. The sub-grids and super-grids technique, first used in the DEMON program in 1972, overcomes this problem in another way.

As clusters of elements and constructs emerge in the conversation time is taken to elaborate the client's understanding of the cluster by eliciting a more differentiated grid. A richer sample of similar elements and constructs with a finer discrimination over a more restricted range of convenience is produced. This increased sensitivity is then fed back into the main grid. Each cluster of elements in the sub-grid can now be represented in the main grid and the clusters of constructs in the sub-grid can be used to generate emergent poles for new constructs in the main grid.

The super-grid serves a complementary purpose. Emergent clusters of elements in the main grid are represented as one element in the super-grid which is then expanded to cover a wider range of convenience. As the super-grid is explored the content of the main grid is defined and its sample of elements can be pruned and/or enriched to more properly span the topic which emerges as the crux of the conversation.

Sustained used of this sub-grid and super-grid procedure can enable clients to explore a domain of their construct system more thoroughly and in a more precise and organised way than the less-integrated verbal laddering techniques. It is however, much more time-consuming and can, in unskilled conversation, become tedious.

Both laddering and the sub-grid — super-grid technique are ways of exploring the levels of organisation in a bi-polar construct system. The question of hierarchies and heterarchies of constructs can be approached more directly.

Sets, networks, hierarchies and heterarchies

The incoherent space of the 'Not Applicables' polluted grid, the entailment networks of the POLE-MAPS technique and the levels of organisation appearing in sub-grids and super-grids all point to the need for a space in which to represent personal meaning which is very different from that implied by the format of the grid. Whilst a full explanation of the implications of this idea is outside the scope of this book, some pointers towards new methods for representing meaning are offered in the final chapter. Here the aim is to offer just sufficient insight into alternate forms for representing meaning to provide a safety net against the more usual errors that can enter into the interpretation of grids.

The idea of bi-polarity in exploring personal meaning is important in identifying the role of 'the submerged pole' or 'the hidden alternative' in making sense of verbal statements. It is as important to recognise what is actively not being said as it is to hear what is actually said. Enough has already been written about bi-polarity for these points to need no further elaboration here. But the apparent simplicity of bi-polarity is too seductive to be thoroughly convincing.

Meaning is more complicated. Construct poles are better thought of as nodes or anchors in a sea of meaning. An emergent pole can be seen to acquire its meaning from its relationship to a number of submerged poles, each of which acquire their own emergent multiplicity of meaning from their relationship to other configurations of submerged poles. In this view meaning is a network of relationships between nodes in the meaning space. On closer scrutiny any node itself turns out to be a network, and so on in all directions. This view has important implications for the whole notion of scaling since scales now turn out to be 'linear' only if and when the elicitation technique forces the responses into a numerical form of scaling. A conversational technique which allowed the client to define their own forms of responses would seem more compatible with the spirit of 'personal meaning' advocated throughout this book. This freedom for the learner to choose their own systems of responses is the basis of the next generation of CSHL technology.

The computer-based versions of this technology are designed to conduct a learning conversation with the client (see chapter 12). As the conversation develops, the computer monitors the structural properties of the patterns of meaning that evolve. It then converses with the users about alternate forms of representations and negotiates which structure best fits with their pattern of thoughts and feelings on the topic.

The alternative structures offered are in effect a data base of personal meaning which can take the form of a complex network. This network can be cut and combined in various ways for various purposes.

When a learner has arrived at a clear-cut definition of purpose, the network is worked through into a hierarchical structure which best represents this intentionality and its consequent anticipations. When learners are less clear about their purposes, the network works out into a 'hierarchy' in which alternative purposes, strategies and outcomes are represented.

The exploration of incoherence is facilitated by representing meaning as having inpermeable boundary conditions within it. This is conceptually equivalent to a set of alternative personal roles or selves which cannot communicate harmoniously with each other. In chapter 11 this idea is developed non-mathematically under the heading of the 'community of selves'.

Another direction in which the representation of personal meaning may be developed starts from questions of provisionality and decisiveness. It is possible to assign measures of doubt or certainty to each response in a grid. This adds a different type of dimensionality to grid analysis. Exploratory work has spanned out from uncertainty measures in grids to the representation of meaning within systems of fuzzy sets of fuzzy logic.

Finally, the POLE-MAPS patterns of construct poles derives from an analysis of the responses in the grid. Another approach to the relating of elements to elements and constructs to constructs is in terms of their verbal labels.

In the following example twenty-two student teachers specialising in mathematics produced grids using exam questions as elements. The investigator then attempted to classify all their constructs to compare and contrast the students. Fig. 7.11 shows his classificatory system. This method of construing the constructions of others is a useful research tool but it is fraught with theoretical and practical problems. Fig. 7.12 shows how each student's constructs distribute within the classification system.

	Construct			*Student's Number*
Problem	1 command	v.	less like a command	17
Preference	1 prefer to do first	v.	tend to avoid or leave	8
Contextual dimensions				
Language	1 verbal explanation	v.	mathematical explanation	8
	2 verbalise	v.	clear pattern	10
	3 expressing oneself	v.	language unnecessary	11
	4 general term	v.	very mathematical	17
	5 written	v.	numerical	18
	6 surface	v.	deep	18
	7 honest	v.	arithmetical	19
	8 linguistic	v.	short calculation	19
	9 sequential	v.	mathematical	19
	10 worded answer	v.	numerical answer	20
	11 questioning	v.	explanatory	20
Difficulty	1 probing	v.	static	1
	2 taxing-trying	v.	simple	4
	3 difficulty-inability	v.	ability-easiness	4
	4 complicated	v.	easy	7
	5 heavy going	v.	light work	7
	6 complicated	v.	easier	8
	7 difficult	v.	attackable	9
	8 hard	v.	easy	12
	9 questioning	v.	accepting	13
	10 awkward	v.	easy	13
	11 testing	v.	reasonable	14
	12 hard	v.	soft	15
	13 less simple	v.	simple word	17
	14 difficult	v.	easy marks	19
	15 extreme concentration	v.	competent	20
	16 deliberation	v.	fairly certain	21
	17 hard work	v.	imitative	22

Definition	1 explicit	v.	more vague	1
	2 specific	v.	exploratory	1
	3 definite	v.	demonstrative	1
	4 clear-cut	v.	difficult	2
	5 coherency	v.	incoherency	4
	6 decisive	v.	alternative	9
	7 definite	v.	indefinite	9
	8 definite	v.	vague	10
	9 secure	v.	insecure	10
	10 known answers	v.	unknown answers	11
	11 clear	v.	confusing	11
	12 definite	v.	unsure	15
	13 definite answer	v.	vague	16
	14 answer given	v.	learned response	16
	15 exact answer	v.	long involved answer	16
	16 definite answer	v.	vaguer	17
	17 answer is clear	v.	answer less clear	17
	18 definitive	v.	diffuse	18
	19 single-minded	v.	enveloping	19
	20 specific answer	v.	answer often given	21
	21 repetitive	v.	constructive	22

Physical	1 tedious	v.	interesting	2
	2 tedious	v.	interesting	3
	3 mundane	v.	taxing	3
	4 laborious	v.	exciting	12
	5 tedious	v.	joyful	12
	6 tiring	v.	pleasing	14
	7 laborious process	v.	simple	19
	8 laborious	v.	possible shortcut	20
	9 exhausting	v.	alert	20
	10 tedious	v.	logical	20
	11 tiring	v.	searching	20
	12 tiring	v.	needing thought	21

Methodological dimensions

Description	1 descriptive	v.	calculative	1
	2 describe	v.	workout	15
	3 describe	v.	brain work searching through	15
	4 descriptive	v.	deductive	18
	5 describing	v.	working out	22

Precision	1 precise	v.	has alternative	2
	2 exact	v.	possible alternatives	2
	3 known	v.	unknown	9
	4 precise	v.	not frightening	9
	5 precision	v.	vague	11
	6 factual	v.	seeking	12
	7 precise	v.	loose	13
	8 enclosing	v.	revealing	13
	9 concise	v.	haphazard	14
	10 set method	v.	general method	16

			v.		
	11	'meat' of question	v.	periphery	16
	12	methodical	v.	exciting	18
	13	precision	v.	difficulty	20

Theoretical	1	theoretical	v.	mechanical	2
	2	display	v.	no proof needed	8
	3	theoretical	v.	practical	9
	4	theoretical	v.	practical	11
	5	algebraic	v.	arithmetical	15
	6	theoretical	v.	practical	22

Learning and memory	1	self-apparent	v.	establishing	1
	2	mechanical	v.	deviations possible	2
	3	repetitive	v.	divergent	3
	4	repetitive	v.	working out	7
	5	book learning	v.	more calculation	8
	6	knowledge of principles	v.	training in use of principles	9
	7	understanding necessary	v.	understanding required	11
	8	memorised	v.	open to error	11
	9	remembering	v.	brain work	15
	10	memory	v.	workable	16
	11	quick answer	v.	calculations	16
	12	requires technique	v.	requires learning	17
	13	previous knowledge	v.	something new	17
	14	memory	v.	mechanical	18
	15	mechanical	v.	thoughtful	22
	16	repetitive	v.	constructive	22

Straight-forward	1	straightforward	v.	problem-solving	1
	2	straightforward	v.	tricky	3
	3	routine working	v.	irregular working	4
	4	straightforward	v.	suspicion	6
	5	explicit	v.	abstract	7
	6	straightforward	v.	more muddling	8
	7	straightforward	v.	needs ingenuity	10
	8	straightforward	v.	round about	11
	9	sure	v.	doubtful	12
	10	general	v.	searching	13
	11	straightforward	v.	involved	16
	12	straightforward	v.	variable solutions	16
	13	straightforward	v.	extensive	19
	14	straightforward	v.	dislike	20

Affect dimensions

Fear	1	horror	v.	joy	4
	2	hollowness	v.	delayed reaction	6
	3	dread	v.	expectation	6
	4	fear	v.	thankfulness	6
	5	horrible	v.	nice	7
	6	revolting	v.	excellent	7
	7	horror	v.	possible	9

8	fill me with terror	v.	fairly happy	10
9	ugly	v.	good	14
10	fear	v.	security	21

Pleasure

1	enjoyable	v.	taxing	2
2	homely	v.	alien	5
3	overjoyed	v.	hate	6
4	liking	v.	loathing	7
5	pleasant	v.	faint-hearted	10
6	pleasure	v.	antipathy	11
7	pleasant	v.	nuisance	13
8	happy	v.	nasty	14
9	joy	v.	maddening	14
10	delight	v.	taxing	14
11	pleasure	v.	daunting	21
12	near to happiness	v.	desperation	21

Worry

1	dismay – anxiety	v.	carefree – worry free	4
2	demanding – worrying	v.	facility	4
3	worry	v.	non-committal	6
4	worrying	v.	easier	8
5	sinking	v.	survivable	14
6	deliberation	v.	fairly certain	21
7	worry	v.	challenging	22

Dislike

1	dislike	v.	like	8
2	dislike	v.	reasonable	9
3	dislike	v.	prefer	17
4	unpopular	v.	acceptable	18

Relief

1	specific	v.	exploratory	1
2	helpful	v.	dull	2
3	relaxing	v.	distasteful	2
4	confidence	v.	failure	3
5	feeling of well-being	v.	disconcerting	3
6	morale booster	v.	off-putting – time to panic	3
7	hopeful	v.	impossible	3
8	reassurance	v.	despair	5
9	assuring	v.	down-heartening	5
10	relief	v.	tenseness	6
11	confident	v.	anxiety	7
12	more-relaxed	v.	anxiety	8
13	calmer	v.	more tense	8
14	confident	v.	reluctant	10
15	more relaxing	v.	uneasy	10
16	positive	v.	apprehensive	12
17	careful	v.	anticipation	14
18	less nervous	v.	makes me nervous	17
19	relief	v.	dismay	20
20	confidence	v.	nervousness	20
21	comforting thought	v.	hesitation	21
22	hope	v.	exasperation	21

Interest	1	interest	v.	non-committal	4
	2	interesting	v.	mundane	5
	3	response	v.	resignment	7
	4	unleashing	v.	inhibiting	13
	5	thoughtful	v.	indifference	14
	6	positive	v.	negative	22
Boring	1	stagnant	v.	leading	1
	2	boring	v.	involving	3
	3	indifferent – bored	v.	curious – questioning	4
	4	disinterested	v.	engaging	5
	5	disinterest	v.	challenging	5
	6	boring	v.	interesting	7

Figure 7.11 Categorisation of constructs from maths exam questions

This classifying of constructs was introduced in chapter 2 where members of a man-management course shared their constructs and produced a classification system as a way of pooling their systems of personal meaning in the topic area. In chapter 11 this approach is developed into the POOL, REFINE and THESAURUS techniques for producing a shared language which contains all non-redundant items of thoughts and feelings elicited from the members of a group. Mathematically these techniques may be represented as a system of sets. The sets may or may not be mutually exclusive and they may or may not be nested into superordinate sets.

CONSTRUING OF MATHS GRID CONSTRUCTS

		STUDENTS																						
TYPES OF CONSTRUCTS		1	2	3	4	5	6	7	8	9	10	11	12	13	14	15	16	17	18	19	20	21	22	
PROBLEM																									
PREFERENCE																									
CONTEXT	LANGUAGE									1						1		1	2	3	2			11
	DIFFICULTY	1						2	1	1		1	1	2	1	1		1	1	1	1	1	1	17
	DEFINITION	3	1		2					2	2	2					3	2	1	1		1	1	21
	PHYSICAL		1	2									2		1					1	4	1		12
	DESCRIPTION		2													2							1	5
	PRECISION		2				1			2		1	1	2	1	1			1		1			13
METHOD	THEORETICAL	1	1				1			1									1				1	6
	LEARNING & MEMORY	1	1				1	1		1	1	2			1		2	2	1				2	16
	STRAIGHTFORWARD	1		1	1		1	1	1	1	1	1	1	1	1					1	1			14
	FEAR						1	2		1	1	1	1	1	1							1		10
	PLEASURE		1				1	1	1	1	1			1	3			1				2	1	14
	WORRY				2		1		1	1					1							1		7
AFFECT	DISLIKE						1	1	1									1						4
	RELIEF	1	2	2		2	1	1	2		2		1	1	1			1			2	2	1	22
	INTEREST		1			1		1						1	1		1							6
	BORING	1			1	2	1	1																6
		9	9	9	9	6	7	10	10	9	8	9	6	7	10	6	9	9	7	7	11	9	8	184

Figure 7.12 Table of categories

Chapter 8

A PCP approach to perception

PART 1 PERCEPTION, SKILL AND LEARNING

An apology

The only apology made for the rather provocative approach taken in this chapter is to place on record the authors' experience in trying to introduce these ideas to undergraduates, postgraduates, teachers, trainers and therapists. Some of them reject the ideas out of hand. (One chairman of a major Industrial Training Board categorically denied the existence of the kinaesthetic sense, which is, in the view of medics, physiologists and psychologists, the basis of most manual skill.) Most claim to understand the ideas. In fact they often appear quite impressed by them. But six months or a year later (or maybe longer) they will come back to say that 'only now am I beginning to see the practical implications of what you were saying about perception'.

Perception — a new idea?

One message intended in this book is the idea that 'the total complex of perceptions, thoughts and feelings' held by any one individual is what 'produces' his or her anticipations and behaviour. The anticipations and behaviour receive, provoke or produce consequences which are then perceived, thought and felt from within the same patterns of personal meanings as gave birth to the earlier perceptions, thoughts and feelings. Thus new ideas are (and can only be) absorbed into existing patterns of meaning. This process of absorption may be deadening or creative. It may merely confirm the existing pattern or enable new growth and development. Many readers will perceive, think and feel that the previous statement is unnecessarily tortuous, and this may be so. But over and over again the authors have found that the reception of new ideas is often still-born because these ideas are forced into the cramped and suffocating spaces to be found within a totally inappropriate pattern of personal meaning which is all too readily perceived, thought and felt to be 'the same kind of

156

approach'. This is why the apparently rather lengthy discussion of the idea of 'personal learning' was offered in chapter 1.

Here it will be argued that perception is a familiar term concealing a powerful pattern of relatively new ideas. These new ideas are not easily combined with commonsense or traditional concepts of learning. The reader is asked to try not to smother these ideas in those patterns of personal meanings which all too obviously represent 'the same approach'.

To help shake open some unexpected spaces in your meaning system consider the following analogy:

> A simple bi-metal thermostat is a temperature-sensitive device which controls some heating appliance such as the electric heater in a hot water system. It can only be in one of two possible conditions. Either the heater is on and the bi-metal strip is warming up and bending in such a way that as the water gets too hot it turns the heater off. Or the heater is off and the water is getting colder. Therefore the bi-metal strip is cooling down, it is bending in the other direction until it eventually gets 'too cold' and turns the heater on. Action and 'perception' are one and the same process. When the heater is on, the thermostat's state of 'perceptual readiness' makes the thermostat sensitive only to becoming 'too hot'. Perceiving 'too hot' is identical with switching the heater off. When the heater is off its state of perceptual readiness makes the thermostat sensitive only to becoming 'too cold'.

Thus with some effort of imagination, the thermostat illustrates a point about the artificiality of a system of meanings which separates perception from thoughts, feelings and actions. The analogy also suggests that in a feedback device different states of activity are merely another way of describing different states of selective perceptual readiness.

For those able to tolerate the idea, a 'feedback mechanism' is a useful analogy to one simple but crucial aspect of human experience and behaviour. The Grey Walter tortoise pushes the anaology further:

> The tortoise is a mechanical 'toy' designed to demonstrate the capabilities of a feedback device. The steering mechanism of this battery-driven trolley has a light-sensitive photo-cell mounted on it. It 'looks' where it is going. Normally it waltzes around in an apparently random epicyclic dance within its enclosure. However, when the amount of light falling on the cell increases the steering mechanism tends to straighten out. This has the effect of sending the tortoise off along a more direct path towards the source of the light. If you walk about shining a torch at it, the tortoise will follow you.

Again the activity and the perceptual sensitivity are indivisible. What is more, the temptation to anthropomorphise is much greater. Most observers talk about the mechanism as if it intended to chase the light.

Finally consider two such mechanisms, one sensitive to green light, and the other to red. They each have a lamp of the contrasting colour mounted on their casing. When placed in an enclosure together they exhibit inter-related behaviours which invite even more anthropomorphic comments. The reader is asked merely to hold these analogies in the fringes of their awareness as they read the remainder of this chapter.

The perceptual components of all human activity

A second approach to appreciating some of the difficulties which may arise in learning about new ideas is to use the repertory grid. It is suggested that before reading the remainder of this chapter the reader explores the personal meaning of 'perception'. After reading the chapter the reader will be invited:

(a) to modify, expand and elaborate the grid they made before reading the chapter to take account of any changes of true personal meaning that have resulted;
(b) to compare their final grid personal constructs with those of the authors.

Thus the authors have seriously applied the CSHL personal learning technology to themselves. The reader is invited to do likewise.

Activity 8.1 Exploring perception

For a grid to yield valid personal meaning the 'items of experience' used as elements within it must be living reconstructions from the experience of the person doing the grid. It is suggested that the reader should identify at least twelve items from the following list. Each 'item of human activity' should then be converted into a specific item of personal experience, i.e. the reader should identify some recent event in which they were involved in that activity. It is their own experience of the activity which leads to the element in their grid. The element in the grid is 'the perceptual processes called into play when I was — for example — driving down to Newquay last Saturday'.

When the readers have identified at least twelve such 'perceptual process' elements they are invited to complete a grid containing at least twelve constructs which are ways in which they perceive, think and/or feel about the processes of perception.

Human activities

E1	Driving a car	E17	Walking home
E2	Reading a book	E18	Getting up in the morning
E3	Visiting an art gallery	E19	Boiling an egg
E4	Translating a piece of prose	E20	Giving a lecture
E5	Chopping wood	E21	Programming a micro-computer
E6	Cooking a meal	E22	Riding a horse
E7	Making love	E23	Ironing clothes
E8	Writing a letter	E24	Conversing creatively
E9	Drawing a picture	E25	Doing personal accounts
E10	Watching television	E26	Checking out a new vacuum cleaner
E11	Raking leaves	E27	Wine tasting
E12	Watching birds	E28	Playing Space Invaders
E13	Playing the piano	E29	Choosing cloth for a suit
E14	Tying a shoe-lace	E30	Taking a photograph
E15	Paddling a canoe	E31	Using a micro-meter
E16	Orienteering	E32	Diagnosing some bodily complaint or disability

Having identified at least twelve elements from the above list, the reader is invited to add at least three more personal experiences (of human activity) from their own set of competences.

Now elicit constructs which depict the similarity and differences between the perceptual processes involved in each activity.

For example obtain a construct from:

> Driving a car
> Playing the piano
> and Visiting an art gallery

Concentrate on comparing what is for you the direct immediate perceptual experience in each case. The reader is now asked to:

(a) Complete the grid.
(b) FOCUS it.
(c) Draw it in SPACED or TRIGRID form.
(d) Reflect upon it.
(e) Modify, expand and refine it until it fully represents your views on the part played by perception in human activity.

When this is done put the grid aside until you have read the remainder of this chapter.

Perception

An example may help to illustrate the nature of perceptual processes.

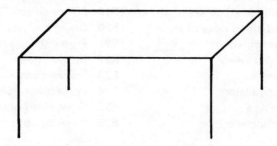

Fig. 8.1 Table A

Fig. 8.1 (Table A) can be seen as 'a table'. To be more precise, most people; most of the time, see it as a table viewed from a distance and from a level slightly above the table top.

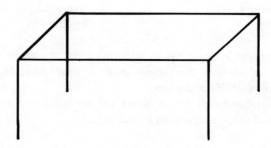

Fig. 8.2 Table B

Many people see Fig. 8.2 (Table B) as a table viewed from underneath, although some people have difficulty in seeing it in this way and see a glass-topped table viewed from above. A little practice can change Table B into an ambiguous figure which can, at will, be seen in either way.

For those who have difficulty in obtaining one of these views there are certain perceptual strategies for looking at Table B. Concentrating on certain parts of it will enhance the probability of seeing it in one way rather than the other. If the lower of the two horizontal lines becomes the centre of attention and is seen as being 'in front of' or nearer than the other one, the figure tends to be seen as the glass-topped table. If the upper horizontal line is 'centred' and thus seen as nearer, then the table appears to be viewed from underneath. Other ways of looking at the figure are to see it as a ceiling with strings hanging down; or to concentrate on the lower middle corner and to see it either as solid or as empty. Readers are asked to practise on Table B until they can flip it forward and back at will to produce either view. Try this now before going any further.

If you can now decide when to see Fig. 8.2 as a table viewed from on top and when to see it from underneath, look back at Table A. Can you now see it as 'a table with one leg missing viewed from underneath and with a piece of string hanging down from the back edge' (or with a cat sitting on it with its tail hanging over the back edge). If you can experience this new perception of the figure, you have achieved (maybe a somewhat trivial example of) perceptual learning.

This rather frivolous exercise has a serious purpose. It is designed to illustrate how we learn to attribute meaning to sensory evidence. Alternative constructions of experience can be achieved by having different systems of meaning available, and by using different perceptual strategies to validate one or other of them. The reader may feel that eight lines on a sheet of paper are sufficiently ambiguous to enable a choice of perceptual illusion which more concrete and detailed evidence would dispel. You may feel that, faced with the full sensory evidence of reality, there is no room for alternative views. But the fact that people do not all perceive their world in the same way is probably the strongest and most agreed finding of modern psychology. So well established and yet intriguing is it that popular books, films and television programmes are continually introducing the general public to the idea that seeing is not necessarily believing. But this is only part of the story. We become purposive by selectively organising our perceptions to achieve our intentions.

In spite of all the 'scientific' psychological evidence, it is very difficult to become conscious of this relativity in perceiving. We are able to attribute meaning unconsciously but directly to even the most incomplete data; but it is difficult to appreciate that our own familiar world of immediate habitual perception may not appear to others as we perceive it. We inevitably assume that everybody must see, hear, feel, taste and smell the outside world in exactly the same way as we do. This is the basis of our belief in the objective reality of the physical world. The truth is very different. One has only to visit a truly foreign country in which the form of almost every apparently familiar object is unexpected and to experience the exhilarating sense of heightened awareness and vividness of perceptual experience, to realise that most of us, most of the time, live in a world of our own habitual constructions. We develop strategies of perception which collect the minimal sensory evidence needed to validate our cosy and familiar working models of the world. So long as our purposes remain the same and the parts of the environment with which we interact allow our actions to produce the consequences we have come to expect, then our perceptions simplify and become habitual. Only when the evidence of our senses fails to validate our habitual expectations do we seek more evidence, and only if this further invalidates the meanings that we 'know' to be out there do we begin to re-acknowledge the need to begin again, actively and consciously to pay attention to the detailed perceptual evidence needed to more adequately explore the 'outside world'. Only then do we again provoke it into yielding new experiences in us through which we can construct meanings which are more personally relevant and therefore more viable in enabling us to pursue our elaborating purposes in interaction with the perceptually enriched 'outside world'.

Activity 8.2 Eliciting perceptual constructs-auditory

Take an example of non-visual perception. Identifying snatches of recorded music (such as are used in the TV and radio programme *Face the Music*) is usually an intuitive act. When asked why you think the music is A, B or C, it is often quite difficult to identify your reasons. Eliciting a system of personal constructs which differentiate between such recordings and which are also firmly described in terms of their auditory qualities can rapidly bring the implicit bases of your musical perception into awareness.

Activity 8.3 Eliciting perceptual constructs-tactile

Blindfold yourself and get a friend to choose 12 objects each small enough to be held comfortably in your hand. Now elicit a system of constructs the poles of which are described solely in terms related to how they feel in the hand.

Activity 8.4 Exercising non-verbal constructs

The grid forces the learner to verbalise their construct pole descriptions. In perception much of the most important construing is not expressed in words. The following exercise is useful in all types of perceptual training, in art, skills for inspection, in fault finding and diagnosis, etc.

Work in pairs. Select 12 to 20 objects, sounds, tastes or other sources of the perceptual experience relevant to your reason for increasing your perceptual activity. Now deal out the objects randomly between you so that you each have the same number of items. Person A orders his or her objects to represent a construct so:

Objects physically distributed to represent
their positions on the construct

Left pole   Right pole

O   O O   O O O   O   O   O O

Person B tries to *visually* empathise with person A's construct.
Person B then tests their visual understanding by juxtapositioning their objects along person A's distribution of objects. Non-discussion beyond a bald yes or no is not permissible and even this is best done by person A removing those of B's objects that do not fit.

It is important that the perceptions are not verbalised either 'out loud' or by silently giving the construct verbal pole names in your head.

Now reverse roles and continue alternatively until your two repertoires of constructs are exhausted.

This exercise is one variation on the EXCHANGE grid technique described more fully in chapter 10.

Activity 8.5 FOCUSing non-verbal constructs

This activity is a continuation and elaboration of Activity 8.4.

If the objects are unobtrusively labelled (e.g. on their base) then the assigning of each object to each construct can be recorded, using whatever scaling or ranking procedure best fits the physical distribution of objects. Constructs are merely numbered and no attempt is made to record any pole descriptions.

The two sets of constructs can be recorded in separate grids or they may be combined in one grid. Once recorded, the grid can be FOCUSed in the usual way.

Activity 8.6 Talkback through a non-verbal grid

This activity continues Activity 8.5.

The FOCUSed grid can be used to talk yourself back through the perceptual construing so that you may *reflect* upon it.

The talkback procedure is similar to that described in chapters 5 and 6, except that the clusters are represented in the physical SPACed layout of elements. Construct clusters are represented by the general layout of elements contained within them.

Perception and competence

Skill or competence in its widest sense of 'purposive personal organisation' depends upon perception. Skills such as driving a car, riding a bicycle, walking, running, jumping or standing still, and activities such as talking, visiting the theatre or concert hall, switching on an electric light, ironing, painting, boxing, tying one's shoelaces, or baking a cake all depend on the pattern of meaning which we attribute to the sensations generated in their performance. Perhaps appreciating and guiding one's bodily processes into achieving a typed manuscript, walking on hot coals, answering mathematics questions, rapidly assembling a printed circuit board, using a burette, juggling seven tennis balls, understanding a lecture or savouring a meal have more in common than is normally acknowledged. Skill, competence and creativity can be considered as patterns of transaction between the person and his physical, physiological, psychological and social environment.

Sometimes the perceptual process may achieve stability in a recognition or naming; but more often the equilibrium is dynamic and perception guides action. Delicate timing, selectivity and precise relative judgment are necessary if the perceptual processes are to become actively incorporated, as feedback, into the organisation and control of the individual's purposive activities. Piaget has identified what he calls the figurative and operative aspects of perception. A similar basic differentiation would appear to be intended. For example, a teacher perceives the learners in the classroom, a manager perceives his subordinates at work and a counsellor perceives her client in the consulting room. Each may choose to become aware of some of their perceptual experience and choose to articulate it with verbal tags, but most of the evidence which is selectively perceived is not recognised descriptively. It takes on meaning within the purposive context of events. It is used to explore, diagnose, check or confirm the continuing effectiveness of the interaction. Equally in observing physical objects, Thomas has described how industrial inspectors visually checking the quality of a product can sort out the defective items without naming the nature of the defect to themselves. Indeed, when challenged, they will either have to check the item again, in a descriptive frame of mind, or they will have to reconstruct the perceptual activity, in memory, to arrive at a naming. Both the descriptive and the control functions of perception may be either conscious or non-conscious. One can recognise something without consciously naming it. One can control something without being aware of the evidence through which control is achieved.

Activity 8.7   Exploring the descriptive and control functions of perception

The reader is asked to consider some simple repetitive skill such as dialling a telephone. Watch somebody performing the skill and record the sequence of actions. Now observe the first action closely and note what perceptions are required to:

(a) initiate the action;
(b) control the action whilst it is being performed;
(c) check that it has been satisfactorily completed.

Repeat this for each action in the sequence required to perform the skill. Now perform the skill yourself and check whether its perceptual requirements fit your description.

Conversational elicitation of a perceptual grid

Perception is difficult to talk or write about; almost inevitably it has become equated with visual perception because these are the easiest examples to use. Perceiving has to be jointly experienced and shared to have any communicable meaning. It is not easy to endow this book with specifically chosen noises, smells, tastes and textures. It may acquire such attributes during manufacture and usage but, whilst we are writing the manuscript, we do not know what these will be. For the purposes of public illustration one is forced to use visual examples.

Ambiguous referents are useless for investigating perception. The objects used as elements in a pereceptual grid must be present and perceived as the grid is being elicited. Our perceiving robot may only need to glimpse them for the robotishly purposeful meaning to become clear; but it (you) does need that glimpse. Our free-self needs the opportunity to explore and develop more subtle new personal meanings.

In eliciting a perceptual grid, care again has to be taken to create a conversational mode and to clarify the purpose of the interaction. The form of the conversation used in eliciting a perceptual grid determines the type of perceptual material that will be placed in it.

Loosely guided conversation has the advantage of offering the clients few leads as to what is expected and, therefore, forces them back to their own uncontaminated construing. This can be very revealing. The client may reveal prejudicially selected views, items unseen by others, blind spots and understandings which a more closely guided elicitation would have ruled out. Sometimes if the purpose is ill-defined, the looseness of the elicitation leaves the client searching for clues which would indicate what it is that the practitioner wishes to hear. Again the crux of the matter is the client's appreciation of the purpose of the grid conversation.

Carefully guided conversation can help the clients to explore the robotish or submerged aspects of their perceptual processes. Most people cannot do this for themselves; they need to be gradually talked down into a detailed appreciation of their own experience. The conversational skill consists in holding the direct perceptual experience at the centre of attention whilst avoiding putting 'words' or 'perceptual categories' into clients' heads when they are having difficulty creating their own.

The twelve prints shown in Fig. 8.3 could become the elements in a perceptual grid. By using the three-card trick and the method explained in chapters 2 and 3, a series of constructs would emerge and each picture could be rated on each construct. Talkback through the FOCUSed grid would provide a very good impression of the general conceptual and perceptual framework within which the client perceives prints of this kind. In the absence of other prints he is not offered the opportunity to explore a wider framework. The prints are used to define the perceptual universe of discourse which the participant is being encouraged to explore. The relevance and meaning of that universe to the particular client and the purpose of the conversation will determine the nature of the perceptual grid which emerges.

There is a feedback process which tends to work during such conversational elicitations. If the prints are irrelevant to the client's experience, they will tend to offer superficial constructs. If these are implicitly welcomed then the tone of

Fig. 8.3 Twelve postcards

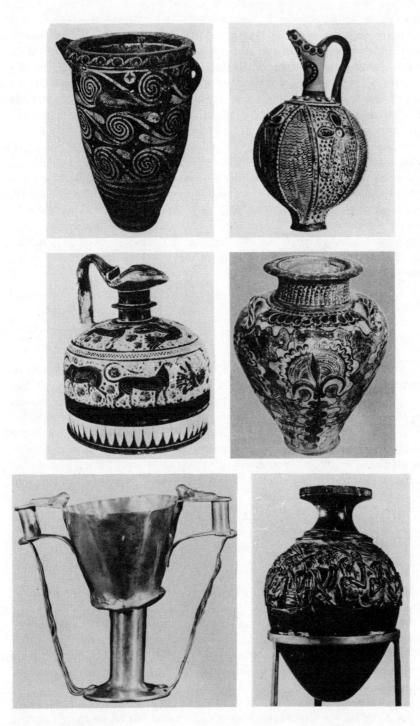

Fig 8.3 (continued)

the conversation can become set at this level. If the superficial constructs are queried or hesitated over the clients may either become alienated and retreat into themselves or if encouraged and supported they may make an effort to dig deeper. The digging can take two forms. It may simply be an uncovering of a structure of meanings which already existed but was not being tapped, or the digging may lead to a creative encounter in which new structures of meanings are evolved and significant perceptual learning ensues. The difference between these two processes is more easily experienced than explained. In the first, the process is experienced as one of recall and recognition, a remembering of earlier perceptual states. In the second, the process is one of spontaneous creation, excitement and surprise. Neither is in itself preferable to the other. The path of the conversation should be laid by the purpose of the interaction. Perceptual grids tend to be both easy and difficult to elicit. They are easy because the elements to be construed are physically present during the elicitation conversation. They are difficult because of the ease with which a subject will slide away into the conceptual world that conceals the exact perceptual sources of his reactions.

Activity 8.8 Identifying a system of perceptual constructs

It is suggested that readers should now identify their own systems of perceptual constructs for the twelve prints in Fig. 8.3. Start by eliciting say 10-12 constructs. Do not as yet assign elements to constructs. Now inspect the constructs and eliminate any which do not directly relate to the similarities or differences between your direct perceptual experiences of the prints. Make sure you can identify the physical referents for each bi-polar differentiation. Proceed with the elicitation of directly perceptual constructs until you have exhausted your repertoire. Consult a friend or colleague and discuss whether they feel your constructs are purely perceptual.

Skilled and unskilled perceptions: a T-C problem

Perception guides all behaviour. Selectivity, precise relative judgment and synchronised timing are necessary if we are effectively to achieve our purposes. It is difficult to learn so to perceive.

To point out the clumsiness of a learner's actions does not help him to acquire greater rhythm, precision and control. The perceptual sensitivities which will enable him to make the discriminations on which to act less clumsily must be acquired. One of the authors occasionally has the following experience whilst driving on a very familiar route; he suddenly 'wakes up' to find himself two or three miles further on than he was aware of having driven. He has stopped at traffic lights, negotiated roundabouts and worked out his morning's lecture.

He is also quite sure that he has driven safely. Tact would lead us to suggest that no reader ever has this experience whilst driving, but in fact everybody has similar experiences! Factory girls chatting away whilst achieving miracles of complicated and precise assembly work, the day-dreaming housewife going about her daily chores and teenagers who respond to routine family questions whilst remaining deep in their own personal world, are all operating in a similar way. A related phenomenon is even more widespread. The driver who is completely aware of where he is and, in a general sense, of what he is doing, may have no consciousness of the detailed activity of driving, braking, changing gear and steering; he may even remain unconscious of negotiating a roundabout.

This explains part of the difficulty which he experiences when he attempts to transmit the skill to someone else. Either he is not aware of the details and is therefore unable to explain what he is perceiving, or as he becomes unusually aware of everything the skill disintegrates, leaving him unable to demonstrate it.

In many learning situations much time is wasted because the T-C practitioner is too concerned with the learner's actions, which she can see, and is not concerned sufficiently with his perceptions, which are invisible. The teacher too often assumes that the learner's perceptions are those which she, the teacher, is herself experiencing. It is this that makes teaching a close friend or relative to drive a car such a nerve-jangling experience. The teacher cannot conceive of her friend acting as she does. The friend must be stupid! Given what I, the teacher, see, hear and feel, how could he, the learner, act like that! The already skilled driver is automatically attributing patterns of meaning to her own sensations. The learner is totally unaware of this subtle, complex and relevant system of meaning. But the teacher/driver assumes that the learner/driver is experiencing the situation as she does.

Unless careful attention is given to the personal perceptual learning of each participant the difficulties associated with the teaching of skill, competence and creativity are indeed formidable.

Given an understanding of the centrality of perceptual organisation in all human activity many seemingly inexplicable failures of T-C resolve themselves into questions of perceptual learning. The issue then becomes that of how to enable and manage various types of perceptual learning. This is discussed in Part 2 of the chapter.

Actitivity 8.9 A taste panel

Select samples of some kind of drink. Tea, coffee, wine, cider or hot chocolate would each serve. Collect some 8 to 12 different brands/types of the particular drink you have chosen. Now, using the professional tasters' method of not swallowing the sample and rinsing the mouth out with water between samples, elicit your system of wine/tea/coffee/cider-tasting constructs.

Activity 8.10 An Indian miniature grid

The Indian miniature shown in Fig. 8.4 can be used to elicit a repertory grid on one object. This is achieved by identifying a series of elements from within the picture. Any aspect of the miniature which is, for you, an 'item of meaning' can be used as an element. Proceed to elicit a perceptual grid in the usual way.

At the end of this chapter two sets of elements and constructs are shown which have been elicited from this Indian miniature.

Conclusions

Before proceeding to Part 2 of the chapter two uncompleted tasks remain to be finished.

The Indian miniature

As was suggested in Activity 8.8, the grid users do not have to explore their picture perception by comparing prints. A more intense analysis of perceptual construing is obtained if they are allowed to focus down and get to grips with just one picture. The elements are elicited, being those aspects or parts of the picture which the clients select as being, for him or her, perceptually significant 'wholes'. The following are the series of elements obtained from 'Clare' when exploring the Indian miniature shown in Fig. 8.4

1	Fat men	8	Woman sitting outside
2	2 Water jugs	9	Group (2 girls)
3	6-petalled flower	10	Third girl
4	2 minarets	11	Blue sky
5	Red wall	12	Foliage
6	Windows	13	Wall
7	Naked girl	14	Staircase
		15	Perspective

'Desmond' selected a rather different set of visual elements from the 'same' picture.

Fig 8.4 An Indian miniature

1 Dirty mark (on roof)	8 Spots on faces
2 3 sides with fences	9 Thing on end of nose (seated woman)
3 1 side without	10 Woman on stairs astride shell
4 Symmetry to pot	11 White fault (in 3rd red arch)
5 Urn (pipe)	12 Pillars missing
6 Piece of hair (by bride's ear)	13 Flatness (pillars missing)
7 Things through nose	14 Ugly man (asexual)
	15 Nine o'clock shadow (on man)

Immediately, it becomes clear that Clare and Desmond are selecting and organising their perceptions of the picture differently. As they generate their constructs, the basis for this selectivity and organisation is partially revealed.

Clare's constructs are as follows:

1	Life	–	Death
2	Life and death	–	Neither
3	Serving girls	–	Bridegroom
4	Impersonal (depicted)	–	Personal (artist's viewpoint)
5	Joined	–	Alone
6	Light symbol	–	Dark symbol
7	Architectural	–	Human
8	Finished object	–	Prior to process
9	Part building	–	Part garden

Desmond described his constructs differently:

1	Single entity	—	Affect different things
2	Details	—	Total painting
3	More visible	—	Extreme detail
4	Relate to people	—	Relate to background
5	Like	—	Don't like
6	In courtyard	—	Not
7	Plainly visible	—	Extreme details
8	Details	—	Part of whole
9	Details	—	Whole
10	Part person	—	Whole person
11	Relates to people	—	Relates to rest of painting
12	Immediately visible	—	Later visible

It is up to each reader to attempt to re-perceive the picture by viewing Desmond's elements through his constructs or by using Clare's constructs to view her elements. Only thus can we begin to enter into their perceptual experience and begin to empathise with their conception of this Indian miniature. But this one arbitrary cross-section through the perceptual experience could be elaborated. Clare and/or Desmond could be taken down into a more detailed analysis nearer to the sensory-data out of which their very different constructions emerge. It is in the nature of man as a species that the nearer we get to the sensory sources the more likely we are to agree. Desmond and/or Clare could on the other hand be encouraged to explore the inferences and implications associated with their perceptions of this picture. This would increase their awareness of the nature of their aesthetic appreciation.

The authors' construing of skill, competence and creativity

When the authors construed their own items of experience provoked by the list of 'human activities' offered in Actitivity 8.1, their purpose was to elaborate and clarify their understanding of the part played by perception in human action, before writing this chapter. They produced the following personal constructs:

aware	— unaware
internal bodily sensations	— oriented towards outside world
evolved and naturally occurring	— learned
recognition and naming	— as feedback to control actions
robot-like	— free-self
single mode of sensation	— multiple modes of sensation
exploratory	— purposively-oriented
shock and exhilaration; raw sensations	— comfortable; selective and highly organised perception
perceptual-motor	— aesthetic appreciative
relaxed	— focused attention
hierarchically organised	— small disconnected units

Part 1 of this chapter and Part 2 following are attempts to communicate the implications of this personal construct system. The ease or difficulty with which readers accept, reject, understand and are able to apply different parts of these chapters may be found to relate to the areas of match and mismatch between their grid and that of the authors.

The reader is asked to compare his or her constructs with those of the authors. Later, in chapter 9, the reader will be introduced to a method for comparing two grids in which the elements are 'shared' but each client has produced their own repertoire of personal constructs. It is suggested that where people are working together they PAIR these grids in the way explained in chapter 9.

PART 2   PERCEPTUAL GRIDS

Learning to perceive: perceiving to learn

Ethologists, for example Tinbergen and Konrad Lorenz, have demonstrated that a dynamic system of selective sensory sensitivity is implicit in the genetic endowment of each living thing. Journalists such as Ardrey and Morris have popularised these findings. Even insects appear to have very complex perceptual organisations although almost totally pre-ordained. In animals higher up the evolutionary scale the capacity for perceptual learning begins to appear. In man, unlike the stickleback or the hyena, the perceived meaning of events appears to be infinitely revisable.

From conception through birth and onwards, the process of perceiving, with its continuing revisions of meaning, is the source of all evidence contributing to our understanding of our outer and inner worlds. The mouth, the skin, the ears, the eyes and the nose are discovered by babies to be sources of evidence which help them to predict what may happen and help them to arrange happenings both within and outside themselves. Psychologists (e.g. Freud, Melanie Klein and Piaget) each have their own construings of the importance of this early search after meaning. In transaction with the world around us we build up patterns of meaning which enable us to remain viable. We learn to meet our basic needs and to achieve at least some of our more elaborated purposes. At the same time we are also beginning to attribute meaning to all the evidence which is generated inside the skin.

Meaning is generated through exploratory transactions in which questions are raised either in action or in exploration of sensations. As evidence is gathered the questions are revised and reformulated (e.g. Postman and Bruner). Gradually the meaning attributed to certain referents stabilises, the perceptual transaction with them simplifies and acquires a fixed form. When this happens we have achieved a viable relationship with the referent. Its meaning, for us, lies in this relationship. For example – the table is for sitting at, for doing homework at, for eating off, for turning upside down and playing pirates in, etc. An oil painting is for appreciating, for looking at in ways that release certain feelings within us. The pendant, given to us by our lover, is for wearing, for adornment and for reminding us of that love and of 3 pm on Friday 17 August 1972. The pain in the stomach comes from eating unripe apples. The meaning of the referent lies in our constructions of the experience we have had with it and in the uses which we can make it serve. The referent thus acquires a personally relevant and viable meaning. Impersonal meanings, acquired at second or tenth hand do not carry this viability. They do not allow the person to fully recruit their experience into anticipating events.

When we perceive, evidence generated in the nervous system and attributed to the senses is almost instantaneously transformed into meaning. We immediately see 'a carpet', we hear 'a clarinet', we put our hand into our pocket and select by touch 'the right coin', we taste 'a grenadine' and we smell 'bad drains'.

The sensory systems are always at work; but the meanings 'carpet', 'clarinet', 'coin', 'grenadine' and 'drain' are not external information, to be taken in through the senses. They are a few of the myriad perceptual meanings which already exist within us. How we come to construct such meanings and how a person learns to perceive more sensitively, more relevantly and/or more purposively is central to understanding the differences between personal and impersonal learning.

Practitioners from all realms of T-C vary in their appreciation of this. They vary in how sensitive and appropriate their methods are for encouraging their clients to develop relevant and viable perceptual meanings. They also differ in commitment to helping their clients to use experience to continue to elaborate, refine and revise their perceptual meanings in the light (smell, taste, sound and feel) of events. All too often the practitioner accepts a perceptual recognition which is demonstrated only verbally as evidence of the dynamically selective perceptual understanding necessary for skilled or competent performance.

Levels in perceptual experience: robots and hierarchical organisation

In a text, letters, words, sentences, paragraphs and larger systems of print are displayed upon the pages. The meanings attributed to each by the reader are both built out of smaller units and lie within the context of the meaning attributed to larger ones. But, as one reads, the focus of awareness appears at only one level at a time. If the going is easy, the units of meaning that are attended to remain large, and may be represented on the page by a sentence or group of sentences. But if, ambiguously, the words, whose order is important, and the letters, which we hardly ever notice, do not lend themselves to intuitive hierarchical interpretation, then the attribution of meaning becomes more difficult. (If you see what we mean.) It becomes necessary first to focus attention on the individual words or phrases and then gradually to construct meanings for large units until the sentence mentally assembles itself into one meaningful whole. Most of the time we are unaware of this constructional activity since it happens non-consciously whilst we are operating with very familiar ideas or materials. However, when we are faced with the need to operate with unfamiliar ideas or in a foreign language the process is forced into awareness.

Much of man's capacity to learn and acquire competence lies in his ability to attribute immediate purposeful meanings to very complex and ambiguous displays, i.e. to recognise, anticipate and predict. If you can remember when you first visited a now familiar situation (e.g. your place of work, a first trip abroad, your house) and contrast it with your most recent experience of the same situation, you will realise that familiarity consists of having already constructed patterns of meaning in our heads, and needing only minimal sensory information from the situation to recognise and anticipate sufficiently to achieve our purposes.

Perhaps better examples are generated by considering a familiar piece of machinery or the playing of a game. Remember when you first unpacked that Gilibuck Rotoknocker? Now notice the ease with which your hand locates the controls. The skilled sportsman has a fantastically sophisticated internal model of how a ball leaves a bat, racket or club and moves through the air. This enables him or her to anticipate its arrival and act accordingly (e.g. cricket, baseball, tennis, golf, etc.). It is useful to think of each of us as having such models of almost every familiar situation, event, person or object. These models allow us to predict and anticipate. Our perception is seldom concerned solely with recognition. Almost always we perceive in a context of action and purpose.

Human beings have an amazing capacity to attribute time-structured dynamic inferential meanings to often very incomplete sensory evidence. This enables members of the human species to become the highly skilled, competent and creative animals that they sometimes are. But this same capacity has its negative aspects. We can become imprisoned within our pre-conceived perceptions. Life can lose its flavour by losing its surprises; and worse, the internal models become nine-tenths submerged, so that we live on a surface of over-familiar meanings that condition both our purposes and actions. In driving, playing tennis, reading, making bread or even making love, we become what Colin Wilson calls 'our own robots'. These robots are incredibly useful in doing many of the routine tasks which would bore us silly if we had to carry them out at the full focus of awareness; and yet these same robots are always with us and can, too easily, take us over, occupying our time and space, leaving very little of our free self available to create and enjoy new experiences. The ability for self-awareness is largely dependent upon a facility for moving between levels of perception. The robot remains in unawareness; but if we are self-organised we retain the freedom to inspect, or even take over, what it is doing, if and when we so choose.

The repertory grid can be used to negotiate ourselves into and out of this roboticism. It can help us to create efficient robots. It can also enable us to free ourselves from the tyranny of those robots that have been with us for so long and have been given such unmonitored reign that they seem to have completely achieved the upper hand.

A partial taxonomy of perceptual processes

All the terms used by a sample of employees and a sample of customers of a food-manufacturing company were pooled. The items in this word pool were categorised for their implications for our understanding of the perceptual processes involved in examining and appreciating the quality of the product.

The following is a simplified version of the category system that emerged:

1   Private company language
2   Special company usage of public language
3   Analogies
4   Sensory references
5   Physical descriptors
6   Inferred causes
7   Objectively measurable
8   Evaluative

Thus the process of perceiving quality might be described as follows:

There is a wealth of sensory evidence available that relates to the consumer's view of the quality of the company's products. Members of the company have constructed images of this consumer and have internalised some view, template or model of good-quality food. This internal model may be refined, reinforced and calibrated against the specifications laid down by the company. But to the extent that day-by-day practice does not match the paper specification the practice seems to exert much more influence on employees' perceptions. When these specifications are not expressed in the day-to-day language of employees they exert almost no real influence on their perceptions.

Mr Production is concerned with output. He will see many faults in terms of inferred causes. He may often use Mr Quality as a reference for what the company requires. A fault such as 'underxxxxed' carries a very specific meaning which is not necessarily implied by the public language or dictionary meaning of the words 'underxxxxing'. It refers to the xxxx manufacturing operation. When Mr Production sees 'underxxxxed faults' he intuitively knows (infers) that they are caused by bad xxxx machinery (or by poor raw material which is not amenable to xxxxing). But what Mr Production actually sees is 'underxxxxed faults'. In spite of the words being descriptive of the process, they are visual faults with a very specific visual appearance. 'Underxxxxing' is different from 'overxxxxing'; so the process of visual perception not only uses the physical cues to infer the state of the production process, it also has evaluative (quality assessment) components in it. The personal meaning in terms like 'dirty xxxx', 'dimple flink', 'overdone', 'unpleasant taste', 'stale', etc. all involve sensory scanning, physical referents, inferences about processing and evaluation of suitability for customers. If a fault appears, people concerned need a language to capture it. The analogies, specialist language and special usage items serve this purpose.

Each of us brings a certain 'visual vocabulary' to seeing any object and each of us is able to construct 'visual meanings' out of this vocabulary by means of a 'visual syntax'. Perhaps an analogy to the aural language of music helps to clarify the problem. A musical score is expressed in a language that needs no verbal construction. To the initiates the hieroglyphics of the musical notation are perceived directly either as sound or as the experience of playing their instrument, or as both. A person's visual language for perceiving pictures should not be confused with the verbal language which we use to describe this experience. The visual building blocks of picture perception are analogous to the meanings that are indicated by the terms such as crochets, bars and cadences of musical language. A motion picture of the eyes scanning the picture shows the visual syntactic processes at work. If an observer does not share the subject's perceptual language, then a visual grid will remain a disconnected haphazard cross-section out of the whole hierarchical organisation of the client's activity.

Specialist non-verbal languages are more numerous than may be apparent at first. The language of ballet, of mathematics, of electronic circuitry, of architecture, of boat design, of maps and of the perceptual recording version of the two-handed operator process chart are all examples of how to express non-verbally coded experience in forms which enable the initiated to reconstruct the perceptual experience. The designer of the language has achieved something special but we do not seem to have appreciated the power of being able to decompose perceptual experience into a code which has been specially designed to contain it. This avoids the need to strain it through the inappropriate constructions of anything but the most sophisticated and complex verbal language.

The repertory grid can serve as a tool for negotiating such languages of perception. Using the grid for this purpose obviously requires a certain amount of practice and careful attention but it does not require half the lifetime of a dedicated specialist to achieve results.

The perceptual grid: three grids in one

If two people have 'the same' items of experience and if they develop 'the same' systems for construing their experience in 'the same' topic area then given similar exposure to 'the same' events they will experience them in 'the same' way. This is the basis of all the socialisation functions of T-C. Since no two people occupy the same place at the same time and since even twins always have 'the other' as a different context in which to generate experience, these theoretical conditions are practically unattainable. However, as with, say, the idea of absolute (temperature) zero in physics, the idea of identity of construing offers a referent against which to make sense of reality. Some items of experience have a greater possibility of being equal than others. Such items, as we have seen, take on their meaning from both the pattern of smaller items out of which they are constructed and from their position within the structure of a larger item of which they are a part. All items have both structure and context.

What is required is an agreed perceptual basis out of which to work. This can be explored, revealed or created using the sense-datum grid. This grid, which takes a very detailed cross-section through the perceptual process, helps to reveal the vocabulary of the perceptual language. It explores the submerged pool of sensory data and thus reveals some of the potential sensory organisation out of which both the robot and the free-self work their meanings.

Clare's elements were all highly integrated percepts embodying her accumulated visual experience in a conventional form. Desmond uses a wider variety of elements; some of them appear to an outsider as arbitrary fragments of the picture. It is only as one tries visually to explore Desmond's or Clare's constructs and their elements together, by gazing at the picture in Fig. 8.4, that one gets glimpses of the sensory data out of which their perceptions were generated. Momentarily the effort to impose their meanings on to the picture leads to perceptual disintegration, releases the sensory basis into awareness and we may see and feel fresh shapes and colours uncontaminated by established meanings.

The elements and constructs continually refer back into the participant's own past experience. These are the inferential components of perception. They acquire their meanings from the personal nexus of the participant. In a sense, all constructs are inferential, but the purpose here is to trace out three cross-sections through the process of perceptual construing. Sufficient for the moment to say that the first two can be divided into a 'sense-datum grid' (the phonemes) and a 'shared or public percepts grid' (the words). These will be explored in more detail later in the chapter. A third level of perceptual construing is revealed in the inferential grid. This may be seen as indicating the syntax of the perceptual language, but the analogy does not hold unless great care is exercised during the elicitation conversation. The inferential grid contains constructs which indicate how the participants build up the sensory construing into nodes of meaning that fit into the pattern of meanings that relate to his purposive state and to his actions.

The sense-datum grid

The purpose of the sense-datum grid is to trace back the process of perceiving towards its origins in the data of the senses. This is, in any absolute sense, impossible, since the data of the senses is strictly in the form of patterns of pulses in the sensory nerves that connect the sense to the brain. Physiological studies of the sensory nervous system, for example of the eye, show that the optic nerve itself has a whole series of integrative and interpretive processes within it. For example, pulses from the semi-circular canals (the organs of body balance) are fed into the optic nerve and transform the data of the moving image on the retina and information about the movement of the head and body into a much more stable pattern of information for transmission to the brain.

If this physiological reference is held in the background, it is possible to locate an 'evidence at the body periphery' which is generated as it transacts with the world around it. Assuming some adequate basis for defining man as one species, this 'evidence at the body periphery' might be seen as a referent common to all men. Konrad Lorenz has in fact published a book on just this issue.

Such a definition of the phonemes of the perceptual language perhaps sharpens our understanding of the problems experienced by the blind or the deaf in building up a common perceptual framework with the rest of mankind. But the existence of a common basis of experience in each of us does not imply that we have any adequate means of locating and exchanging that experience. The assumption that the same word makes reference to similar sensory experiences in two different bodies is almost always somewhat misguided. Only when much common experience has been explicitly explored and coded does such an assumption begin to hold water. It is, or should be, one function of education to build up shared systems of verbal and non-verbal reference to sensory perception which is shared by all members of a culture, sub-culture or technical group.

A little time spent on any training activity in which perception plays a dominant role soon disabuses us of the naïve view that education succeeds in this endeavour. Art, science, cookery, industrial inspection, clinical medicine, all require that perceptions be shared and exchanged. The art of pursuing the perceptual process back to its referents in the senses is only very partially understood. The length of many apprenticeships results from having to rely on a dumb, unarticulated sharing of experience. The learner wallows in a sea of sensation and like a blind man he feels his way towards the sophisticated patterns of perception which it is necessary for him to evolve if he is to acquire the skills of his trade. The sensory grid can help to articulate this process of groping for sensory awareness, converting it into the joy of primary learning.

Sense-datum grids are very difficult to elicit. Intending subjects can train themselves by exercises which isolate the different senses. For example, a 'touch' description of a door key can be obtained as follows:

Blindfold the subject (or ask him to close his eyes) and place his hand, palm up, on a tabletop. Now place an 'unknown' object on the palm of the hand and insist that the hand remains still. The subject will need time to recognise the nature of the sensations which he experiences. Coldness, weight and vague feelings about size and shape will gradually consolidate. Most subjects cannot resist moving the hand or the fingers to create more sensory information. If this is allowed in a carefully controlled way, the evidence comes slowly until some cue produces a flood of recognition and many other properties are then immediately inferred. Some people suddenly 'see' the key even though they are blindfolded. It is at this point of recognition that the process ceases to be an exploration; organisation sets in and the sense data is integrated into a larger network of meanings.

The reader is advised to play sensory exchange games with one or more others at this point. Any set of objects will serve. By comparing and contrasting the 'feel' of different objects, sense-datum constructs can be elicited. It is as well to avoid oversimplified verbal labels in your descriptions because these magnify the tendency to stay with the robotish perceptual framework into which one is habituated and imprisoned. It is this property of sense-datum grids that make them difficult to report. They are concerned with immediate sensory experience. This loses much of its meaning when expressed in public verbal terms.

The public perception grid

The sense-datum grid is often a tediously long way back from day-to-day perception. The difficulty that one experiences in pushing people back into becoming aware of their 'really pure' sensations, unencumbered by the masks of cumulative experience, demonstrates just how unusual it is to pursue these levels of awareness. Perhaps this is one of the attractions of hallucinatory drugs. However this may be, experience in eliciting 'sensory' grids reveals over and over again that skilled and experienced people directly perceive characteristics which would involve the less skilled and experienced in long chains of conscious inference.

In all areas of life people share sophisticated perceptions. These are built out of common experience which is recognised, made explicit and shared. The Grand Prix driver who recognises an opportunity to overtake at 180 m.p.h. may share his view of 'an opening or a gap' with only forty or fifty other people in the world. The spring song of the cukoo is recognised by rather more of us. The recognition of a 'sixteenth-century refectory table', a 'second-grind fault' on a razor blade, 'green stick' in the tasting of whisky and a 'David Hockney picture' are all shared by certain specialist groups. To the uninitiated the set of referents that are indicated by any one of these descriptions have little or no common sensory basis. The percept is an aspect of the internal model, an organising principle that produces categorisations in thought, feeling and perception. When a percept is familiar enough and the situation demands no greater differentiation, it will produce a direct perception of the object as an exemplar. Great familiarity leads to an unconscious organisation of perception.

It is often difficult to break out of this stable network of meanings. An everyday example of public percept is 'chair'. No sensory referent or group of referents defines a chair. Materials, shapes, legs, size, backs, all vary; in fact a hanging chair has no legs at all, but the concept 'designed to be sat in' unifies perception for all those for whom sitting in a chair is a recognisable function. Although both a bed and a stone may serve the function, not having been designed specifically for this purpose excludes them.

One perceptual organising principle serves to combine many different patterns of sensation into one mode of meaning. This mode has a unique position within a wider pattern of meanings. The pattern of meanings is the product of a group's similar interactions with the world around them, i.e. tasting Scotch whisky, racing cars or sitting on chairs.

The public percept grid allows a group to explore their shared perceptual language. Exemplars of the percept can be placed among elements that define a larger universe of discourse and the position of the exemplars within the focused grid will reveal the percept's defining characteristics. 'Grid games' with chairs and tables are played in nursery schools, whereas a detailed exploration of the taste percept 'green stick' may be a matter of crucial importance in the boardroom of a distillery.

It is interesting to note that the producers and salesmen of the same product often do not share the same perceptions of it. They share the same referent, the source of sensory data, but their purposes and their transactions with the product are so different that their percepts develop quite differently, linked into quite different patterns of meaning. Thus their views about quality and what constitutes a fault can easily be at variance.

The inferential grid

The sensory and public percept grids are both 'object related'. Their function is to enable a person or a group to identify a common referent or set of common referents. But earlier it was suggested that the process of perceiving is itself functional. The ball player was given as one example. The purpose is not to identify the ball. It is already identified in the dynamic context of the game. It is that which leaves the bowler's hand. What the ball player does is to perceive by anticipating and acting.

The inferential grid is a tool for exploring the networks of inference through which the immediate process of perceiving is linked into prediction for a specific purpose.

Our inspector of razor blades might be a quality control operative concerned to feed back information down the production line for adjustments to be made to the processing machinery. If so, his identification of 'second-grind fault' is no longer just a public percept, it becomes a basis for action. The pattern of meaning into which it fits is an operational one. It implies that the second grinder needs looking at. In actual fact, there are three adjustments that can be made to the second grinder and the quality controller can pick out eccentricity, worn stone and speed faults quite easily since he is continually checking out the validity of his perceptual categorisation against the results of the anticipations on which his actions are based.

But many inferences are mistaken. There is always a very peculiar mix of amazing insight and strongly, but wrongly, held mythology in the personal structure of meaning which a skilled man attributes to the tools, materials and products of his trade.

The mythologies of skill

Many coincidences in life are probabilistic. Sometimes A follows B. Sometimes it doesn't. Many consequences of actions are delayed and, therefore, overlaid by a series of alternative contributory causes. Most consequences of any value have a pattern of inter-related causes which are not easily isolated. Each of us makes what sense we can of our transactions with the world around us; building up our own mythology, a mix of operational understandings and rituals that give us the actuality or illusion of control.

The inferential grid is a tool for exploring such mythologies. The blood-letting witch-doctor, Merlin, and the medieval sword-maker all had mythologies proven to be effective in their contexts. We should exercise caution in being too quick to accept or reject the hard-won mythologies of the master craftsmen, be they teachers, trainers, therapists, coaches, counsellors or consultants. The pattern of 'mumbo-jumbo' words may well map on to the repeating patterns of personal experience. For two extreme examples we can look to the description of mental processes which lie embedded in the sacred books of Buddhism, and we can look to the workshop manual for 'landrover' maintenance. Psychologists are only now beginning to recognise the precision, coherence and relevance of the Buddhist perceptions. Users of the landrover manual will recognise how difficult it is to learn to perceive the real world under the bonnet in the terms of the motor mechanic.

To explore the mythologies of electronics is to enter into a world no less magical than Merlin's. The inference about performance and service life to be made from perceiving a pattern of soldered joints could be a life-time's psychological study in itself.

The inferential grid can articulate the evidence of hard-won beliefs from within which the pure gold of valid understanding can be mined. The intuitive technologies of one generation may disappear without trace or become the new sciences of the next. Acupuncture, homeopathic medicine, cordon bleu cookery, bricklaying, dog breeding, aesthetics, drain cleaning and cheese are all rich pools of inferential constructs. Which of them will generate pure gold?

The conversation for eliciting the elements of an inferential grid must crisscross back and forth between the source of the perceptual evidence and the consequences that are valued, or to be avoided. Gradually, the inferential chain emerges.

Using the three perceptual grids

In practice, the seemingly logical progression from sense-datum to percept to inference is not psychologically economic.

The technique which proves most successful is a pragmatic one. One can start by eliciting a set of elements relevant to the area of investigation and eliciting as many and as varied a set of constructs as possible. Now, keeping both the skill which is being explored and the sensation-percept-inference sequence in mind, the constructs can themselves be construed by the client. It is often useful to pool the constructs from the grids of a number of skilled practitioners and for each to complete a grid containing everybody's constructs. In discussion all the participants can then together decide which are sensory, which perceptual and which inferential. Then, by FOCUSing (chapter 4) all the grids, the patterns of relationships emerge.

This 'construing of constructs' grid can be used to move the focus of awareness up into inferences or down into sense data. The elements can be renegotiated and separate grids at each level can be elicited. Each grid can be FOCUSed. Then, by mapping the grids back on to each other, it becomes

possible to trace out how sense data cluster on to percepts and percepts lead
to inferences. The next section offers a systematic procedure by which this can
be done. The PERCEPTUAL GRIDS program takes the user conversationally
through the whole 'categorise, elaborate and recombine' activity. Fig. 8.5 shows
an algorithm of the perceptual grid procedure.

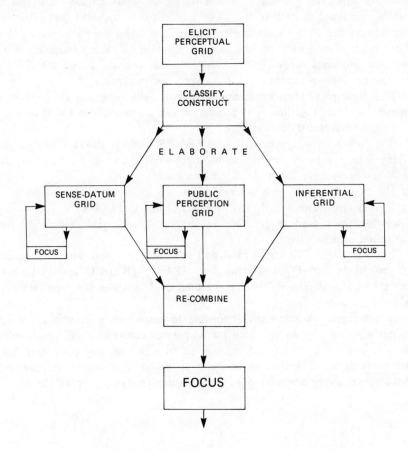

Fig 8.5 Perceptual grids: an algorithm

PAIRS: a method for re-combining the perceptual grids

Thus that part of construing which we have here called perception was usefully
seen to contain three types of construct:

(a) the sensory;
(b) the public percept;
(c) the inferential.

It is suggested that the same 'items of experience' which are attributed to referents which are physically present during the grid-elicitation conversation can be construed in each of these ways. Indeed it is suggested that all perception always has all three components in it. The technique of separating these three types of construct is introduced as a device for raising awareness of the personal processes of perception. This artificial analysis allows the client to explore one level of construing systematically and in depth.

It is now possible to synthesise these artificially separated components of perception back together. This process of successive analysis and synthesis is one key to perceptual development.

The technique of synthesis is called PAIRS, since it allows a pair of grids which share the same elements to be superimposed one on to the other. The technique is no more than FOCUS in a new guise.

The two perceptual grids are drawn on two differently coloured pieces of card. They are drawn exactly as if one were going to FOCUS them separately. Following the procedure described in chapter 4, each grid card is cut into horizontal construct strips.

But instead of FOCUSing each grid separately the two sets of constructs are combined and FOCUSed together. SPACE, TRIGRID and POLE-MAP can then be used. The differently coloured card indicates the type or source of the constructs.

It now becomes immediately possible to see which inferential constructs cluster with or map on to which public percept constructs: and which public percept constructs cluster with or map on to which sensory constructs. Used iteratively as was described in the stages of the grid conversation in chapter 6, this becomes a very powerful tool for the development of perceptual skills.

Chapter 9

The critical self: conversational self-assessment

Perceiving from within

Perhaps the potentially most useful area of application of perceptual grids is in the perceiving of our own inner processes. The brain receives sensory evidence from almost every part of the body. It selects and organises this and regulates the body accordingly. It is the 'special-hell' of Western modern man that he makes rather a mess of perceiving his own processes in terms which are physiologically, psychologically or emotionally predictive and operationally useful to him. His mythology of body processes misleads him into continual abuse of an incredibly complex, robust but sensitive system. As his misconstruing stabilises, he becomes beset by ill-health: from schizophrenia to migraine and from ulcer to backache. We need a perceptual language (non-verbal) for effectively perceiving and using what goes on inside us.

Skill always involves the perceptual organisation of sensory evidence from both inside and outside. In many jobs, a large component of the skill consists in handling one's inner processes effectively. Anger, joy, fear, elation, alienation, love and guilt are all valid and useful feelings, but often they are disruptive to the achievement of our purposes through our skills.

A careful elicitation and selection of elements can prove the starting point of an exploration of the relationships between internal states and external events. The nature of the skill to be explored will determine the choice of appropriate elements.

Perception can be seen as the process by which an individual imposes meaning on the outside and inner worlds of sensation. At the same time it can be seen as the process by which we can discover and explore meanings that do not yet lie within us. These two approaches to perception relate to two extreme modes in which it can operate. In skilled behaviour such as talking, perception is used to monitor a very familiar and well-tried activity. Most of the time we are unaware of hearing ourselves talk. It is only under exceptional conditions, such as delayed auditory feedback, that an interference with this monitoring process displays our normally unthinking dependence upon it. Under familiar skilled conditions perception operates to reduce redundancy and is channelled within pre-determining categories. When the situation is unfamiliar and our needs are muddled or complex, perception relaxes its organisation and search activity ensues. But modern man, perhaps all mankind, seems to very easily succumb to a rigidification of the perceptual process and becomes imprisoned in worlds of his own construction. Each of us manufactures our own robots. At first they serve us well, but unless we are careful these robots gradually steal away our spontaneity and openness to fresh experience. The sensory, public percept and inferential grids discussed in chapter 8 offer mechanisms for breaking out of such dogmatic perceptual construing of one's own processes. In this chapter we argue that self-organised learning depends upon the ability to monitor one's own inner world not only at the perceptual level but also evaluatively at the emotional and intellectual levels.

The critical self

The criticism of many practitioners of T-C which has been developed through-out this book might be summarised as follows. The educated man or woman is supposed to be autonomous, self-organised, informed, socialised and creative. But our educational experience appears to leave many of us disabled as learners. Organised learning experiences leave us far less than fully functioning. Being at school, in the family, at college, at play, at work or at university sometimes suppresses the positive self-evaluative capacity inherent in every man, woman and child. In the context of contemporary society this self-evaluation process appears to go wrong. It either becomes punitive, and the person becomes their own worst enemy, or it ceases to function adequately and the person becomes self-indulgent and uncontrolled. Often people suffer from some mix of both of these malfunctionings of the self-evaluative faculty at the same time. For example, whilst writing, many people (including the authors) are not able to monitor the quality of what is being written. The style and organisation of the content may therefore become sloppy, self-indulgent and uncontrolled. When the piece is written and then typed the writer becomes hypercritical and self-punitive, rejecting what has been written and either giving up or starting again from scratch.

The art of constructive self-assessment is to bring the full range of different self-evaluation processes into effective relationship one with another, rather than having them act out a series of incompatible self-confrontations. This process is described more fully in chapter 11 under 'the community of selves'.

The grid can be used to reveal the nature of the critical self not as an inner representation of some tyrannical significant other, but as an observant sympathetic but realistic companion able to converse fully with us. For example, a factory supervisor was encouraged to keep a diary of what he felt to be man-management incidents occurring during a week. He was then asked to do two grids, or rather to develop two sets of constructs within one grid (see the PAIRS section of this chapter for the EVALUATIVE grid). The elements were negotiated and clarified, being short events during his working day in which he had to 'handle someone'. A collaborative elicitation revealed both descriptive and evaluative constructs. The elicitation conversation is conducted to enable this foreman to reflect on his practical understanding of how he operates in these situations, and also to examine how he evaluates himself. Rating and FOCUS-ing revealed the pattern of his construing, and talkback through the FOCUSed EVALUATIVE grid helped him to begin to bring his critical self under review, moulding an over-anxious worrier into a helpful sympathetic but usefully evaluative comrade. As in industry, so in education: head teachers and children, professors and students can all be encouraged to review the critical processes they bring to bear in teaching/learning situations.

Referents and comment from the outside world

Most people are not short in critical comment about others and their perform-ances. The teenager in the family, the child in the classroom, the young adult at work and the wife and/or husband in the home are all liable to be offered a commentary on how some other people feel about the ways in which they behave. Education does not equip us to make effective use of such criticism. Nor does it enable us to generate conversation which would transform unusable but destructive commentary into a constructive source of reflective evaluative opinion.

Evaluative information offered by another has no direct influence over our actions. If we were deaf and did not know that it was being offered, we would go on as before. It is the meaning which we attribute to it as we listen to such evaluative information which influences us. Examination results, a manager's six-monthly appraisal, the comments of peers, or the praise and chastisement of teacher or parent, all have meaning; but the meaning attributed to the same comment will vary with different recipients. For example, there is a very real difference between accepting an examination result as a comment on one's current learning skill and application, as against becoming resigned to it as a classification of one's general innate ability. Most of us, most of the time, remain locked in our evaluative systems, stubbornly resisting or failing to make use of others' comments or being alternatively overwhelmed by them.

A central weakness of our formal educational system is that many people passing through it learn not to question and explore the extended meanings and implications that can be drawn from its evaluative operations. They never learn to evaluate the evaluation and to use the results optimistically, critically but constructively. The public pseudo-objective assessment offered is the per-sonal meaning which is all too often uncritically received. Since many of the evaluative operations in our society arise out of organisational and economic 'necessities' (e.g. 'A' levels, 'O' levels, apprenticeships, obtaining promotion, getting a bit of quiet, selecting sales staff, or sorting out university entrants), the pass-fail, good-bad connotations arise out of quite different perspectives than those within which they are received. This has the double-edged effect of producing an apparently docile acceptance of evaluative comment, until inner questioning, which has no negotiating outlet, builds up enough pressure for a forcible rejection of whole parts of the system. This can be equally as true for the academically 'successful' as for the academic 'failures'. In fact, to fail can be a liberating experience since it offers the possibility of withdrawal from the system and an opportunity to view the evaluation comment from a new perspective.

Holistic acceptance or rejection of the evaluative commentary offered by others always eventually results in alienation. A pathological splitting up of the integral inner self is induced. Structures of unaccepted evaluative meaning become encapsulated in the experiential world without that fine structure of interpretations which would enable them to play a coherent, detailed and constructive part in the orientation, guidance and control of one's inner life and externally oriented activities. Any monolithic internal evaluative system must inevitably be disruptive to the carefully evolved systems of meaning (the models) through which the individual is perceiving and acting upon the world. If as well as being disruptive they remain impervious to review, then they can become destructive to the whole effect to achieve competence in a given area of endeavour. Any family, commercial, educational or industrial milieu which builds such monolithic self-critical systems in its participants is a pernicious and dangerous threat both to its own well-being and to the mental health of the community or culture.

A radical change in the negotiation of evaluative comment as an informal aspect of the formal educational structure is a high priority for change. The change can only come if our images of man contain a much better and more elaborated understanding of the nature of this interpretive activity.

The meanings which may be attributed to the evaluative comments of others can take various forms.

1 Reference to the person

(a) The individual may attribute positive or negative value to himself as a person and therefore the effect may be to decrease or increase his self-esteem.

(b) Depending on the form which this takes, it may remain as purely classificatory self-esteem, e.g. 'I'm a good boy', 'I'm no good', or it may be inferential, leading on to 'I must try to . . .'.

2 Reference to the product

(a) The individual may attribute purely positive or negative value to the product of his performance, e.g. tear up an essay or painting; secretly keep a poem and read it to himself every so often.

(b) Or the person may be analytic and attempt to construe the offered evaluation into aspects or characteristics of the product which they can then attempt to change.

(c) The evaluation of product may be functional in terms of the conse-quences it achieves, e.g. 'the product is a good piece of writing because it gets across my message'.

(d) It may have implications for performance, i.e. 'the painting is good because of the play of light. I achieved that by the brushwork but it does not quite work for her shoe; what's wrong?'

3 Reference to performance

The comment may be interpreted as being about the process of the performance, i.e. the style of a cricketer. It may be derived as a measure of the product, e.g. batting average or number of wickets taken.

4 Reference to feelings

The evaluative comment may be directly about feelings, e.g. 'You are always so moody', or it may be formed to have such implications, e.g. 'Why are you always so bloody-minded?' Either way feelings are very difficult to control, change or constructively review. The trick is to track the source of the feeling and to handle it, or to diagnose the result of the feeling and to persevere through to new, more welcome results so that the causal chain of feelings is changed. On the other hand, 'good feelings' should be harnessed into the self-evaluative system so that productive and successful activity becomes self-sustaining.

5 Back to the person

The offered comment which is interpreted as being about the person can have a positive result. If recognised, questioned, carefully reviewed and still found to have good justification and to be based on realistic evidence, it can become a spur to creative change. This is achieved not by reflecting on the earlier self and trying to be different; that seldom works. The trick is to accept the earlier self using the good and gradually revising and reviewing feelings and performance to become more as one wishes to be.

Thus conscience may be a fully accepted quiet voice offering a useful and fully integrated meta-commentary on the process of learning and living, or it may be an alien tyrant continually shouting at, but never negotiating with, the everyday-living self.

The knotted ones: human components of self-evaluation

The images of man invented by Freud have enriched our understanding, but as a complete construing of the human condition they leave many people uneasy. Is it useful to believe that we are born split and possessed? Are we inhabited by a rapacious idiot out of which emerges a phantom unconscious that unbeknown to us pursues ends and meanings of its own? Are we dominated by a super-ego, that must be obeyed or placated if we are to experience peace? This community of incompatible selves is in some ways a seductive view of the inner world. It

offers hopes of salvation through a greater feudal communion. But the metaphor
has lost much of its power with the passing of the system of public meanings
from which it drew its strength: the culture and morality of pre-1914 Imperial
Vienna.

In our own time R. D. Laing has approached 'the same' experiential phenomena in a different way. For him it is a question of 'knots'. Faced with recurrent
incompatibilities in the 'real' world of direct sensory experience and perception
(e.g. the family), rational man or woman creates meanings that map on to these
incompatibilities. Thus the experiential world gets knotted, and the normally
neurotic man lives among his knots. To become unknotted requires the invention of a series of transitional meanings that are largely unacceptable to the
knotted person and to the knotted society in which they must be worked
through. Some of the knotted ones may be lucky enough to become involved
with others who can share an unravelling search for personally viable and relevant meanings. Most of us stay variously knotted. Gradually we ease our knots
into the comfortable havens and pastures of society's protective asylums. Marriage or a commune, boardrooms, toolrooms, mental hospitals or mental gym-
nasiums, the union branch, park benches or local government thrones, theatres
and the civil service, suburbia or Utopia, all accommodate man, loosening or
tightening his knots into more or less comfortable close-fitting chain-mail. Reich
has called this character armour. Laing himself has explored a few such havens
in his time from the Tavistock Clinic to a Tibetan monastery. Most of us prefer
the continuing sanctuary of the familiar.

Self-assessment is concerned with these problems. In every thought and
action there is a thread of evaluation or review. But familiarity breeds invi-
sibility and we remain unaware of the heavy constraints apparently imposed on
us by the structure of our species and the accumulation of personal experience.

The identification of feedback

If a tape recorder and headphones are arranged to delay the hearing of one's
own voice for about half a second, most people begin to stutter. If a mathematician gets a feeling that his calculation has gone astray, he is probably correct, but it may take him a considerable time to discover exactly what is wrong.
If our leg 'goes to sleep', we lose the feeling in it and we cannot walk. If we are
blindfold, and a very small electric current is passed between the ears, we fall
flat on our face because it disrupts the feedback from the semi-circular canals
upon which our balance depends. All-pervasive, the feedback on which our
stabilities are based is mostly non-conscious. Awareness usually occurs only
when the familiar feedback is disrupted.

To demonstrate the existence of feedback, put your arm behind you, away
from the body and out of view. Now spread the fingers of one hand and waggle
the forefinger. How do you know that it is waggling? You feel it! The kinaesthetic
sense, the sense organ in the muscles, is continually sending messages back to

the brain and all of our muscular co-ordination depends upon this. But only under exceptional circumstances, for example learning some new motor skill such as typing, juggling, winking, or wiggling the ears, does the familiar sensory information take on new meanings out of which we can generate new awareness.

A similar awareness may result from the disruption of the familiar pattern of established feedback in any area of skill or incompetence. In reading, writing, talking, feeding, sleeping, thinking, shivering or feeling, we use long-established models to generate the familiar patterns of meaning which we attribute to the consequences of our activities. So much so that biologists have until recently assumed that the control of most of our totally familiar body processes, for example blood pressure, pupil size, blood sugar concentration and so on was outside the range of conscious influence. The pioneer work of Neil Miller and the popularising phrase 'bio-feedback' indicate what was perhaps already well known to the Yogi.

Self-assessment is attributing meaning to the consequences of experiencing and behaving. The argument of this chapter is that such self-assessment is the vehicle of all self-organisation and control. Unfamiliar modes of feedback can be used to disrupt the robots, disturbing the existing patterns of feedback until they are reconstructed and again become familiar enough to drop back into non-conscious roboticism. But the patterns which emerge may produce 'knots' for Laing to unravel or new twists in the super-ego and the unconscious for the followers of Freud to explore. The patterns of meaning which are attributed to the consequences of our experience may not map on to the patterns of meaning out of which those consequences arose. The inner life may become split, but unaided we are unable to construe this incompatibility in ways that allow us to shift or release it. We simply get into hopeless cycles of good intentions and 'wrong outcomes' that lead into resigned if negative re-classifications of the self. 'Stupid', 'unmusical', 'psychotic', 'intellectually brilliant but emotionally unstable', 'a good solid plodder', 'I'm a bad person', are all terms for classifying the self into stability and then ultra-stability. They may be true of what you do. They are never completely true of what you are.

Self-assessment as a perceptual process

In chapter 8 perception was dissected into sensory, perceptual and inferential sources of meaning. Each perceptual act contained all three, but consciousness was focused only at one level at a time. Thus if a young art student is locked up for eight hours a day, for five consecutive days, with a wheelbarrow full of bricks, forbidden to talk, and asked to produce something, he is likely to experience some unusual sensory, perceptual, inferential and emotional construing of bricks. Inevitably this description plays itself out, either through the instabilities of his inner processes or through the creation of new externally viable forms; either way he will probably never feel the same again. For one student they may re-appear as a continuing theme in his artistic after-life, continually and creatively transmuted. For another they may become a recurrent source of dreams and nightmares. Basic perceptual processes of feedback, evaluation and self-assessment have been changed, but the new meanings achieved are different for each person.

This experiment, which actually happened, seems to me to have been perhaps an unwarranted intrusion into the private world of the student, and yet how many of us have escaped from being the victim of comparable experiences at school. Our later enjoyment, or emotionally charged avoidance, of mathematics, languages, music, cricket or some other subject or activity, can often be traced back to an enforced close continuing interaction with an originally unsought and unappreciated topic. The meaning we were able to create set up a feedback system which has influenced and controlled all of our subsequent interaction with the topic. It is not the teaching/learning events in themselves which produce these effects. It is the meanings which are attributed to the experiences as they develop. Thus the process of self-assessment during each event establishes the pattern of self-assessment which is brought forward to the next event. In the absence of personally sensitive learning conversations offering external support and focused review, this cumulative process rapidly stabilises and soon reaches an ultra-stable state. The learner becomes imprisoned within his own self-perpetuating system of evaluative meaning. This limits the range of events to which he is willing to expose himself. It also limits the actions he will take within any acceptable event and limits his perception of appreciable outcomes to those attributable within his own patterns of personal meaning. The emotional concomitants of each meaning gradually seal him in. This is how emotional blocks to learning are created.

This is our 'Learning-to-learn' perspective of what Laing, Freud and many other therapists from Christ to Perls are talking about.

The freedom created by a flexible sensitivity to sensory experience is diminished by the category systems which habit develops until at last a robot forms. This can lead to the acceptance of public percepts as the only coinage of sensory experience. The tourist who uses the guide (book) to structure his looking, rather than using it later to add meaning to his unique sensory exploration of new realms of experience, is a typical example.

Finally, the inferential meanings of events can lead to predictions and expectations that structure subsequent experience. This hierarchically structured pattern of meanings is the source of all stability. Mostly this is to be valued as the vehicle for continuing personal and social coherence. But in learning it can form a solid blockage to the achievement of all but the most trivial reconstruings. This situation can be seen repeated again and again throughout the educational system. The resources of the 'testing' psychologist and the beliefs of teachers and parents combine to reinforce the misconception that the many arbitrarily achieved, experientially stable conditions in the individual are biologically endowed. The repertory grid, particularly in its PERCEPTUAL and EVALUATIVE forms, offers one tool by which such stabilities can be challenged. From this base a fresh negotiation of evaluative processes can begin.

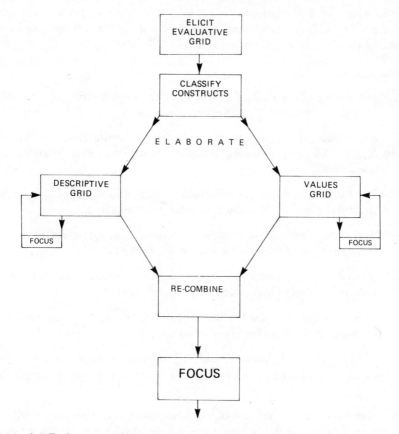

Figure 9.1 Evaluative grid: an algorithm

Self-evaluation of the reading process

In reading we consciously or unconsciously monitor the attribution of meaning to the printed hieroglyphics on the page. When the meanings in our head and the structure of black and white squiggles on the page agree, our eyes move on. When there is disagreement, the smooth forward flow of the reading is disrupted. The eyes hesitate, check, backtrack or skip forward and the 'meaning generator' in the head creates alternatives which are then tried out until a match is achieved.

The Brunel Reading Recorder traces out the behavioural aspects of this process. The repertory grid enables us to explore the nature of the self-evaluative monitoring processes at work. The READING-FOR-LEARNING computer package pursues this further (see Appendix B).

The following sentences were used as the reading material in a reading-to-learn experiment with sixth-form students studying biology. Three types of sentence were used: normal English, English with German syntax and scrambled English. The students were asked to read the sentences for the purpose of assessing the meaning in their own words.

The sentences

1   The pairing of codon and anticodon at the third position of the codon, to explain the wobble hypothesis rules provides.

2   Direct recognition for disease demonstrated acute notches, that the formylatable variety during catalytic reductions, failed to confirm in black time.

3   The fertilised egg has the remarkable ability to form all the complicated structures which are characteristic of the adult organism.

4   Which serve specific functions, a trend toward the specialization of cells, in the progression from simple to complex animals exists.

5   Information concerning the shapes of intact protein molecules can be obtained by X-ray structural analysis of crystals of the protein.

6   It is unfortunately possible that a few codons may be ambiguous, that is, may code for more than one amino acid.

7   A virus interfering substance called interferon is formed in appreciable quantities when heat-inactivated influenza virus is incubated in suitable cells.

8   There is no tailor made building determined cofactors since analysing knowledge grows in low magnesium circumferences involving penetration much faster.

9   Every cell normally contains equivalent chromosomes and identical DNA as a result of mitosis and this mechanism ensures genetic continuity.

10   The decipherment of groups of atoms takes place according to unknown enzymes therefore transcription is generated in bonds reading off.

11   As the fertilised egg passes into the uterus it adapted to receive the embryo, providing food and disposing waste is.

12   Mendel did not find gene linkage groups in the pea plant but he only tested seven pairs of alternative traits.

If the reader inspects sentences 3 and 4 they will find that whilst they both contain 20 words the syntactic (or grammatical) structure is very different.

A 'good' reader, i.e. one who scores high on the criteria tests, read these two sentences in the following way:

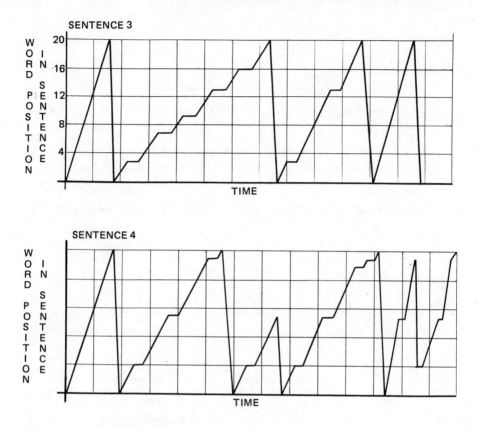

Figure 9.2 Sentence-reading patterns for a 'good' reader

The record of how sentence 3 was read showed that the reader was familiar with this syntactic structure. The record obtained when reading sentence 4 shows that a considerable amount of mental re-ordering of the words was necessary before they fitted into an internal syntax from which the reader could produce an acceptable outcome. A grid using the sentences as elements revealed the following constructs (Fig. 9.3).

It can be seen that this grid enables us to 'see into' the internal-review process which is going on whilst the sentence is read. The elaborate pattern of meaning available for assessing the matching process generates a subtle system of feedback which enables the reader to get to grips with the sentence purposefully and thus achieve his (evaluative) purpose.

In contrast the grids from unsuccessful readers showed: either

(a) an unelaborated feedback system yielding no control; or

(b) an irrelevantly elaborated system yielding inappropriate control and no success on the assigned task.

The read records (not shown) obtained from these unsuccessful readers show

WITH VERBAL LABELS

ELEMENTS

CONSTRUCT POLE RATED - 1 -   CONSTRUCT POLE RATED - 5 -

		E10	E2	E8	E1	E4	E11	E6	E12	E3	E7	E9	E5			
METHOD	RC8	5	5	5	5	4	4	3	4	2	2	4	1	RC8	FACTUAL
SIMPLE	C4	5	5	5	5	4	2	1	1	2	2	2	2	C4	COMPLEX
EASY	C2	5	5	5	3	3	3	1	1	1	2	2	2	C2	DIFFICULT
STRAIGHTFORWARD	C5	5	5	5	4	4	4	1	1	1	1	1	2	C5	INVOLUTED
MAKES SENSE WITH EFFORT	C10	5	5	5	4	4	4	1	1	1	1	1	1	C10	NEVER MAKES SENSE
DOES NOT WORRY ME	C9	5	5	5	3	4	3	2	1	1	1	1	1	C9	WORRIES ME
SENSIBLE	C3	5	5	5	3	3	3	1	1	1	1	1	1	C3	RUBBISH
READABLE	C6	5	5	5	3	2	2	1	1	1	1	1	1	C6	UNREADABLE
STRAIGHT	C11	5	5	5	1	3	3	1	1	1	1	1	1	C11	TWISTED
SHORT	C1	3	5	5	2	4	2	1	1	3	4	3	4	C1	LONG
BIOLOGICAL	RC7	5	2	3	3	2	2	3	1	1	3	3	4	RC7	CHEMICAL
LIVING TISSUES	RC12	5	4	2	2	2	1	4	2	1	2	3	4	RC12	ATOMS AND MOLECULES

*SENTENCE 5
*SENTENCE 9
*SENTENCE 7
*SENTENCE 3
*SENTENCE 12
*SENTENCE 6
*SENTENCE 11
*SENTENCE 4
*SENTENCE 1
*SENTENCE 8
*SENTENCE 2
*SENTENCE 10

Figure 9.3 Fred D'Arcy's FOCUSed grid with verbal labels

that they were unable to make sense of the sentence. Thus the grid indicates the un-organised reading behaviour, and the read record leads us to expect an unviable pattern of personal meaning in the grid.

Moving from the private to the public world of evaluation

Having explored the possibilities that evaluative meanings can be exchanged systematically and that differences in meaning can be measured and identified between private personally viable meanings and publically acceptable meanings more precisely, we are able to consider what Rogers has suggested as 'three types of knowing' in precise yet personally valid terms. Roger's three types are:

    (i) private knowing;
   (ii) interpersonal knowing;
  (iii) public knowing

For the purpose of self-assessment it is useful firstly to add a dimension of viability, i.e. 'It works when I use it' versus 'Does not work when I use it', and to differentiate the knowing into three: 'shares my meaning', and 'shares some part of my meaning', or 'does not share my meaning'. This enables us to differentiate modes of self-assessment:

1 Private inner defined criteria,
   i.e. feels right or wrong or incoherent
      v.
   consistent with my other knowing or inconsistent;
   coherent within itself.

2 Private (unshared by others) outer-defined criteria,
   i.e. enables me to achieve a certain range of purpose in a certain range of situations.

3 Interpersonal (shared with one other),
   i.e. meets with A's understanding;
   meets with A's critical evaluation;
   meets with A's approval.

4 Differentiated referents,
   i.e. certain knowing stands up to perusal by certain people or groups of people who serve as referents.

This way of construing self-assessment allows us to build up an effective and systematically varied and flexible reference network. Self-criticism is primary, but others' evaluative comment becomes part of the conversational encounter which promotes creative change. Grid techniques which allow inner and outer comparison to be made, thus making the self-reference explicit and raising awareness of the critical self, offer powerful aids for self-assessment. PAIRS, DIFF. and CORE are grid techniques for comparison.

The CHANGE grid procedures described later in this chapter offer the critical self systematic aids for monitoring personal change over time, and to reflect upon the uniquely personal principles of causality which influences this.

Extending the use of the PAIRS technique

Once the power of the PAIRS technique is recognised, it can be applied to a wide range of different types of grids and grid conversations. The algorithm of simple PAIRS shown in Fig. 9.4 summarises the procedure first introduced at the end of chapter 8. Figs 9.21(i)-(iii) at the end of this chapter illustrate how a married couple used this technique to explore their construing of mutual acquaintances. In the example in Activity 8.1 the reader was asked to elicit a grid from themselves on 'the perceptual components of human activities'. At the end of part 1 of chapter 8 the authors' construing of a list of such activities was offered and the reader was asked to compare their constructs with those of their partner. If the reader extracts those elements which are common between their partner's grid and their own they can use the PAIRS procedure to discover which of their constructs cluster with which of their partner's, and which of their construct poles map on to which of their partner's. This interpersonal use of the PAIRS technique is more fully developed in chapters 10 and 11.

Here the main theme of the chapter is how to achieve greater self-organisation. The PAIRS technique lends itself to this process in various ways. Firstly the constructs in a grid on a topic of central interest to a client can be categorised in various ways. For example, if readers elicit a grid from a T-C using events in the T-C activity as elements they might find it both interesting and useful to separate the descriptive constructs from the evaluative ones.

Two separate grids can then be independently developed in two separate grid conversations. When the readers feel they have sufficiently analysed their descriptions and their evaluations they can have a third conversation around the process of doing a FOCUSed PAIRS analysis. Similarly mathematics students can be encouraged to construe exam questions firstly in content terms, secondly in process terms and thirdly in terms of their emotional reactions to the questions. The list at the end of this chapter shows some of the constructs which were elicited from a group of students during such an activity. The uses of this technique for helping people to systematically explore how one type or area of their construing maps on to another is restricted only by lack of ingenuity on the part of practitioners and clients in identifying topics, elements and construct categories that facilitate such grid conversations. The INTERACTIVE PAIRS program allows two users to conversationally compare their grids. The

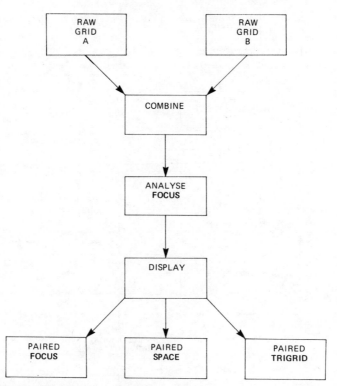

Figure 9.4 Simple PAIRS: an algorithm

reader may find it useful to construe the successive stages of analysis and synthesis in the FOCUSed PAIRS conversation as a cycle involving alternate phases of provisionality and decisiveness.

A more complete comparison of two grids can be achieved by the construct-by-construct PAIRS comparison summarised in Fig. 9.5. Every construct in each grid is compared with every construct in the other grid.

DIFF. and CORE

PAIRS is only one of a number of possible ways of comparing one grid with another. The method of comparison which is most suitable for any given project is that which the client in the learning conversation is best able to use. Choosing a method depends upon three considerations:
(a) the nature of the grids which are being compared;
(b) the purpose for which the grids are being used;
(c) the client's state of readiness for dealing with various forms of analysis.

A client may have elicited a grid and then later used 'the same' elements and constructs to complete a second version of the grid to record and make

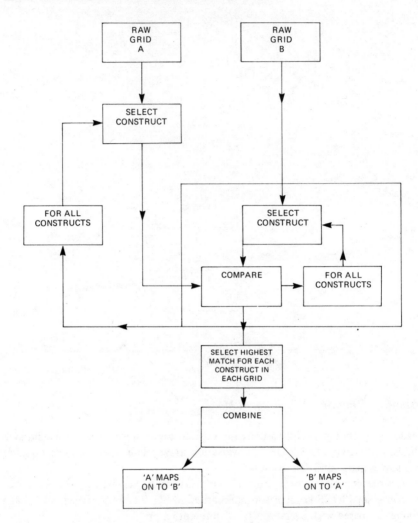

Figure 9.5 Construct-by-construct PAIRS: an algorithm

explicit any changes in construing which have occurred in the meantime.

DIFF. and CORE are methods for analysing two grids in which both elements and constructs are shared. Mr Production's 50 element by 30 constructs grid was used (but not shown) as the basis of one talkback conversation in chapter 5. Here part of his grid is compared with the equivalent part of one which he did two months later. A grid from this study is shown in chapter 11.

He used exactly the same constructs and elements on each occasion. It follows therefore that a comparison of the two grids will reveal where changes have accrued. The diagrams shown as Fig. 9.6 and Fig. 9.7 show the calculation for a segment of the complete grid. They show the first 10 elements and the first 10 constructs. He was using a five-point scale.

ELEMENTS

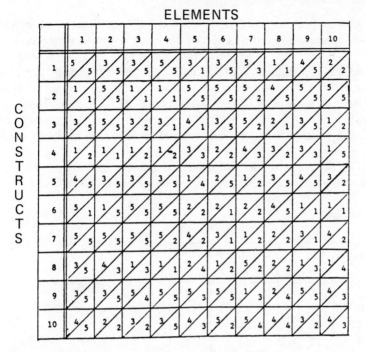

Figure 9.6 The double grid: ratings on two successive grids

ELEMENTS

	1	2	3	4	5	6	7	8	9	10	
1	0	+2	+2	0	−2	+2	−2	0	+1	0	11
2	0	0	0	0	0	0	−3	+1	0	0	4
3	+2	0	−1	−2	−3	+2	−3	−1	+2	+1	17
4	+1	0	+1	+1	0	0	−1	−1	0	+4	9
5	+1	+2	+2	+2	+3	+3	+1	+2	+1	−1	18
6	−4	+4	0	0	0	−1	0	+1	0	0	10
7	0	0	0	−3	−2	−2	+1	0	−2	−2	12
8	+2	−1	+2	0	+2	+1	−3	0	+2	+3	16
9	+2	+2	−1	0	−2	0	+2	+2	0	−1	12
10	+1	0	−1	+2	−1	−3	−1	0	−1	−1	11
	13	11	10	10	15	14	17	8	9	13	

CONSTRUCTS

Figure 9.7 The difference matrix

In the first diagram the numbers in the top left half of each cell are the ratings which appeared in the first grid and those in the bottom right hand half of each cell are those that appeared in the second grid. The second diagram shows the cells as containing the difference for each pair of ratings. By summing the differences in each column the amount of change in each element is calculated. The sum of differences in each row identifies the amount of change in each element.

This analysis revealed that some elements and some constructs change much more than others.

This DIFF. analysis is simple to calculate if the responses from both grids are entered on the same matrix. The results can be summarised as follows:

From least change

Elements	Diff.	Constructs	Diff.
E8	8	C2	4
E9	9	C4	9
E3	10	C6	10
E4	10	C1	11
E2	11	C10	11
E1	13	C7	12
E10	13	C9	12
E6	14	C8	16
E5	15	C3	17
E7	17	C5	18

To most change

To illustrate the method without becoming unduly elaborate this example has been simplified. These figures apply only to the 10 elements and 10 constructs that are shown and do not reflect the actual results for the 50 by 30 gird. Once the client has appreciated the nature of these changes reference back to the numerical matrix allows them to see exactly how the changes have proceeded.

CORE takes this process of comparison further. The differences shown above reveal E7 as the element which has changed most. E7 is therefore contributing most to the changes which have occurred in the constructs. Removing the most changed element reduces the amount of change in the constructs.

The following figures illustrate how successive removal of the most changed element and then the most changed construct rapidly reveals a CORE grid in which the most stable elements and constructs remain (Fig. 9.8A-K). The client can then be talked back through the changes by going back through the matrixes in reverse order.

	1	2	3	4	5	6	7	8	9	10	
1	0	+2	+2	0	-2	+2	-2	0	+1	0	9
2	0	0	0	0	0	0	-3	+1	0	0	1
3	+2	0	-1	-2	-3	+2	-3	-1	+2	+1	14
4	+1	0	+1	+1	0	0	-1	-1	0	+4	8
5	+1	+2	+2	+2	+3	+3	+1	+2	+1	-1	17
6	-4	+4	0	0	0	-1	0	+1	0	0	10
7	0	0	0	-3	-2	-2	+1	0	-2	-2	11
8	+2	-1	+2	0	+2	+1	-3	0	+2	+3	13
9	+2	+2	-1	0	-2	0	+2	+2	0	-1	10
10	+1	0	-1	+2	-1	-3	-?	0	-1	-1	10

Remove
E7

Figure 9.8A Revealing the CORE grid: step one

	1	2	3	4	5	6	7	8	9	10
1	0	+2	+2	0	-2	+2	-2	0	+1	0
2	0	0	0	0	0	0	-3	+1	0	0
3	+2	0	-1	-2	-3	+2	-3	-1	+2	+1
4	+1	0	+1	+1	0	0	-1	-1	0	+4
~~5~~	~~+1~~	~~+2~~	~~+2~~	~~+2~~	~~+3~~	~~+3~~	~~+1~~	~~+2~~	~~+1~~	~~-1~~
6	-4	+4	0	0	0	-1	0	+1	0	0
7	0	0	0	-3	-2	-2	+1	0	-2	-2
8	+2	-1	+2	0	+2	+1	-3	0	+2	+3
9	+2	+2	-1	0	-2	0	+2	+2	0	-1
10	+1	0	-1	+2	-1	-3	-3	0	-1	-1
	12	9	8	8	12	11		6	8	12

Remove
C5

Figure 9.8B Revealing the CORE grid: step two

	1	2	3	4	5	6	7	8	9	10	
1	0	+2	+2	0	−2	+2	−2	0	+1	0	9
2	0	0	0	0	0	0	−3	+1	0	0	1
3	+2	0	−1	−2	−3	+2	−3	−1	+2	+1	13
4	+1	0	+1	+1	0	0	−1	−1	0	+4	4
5	+1	+2	+2	+2	+3	+3	+1	+2	+1	−1	
6	−4	+4	0	0	0	−1	0	+1	0	0	10
7	0	0	0	−3	−2	−2	+1	0	−2	−2	9
8	+2	−1	+2	0	+2	+1	−3	0	+2	+3	10
9	+2	+2	−1	0	−2	0	+2	+2	0	−1	9
10	+1	0	−1	+2	−1	−3	−1	0	−1	−1	9

Remove E10

Figure 9.8C Revealing the CORE grid: step three

	1	2	3	4	5	6	7	8	9	10
1	0	+2	+2	0	−2	+2	−2	0	+1	0
2	0	0	0	0	0	0	−3	+1	0	0
3	+2	0	−1	−2	−3	+2	−3	−1	+2	+1
4	+1	0	+1	+1	0	0	−1	−1	0	+4
5	+1	+2	+2	+2	+3	+3	+1	+2	+1	−1
6	−4	+4	0	0	0	−1	0	+1	0	0
7	0	0	0	−3	−2	−2	+1	0	−2	−2
8	+2	−1	+2	0	+2	+1	−3	0	+2	+3
9	+2	+2	−1	0	−2	0	+2	+2	0	−1
10	+1	0	−1	+2	−1	−3	−1	0	−1	−1

Remove C3

10 9 7 6 9 9   5 6

Figure 9.8D Revealing the CORE grid: step four

	1	2	3	4	5	6	7	8	9	10	
1	0	+2	+2	0	-2	+2	-2	0	+1	0	9
2	0	0	0	0	0	0	-3	+1	0	0	1
3	+2	0	-1	-2	-3	+2	-3	-1	+2	+1	
4	+1	0	+1	+1	0	0	-1	-1	0	+4	3
5	+1	+2	+2	+2	+3	+3	+1	+2	+1	-1	
6	-4	+4	0	0	0	-1	0	+1	0	0	6
7	0	0	0	-3	-2	-2	+1	0	-2	+2	9
8	+2	-1	+2	0	+2	+1	-3	0	+2	+3	8
9	+2	+2	-1	0	-2	0	+2	+2	0	-1	7
10	+1	0	-1	+2	-1	-3	-1	0	-1	-1	8

Remove
E1

Figure 9.8E Revealing the CORE grid: step five

	1	2	3	4	5	6	7	8	9	10
1	0	+2	+2	0	-2	+2	-2	0	+1	0
2	0	0	0	0	0	0	-3	+1	0	0
3	+2	0	-1	-2	-3	+2	-3	-1	+2	+1
4	+1	0	+1	+1	0	0	-1	-1	0	+4
5	+1	+2	+2	+2	+3	+3	+1	+2	+1	-1
6	-4	+4	0	0	0	-1	0	+1	0	0
7	0	0	0	-3	-2	-2	+1	0	-2	+2
8	+2	-1	+2	0	+2	+1	-3	0	+2	+3
9	+2	+2	-1	0	-2	0	+2	+2	0	-1
10	+1	0	-1	+2	-1	-3	-1	0	-1	-1
	7	7	6	7	7		5	5		

Remove
C1

Figure 9.8F Revealing the CORE grid: step six

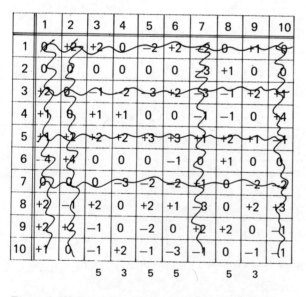

	1	2	3	4	5	6	7	8	9	10		
1	0	+2	+2	0	-2	+2	-2	0	+1	0	1	
2	0	0	0	0	0	0	-3	+1	0	0		
3	+2	0	-1	-2	-3	+2	-3	-1	+2	+1	3	
4	+1	0	+1	+1	0	0	-1	-1	0	+4		
5	+1	+2	+2	+2	+3	+3	+1	+2	+1	-1	2	Remove E2
6	-4	+4	0	0	0	-1	0	+1	0	0	9	
7	0	0	0	-3	-2	-2	+1	0	-2	-2	7	
8	+2	-1	+2	0	+2	+1	-3	0	+2	+3	5	
9	+2	+2	-1	0	-2	0	+2	+2	0	-1	8	
10	+1	0	-1	+2	-1	-3	-1	0	-1	-1		

Figure 9.8G Revealing the CORE grid: step seven

	1	2	3	4	5	6	7	8	9	10		
1	0	+2	+2	0	-2	+2	-2	0	+1	0		
2	0	0	0	0	0	0	-3	+1	0	0		
3	+2	0	-1	-2	-3	+2	-3	-1	+2	+1		
4	+1	0	+1	+1	0	0	-1	-1	0	+4		Remove C7
5	+1	+2	+2	+2	+3	+3	+1	+2	+1	-1		
6	-4	+4	0	0	0	-1	0	+1	0	0		
7	0	0	0	-3	-2	-2	+1	0	-2	-2		
8	+2	-1	+2	0	+2	+1	-3	0	+2	+3		
9	+2	+2	-1	0	-2	0	+2	+2	0	-1		
10	+1	0	-1	+2	-1	-3	-1	0	-1	-1		
			5	3	5	5		5	3			

Figure 9.8H Revealing the CORE grid: step eight

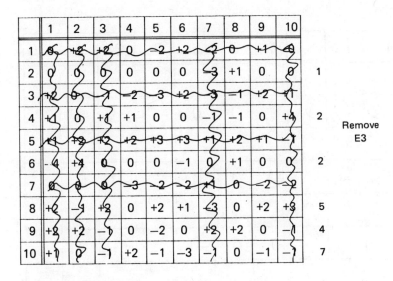

Figure 9.8I Revealing the CORE grid: step nine

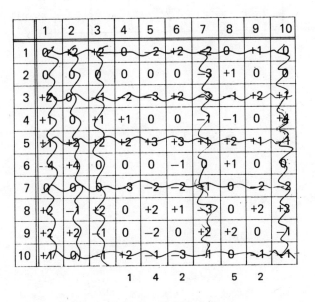

Figure 9.8J Revealing the CORE grid: step ten

	1	2	3	4	5	6	7	8	9	10
1										
2				0	0	0		+1	0	
3										
4				+1	0	0		−1	0	
5										
6				0	0	−1		+1	0	
7										
8				0	+2	+1		0	+2	
9				0	−2	0		+2	0	
10										

Figure 9.8K The CORE grid

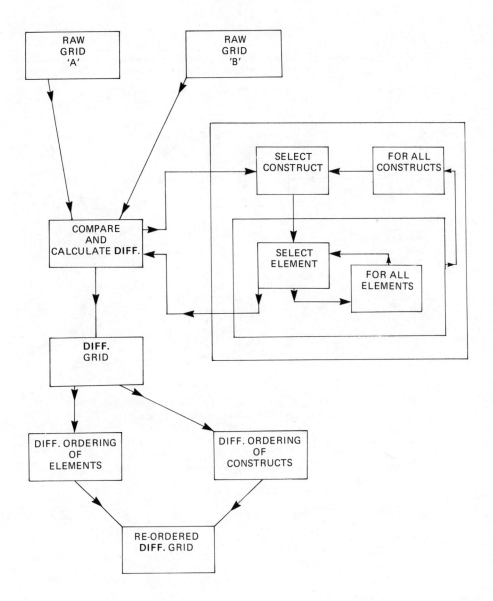

Figure 9.9 DIFF. – the difference grid: an algorithm

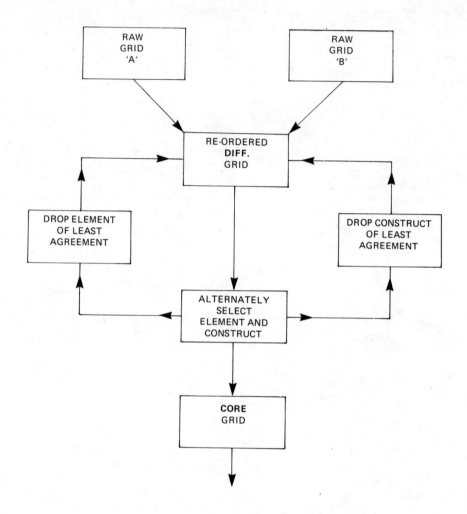

Figure 9.10 CORE grid: an algorithm

The CHANGE grid: a conversational heuristic for self-development

Helping the individual become aware of the nature of personal change involves a reconsideration of a person's views of causality. It forces them to re-evaluate their ideas about what goes with what. For the practitioner this is a crucial issue since it influences what the T-C chooses to deal with so that individuals may be enabled to develop themselves. In chapter 1 the idea of personal myths about learning was introduced. Here the concern is with those components of the process of learning that appear to influence personal change. One obvious fact is that a person's capacity for change is a function of their ability to imagine alternative futures. Imagination is prior in the sense that it is our means of interpreting the world. It is our means for forming images in the mind. It is the process by which we construct meaning. The images are not separate from our interpretations of the world. They are our way of thinking and feeling about the objects in the world. We see the forms in our mind's eye and we see these forms in the world. We could not do one without the other. The two abilities are joined in our ability to understand that the forms have a certain meaning. They have a quality that signifies other things beyond themselves. It may be useful to use the term imagination for what allows us to go beyond the barely sensory into the thought and emotion-endowed territory of perception. This is what the inferential grid aims to illuminate.

The viewpoint which has been emerging out of the work of CSHL is that the process of creating meaning is prior. This process is essentially conversational in the sense that we used this term in chapter 6 with respect of the grid conversation.

What is required is a technology which can take the individual beyond the mere awareness of personal meaning into an awareness of how meaning is created, changed and developed. When the repertory grid is used to explore the nature of personal change one must go beyond the reflection of just one grid to a consideration of how the person's construing is changing and developing over some period of time. A sequence of grids can be used to trace this change. Earlier the techniques of PAIRS, DIFF. and CORE have introduced the idea of comparing the sensory grid with the inferential grid. These all superimpose one grid upon another. Here these methods are combined.

The CHANGE grid is essentially a FOCUSed grid of events as seen by one person at a certain point in time. Superimposed on this is information about how his or her construing has changed from that elicited about 'the same topic' at an earlier point in time. Specifically it is a comparison of two grids displayed on a FOCUSed version of the second. In addition to a direct comparison of how the assigning of elements to constructs has changed, new elements and new constructs may be introduced to reveal changes in the scope and definition of the topic. Fig. 9.11 illustrates the CHANGE grid of a company manager. Personally known managers were used as elements.

The overall pattern shows differentiation of elements and constructs. E8 is rated on the same pole ($\sqrt{}$) of all constructs. E7 is rated on the opposite pole

Figure 9.11 A CHANGE grid for a manager

of all constructs (X). The circles around certain responses indicate the ones that have changed between the first and second grids. E9 shows five changes out of fifteen. RC9 also demonstrates five changes.

Most of the six new elements (i.e. E10-15) have FOCUSed into the right-hand side of the grid extending and differentiating this aspect of the topic. These are indicated by the responses contained within the enclosing lines in the grid. Four of the six new constructs (i.e. C10-15) have clustered together showing a new emphasis in the client's construing of the topic.

Thus the CHANGE grid is designed as a transparent display of how the client's construing appears to be changing. In talkback through the CHANGE grid the client is encouraged to explore the personal causality of these changes. The CHANGE grid program does this complete analysis. Figs. 9.12, 9.13, 9.14 illustrate the CHANGE grid procedures.

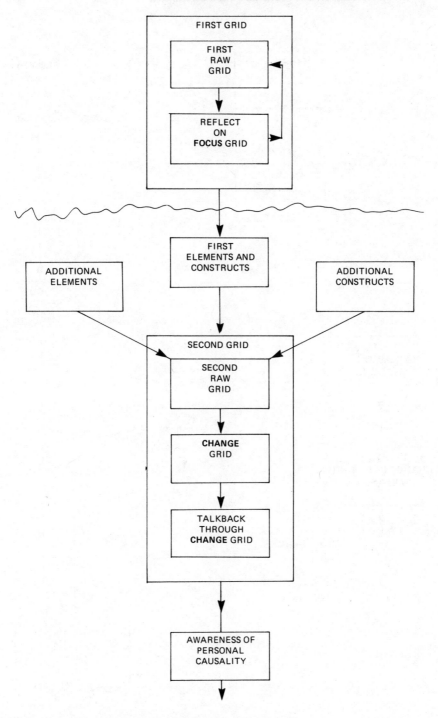

Figure 9.12 The CHANGE grid conversation: an algorithm

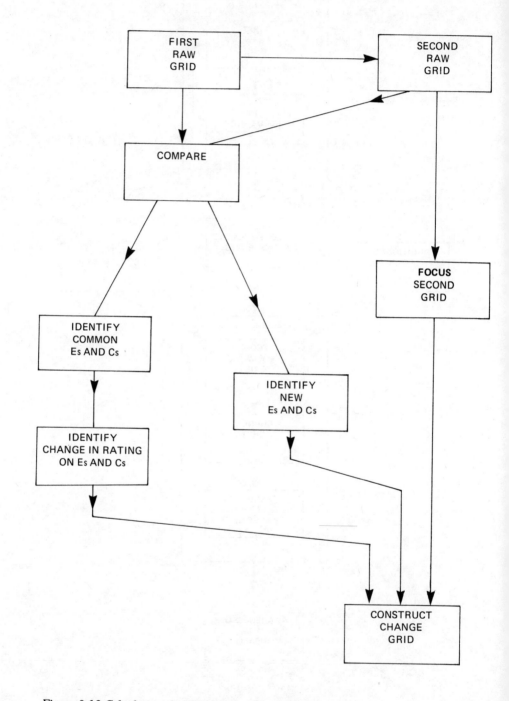

Figure 9.13 Calculating the CHANGE grid:an algorithm

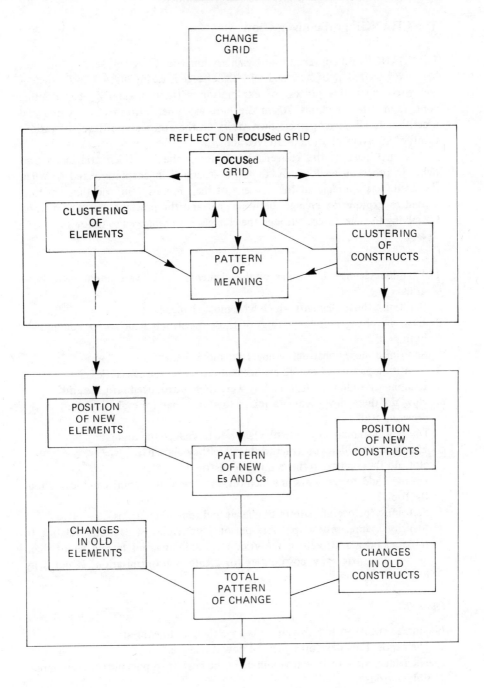

Figure 9.14 Talkback through the CHANGE grid: an algorithm

The CHANGE grid conversation

The CHANGE grid conversation is again asymmetric. The client seeks to discover her or his own view of how and why the change is taking place. The T-C guides and encourages this process of exploration without necessarily contributing content or interpretations. Again the pure asymmetric form rarely exists and practitioners all develop their own views on the ethics and efficacy of various forms of intervention or non-intervention.

The first part of the conversation is about the FOCUSed grid in its own right. It proceeds analogously to those described in chapters 5 and 6. When the client has appreciated the content of their more recent grid they are then invited to explore the changes between that and the previous one. The method for talking the client back through the changes is summarised as follows:

Phase A

1 Examine changes in ratings of the elements which were common to both grids.
   Scrutinise those elements which have most changed.
2 Examine changes in the ratings of those constructs which were common to both grids.
   Scrutinise those constructs which have most changed.
3 Identify a pattern of overall change and reflect on the causalities.
4 Examine the added elements. Why were these introduced into the grid?
   How do these new elements relate to those that were already used in the previous grid?
   Do they systematically extend, elaborate or change the topic?
5 Examine the added constructs. Why were they chosen?
   How do these relate to the common constructs?
   Do they add to the ways in which the client perceives, thinks and feels about the topic?
6 Scrutinise the overall pattern of change and reflect upon this.
7 Identify as precisely as possible personal principles of causality relating to those changes reflected in the grid. Does thinking and feeling about them in this way offer any possibilities for greater self-organisation? If not, why not?

Phase B

Encourage clients to add, discard or change the grid to express:
1 Their most fully developed view of how it really is.
2 Their ideal view of how it would be in the best of all possible (or even impossible) worlds.
3 Their view of what they can realistically hope for in the near or foreseeable future.

Conversational examples

Example A

Gwen, an Open University post-experience student taking a Reading Development Course, was concerned about improving the range and operational efficiency of her purposes for reading. An individual elicitation interview enabled Gwen to explore reading experiences which were personally relevant and representative of her approach to learning. This was reported in chapter 5.

Gwen continued with her studies for six weeks and was taken through a second elicitation interview to identify a set of reading purposes. Gwen was asked to match 'new' purposes on to her original 9 purposes and to identify the *really new* purposes. These were combined with the old set to produce a second grid. This grid elicitation procedure comprised two stages. All the new and old elements were assigned to the poles of the original constructs. The original ratings were not made available. New constructs were elicited which Gwen felt now fully represented her view of purposes to be achieved by reading. All the new and old elements were assigned to the poles of these new constructs. This second grid was FOCUSed and displayed in the form of a CHANGE grid (Fig. 9.15).

Talkback through the CHANGE grid

The following explanations were offered by her:

T-C: If we examine the changes you have made in your ratings of all the elements on all the constructs it does appear that you have modified your views on:

E2   'To learn the photosynthesis equation'
E13   'To evaluate the author's argument'
E3   'To find out how to do an experiment'
E1   'To find out what materials a plant needs for photosynthesis'
E11   'To summarise the author's main ideas'

Gwen: I don't think my view of E2 has changed much except that I see this more clearly as a 'literal' Barrett-type learning task. In one sense this purpose sounds fairly complicated but since all the information is in the teacher-notes all I have to do is 'learn' it, i.e. memorise.

I think changes in E13, 3 and 1 are more significant to me. You remember in our first grid conversation I wanted to explore further my construct 'Elucidate my own view'. Well, I had a good look at various purpose taxonomies offered on the Reading Course, Barrett's and Bloom's in particular, and I decided to make real efforts to categorise my own reading purposes more clearly. I now see E13, 3 and 1 as more open-ended reflective tasks where I can put a lot more of *me* into them. . . . But I see E11 like E2 as more factual and disciplined. . . .

T-C: Let's look at some constructs. . . .

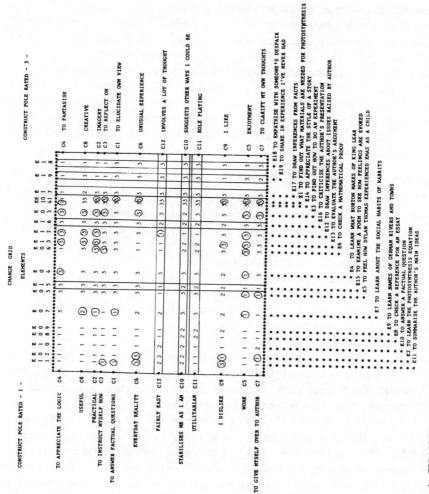

Figure 9.15 Gwen's CHANGE grid on purposes for reading

Gwen: Yes, C2 and 8. I have used far more of the 'Imagery' and 'Creative' poles of these constructs. This again ties up with my concern to develop further 'Elucidate my own view', C1. As you see, I have remained fairly stable on this one. Again, construct 5 is a very important one — here I have distinctly changed my views of reading purposes E6, E13, E12, E3 and E1. I now *enjoy* these because I see them in a different light — as reflective tasks, whereas before I saw them as more to do with academic learning and factual.

It surprises me a bit to find that I now see E4, 5 and 1 as 'More to do with work' than 'Enjoyment' but I think this is because I have tried to view these purposes through the eyes of Barrett and I have become very analytical about them... but I still enjoy these. I think the C5 which distinguishes between 'work' and 'enjoyment' is beginning to become artificial. . . .

Again, I think getting to know more about how to define reading purposes and about types of comprehension by doing all these activities on the course has influenced me here, I really do *like* most reading I do now.

T-C: Now, if we look at the added elements. . . .

E15 aligns very closely with E5
and
E16 with E3
so neither of these 'reading purposes' have extended your range of thinking. . . .

Gwen: No, I see that E15 is almost a paraphrase of E5 and E16 goes with E3 because I see both as being open-ended. . . .

E17 has added something new though, not so much because of the Reading Course but because of another course I'm taking on social reality. . . . facts need not be reified. . . .

Again, E18 and 19 are similar but together do add something new, which is to more deliberately, i.e. consciously, give myself over to the world of a good prose writer. . . .

Again, the work we did on 'literature' on the Reading Course influenced me here I think... the idea of the 'inner' and the 'outer' worlds of reality and of how these can be expressed in prose. . . . Of the added constructs, C10 is the most significant for me. . . . I am much more aware in going through my Reading Course of alternate realities... different ways of assessing things... the relativism of all knowledge. . ., I see myself in a different light. . . . But this is becoming a real problem for me... at work... in my job as a teacher and as a post-experience student. . ., I am finding it hard to keep this changing view in mind. . . . I find myself slipping back to my old ways of thinking about things — when one's in a rush and the kids are undisciplined its easy to slip back and on the whole one gets better credit from my headmaster if I keep the class quiet . . . and give them straight factual things to learn, Literal Purposes à la Barrett *in fact*!

Gwen was awarded a Grade 1 on her course. According to her, the awareness-raising and review opportunities offered to her in tutorial had significantly contributed to her award. Each member of the tutorial group were given similar opportunities. The examination results of the group showed a significantly higher distribution of Grades 1 and 2 than any other tutorial group in the country.

Example B

Sam and Harry were middle managers participating in a course in management development. Conversational grids were used to encourage them to reflect upon their job and to develop new ways of effective management. The elements in their grids were 'management events'. Three grids were elicited; one at the beginning, the second in the middle and the third three months after the course. In the first grid 12 elements were elicited. In the second grid they added 3 new elements and 3 new constructs. In the third they added yet another set of 3 new elements and constructs.

> Sam: When trying to find explanations for the correlation of constructs and elements in my first grid I experienced a real insight. Working closely over the last 1½ years with a new computer system, I tended to see PROBLEMS as a job problem relating to MACHINERY and SYSTEMS. My grid showed me that my PROBLEMS were PEOPLE PROBLEMS, and not as my 'blinkered' approach was showing. When reflecting on this in relation to other parts of the training course, certain specific problems I had at work were positively resolved.
>
> Two added constructs which extended my repertoire were highly correlated. Both these were to do with people.
>
> Constructive response from   v.   Unconstructive response
> affected parties
>
> Satisfactory outcome   v.   Unsatisfactory outcome
>
> This was a new way of thinking for me.
>
> Another added construct which extended my thinking consisted of seeing problems as:
>
> Single   v.   Multiple
>
> On examining my third grid, one additional construct was new for me –
>
> Act as management   v.   Act as employee

This relates to one experience at work after the course. With the absence of higher line management, I became involved in a personal staff problem where two members of staff had not in recent months hidden their dislike of each other. There was a confrontation where the senior male member of staff expressed his displeasure at the junior female member in her presentation of figures. Whereas in the past I would have tried to avoid the situation and hope for extinction, I felt confident in dealing with the situation. With unconscious and then conscious use of TA and B MOD techniques I was able to deal with the situation with greater confidence, knowing I could control it and take satisfactory action, which I am sure I would not have been in a situation to do some time ago.

Harry: Several aspects of the grid were very revealing for me. The evidence of change from the first to the second grid and from the second to the third grid has pushed me to consider whether these are really valid for me and the influences which might have caused them.

The addition of the construct

C14: Giving insight into personality   v.   Does not give insight

was definitely influenced by the course, which throughout stressed the importance of understanding personalities and behaviour.

Influenced by this impact, I changed my ideas about a number of elements and their construct relationships.

Construct 1 showed me that a number of —

informal   v.   formal

relationships had changed and that informal relationships are increasingly important to me.

Construct 4 Important consequences   v.   Unimportant

revealed that the events I now regard as important consequences tended to be the 'relation' type and not the 'result' type.

Constructs 13 and 15 were added between the first and second week of the course and these show up to be very similar.

Aids future strategies   v.   No value to future strategy
Enables more effective effort   v.   Worsens or at best maintains

Together they do expand my thinking beyond the majority of the original constructs, which are 'ME' orientated, to include a company importance as if I were taking a detached viewpoint.

Upon examining how I now feel, I must say that it suddenly occurs to me that I identify more with my position in my first grid. I feel that in my second grid I was exhibiting the 'fresh' influence of the course, which manifests itself in the changed constructs, whereas now the effects of the course are diminishing and I am reverting to my original stereotyped view.

Upon reflection of my *third grid*, several personal comments seem valid. Constructs 13 and 15, which I added in the second grid and at the time I saw these as very similar, have now become devastatingly different. I now find that in the light of examining the reasons behind people's actions I am relating Construct 13 —

      Aids future strategy   v.   No value to future strategy

more *personally to me*, while Construct 15 —

      Enables more effective effort   v.   Worsens or at best maintains

I still relate *companywise*. This ties in with Construct 11 —

      Solving problems   v.   Leading to problems,

which is also company orientated.

> *In the general sense I still feel that I am relating to my original responses but now in the light of knowledge gained on the course, this response is from a more informed outlook on situations in the real world, and an understanding of why particular things happen and why particular people react in a specific way.*
>
> Constructs and elements group into clusters that I am now expecting to be similar whereas before the course I may not have been able to comprehend and get insight into these similarities between the ways in which I view events.
>
> Element 14 — 'Meeting in Technical Manager's Office'
>
> I have changed my view of this considerably in the light of more experience, enabling me to look beneath the surface of this event and the reasons and the consequences of it. *I now begin to see that there were entirely different reasons and results for the events that took place.*
>
> Whereas I once related formal relationships with company positions, I now feel that there is an unstated series of relationships between individuals which may in fact be very formal.

Sam's appraisal in the company has moved from Grade D to Grade A. Harry has left to take up a post of higher responsibility in another company. Fig. 9.16 summarises an awareness-raising heuristic for personal learning and change.

Conversation: the mind's construction of the mind

Despite the validity of some philosophical and scientific arguments against the concept of mind, it can be very useful in practical everyday affairs. But the illusion that there is in any one person a finite, fixed and static mind is a fundamental flaw in any approach to learning. It is an even greater impediment to using a conversational approach for enhancing people's capacity for learning. Mechanistic views of mind are embodied in many people's personal myths about themselves and about others. Such personal myths are so firmly embedded in most Western minds that people in education, medicine and psychology have developed tests of intelligence, natural abilities, aptitudes and personality

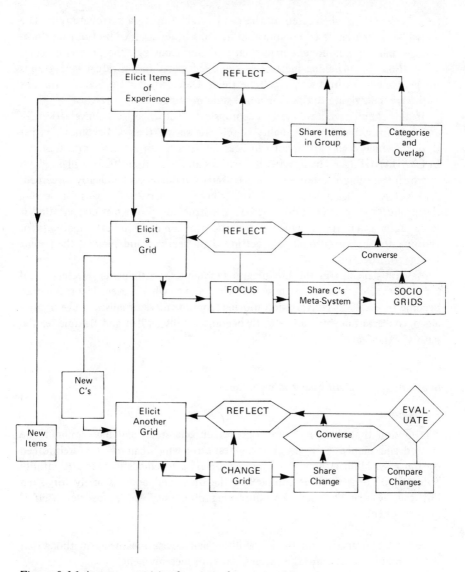

Figure 9.16 Awareness-raising heuristic for personal learning

which assume fixed and limited potential. In so classifying people at important points in their life these perpetuate such myths even unto the third and fourth generation. Much modern public knowledge has either rejected subjectivity as being too ephemeral for serious study or it so restricts its constructions of the mind that it denies the natural structure and infinite potential of human conversation.

Brains in bodies communicating with other brains in other bodies are all too easily under-estimated. The capacity of the mind to reconstruct and thus transcend itself is obstructed by the dead hand of many a personal myth. The incredible potential of communicating humans is undermined by these mythical sources and the consequent inadequacy of our models of the process of communication. In mistaking ineffective stabilised states in individuals and groups for permanent features we perpetuate them. Descriptive and psychometric uses of the grid contribute to this embalmed state of mind.

In this chapter we have tried to demonstrate that when used conversationally as a tool for enhancing the quality of self-assessment, the grid becomes a mirror through which each participant can become more aware of their critical selves. In EXCHANGE (see chapter 10) it becomes an image-intensifier (or night glass) in which the mind of another which is usually hidden can be clearly discerned. As EXCHANGE leads to a shared grid, it begins to serve as a means for viewing the products of conversation. Used to construe the process of conversation it serves again as a mirror in which each participant can develop better methods for charting the conversational sea, getting their bearings and making their joint voyages of discovery.

As skill develops in the use of grid techniques, participants develop a feel for which techniques to use, how and when and to what degree. The techniques become true aids to conversation moving from the mere ritualistic usage of grid-aided conversation 'by numbers' to become a fully skilled and flexible 'explanatory' experience.

Self-assessment: additional grid techniques

1 Talkdown

The illusion that there is in any one person one static and basic mind to be fixated and pinned up is the fundamental error which can easily be reinforced by the grid. Mind is now the construction of a mechanistic age. The infinite potential of a network as complex as the brain and body is easily forgotten but can be demonstrated. Its continuing propensity to reconstruct itself is ignored when:

(a) we concentrate on these stabilities and devise measuring methods that build stability into the social context of measurement;
(b) the psychological and social context creates the conditions of self-fulfilling hypotheses or self-reinforcing habitual mechanisms.

As a tool for enhancing conversation inside one person the grid becomes something else again. It becomes a mirror and must take on mirror-like qualities.

The one property of a mirror is the immediacy of its reflection. Yesterday's grid becomes merely a discarded image. The grid must produce a rapid reflection (self-administered FOCUSing methods aim at this). A 90 per cent reliable image now is worth a hundred 99 per cent reliable images next week. This is one point of departure between grid describers and grid conversationalists. Only if the image is quickly available can the conversation proceed.

If the grid is a mirror we must learn how to look into it. If we posture, we are seen to posture. We need magnifying mirrors for close work. A hand mirror does not give us a full-length view. Looking into the mirror is analogous to the elicitation of the grid. What we see depends on how and where we look. The talkdown is all important. The range of elements determines the size of the mirror but the type of construct elicited will depend upon the state of mind into which the participant is placed or places himself. All the expertise and difficulty of interviewing technique applies to the elicitation of grids. Depth interviews, open-ended interviews, structured interviews, all have their grid elicitation counterparts. The skill is in guiding and orienting the process without putting words or ideas into the mouths of the participants and thus into their grid.

In talkdown there are three methods of orientation:

(a) the role grid
(b) the task grid
(c) the situation grid

(a) The role grid: This helps in talking the participant down into his or her view of a particular role, e.g. father, manager of X's department, 2nd-year engineering student, playmate, lover, mathematician, counsellor, supporter of the family, leader of the community, scientist, public figure and so on.

Used in its *self-awareness form*, the chosen role is one the participant already occupies.

In its *communication* or *exchange form* the role is some other particular person.

In its *alternative futures form* the role is some aspiration or intention.

In practice getting inside a role needs careful and elaborate talkdown. ARGUS, a variant of the DEMON, PEGASUS, ICARUS interactive computer program in which different roles are compared and contrasted, is designed to achieve this.

(b) The task grid: This consists of talking oneself down into one's approach to a task. Often we are only partially aware of the intentions which underlie our activities. As a consequence, our approach to a task is vague and fragmented. The sub-tasks and related actions can be elicited and reflected upon. They can then be rebuilt into a personal taxonomy of integrated activities relating to a task.

(c) The situation grid: This method of orientation consists in talking (thinking) oneself down into a specific situation (e.g. that row I had with the English teacher on Monday afternoon). Getting right inside it may involve video-tapes, writing a story, handling certain objects or photographs, or using other systematic ploys for reviving, recreating or creating experiences. Again the situation can come from one's own past, from another's past (or from fiction), or it can be a projection into the future.

2 The Real Me grid

This is the most difficult, and in a sense is impossible. But it is the most reward-ing to attempt. The victim talks to himself for five minutes with a tape recorder running, then listens to the recording a couple of times and wipes the tape clean. Nobody ever knows what he said. Then he does a ten-minute session, similarly, and finally a half-hour session. The experience is traumatic. The question which gradually clarifies itself is 'What do I have to say to myself?' when I have no need to make images for others and have no structured situation against which to work out my meanings.

The private self-destruct, never-to-be-seen-by-others grid, using 'What I want to say but never do' items as elements is similarly confronting, parti-cularily if 'What I do say' items are used in the same grid to provoke the self-monitoring constructs.

The choice of element

The choice of elements is crucial in using the grid as a self-conversation tool. Many of the limitations of the grid lie in the constraints imposed by the defini-tion of inadequate elements. Conversationally it may often be appropriate to start with a pilot grid and then after 10-30 minutes, discard it and generate a 'better' set of elements in the light of the earlier experience. PEGASUS/ICARUS is designed to achieve this.

Specific concrete elements are necessary for sensory grids (see chapter 8) but the problem quickly expands, for example spaces in architecture are not 'things' and yet the architect must differentiate between spaces. The problem of how to get 15 spaces personally specified as elements in a grid is mind-expanding in itself.

Similarly one's experience of the relationship between two people can become an element in a grid. A grid which uses a set of such dyadic relationships can be used to explore the system of personal meaning within which we approach others. One teacher training student confronted her relationship with each member of her family, teachers who were seen as significant in her life, close friends and favourite pupils. This profoundly influenced her attitude to learning and to the ways she herself later taught (Fig. 9.17).

Again for a pseudo-physicist a grid using:

weight	entropy
mass	heat
time	temperature
gravity	information
electricity	energy
heat	frequency
temperature	ether
velocity	energy
space	sound

ELEMENTS

CONSTRUCT POLE RATED - 1 -		E1	E2	E3	E4	E5	E6	E7	E8	E9	E10		CONSTRUCT POLE RATED - 5 -
MORE ADULT RELATIONSHIP	C1	5	4	2	4	5	3	3	3	4	5	C1	MORE IMMATURE RELATIONSHIP
DEEPER RELATIONSHIP	C2	5	5	4	2	5	5	2	4	1	4	C2	SHALLOWER RELATIONSHIP
INSINCERITY IN RELATIONSHIP	C3	1	2	2	3	1	1	4	2	4	1	C3	SINCERE RELATIONSHIP
POLITELY SOCIABLE	C4	1	1	1	4	1	2	5	2	5	3	C4	REAL
FRANK RELATIONSHIP	C5	5	4	3	2	2	4	1	5	2	4	C5	GUARDED
HONEST RELATIONSHIP	C6	5	4	3	2	3	4	1	4	1	4	C6	DISHONEST RELATIONSHIP
SIMILAR SENSE OF HUMOUR	C7	5	4	3	3	3	2	1	4	2	5	C7	DIFFERENT SENSE OF HUMOUR
CANNOT LAUGH WITH EACH OTHER	C8	1	2	4	4	2	2	4	2	4	2	C8	CAN LAUGH TOGETHER
SCORN IN RELATIONSHIP	C9	1	2	3	4	2	4	4	3	5	1	C9	NO SCORN
UNDERSTAND EACH OTHER'S NEED	C10	5	4	4	3	3	4	1	4	2	5	C10	NO REGARD FOR OTHER'S NEEDS

```
*   *   *   *   *   *   *   *   *   *
*   *   *   *   *   *   *   *   *   *SISTER - COUSIN
*   *   *   *   *   *   *   *   *
*   *   *   *   *   *   *   *   *KERRY - COUSIN
*   *   *   *   *   *   *   *
*   *   *   *   *   *   *   *KERRY - SISTER
*   *   *   *   *   *   *
*   *   *   *   *   *   *DAD - COUSIN
*   *   *   *   *   *
*   *   *   *   *   *DAD - SISTER
*   *   *   *   *
*   *   *   *   *DAD - KERRY
*   *   *   *
*   *   *   *MUM - COUSIN
*   *   *
*   *   *MUM - SISTER
*   *
*   *MUM - KERRY
*
*MUM - DAD
```

Figure 9.17 Kerry's dyadic grid

will quickly loosen some of his over-confidence in the clarity and absoluteness of his subject matter.

3 The Raiffa technique (construing and action)

Looking at someone else's grid often gives you the feeling that you know what their attitude would be in a certain situation and that you could guess how they would act. But the more we try to pin down such a prediction, the more we realise one of the major defects of the grid as a tool for revealing anticipations. It does not immediately or easily relate to action. There is no way in which to move directly from the construing to the behavioural consequences of this construing. To anticipate the action we have to EXCHANGE (chapter 10) with the other's grid and then imagine how we would act if we were construing like that.

What is needed is:

(a) A grid in which the elements are the behavioural alternatives or the consequences of such behaviour.
(b) A method for weighting the constructs so that we can obtain a combined weighted construct score for each alternative action.

Such an approach is very attractive because it reveals the alternatives behind the eventual behaviour. What might have been done is included alongside what was done. This enriches the learning conversation out of reach of any behaviourist's fixed-future dreamland of social engineering. It allows validation of construing against behaviour. It reveals how much each construct contributes to the decision. Members of the Centre have used it to explore consumer preferences, the thoughts and feelings that contribute to a magistrate's decisions about 'sentencing', an artist's choice of materials, a gourmet's choice of meals, a pharmaceutical research director's choice of projects and a student's selection of background music.

In chapter 10 an example is given on the selection of examination questions. Used in conjunction with the 'role', 'task' or 'situation' grids, it can help one to explore how the weighting of constructs varies from role to role, task to task and situation to situation. It is a systematic tool for investigating the selectivity of attention or perceptual set.

4 The overlap grid

Suppose one has two grids elicited, one from the examiner and one from the examinee on the subject topic. The identification of understanding, agreement and assessment is not easy. If we insist that the 'same' constructs and 'same' elements are used by each we probably miss most of the important changes in construing that have occurred. On the other hand, two completely arbitrary grids of different elements and different constructs allow for no comparison. It is therefore useful to envisage a GROWTH grid or OVERLAP grid. The growth grid incorporates all of the first grid into the second but allows additional constructs and elements to be introduced. The overlap grid is similar but it allows for the discarding of some old elements and constructs when new ones are introduced, thus it can economically be used over longer sequences. This is the basis of the CHANGE grid procedure described earlier in this chapter. But as we have seen, the same verbal labels do not necessarily mean the same construing, so we need special techniques to identify how one person's constructs map on to another's.

Let us start by assuming that we have two verbally similar grids, taken on occasions A and B.

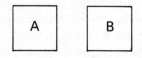

Figure 9.18 Two verbally similar grids

We can construct two larger grids. In one, we assume that the Es remain the same, and the Cs change. In the other we assume that the Cs remain the same and the Es change. Now with Es constant we get:

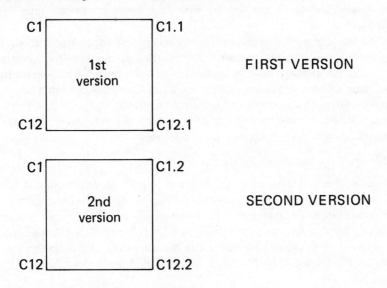

Figure 9.19 Matching all Cs with all Cs

If the two people use the verbal labels in the same way C1 (A) should match 100 per cent with C1 (B) and so on. But if the participants' view of any E has changed, all the AB comparisons will drop. We can therefore proceed with an alternating procedure.

Identify the construct which has changed most (i.e. matches least between A and B (say C3)). The CORE technique (pp. 201-12) is designed to achieve this.

Now construct the Cs constant, Es changed double grid:

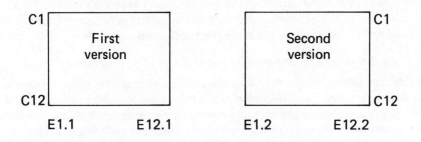

Figure 9.20 The double grid, Cs constant, Es changeable

The Es should match 100 per cent if not changed. Identify the E of least exchange, i.e. least match. Remove it and proceed back to the construct comparison. Es and Cs are removed until the matching matrices reveal an acceptable level of stability. The Es and Cs that remain constitute the stable unchanged construing between A and B, i.e. there is a stable overlap.

The stable overlapping grid is identified. The AB can now be FOCUSed and the A grid and the B grid can be separately resorted into this common FOCUSed grid.

Now having identified the areas of least exchange in apparently (verbally) identical grids, it is possible to search for 'no change' in verbally disparate grids. The 'same' element may be named differently on different occasions and the same differentiation may be given different verbal construct labels. Overlap grids offer the starting point for such explorations.

The EXCHANGE conversation can be systematically articulated. This has significant implications for examination and assessment.

5 FOCUSing a non-coherent grid: 'Not Applicables'

It is possible that not all constructs elicited in a grid can be (or should be) applied to all the elements. This is equivalent to saying that different constructs have different ranges of convenience (universe of discourse). A simple version of the 'FOCUSing' technique which simply uses 'Applicable – Not Applicable' as its criterion very quickly identifies this structure and allows enrichment sub-grids to be defined. The Ms Shop Assistant grid in chapter 7, Fig. 7.3, illustrates this.

6 Enrichment sub-grids

When a close cluster of elements (or constructs) is identified in a grid, it is often useful to extract the cluster as the core elements and constructs for a new sub-grid. This allows a greater concentration upon detailed differentiation over a restricted range of convenience. New additional elements can be added to enrich but not extend the range of convenience. The experience of concentration on such a detailed sub-grid can often change and enhance the differentiation in the main grid by refining the selection of elements and constructs. FOCUSing the sub-grid throws up the major clusters of elements and constructs. A re-naming of salient members of each cluster may then be used to represent the sub-grid in the main grid in a more evenly differentiated form.

7 Non-verbal grids: a process of silent conversation

Words can often impede the blossoming of experience. To name a thing is to assume you know it. To know it is to cease to explore. The non-verbal grid uses physical objects in the here and now as its elements, i.e. it offers continuing opportunities for referring back to the real world and gathering new data.

The objects are divided equally between two people. Person A considers three of his objects, identifies a pair and a singleton and sorts the remainder of his objects accordingly. (Alternatively five or seven point scales or ranking can each be used and a 'Not Applicable' category can be allowed.)

Person B contemplates A's patterning and attempts to sort his objects into the other's categories. When this is completed A simply re-sorts B's objects

```
        CONSTRUCT POLE RATED - 1 -              ELEMENTS                    CONSTRUCT POLE RATED - 2 -

                                          E E E E E E E E E E E E
                                          0 0 0 0 0 0 0 0 0 1 1 1
                                          1 2 3 4 5 6 7 8 9 0 1 2
                                          ****************************
INTENSITY, THEY BOTH ARE INTERESTED IN     *                          *      HUMOROUS, CREATIVE
PEOPLE, CONCERNED WITH WORLD PROBL-    C1 * 2 2 1 1 2 1 1 2 1 2 1 1 * C1      UNCONVENTIONAL, APPROACH TO WORK
-EMS, AMBITIOUS, SLIGHTLY DETACHED         *                          *      AND RELATIONSHIPS EXCITABLE
                                           *                          *
INDIVIDUALISTIC, MUSICAL, CALM(EXTERIORALLY),*                        *      SELF-AWARE, CONTROLLED, SPORTING, EXPERIENCED
UNCONVENTIONAL, NON-AGGRESSIVE, LOYAL, INTER- * 1 1 1 1 2 2 1 1 1 1 2 1 *    IN RELATIONSHIPS, ATTRACTED TO SOPHISTICATION
-ESTED IN MYTH & FANTASY, HOMELY, LAND-LOVING, C2 *              * C2       AND THE EXOTIC, EXTROVERTED, LIGHT-HEARTED
                                           *                          *
GENEROUS, INTERESTED IN HISTORY, SLOW LIVING, *                       *      DIRECT, POLITICAL,
PERFECTIONIST IN WORK, UNUSUAL         C3 * 1 1 1 1 2 2 2 1 2 1 2 1 * C3      SUPER ACTIVE,
RELATIONSHIPS                              *                          *      STRONG INTEGRITY, COMMITTED
                                           *                          *
AMBITIOUS, QUESTIONING, QUICK MINDS,       *                          *      ARTISTIC, CAPABLE,
CONFIDENT, INTERESTED IN               C4 * 2 2 2 2 1 1 1 2 1 2 1 2 * C4      GENTLE, ROMANTIC,
SOCIETY'S ILLS                             *                          *      EXPLORATORY
                                           *                          *
OUTDOOR ENTHUSIAST, ANXIOUS TO SUCCEED,    *                          *      CREATIVE,
ANXIOUS ABOUT SUCCESS WITH OTHER SEX,  C5 * 2 2 2 2 1 1 1 2 1 1 1 2 * C5      ENJOYS COMFORT,
ACTIVE, ENIGMATIC, NEED MENTAL STIMULATION *                          *      RELAXED
                                           *                          *
ENJOY INTELLECTUAL DISCUSSION, DIFFICULT   *                          *      AFFECTIONATE, HUMBLE, SENSITIVE, MUSICAL,
TO UNDERSTAND INITIALLY, CITY LOVERS,  C6 * 1 2 2 2 1 1 2 2 2 2 1 2 * C6      INVOLVED WITH THOSE IMMEDIATELY AROUND,
SEEKS CHALLENGES, INSECURE BACKGROUND      *                          *      COMPASSIONATE, PHILOSOPHICAL
                                           *                          *
ENERGETIC, SOCIABLE, POLITICALLY CONCERNED, *                         *      THOROUGH, CARE FOR DETAIL, EXTREMELY
INTERESTS, DYNAMIC, RESTLESS, FACTUAL APPROACH C7 * 2 2 2 2 1 1 2 2 1 1 2 * C7  CREATIVE, NOT CONCERNED WITH
AS OPPOSED TO INTEREST IN FANTASY WORLD    *                          *      SOCIAL SUCCESS, GENTLE, PERCEPTIVE
                                           *                          *
BOTH NEED COMPANY, GREGARIOUS, PREPARED    *                          *      MUSICAL, SCIENTIFIC BUT
TO COMPROMISE, FACTUAL APPROACH,       C8 * 2 2 2 2 1 1 1 2 2 2 1 2 * C8      ALSO KEEN ON THE
ENJOY DISCUSSION                           *                          *      UNREAL WORLD, FANTASTICAL
                                          ****************************
                                           * * * * * * * * * * * *
                                           * * * * * * * * * * * * * ACQUAINTANCE 1
                                           * * * * * * * * * * *
                                           * * * * * * * * * * * * ACQUAINTANCE 2
                                           * * * * * * * * * *
                                           * * * * * * * * * * * ACQUAINTANCE 3
                                           * * * * * * * * *
                                           * * * * * * * * * ACQUAINTANCE 4
                                           * * * * * * * *
                                           * * * * * * * ACQUAINTANCE 5
                                           * * * * * * *
                                           * * * * * * ACQUAINTANCE 6
                                           * * * * * *
                                           * * * * * ACQUAINTANCE 7
                                           * * * * *
                                           * * * * ACQUAINTANCE 8
                                           * * * *
                                           * * * ACQUAINTANCE 9
                                           * * *
                                           * * ACQUAINTANCE 10
                                           * *
                                           * ACQUAINTANCE 11
                                           *
                                           ACQUAINTANCE 12
```

Figure 9.21(i) Jane's acquaintance grid

ELEMENTS

CONSTRUCT POLE RATED - 1 -   CONSTRUCT POLE RATED - 2 -

		E1	E2	E3	E4	E5	E6	E7	E8	E9	E10	E11	E12		
LESS HUMOROUS	C1	2	2	1	1	2	1	1	2	2	1	1	2	C1	MORE HUMOROUS
LACKING A SENSE OF WONDER	C2	2	2	2	2	1	1	2	1	1	1	1	1	C2	HAVING A SENSE OF WONDER
WEAK PERSONAL INTEGRITY	C3	1	2	1	1	2	1	1	1	2	2	1	1	C3	STRONG PERSONAL INTEGRITY
EXPLICIT PERSONALITY	C4	2	1	2	1	2	1	1	2	2	1	1	2	C4	IMPLICIT PERSONALITY
INDIVIDUALITY	C5	1	1	1	2	1	2	2	2	1	2	2	2	C5	LESS INDIVIDUALITY
AMBITIOUS	C6	2	2	2	1	1	1	1	2	2	2	1	2	C6	LESS AMBITIOUS
SENSE OF HUMILITY	C7	2	1	1	1	2	2	1	2	1	1	2	2	C7	LESS SENSE OF HUMILITY
FRANK	C8	2	1	2	2	1	2	2	2	1	2	1	2	C8	LESS FRANK

*ACQUAINTANCE 12
*ACQUAINTANCE 11
*ACQUAINTANCE 10
*ACQUAINTANCE 9
*ACQUAINTANCE 8
*ACQUAINTANCE 7
*ACQUAINTANCE 6
*ACQUAINTANCE 5
*ACQUAINTANCE 4
*ACQUAINTANCE 3
*ACQUAINTANCE 2
*ACQUAINTANCE 1

Figure 9.21(iii) Jane and Dave's PAIRS grid

```
                              PAIRS GRID

CONSTRUCT POLE RATED - 1 -              ELEMENTS              CONSTRUCT POLE RATED - 2 -

                           E E E E E E E E E E E
                           1 0 0 0 0 0 0 1 0 0 0 1
                           2 8 1 3 4 7 6 1 5 9 2 0
                           ****************************
              INTENSITY J C9 * 2 1 1 2 2 2 2 2 1 2 1 1 * C9 J HUMOROUS
WEAK PERSONAL INTEGRITY D C3 * 2 2 2 2 2 2 2 2 1 1 1 1 * C3 D STRONG PERSONAL INTEGRITY
             LESS FRANK D C8 * 2 2 2 2 2 2 2 1 1 1 1 2 * C8 D FRANK
      LESS INDIVIDUALITY D C5 * 2 2 1 1 2 2 2 2 1 1 1 2 * C5 D INDIVIDUALITY
    EXPLICIT PERSONALITY D C4 * 1 1 1 1 2 2 2 2 1 1 2 2 * C4 D IMPLICIT PERSONALITY
          LESS HUMOROUS D C1 * 1 1 1 2 2 2 2 2 1 1 1 2 * C1 D MORE HUMOROUS
              AMBITIOUS D C6 * 1 1 1 1 2 2 2 2 2 1 1 1 * C6 D LESS AMBITIOUS
             GREGARIOUS J C16 * 1 1 1 1 1 2 2 2 2 1 1 1 * C16 J FANTASTICAL
                DYNAMIC J C15 * 1 1 1 1 1 2 2 2 2 1 1 2 * C15 J CARE FOR DETAIL
               ENIGMATIC J C13 * 1 1 1 1 1 2 2 2 2 2 1 2 * C13 J ENJOYS COMFORT
              AMBITIOUS J C12 * 1 1 1 1 1 2 2 2 2 2 1 1 * C12 J ARTISTIC
                 DIRECT J C11 * 1 1 1 1 1 2 2 2 2 2 1 1 * C11 J GENEROUS
             SELF-AWARE J C10 * 1 1 1 1 1 1 2 2 2 1 1 1 * C10 J INDIVIDUALISTIC
         SEEKS CHALLENGES J C14 * 1 1 2 1 1 2 2 2 1 1 1 * C14 J COMPASSIONATE
   LESS SENSE OF HUMILITY D C7 * 2 2 2 1 1 1 2 2 2 1 1 1 * C7 D SENSE OF HUMILITY
  LACKING A SENSE OF WONDER D C2 * 2 2 1 1 1 1 2 2 2 2 1 2 * C2 D HAVING A SENSE OF WONDER
                           ****************************
                            * * * * * * * * * * * *
                            * * * * * * * * * * * * * ACQUAINTANCE 10
                            * * * * * * * * * * *
                            * * * * * * * * * * * * ACQUAINTANCE 2
                            * * * * * * * * * *
                            * * * * * * * * * * * ACQUAINTANCE 9
                            * * * * * * * * *
                            * * * * * * * * * ACQUAINTANCE 5
                            * * * * * * * *
                            * * * * * * * * ACQUAINTANCE 11
                            * * * * * * *
                            * * * * * * ACQUAINTANCE 6
                            * * * * * *
                            * * * * * ACQUAINTANCE 7
                            * * * * *
                            * * * * ACQUAINTANCE 4
                            * * * *
                            * * * ACQUAINTANCE 3
                            * * *
                            * * ACQUAINTANCE 1
                            * *
                            * ACQUAINTANCE 8
                            *
                            * ACQUAINTANCE 12
```

D = Dave's construct

J = Jane's construct

Figure 9.21(iii) Jane and Dave's PAIRs grid

to conform with his own construing. The objects are then re-allocated equally between the two and B construes. If no talk is allowed and if participants try to avoid verbalising to themselves then this game produces a high degree of sensory awareness. For conceptual awareness non-verbal artifacts such as computer programs, engineering drawings, musical scores or Victor Silvester dance patterns (on cards) might be used. A variant is to restrict the game to one sense, i.e. touch, smell, sound, etc. Activities based on this procedure were offered in chapter 8.

Critical selves

In this chapter we have sought to demonstrate how various conversational grid techniques can be recruited for self-assessment. These procedures can also be used by two or more people as a resource. Evaluation in their own terms enables them to develop their critical selves. Figs 9.2(i)-(iii) illustrate how a young married couple used the PAIRS technique to evaluate their views of joint friends. Their social life together was an important aspect of their developing relationship. The next chapter extends this approach to achieve conversations for the sharing of meaning.

Chapter 10

Grid conversations for the sharing of meaning

PART 1 EXCHANGE GRIDS AND THE PROCESS OF CONVERSATION

Articulating a conversation both as content and process

This chapter demonstrates how a conversation may be articulated: and how grid techniques can contribute to this process by making the exchange of meaning explicit.

A recurrent theme throughout this book has been the proposition that the process of learning is necessarily conversational. The conversation may be between teacher and learner or between peer learners; or it may be between the learner and him- or herself. Indeed, it has been argued that the very essence of becoming a self-organised learner is the development of an ability to conduct the teaching/learning conversation within oneself. The question of self-organised learning is taken up again in the second part of this chapter and is expanded in chapter 12.

In chapter 6 the asymmetric grid conversation was described. This was partly to differentiate the employment of the grid as a psychological test or measuring device from its use as a tool for enabling self-awareness. It was also to highlight the difference between the process of a conversation and its content. To achieve this the authors described a model and algorithm of the grid conversation which might guide and inform the process for eliciting a grid and reflecting upon the pattern of personal meaning within it. Here the emphasis is reversed: from describing a conversational method for eliciting a grid the focus of attention is moved to the use of grids as aids to conversation.

The art of conversation is elusive. Much colloquial chit-chat does not contain the main ingredients of what people would mean by the word 'conversation' when seriously conversing about it. What is conversation? It is not chit-chat. It is not the empty interchange of sentences, phrases and words. Let us label such exchange of nothings as frozen conversation.

The first less trivial level of exchange might be designated *factual* or *ritualistic*. A mother helping her child to memorise a shopping list before going to the local store for her might be said to be generating a factual conversation.

Equally the airline pilot checking through her pre-flight procedures with the people in the control tower might describe her conversation in the same way. Information does pass, meaning is exchanged and checked, but the purpose is fairly short-term and the conversation, whilst essential at the time, is not intended to produce any permanent change in the personal meaning systems of either participant. Some revision and preparation for examinations might fall into this category.

The next level of conversation might be designated as *instructional* or *informational*. Here the child is learning to say her prayers, or brush his teeth; the airline pilot is being taught her pre-flight procedures; and the trainee teacher is being told that the art of good teaching is never to turn your back on the class, to have well-prepared lesson plans with clear visuals and 'to say what you are going to say, say it, and then say what you have said'. The exchange is factual but the factual material comes in larger lumps which are judged to be important and are meant to be retained. The reader may examine their own experience to assess what percentage of organised opportunities for learning fall into this category of conversation. Study skills books often over-emphasise the factual and instructional levels of learning with memory aids and mnemonics for the retention of items of information which are valued for their own sake.

The third level of conversation might be designated *explanatory*. Here the meaning to be exchanged is in the form of explanations, models or systems. These, when fully understood, are capable of generating more than is passed in the conversation, since they represent (and therefore offer an opportunity for transacting with) some part of the personal, physical, conceptual or social environment of the conversationalists. Here children are learning to brush their teeth to keep them clean and thus prevent them from later hurting, decaying, or falling out. Again readers will be able to supply themselves with examples and will be able to comment upon the quality and negotiability of the explanations given within teaching situations with which they are familiar.

Before proceeding, we, the authors, feel the need to temporarily re-emerge from the veils of third-person exposition. This is because we wish to invite the reader to converse with us about the nature of conversation.

Before exploring the implications of these three ways of regarding conversation we feel that it is only fair to indicate that we will be introducing two more forms in which conversation can be constructed or created. These are the 'constructional' and 'creative' levels of conversation. Having offered you the 'fact' that they are coming, we will instruct you about them and explain them to you later in the chapter. You, the reader, may then wish to make them part of your personal knowing by re-constructing, developing and creatively transforming them to suit your own needs and purposes.

However, now, before climbing any further up our conversational ladder, let us traverse. Let us expand and elaborate our understanding of these first three levels.

So far we have suggested that there are asymmetric and symmetric conversations. In the symmetric form each participant is free, willing and able to make any type of contribution. In the asymmetric form each participant makes a different type of contribution, they have separate and distinct roles within the conversation and these remain fixed. In chapter 6 the grid conversation was originally offered in its asymmetric form. The client offered the content and the practitioner controlled the process. Each reader will have appreciated that when used among peers the asymmetric form is either a consequence of purpose (i.e. when one participant wants to elicit a grid and the other is helping him or her to do so), or it is a consequence of the restricted timespan of the observer. Observation over longer periods would reveal an exchange of roles and the conversation would be seen to become symmetric. In chapter 6 the initial emphasis on asymmetry was used as a method for emphasising the distinction between content and process. Assigning control of the process of conversation to one participant and control of the content to the other made the explanation easier to write and hopefully to follow. Towards the end of the chapter a shared understanding of the algorithms was seen to free the participants for more symmetric conversation. Peers working together can, if they share an understanding of the process, exchange roles and pass various forms and parts of the conversation back and forth between them. Thus, for example, two people may decide to work together to produce one 'shared' repertory grid. They could both contribute equally to the content and to guiding the process.

The algorithms in each chapter have described content-free conversational procedures. Each algorithm articulated a particular type of conversation designed to contribute to personal learning, to help the learner achieve greater self-organisation and to enable them to learn-how-to-learn. These content-free procedures control the form of the conversation whilst the experience of the participants determines its content. At first readers may have applied each algorithm as a step-by-step ritual to be rote learned and dogmatically followed. As users gained experience with the grid technology these algorithms should have taken on a more flexible and adaptable meaning, serving as instructional guides to the quality and completeness of the grid conversation. Finally as the reader becomes familiar with the complete range of techniques the separate algorithms coalesce to become a personal pattern of meaning around the explanatory theme of a learning conversation. *There are therefore not only levels of content to be contributed to a conversation but also levels of process by which it may be guided. These are two distinct modes of contribution to a conversation.*

This elaboration to our description of 'conversation' adds considerably to our ability to articulate it. Our classification of content exchange into:

(1) factual or ritualistic;
(2) informed or instructional;
(3) explanatory;

can be usefully transferred to the classification of the content-free processes through which the conversation is controlled and guided.

A conversation guided by a *factual* or *ritualistic process* proceeds as a mere sequence of steps: i.e. first do this, then do this, then this and this and this. . . .

At the *informational* or *instructional level* of process the model guiding the form of the exchange is more adaptive. Contributions are not made in one predetermined order but they cohere within the organisation of the process as a whole. This informed or instructional model of process is best thought of as organised at more than one level, each of which generates its own feedback. For example, if the contents of this section were being delivered within an asymmetric conversation guided by an instructional model of process the authors would be checking whether we had conveyed each point as we made it. We would be asking for examples and examining these to diagnose areas of misunderstanding. Thus the exact sequence of the conversation would not be predictable since the participants' responses might lead us to jump back and forward through the content as we were guided by our inferences about the participants' experience and understandings. If we used a symmetric instructional model, we would find that the participant was using their interpretation of their understanding to ask questions and even to offer their own views about the nature of conversation.

Thus the conversation could be symmetric at the process level and asymmetric at the content level, i.e. *our* view of 'conversation' is the *content*, but both readers and authors explore this view together.

Finally, the *explanatory level* of modelling the process contains assumptions, understandings and/or prejudices about 'cause and effect' or 'system characteristics'. These influence the way in which the conversation unfolds and predict the consequences that may result.

A conversation in which one participant alone defines the process may mean that the other participant is totally unaware that the conversation has a form or that she or he totally accepts the form it is taking. Or for one reason or another, one participant may decide not to interfere. They just go along, contributing to the content but letting the process take its other determined course.

A ritualistic process does not prevent content contributions being made at other levels. Thus we could have an asymmetric ritualistic conversation about a Chomsky model of linguistic analysis, about Regnault's constant flow method of calorimetry or about why my lavatory gets blocked up, i.e. the content could be at an explanatory level.

Again, the reader may, from his or her own experience, like to estimate the proportion of technical and science teaching, of sports coaching, or of therapy which deals ritualistically with explanatory content.

Gradually our ability to illuminate the process of conversation increases. In a symmetric ritualistic conversation each participant would feel equally free to make the appropriate contribution at each step. The conversational science paradigm now begins to take on structure and precision; action research and other essentially interactive techniques can all be usefully described as learning conversations (see chapter 12) and therefore subsumed within the conversational science paradigm.

We are now equipped to explore the rather murky regions of the reality of many T-C conversations. We can contemplate the ramification of a conversation in which the participants each hold different models of the process but do not discuss them, and have often conflicting expectations about the topic.

Participant A   Participant B

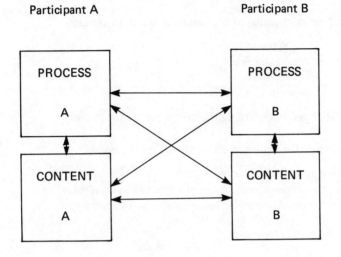

Figure 10.1 Conversation as content and process

Activity 10.1 Conceptual analysis of conversations

The reader is invited to reflect upon a particular example of a two-person teaching/learning conversation which is well known to them. Tick off the levels of content and process contributed by each participant. Are they explicitly or only implicitly aware of each?

Participant A . . . .

Content   Factual
                       Instructional
                       Explanatory
                  Implicit v. Explicit

Content Brief description of the nature of the content contributions:

Process   Ritualistic
                       Instructional
                       Explanatory
                  Implicit v. Explicit

Process Brief description of the nature of the process:

Participant B . . . .

Content	Factual
	Instructional
	Explanatory
	Implicit v. Explicit

Content Brief description of the nature of the contributions:

Process	Ritualistic
	Instructional
	Explanatory
	Implicit v. Explicit

Process Brief description of the nature of the contributions:

In reflecting on the nature of the conversation as a whole:

   (i) Was it symmetric or asymmetric?
  (ii) Was the content fixed or negotiable? If so in what ways?
 (iii) Was the process fixed or negotiable? If so in what ways?

Activity 10.2 Observational analysis of conversations

If the reader wishes to pursue this way of thinking about teaching/learning conversations then the following exercise will prove illuminating.

Record (either on audio-tape or preferably on video-tape), a session of the teaching/learning conversation which formed the basis of Activity 10.1.

Listen to, and/or watch it (more than once if necessary).

Classify each contribution as either content or process e.g.:

Process	Content	Tape counter	
A		23	A and B are the
	B	50	participants
	A	61	
	A	72	
	B	85	
A		99	
	A	130	

Figure 10.2 Observational analysis of conversation

Having analysed the conversation in this way, check through the sequence of content contributions. Are they compatible with your understanding of the process model guiding each participant? Do you feel that you could have anticipated their process interventions? Given the purpose of the enterprise, how would you yourself have guided it:

    (a) given their models;
    (b) given what you consider to be better or optimal models?

Agreement, understanding and judgment as exchange of meaning

What is shared personal meaning? Almost every major thinker from Socrates to Kant, from Confucius to Wittgenstein, from Shakespeare to Solzhenitzyn and from Lucretius to Liebnitz to Einstein, has attempted to explore the question of how human beings can communicate. Is the meaning in one head the same as the meaning in another head? If communication is possible how does it take place? Modern writers such as B. Russell, J. P. Sartre, Shannon and Weaver, K. Lorenz, M. Macluan and N. Chomsky and almost all serious novelists have confronted this question of the nature and feasibility of communication.

The state of public knowledge about this philosophical issue is less relevant than recognising the need to make the optimistic assumption that some serious communication is possible. This is necessary for all practitioners of T-C. Once this quite reasonable assumption has been made and accepted then various conclusions follow. If some communication is possible then more must be possible. The philosophical questions about human communication are transformed by inventing, refining and elaborating a technology for enhancing the speed and quality of the processes by which personal meaning may be shared.

The sharing of meaning is a peculiar activity. Personal meaning is constructed internally from items of experience. But no one item of experience acquires meaning in isolation. Items of experience acquire meaning as they are compared and contrasted with other items. They acquire their personal meanings within a larger pattern of relationships.

Isolated local meanings can be generated out of impoverished items of experience which have little or no relationship to other areas of personal meaning. Thus it is possible to begin to learn a new topic in isolation from all past experience. This can be a periodically useful way in which to proceed. But, taken too far, or used too often, it produces the alienated knowledge which is perhaps the outstanding hallmark of much institutional learning.

The method for checking or validating a meaning can be factual, informational or explanatory, i.e. meanings can be checked:

factually, i.e. item by item against an inventory;
instructionally, i.e. pattern by pattern for internal coherence and consistency, against an authoritative referent;

for *explanatory* power, i.e. in terms of effectiveness, i.e. by using it to achieve results in some area of application.

The sharing of personal meaning has another dimension to it. Are the feelings associated with similar thoughts also similar? Only if the meaning has been thoroughly re-constructed within the person will it become personal. The 'as if' reconstruction of experience creates an opportunity for the client to test their capacity to sympathise or empathise, i.e. to fully enter into the 'other's' personal meaning.

In chapter 9 the process of self-assessment was shown to be a question of internalising referents. The nature of performance referents, explanatory referents and social referents was discussed. Such referents can be internalised to provide a capacity for personal judgment and thus for self-organisation. The danger with such internalisation is that all too often it can become isolated from reality. If a parody of the original external referent is constructed in the head and remains unreviewed, it may become an uncommunicating tyrant which merely issues unexplained but powerful judgments in the way that Freud viewed the working of his super-ego. A technique is required for entering into reflective communication with a referent whether internal or external. It is also useful to identify multiple referents which serve both as anchor points and signposts to quality and yet, by offering alternatives, leave the individual free to make his or her own judgments.

Before going on to discuss the technology of EXCHANGE grids, it is necessary to define different ways of sharing meaning with the use of grids.

(a) Agreement

The meaning of the word agreement is difficult to agree. There are two rather different nodes of meaning. What is meant by making an agreement is rather different from what is meant by being in agreement. Is an internal personal 'state of being' referred to or an external public state of affairs? Another difference has to do with time-span. Is the agreement about an immediate but transitory state or is it intended to last for some significant period of time? There is also the question of commitment. Is agreement an observed similarity between two sets of personal meaning which were arrived at independently (i.e. being in agreement); or is it the result of joint work and negotiation which changes one or both sets of personal meaning until they come together (i.e. coming to an agreement). Being in agreement implies a similarity of thoughts and a similarity of emotional position. Ideas are shared, but attitudes, values and commitments are also shared.

In grid terms, being in agreement implies that two naturally occurring grids elicited from different people turn out to be identical. This would mean that in any one topic the same elements came to mind, that on construing these elements the same constructs were brought into action and that each participant assigned the elements to the constructs in the same way.

Making an agreement implies that two people have decided or contracted to act as if they were in agreement on a clearly defined and limited topic. The problem with written or verbal agreements is that later a situation often arises in which the agreement is broken, or kept in the letter but not in the spirit. A stored agreed repertory grid may, if it contains the appropriate elements and constructs, be used as a referent to the spirit of an agreement.

(b) Understanding

Understanding does not imply agreement, but it does imply that one person can enter into the personal meaning system of another. It implies that one person can appreciate how another person is construing certain items of experience and can temporarily take on this point of view. Teaching and all other forms of T-C require this skill of understanding, this skill of being able to empathise with another's point of view. Understanding, also, has a variety of meanings. To be understanding, to reach an understanding and understanding a theorem carry rather different implications. The relationship between thought and feelings is different.

In grid terms understanding involves being able to enter sufficiently into another's system of personal meaning to be able to reproduce a repertory grid on a topic in the form in which they would produce it. This does not at all imply that, left to one's own devices, one would express one's own personal meaning in the same way.

(c) Judgment

The term judgment (or assessment), which was used extensively in chapter 9 stands in a unique configuration with agreement and understanding. To make a judgment, to carry out an assessment or to evaluate requires that a referent position be defined. This referent may lie within another person (i.e. the judge, assessor, evaluator or examiner), within oneself (self-assessment) or the referent may be embedded in an institution (i.e. examining board, professional institution, doctor, etc.). The standards which are contained therein can usefully be construed as a system of constructs. Attempting to formulate the process of judgment in grid terms clarifies a number of otherwise obscure issues.

(a) The 'thing' to be judged, be it an essay, a crime, a person, the solution to a problem, a manufactured product, or a course of action, may be placed in a grid as one element among a sample or population of similar elements. The constructs are evaluative (see chapter 8). The judgment is relative to the sample, and the criteria arise from an immediate and direct elicitation of constructs.

(b) The construct system may have evolved over a period of time but other elements (i.e. unrecorded events or performances such as an actor's performance or an interview) may no longer exist for direct comparison.

(c) The thing to be judged may not be evaluated for its own sake, but as the embodiment of a person (i.e. construct system). All appraisal and selection interviews and many examinations have this purpose. The question then is how does the construct system being evaluated map on to the referent or ideal construct system?

Activity 10.3 Carl Rogers's conditions of learning

Carl Rogers has suggested that personal learning is facilitated and enabled in a conversation in which the T-C practitioner exhibits:

(a) unconditional positive regard;
(b) empathy;
(c) congruence.

Identify a teaching/learning situation known well to you. Identify a practitioner and a client. Design a method based on grid techniques which would enable you to judge the likelihood that your practitioner could, if he or she so chose, conduct a Rogerian conversation with your client. For a full appreciation of Rogers's three categories, the reader should refer to *Freedom to Learn* (Bibliography to chapter 1).

EXCHANGE grids: a basic tool for enabling conversation

The problem of improving conversation is not simply one of achieving verbal agreement. It requires the understanding and exchange of patterns of meaning. The inability to do this is the cause of much misunderstanding and strife. 'But I told you', 'Yes, but I didn't think you meant it like that' is an epitaph to many attempts to achieve personal and professional understanding.

Teachers, architects, scientists, town-planners, politicians, industrial designers, doctors and sculptors all suffer in their various ways from the inadequacy of our methods for fully sharing personally viable and relevant meanings. The client who after long discussions with an architect reaches a point-by-point agreement about the 'plans for a house' is disagreeably (or occasionally agreeably) surprised when he enters and starts to live in his new home. In spite of detailed verbal agreement the meanings in the head of the architect have never fully meshed with those expected by the client.

The problem is universal. We hardly ever see the world as another sees it. When we do it often carries the impact of a revelation. Usually our view of another's view has acquired the facile attributes of loosely held verbal opinion rather than confronting us with a different personal reality. But if our realities are different, how do those of us who have neither the skill of Shakespeare nor the precision of Proust offer our view of the world to another, or enter into theirs?

The EXCHANGE grid is an attempt to develop a methodology which will enable each of us to achieve this.

The essential mechanism of the EXCHANGE grid is very simple. Person B is asked to 'do a grid' on a given topic. B produces his own elements and his own constructs and his own assignings of the one on the other. Person A then uses Person B's elements and constructs in an attempt to reproduce B's pattern of meaning. A rates each of B's elements on each of B's constructs. B's original grid is then compared with A's version of B's grid. Any mismatch between B's grid and A's version of B's grid is then discussed to reveal the areas of mis-understanding or disagreement. This procedure can be repeated until a certain predetermined degree of understanding or agreement is achieved. Person A is then thought to be able to enter into that component of B's phenomenological world which has been defined by the elements in the grid. The term EXCHANGE was invented because it is practically useful and administratively convenient for A to do a 'like-B' grid whilst B does a 'like-A' grid.

The detailed procedure

A does a grid, identifies elements, elicits constructs and assigns elements to constructs. The verbal descriptions of the elements and constructs are copied on to a blank grid form. A may or may not then 'explain' his constructs (and his elements) to B. If he does, various safeguards are required to check that the ratings are not communicated without any real exchange of meaning. This aspect of the methodology is explained later. Here let us assume that no dis-cussion takes place.

B is presented with A's empty grid. He is asked to think himself into A's frame of mind. If the purpose of the exchange is to explore 'understanding' then B is asked to fill in the ratings in the grid as he 'B' thinks and feels 'A' would fill them in.

If the purpose of the exchange is to explore 'agreement' then B is asked to fill in the grid as he thinks and feels it should be filled in.

This procedure can be carried out without more ado if A is well known to B: otherwise an initial discussion should be arranged in which B gets to know A (and vice versa) and explores A's views about the topic in hand. Neither should at this stage know specifically what the elements in the EXCHANGE grid will be, e.g. in the following example the participants were friends who shared a common interest in art. The universe of discourse was the Indian miniature introduced in chapter 7. B was offered A's empty grid and filled it in as she thought A would do it (see Fig. 10.3).

The two grids can be superimposed and a difference grid can be calculated by subtraction cell from cell (see Fig. 10.6).

Now if the signs of the differences are ignored (or if in true statistical style the differences are squared to make them all positive) the sum of the differences in the columns is a measure of disagreement about elements. And the sums of differences across rows is a measure of disagreement of constructs.

The elements and constructs can be placed in ascending order of disagreement

RAW GRID

ELEMENTS

```
CONSTRUCT POLE RATED - 1 -                                                    CONSTRUCT POLE RATED - 5 -
              E1 E2 E3 E4 E5 E6 E7 E8 E9 E10 E11 E12 E13 E14 E15
           *************************************************************
           *                                                         *
   BUILT  C1 * 1  5  2  5  2  4  2  1  3  5   1   2   5   3   2 *  C1  JUST IS
           *                                                         *
INVOLVED  C2 * 5  5  3  5  4  5  2  3  2  5   3   2   1   5   5 *  C2  UNINVOLVED
           *                                                         *
   MOVE   C3 * 4  5  2  4  2  5  3  2  2  5   4   2   4   5   1 *  C3  STATIC
           *                                                         *
ENCLOSE   C4 * 5  5  1  3  1  4  3  1  2  1   1   2   2   1   4 *  C4  FLAT TO SPACE
           *                                                         *
  ALIVE   C5 * 4  2  4  1  2  4  3  5  2  2   4   2   1   4   2 *  C5  DEAD
           *                                                         *
COMMUNICATE C6 * 3 5  3  4  2  2  2  4  2  5   4   1   2   5   2 *  C6  DO NOT COMMUNICATE
           *                                                         *
   FULL   C7 * 4  2  2  3  2  5  2  1  3  4   4   2   3   1   2 *  C7  EMPTY
           *                                                         *
DO NOT COVER C8 * 4 4  1  2  3  3  1  4  2  4   4   2   3   2   5 *  C8  COVER
           *                                                         *
HEAD UP   C9 * 5  3  2  2  1  3  2  4  4  1   2   1   3   4   5 *  C9  DO NOT HEAD UP
           *************************************************************
              *  *  *  *  *  *  *  *  *  *   *   *   *   *  *
              *  *  *  *  *  *  *  *  *  *   *   *   *   *  * *COLOURED PATTERNS
              *  *  *  *  *  *  *  *  *  *   *   *   *   *
              *  *  *  *  *  *  *  *  *  *   *   *   *  *VASES
              *  *  *  *  *  *  *  *  *  *   *   *   *
              *  *  *  *  *  *  *  *  *  *   *   *  *PEOPLE
              *  *  *  *  *  *  *  *  *  *   *   *
              *  *  *  *  *  *  *  *  *  *   *  *SHAPES
              *  *  *  *  *  *  *  *  *  *   *
              *  *  *  *  *  *  *  *  *  *  *HOUSE
              *  *  *  *  *  *  *  *  *  *
              *  *  *  *  *  *  *  *  *  *SKY
              *  *  *  *  *  *  *  *  *
              *  *  *  *  *  *  *  *  *MATERIALS
              *  *  *  *  *  *  *  *
              *  *  *  *  *  *  *  *BARRIERS
              *  *  *  *  *  *  *
              *  *  *  *  *  *  *GESTURES
              *  *  *  *  *  *
              *  *  *  *  *  *PERSON OUTSIDE
              *  *  *  *  *
              *  *  *  *  *PERSPECTIVES
              *  *  *  *
              *  *  *  *PLANTS
              *  *  *
              *  *  *OPENINGS
              *  *
              *  *EARTH
              *
              *PATHWAYS
```

Figure 10.3(i) A's completed grid⁻

```
                          RAW GRID

CONSTRUCT POLE RATED - 1 -      ELEMENTS      CONSTRUCT POLE RATED - 5 -

                  E E E E E E E E E E E E E E E
                  0 0 0 0 0 0 0 0 0 1 1 1 1 1 1
                  1 2 3 4 5 6 7 8 9 0 1 2 3 4 5
                  *******************************
        BUILT  C1 * . . . . . . . . . . . . . . * C1  JUST IS
     INVOLVED  C2 * . . . . . . . . . . . . . . * C2  UNINVOLVED
         MOVE  C3 * . . . . . . . . . . . . . . * C3  STATIC
      ENCLOSE  C4 * . . . . . . . . . . . . . . * C4  FLAT TO SPACE
        ALIVE  C5 * . . . . . . . . . . . . . . * C5  DEAD
  COMMUNICATE  C6 * . . . . . . . . . . . . . . * C6  DO NOT COMMUNICATE
         FULL  C7 * . . . . . . . . . . . . . . * C7  EMPTY
 DO NOT COVER  C8 * . . . . . . . . . . . . . . * C8  COVER
      HEAD UP  C9 * . . . . . . . . . . . . . . * C9  DO NOT HEAD UP
                  *******************************
                 * * * * * * * * * * * * * *COLOURED PATTERNS
                 * * * * * * * * * * * * *VASES
                 * * * * * * * * * * * *PEOPLE
                 * * * * * * * * * * *SHAPES
                 * * * * * * * * * *HOUSE
                 * * * * * * * * *SKY
                 * * * * * * * *MATERIALS
                 * * * * * * *BARRIERS
                 * * * * * *GESTURES
                 * * * * *PERSON OUTSIDE
                 * * * *PERSPECTIVES
                 * * *PLANTS
                 * * *OPENINGS
                 * *EARTH
                 *PATHWAYS
```

Figure 10.3(ii) A's empty grid to be completed by B

RAW GRID

ELEMENTS

CONSTRUCT POLE RATED - 1 -   CONSTRUCT POLE RATED - 5 -

```
                    E E E E E E E E E E E E E E E
                    0 0 0 0 0 0 0 0 0 1 1 1 1 1 1
                    1 2 3 4 5 6 7 8 9 0 1 2 3 4 5
                    *******************************
         BUILT   C1 * 1 5 2 5 2 4 3 1 2 5 1 2 5 2 2 * C1  JUST IS
      INVOLVED   C2 * 4 5 5 5 2 2 1 3 2 3 2 1 3 3 3 * C2  UNINVOLVED
          MOVE   C3 * 5 5 5 2 5 1 2 4 1 3 4 1 2 3 2 * C3  STATIC
       ENCLOSE   C4 * 5 5 5 2 1 2 2 1 2 5 1 2 2 1 3 * C4  FLAT TO SPACE
         ALIVE   C5 * 5 2 4 1 2 1 1 5 2 2 3 1 1 3 2 * C5  DEAD
   COMMUNICATE   C6 * 5 4 3 4 2 1 1 5 2 5 3 1 2 2 2 * C6  DO NOT COMMUNICATE
          FULL   C7 * 5 3 1 2 3 2 2 1 5 4 3 1 2 2 2 * C7  EMPTY
  DO NOT COVER   C8 * 5 3 1 2 3 1 1 4 2 3 4 2 3 2 5 * C8  COVER
       HEAD UP   C9 * 5 4 2 2 1 1 4 4 1 1 1 3 4 * C9  DO NOT HEAD UP
                    * * * * * * * * * * * * * * *COLOURED PATTERNS
                    * * * * * * * * * * * * * *VASES
                    * * * * * * * * * * * * *PEOPLE
                    * * * * * * * * * * * *SHAPES
                    * * * * * * * * * * *HOUSE
                    * * * * * * * * * *SKY
                    * * * * * * * * *MATERIALS
                    * * * * * * * *BARRIERS
                    * * * * * * *GESTURES
                    * * * * * *PERSON OUTSIDE
                    * * * * *PERSPECTIVES
                    * * * *PLANTS
                    * * *OPENINGS
                    * *EARTH
                    *PATHWAYS
```

Figure 10.3(iii) B's version of A's grid

DIFFERENCE GRID

CONSTRUCT POLE RATED - 1 -   CONSTRUCT POLE RATED - 5 -

ELEMENTS

```
                    E E E E E E E E E E E E E E E
                    0 0 0 0 0 0 0 0 0 1 1 1 1 1 1
                    1 2 3 4 5 6 7 8 9 0 1 2 3 4 5
                    *******************************
        BUILT   C1 * . . . . 1 . 1 . . . 1 . *  C1  JUST IS
     INVOLVED   C2 * 1 . 2 . 2 3 1 . 2 1 . 2 2 * C2  UNINVOLVED
         MOVE   C3 * 1 . 3 2 3 . 2 1 2 4 3 3 2 * C3  STATIC
      ENCLOSE   C4 * . . 1 1 . 2 1 . 4 . . 1 *   C4  FLAT TO SPACE
        ALIVE   C5 * . . . 3 2 . . 1 1 . 1 . *   C5  DEAD
   COMMUNICATE  C6 * 2 1 . . 1 1 1 . 1 . 3 . *   C6  DO NOT COMMUNICATE
         FULL   C7 * 1 1 1 3 1 1 . 1 . 1 2 1 *   C7  EMPTY
  DO NOT COVER  C8 * 1 1 . 2 . . 1 . 2 1 . *     C8  COVER
      HEAD UP   C9 * . 1 . 1 2 1 . 3 1 . 2 1 1 * C9  DO NOT HEAD UP
                    *******************************
                    * * * * * * * * * * *COLOURED PATTERNS
                    * * * * * * * * * *VASES
                    * * * * * * * * *PEOPLE
                    * * * * * * * *SHAPES
                    * * * * * * *HOUSE
                    * * * * * *SKY
                    * * * * *MATERIALS
                    * * * *BARRIERS
                    * * *GESTURES
                    * * *PERSON OUTSIDE
                    * * *PERSPECTIVES
                    * *PLANTS
                    * *OPENINGS
                    * *EARTH
                    *PATHWAYS
```

Figure 10.3(iv) The difference grid

RE-ORDERED DIFFERENCE GRID

```
CONSTRUCT POLE RATED - 1 -           ELEMENTS            CONSTRUCT POLE RATED - 5 -

                        E E E E E E E E E E E E E
                        0 0 0 0 1 1 0 1 0 0 1 1 0
                        8 9 2 4 2 1 5 5 1 3 7 4 0
                                                6
                        *************************
        BUILT        C1 * - 1 . . . . . . 1 1 . . * C1  JUST IS              (3)
 DO NOT COVER        C8 * . . . 1 . . 1 . . 1 2 * C8  COVER                (5)
        ALIVE        C5 * . . 1 1 . . 2 1 . 3 . 3 * C5  DEAD                 (9)
  COMMUNICATE        C6 * 1 . 1 . . 1 . 2 . 1 3 . 1 * C6  DO NOT COMMUNICATE (10)
      ENCLOSE        C4 * . . . 1 . 1 . 1 . 4 2 * C4  FLAT TO SPACE       (10)
      HEAD UP        C9 * . . 1 1 1 . 2 1 1 3 2 * C9  DO NOT HEAD UP      (14)
         FULL        C7 * 1 . 1 1 1 . 2 1 1 3 * C7  EMPTY                (14)
     INVOLVED        C2 * . . . 1 2 2 1 1 2 2 2 3 * C2  UNINVOLVED          (16)
         MOVE        C3 * 1 2 . 2 1 3 2 1 3 2 3 4 . * C3  STATIC             (29)

                        *************************
                        * * * * * * * * * *PERSON OUTSIDE  (16)
                        * * * * * * * * *SKY  (15)
                        * * * * * * * *VASES  (12)
                        * * * * * * *GESTURES  (10)
                        * * * * * *PEOPLE  (7)
                        * * * * *OPENINGS  (7)
                        * * * *PATHWAYS  (7)
                        * * *COLOURED PATTERNS  (6)
                        * * *PERSPECTIVES  (6)
                        * *HOUSE  (5)
                        * *SHAPES  (4)
                        * *PLANTS  (4)
                        *EARTH  (4)
                        *MATERIALS  (3)
                        *BARRIERS  (3)
```

Figure 10.3(v) The re-organised difference grid

giving the re-organised difference grid. Reference back to the difference grid indicates exactly where the areas of disagreement lie. It is possible to FOCUS the difference grid highlighting areas of agreement and disagreement but this is not strictly necessary.

The identification of specific element and construct disagreement is the starting point for a new discussion in which meaning is explored and shared.

Introspective reports

Many couples have reported that the processes of EXCHANGE and of subsequent EXCHANGE grid discussion result in a much greater refinement of understanding and often lead to a creative experience of perceiving the picture (or whatever other topic has been the focus of the EXCHANGE) entirely afresh. A new pattern of meaning becomes apparent. Perceptually this may take the form of a new organisation of figure/ground. Conceptually new insights or implications emerge. Emotionally the feelings associated with the topic may be re-organised or completely transformed. The perceptual illusion of the table in chapter 8 gave a simple experience of perceptual change. The TRIGRID display provided the reader with the opportunity to think through the idea of cluster analysis and achieve some new conceptual insights.

Refinements in the EXCHANGE grid technique

1 Mutual exchange

There is an advantage to having A fill in B's grid, whilst B is filling in A's. Each has had to commit himself to his own grid and therefore has had to commit himself to a specific personal pattern of meaning before attempting to enter the experiential world of the other. This gives the experience the flavour of discussion or argument, in which each starts from a stated position. It therefore highlights the nature of the moves that have to be made to enter the other's world.

2 The paired elements method

It is useful to set up two comparable grids so that a 'before' and 'after' comparison may be carried out. This is done by asking each participant to select pairs of elements which are for them similar items of experience in the area of the topic. One from each pair is used in the first exchange and the others in the second. This allows a 'total mismatch' score (i.e. the sum of all cell differences) to be computed. The change in the degree of agreement (or understanding) can thus be measured. This gives an independent indicator of the quality of the EXCHANGE discussion.

General comment

The quality of an EXCHANGE discussion depends on the ability of the participants to 'take the constructs and elements apart' and ladder down through the hierarchy of meaning until disagreement or misunderstanding is identified and resolved in an area of shared experience. This can only be done by direct reference to well-identified shared events or experiences. Metaphor, simile and analogy are very helpful in the intermediate stages but specificity is necessary in the 'crunch' points of the discussion.

It soon becomes possible to recognise a 'good' EXCHANGE discussion and this is a learning experience which has a longer-term value for the participants apart from any continuing use of grid techniques. There follows some examples of EXCHANGE:

In chapter 3 the elicitation of a grid was illustrated by reference to Mick's construing of radio programmes. This was, in fact, part of a rather crucial negotiation between Mick, a teenager, his father, and Auntie Ada who lived with them. The original choice of programmes by each was:

Mick	Auntie Ada	Dad
Double Top Ten Show	–	–
The News	The News	The News
The Archers	*The Archers*	*The Archers*
Study on 3	–	–
Sports Desk	–	*Sports Desk*
Tony Blackburn Show	–	–
A Book at Bedtime	*A Book at Bedtime*	–
Jazz Today	Saturday Night Theatre	–
–	*Woman's Hour*	–
–	*Lighten our Darkness*	*Lighten our Darkness*
–	*Talking about Antiques*	*Talking about Antiques*
–	*Any Questions*	*Any Questions*
–	–	Financial World Tonight

Negotiation produced an agreed set of nine elements (which were those indicated above), but inspection of the original selections throws light on Mick's, Auntie Ada's and Dad's listening habits. When they did EXCHANGE grids they used the nine agreed elements, but additional light might have been thrown on their relationships if their original selections had been used in the grids for EXCHANGE. One trick is to get everybody using an agreed set of elements but then allow them to add their own selections to the grid.

For completeness all three grids are given.

FOCUSED GRID

CONSTRUCT POLE RATED - √ -   ELEMENTS   CONSTRUCT POLE RATED - ✕ -

```
                      E E E E E E E E
                      0 0 0 0 0 0 0 0 0
                      6 1 4 3 9 2 5 7 8
                      **********************
     TOO CLEVER   RC4 * ✓✓✓✕✕✕✕✕✕ ✕ * RC4  DOWN TO EARTH
  OLD AND BORING  RC1 * ✓✓✓✓ ✕✕✕✕✕ * RC1  WITH IT
          CHATTY  C3  *✓✓✓✓✓✓✕ ✕✕✕✕ * C3   REAL
 OKAY WITH FATHER C2  * ✕✓✓✓✓ ✓✕✕✕✕ * C2   LIKELY TO UPSET FATHER
     GOOD FOR ME  C5  * ✕✓ ✓ ✓✕ ✕✕✓✓* C5   I ENJOY BUT FEEL GUILTY
       ONE THING  C6  * ✕✓✓✓ ✓✕✕✕ ✓ ✓* C6  LIVELY AND CHANGING
                      **********************
                      * * * * * * * * *A BOOK AT BEDTIME
                      * * * * * * * *STUDY ON 3
                      * * * * * * *THE ARCHERS
                      * * * * * *DOUBLE TOP TEN SHOW
                      * * * * *SPORTS DESK
                      * * * *LIGHTEN OUR DARKNESS
                      * * *ANY QUESTIONS
                      * *TALKING ABOUT ANTIQUES
                      *WOMAN'S HOUR
```

Figure 10.4(i) Mick's FOCUSed grid

FOCUSED GRID

CONSTRUCT POLE RATED - √ -   ELEMENTS   CONSTRUCT POLE RATED - ✕ -

```
                      E E E E E E E E
                      0 0 0 0 0 0 0 0 0
                      1 4 9 3 5 7 8 6 2
                      **********************
    INTERESTING  C3 * ✓ ✓✓ ✓ ✓ ✕✕✕✕ * C3   IRRITATING
    INFORMATIVE  C2 * ✓ ✓✓ ✓ ✓ ✕✕✕✕ * C2   WASTE OF TIME
           GOOD  C5 * ✓ ✓✓ ✓ ✓ ✕✕✕✕ * C5   POOR STUFF
         I LIKE  C1 * ✓ ✓✓ ✓ ✓ ✕✕✕✕ * C1   I DISLIKE
    EDUCATIONAL  C6 * ✓✓✓✕✕ ✓✓ ✕✕ * C6   RADIO RUBBISH
         CLEVER  C4 * ✓ ✓ ✓ ✓✓ ✓✓✕✕ * C4   NOT CLEVER
                      **********************
                      * * * * * * * * *DOUBLE TOP TEN SHOW
                      * * * * * * * *WOMAN'S HOUR
                      * * * * * * *A BOOK AT BEDTIME
                      * * * * * *STUDY ON 3
                      * * * * *THE ARCHERS
                      * * * *LIGHTEN OUR DARKNESS
                      * * *SPORTS DESK
                      * *ANY QUESTIONS
                      *TALKING ABOUT ANTIQUES
```

Figure 10.4(ii) Father's FOCUSed grid

```
                            FOCUSED GRID

CONSTRUCT POLE RATED - ✓ -      ELEMENTS    CONSTRUCT POLE RATED - X -

                         E E E E E E E E
                         0 0 0 0 0 0 0 0
                         5 1 2 6 8 3 7 4 9
ABOUT LUCKY              *********************
& INTERESTING PEOPLE  C5 * ✓ ✓ ✓ ✓ ✓ X X X X * C5   ALL POLITICS
            AMUSING   C3 * ✓ ✓ ✓ ✓ ✓ X X X X * C3   SERIOUS
             I LIKE   C6 * ✓ ✓ ✓ ✓ ✓ ✓ ✓ X X * C6   I DISLIKE
          ALL RIGHT   C1 * ✓ ✓ ✓ ✓ ✓ ✓ ✓ X X * C1   TOO MUCH TALK
      UNDERSTANDABLE   C4 * ✓ ✓ ✓ ✓ ✓ ✓ X X X * C4   OVER MY HEAD
            A STORY   C2 * ✓ X X X ✓ ✓ ✓ X X * C2   BITSY
                         *********************
                         * * * * * * * * *SPORTS DESK
                         * * * * * * * *ANY QUESTIONS
                         * * * * * * *STUDY ON 3
                         * * * * * *LIGHTEN OUR DARKNESS
                         * * * * *A BOOK AT BEDTIME
                         * * * *WOMAN'S HOUR
                         * * *DOUBLE TOP TEN SHOW
                         * *TALKING ABOUT ANTIQUES
                         *THE ARCHERS
```

Figure 10.4(iii) Auntie Ada's FOCUSed grid

When Father EXCHANGEd with Mick he gave:

```
                           EXCHANGE  GRID

CONSTRUCT POLE RATED - ✓ -     ELEMENTS    CONSTRUCT POLE RATED - X -

                        E E E E E E E E
                        0 0 0 0 0 0 0 0
                        1 2 3 4 5 6 7 8 9
                        *********************
       WITH IT      C1 * ✓ X X ✓ X X ✓ ✓ ✓ * C1   OLD AND BORING
 OKAY WITH FATHER   C2 * X ✓ ✓ X ✓ X X X ✓ * C2   LIKELY TO UPSET FATHER
        CHATTY      C3 * X ✓ X ✓ ✓ X ✓ ✓ X * C3   REAL
  DOWN TO EARTH     C4 * X ✓ X X X ✓ X X ✓ * C4   TOO CLEVER
   GOOD FOR ME      C5 * X ✓ ✓ X ✓ X ✓ ✓ X * C5   I ENJOY BUT FEEL GUILTY
     ONE THING      C6 * ✓ X X X X ✓ X X X * C6   LIVELY AND CHANGING
                        *********************
                        * * * * * * * * *SPORTS DESK
                        * * * * * * * *A BOOK AT BEDTIME
                        * * * * * * *STUDY ON 3
                        * * * * * *WOMAN'S HOUR
                        * * * * *THE ARCHERS
                        * * * *ANY QUESTIONS
                        * * *LIGHTEN OUR DARKNESS
                        * *DOUBLE TOP TEN SHOW
                        *TALKING ABOUT ANTIQUES
```

Figure 10.4(iv) Father's version of Mick's grid

Giving a DIFF. grid of:

```
CONSTRUCT POLE RATED - / -        ELEMENTS        CONSTRUCT POLE RATED - — -

                       E E E E E E E E
                       0 0 0 0 0 0 0 0 0
                       1 2 3 4 5 6 7 8 9
                       ********************
           WITH IT  C1 * / / - / / - - - - * C1   OLD AND BORING
  OKAY WITH FATHER  C2 * / / - / - - - - - * C2   LIKELY TO UPSET FATHER
            CHATTY  C3 * / / / - / / / / / * C3   REAL
     DOWN TO EARTH  C4 * - - / - / / / / - * C4   TOO CLEVER
       GOOD FOR ME  C5 * / / - / / - - - - * C5   I ENJOY BUT FEEL GUILTY
         ONE THING  C6 * - - / / / - / / / - * C6 LIVELY AND CHANGING
                       ********************
                       * * * * * * * * *SPORTS DESK
                       * * * * * * * *A BOOK AT BEDTIME
                       * * * * * * *STUDY ON 3
                       * * * * * *WOMAN'S HOUR
                       * * * * *THE ARCHERS
                       * * * *ANY QUESTIONS
                       * * *LIGHTEN OUR DARKNESS
                       * *DOUBLE TOP TEN SHOW
                       *TALKING ABOUT ANTIQUES
```

Key:
/ Different
— Similar

Figure 10.4(v) Difference grid: Father on Mick

Confronted with these differences, Dad was very annoyed and tried to persuade Mick that he was wrong. Gradually it dawned on him that Mick using Mick's constructs could not be wrong and he went very quiet. *This event was seen as a turning point in the relationship.*

Mick doing Father's grid as he thought Father would produce it gave a DIFF. grid of zero. But when asked to fill it in as he thought it should be filled in he refused. He could understand Father but was unwilling to explore their disagreements. This was taken up in conversation and it transpired that Mick was unable to contemplate making an explicit statement in Father's terms since this would reveal wide areas of disagreement. Mick felt that since he understood Father that should be sufficient. Without reproducing all the grids it transpired that:

	FATHER	AUNTIE ADA	MICK
MICK	U.DA	NU.A	
FATHER		NU.DA	NU.DA
AUNTIE ADA	U.A		U.A

U = understand   NU = not understand
A = agree   DA = disagree

Figure 10.5 Summary of EXCHANGE

These results throw light on the relationships and the detailed similarity and the differences between grids provides sufficient material to get the conversation going. Subsequent conversation was progressively more realistic and the negotiation of radio programmes became much easier. These three went on to do grids on 'shared acquaintances' and on 'crucial events' and the whole group counselling process was enhanced by the negotiations.

Entering the phenomenological world of others is a difficult business. Re-entering, exploring and re-organising one's own phenomenological world needs specific techniques; of which, as we have seen, the repertory grid is a powerful example. But to enter is only the first move. The structure of the mind is man-made. The differentiations which we can achieve and the patterns of meaning which we can generate are themselves the products of the rules for thinking and feeling which the structure of the species, the pressures of our culture and the constraints of accumulating experience impose upon us. This imposition exists only for as long as we lack tools for re-structuring our own experience. This is the powerful attraction of religious conversion, of psychedelic drugs and of the encounter group explosion in the 1960s and 1970s. Each offers opportunities for the individual to break his own un-reviewed past-bound constraints. Unfortunately, in breaking bounds there is a real danger of psychic chaos. The mind flows out of its broken container. The aim of conventional tool-making is to add opportunities for re-building and re-furbishing to the excitement of the break-out.

The FOCUSed grid and its manifestations in the EXCHANGE grid procedures, is one such tool. Fig. 10.6 shows the algorithm for EXCHANGE. It allows us to see the pattern underlying a series of discrete differentiations. Each construct is, ideally, elicited without reference to any other. Freud's free-association technique also aimed to release the mind from its strong but superficial habits of thought and feeling. 'What should go with what, rationally', is no longer the important criteria against which all out-putting is monitored. Released from rationality, the underlying principles of patterning are free to reveal themselves. When the elicitation of constructs becomes such a free-flowing cognitive process the FOCUSed grid can reveal the deeper patterning.

But this is only true when the participant is talked down (or talks himself down) into the free-associative state of mind. Other states of mind also have their uses. Free association is only useful when the deepest patterns are to be explored. Other principles of association are necessary to living. What Freud called the ego is highly structured and reality oriented.

These structures can also be explored. In this chapter we are concerned not only with what is, but also with what might be, in the grid technology of tomorrow. In chapter 12 we discuss how the structure of the grid itself is too restricted and simplistic and how the exploration of phenomenological worlds might become more flexible with techniques that can respond to the structure of the mind without continually overlaying it with irrelevant constraints of their own forms.

The grid is a method for revealing the constructions of the mind. But it

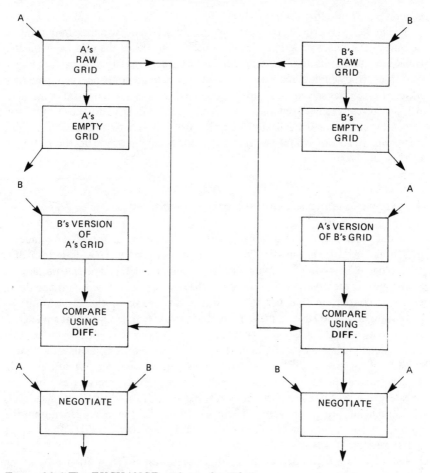

Figure 10.6 The EXCHANGE grid: an algorithm

only allows one component of all structures to emerge, i.e. the dimensions of differentiation, the personal constructs. It is also only a cross-section at one point in time. Thirdly, it is only concerned with differentiations between 'equal' elements. The hierarchical/heterarchical nature of thought and feelings is un-revealed. Extensions of grid technology can move some distance towards over-coming these limitations. Each new step in methodology is a new freedom for articulating the structure of thought and feeling and is therefore equally usable in the descriptive and cognitive mirroring modes. It can be used descriptively or conversationally, as a pin for fixating the dead butterfly of mind in the museum showcase of psychological and pedagogical expertise or as one in a battery of multi-faceted mirrors which can be used to encourage and enhance personal growth and development. These two approaches to grid technology carry quite different systems of value. Accuracy and validity are obviously as important in mirroring as in description, but the criteria which each position generates lead in rather different directions.

When the grid is used as a descriptive technique, it becomes important to be able to compare all grids with each other. This leads the grid psychometricians into standardisation procedures. Elements and constructs must be shared, but since true sharing requires techniques which are outside their paradigm of legitimate science they end up using offered elements and offered constructs. All too often these degenerate into dead verbal forms which have quite different meanings for each living butterfly. When it is movements of the living mind which are important, to fixate it with a pin may not be the optimum method of investigation.

A systematic approach to the creative encounter

Now our reflective learning tool-bag is beginning to look formidable. Indeed, it is beginning to warrant the title of a new technology. One definition of a technology is a system of tools which are self-referent and therefore able to contribute to the creation of new tools which supersede those that made them. It is our contention that just as the wind-driven tools of the early industrial revolution could be used to make parts that were assembled into a steam engine, and just as a lathe capable of an accuracy of + or − 0.01 inches can be used with human ingenuity to produce parts that can be assembled into a lathe capable of an accuracy of + or − 0.001 inches, so our tool-bag of grid techniques and the models of personal and conversational processes can be used to produce a new bag of tools and a new set of models which can enable levels of learning at present beyond our imagination. To the next generation the schools of today will appear almost identical in approach to those that appear in the pages of Dickens.

Let us take a hesitant peep into this future. Maslow has written of what he called the creative encounter. This is a conventional event in which apparently 'magical' things happen. Something − an idea, an attitude change, an imaginative leap, a new skill − emerges out of the white heat of the encounter, or a completely new level of relationship between the participants is achieved.

Most of us have experienced this type of encounter a few times in our life. Some of us have been to encounter groups or brainstorming sessions which were designed to produce such an effect, but not many of us are able to produce such events at will. It might be claimed that the outstanding exponent in any area of T-C has this apparently 'magical' ability to occasionally get such a session going and to set it alight. Here it is suggested that such an ability is an intuitive or tacit skill which is not gene-given but has itself been learned.

The authors' developing understanding of the construction and exchange of personal meaning allows us more and more frequently to produce such events.

The mechanism seems to be as follows:

1   Construct such events (e.g. grid sessions) as will challenge and loosen the personal myths of the participants about their own and other people's

capacity for creative learning.

2   Introduce the idea of factual, instructional and explanatory levels of conversational content. Design some exercises which offer operational experiences of this classification in a content area of relevance and significance to the participant.

3   Collect first-hand examples of content exchanges in the group which do not fall easily into these three categories. Examine them. Among other possibilities as we shall see later some of these exchanges will begin to show apparently 'magical' (i.e. unpredicted) properties. What is received is more than or different from what was sent. Within the criteria which the participants are using to judge the quality of content these new items are as good or better than those items which were known to one or other of the participants before the conversation started.

4   Now begin a discussion and reflect upon the process whereby such newly constructed items have evolved. If necessary bring the conversational grid techniques into play if they hasten or heighten understanding.

5   We have now identified a new 'constructional' level in our content events. They may arise from one individual participant having indulged in the process of personally constructing new meaning. This is interesting and may be very useful for the individual to reflect upon. Indeed this is the key to personal learning, but is not here our primary concern.

6   Records of any conversation often show a series of such apparently newly constructed content contributions. On closer examination most of these will turn out not to be new to the contributor but to have been dredged up whole out of previous experience. Either way your record of the conversation will reveal that sometimes such new contributions disappear without trace. At other times they bounce back and forth, gaining in significance and coherence.

7   Try to identify the process assumptions shared by participants during such constructive group events. Here an interesting phenomenon emerges. The process may be ritualistic. People may have evolved or been taught a totally fixed algorithm for 'brainstorming' or being 'creative in a group'.

8   Try to get participants to construct an explanatory model of how such ritualistic or instructional processes produce their effects.

9   Get them to:
   (a) try to continue their significant content conversation using this newly constructed explanatory model of process;
   (b) reflect upon the process by which they arrived at their explanatory model;
   (c) decide whether their descriptions of group processes contain any self-developing or constructional features?

10 If so we have identified a new level of process description in which the process is itself being constructed within the conversation. This constructional level of process has a 'bootstrapping', 'positive feedback' or 'growth impact' on the conversation. It takes off.

11   This ability to 'take off' is one crucial mechanism in producing an encounter. Many people will classify such an event as a creative encounter
but it does not necessarily meet Maslow's criteria. He saw the creative
encounter as an event which not only 'takes off' but which does so in
such a way that it transcends the evaluative system out of which it arose.
It must and can only be valued from a perspective which evolves out of
the event itself. It is both transcendent and self-referent.

12   The definition of creative content in a conversation is that it is valued
highly by the participants but for reasons arising out of criteria which
did not exist at the commencement of the conversation.

13   The definition of creative process in a conversation is that it is valued
highly by the participants but it transcends their original models of the
conversational process and justifies itself by producing experiences which
are valued for reasons which did not exist at the commencement of the
conversation.

14   This description of the creative encounter yields some interesting conclusions.

(a) The constructive and creative levels of content offer the minimum conditions of personal learning. It is the construction, reconstruction and negotiation and exchange of personally relevant and viable meaning which typifies
self-organised learning.

(b) The factual, instructional and explanatory levels of content in the absence
of construction and creativity will build up layers of impersonal or alienated
learning which must later be destructured and reconstructed if personal learning is to be achieved.

(c) The constructive level of content implies development within the existing
evaluative framework, and the creative level of content implies a symbiotic
change in content and values.

(d) The constructive and creative content is inevitably the consequence of
self-organisation at work.

(e) Ritualistic conversational process can produce any level of conversational
content if the ritual plays out through compatible algorithms. The instructional
and explanatory process levels are more flexible and more adoptive and therefore more likely to succeed, but they also imply increasing insight into the
conversational process.

(f) The constructive levels of conversational process can have an experiential
effect on the quantity of personal learning since it is in effect the core of learning-
to-learn.

(g) The creative level of conversational process can have an experiential impact
on the quality of personal learning since each time it operates it is engender-
ing a change in a personal and/or group paradigm.

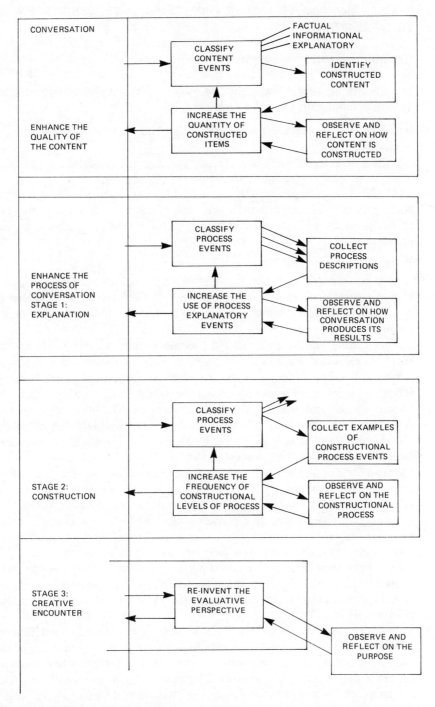

Figure 10.7 The creative encounter: an algorithm

PART 2 ASSESSMENT AND EXAMINATIONS: A PECULIAR FORM OF CONVERSATION

Examinations and assessment

The exercise of judgment and the processes of evaluation and assessment are necessary components of any learning event. But:

(a) There is a considerable amount of rubbish talked about written assessment of examinations.
(b) There is a considerable amount of hypocrisy and double-think operating in the practice of 'continuous' assessment.
(c) There is an infinite amount of damage done to teachers and to learners, both to those who pass and those who fail, as the result of misunderstanding of the processes of 'subjective judgment' as they operate in assessment and examinations.

Why is this?

It is because the exercise of certain key processes of evaluative judgment are not incorporated into the ongoing conversation between teacher and learner. The learner is in fact often deliberately isolated from the constructions of the examiner's mind.

Thus the topic of examinations and assessment provides a very good sounding board for exploring just how useful personal construct theory can be, or might prove to be in the future, as a new approach to educational issues. Firstly it allows us to see many educational controversies as conflicts or gaps between systems of personal meaning developed for coping with different roles and person/life situations. These involve social status, vulnerability, job prospects, personal relationships and self-image. In chapter 1 the whole question of how learning is to be construed was clarified by recognising that learning is itself a construct. It can be seen from within the learner's construct system as valued changes in personal meaning, or it can be seen through the eyes of an observer as valued changes in behaviour. The teacher (or experimenter) construes the learner's performance through a particular pattern of personal meanings. Some examiners are not prepared to discuss, or be challenged, about the basis of their judgements. For examining purposes learning is evaluated from within the teacher's value system. For other purposes different criteria may be more relevant. These differing perspectives for evaluating learning will be explored in more depth in chapter 12. They produce a variety of confusions among practitioners of T-C.

Basically, changes in construing will be seen as academically valid learning only in as much as a change is visible through the personal constructs of the teacher, and then only in so far as the movement is in the positive direction, i.e. from the unpreferred to preferred poles of the teacher's constructs. This movement may not be in the best long-term interests of the learner. For example, there is often a period of mid-course doldrums in which students appear to be marking time or even to be degenerating, when their performance is viewed through the eyes of a 'subject or course-oriented' tutor. From within the construct system of the learner himself it can appear quite differently. It may be a period of very rapid change for which the implications of partially digested reconstruings, which have been developed during the early part of the course, are worked through into a wider pattern of personal meanings. This could be the crucial learning period when originally isolated academic meanings acquire greater personal significance and durability.

This taking apart and reconstructing of whole systems of construing is important if education is to lead to profound changes in an individual's pattern of life. During this period of change a necessary confusion and provisionality in his interim construings may work itself out as withdrawal or as a significant drop in overt performance. Sympathetic tutoring would seek insight into this process and offer support and guidance through this period of personal change. Too insistent a pressure for sustained overt performance at such points in students' or children's development may drive them back to the security of their earlier construings which have, up to then, enabled them to 'get by' in tests and examinations.

For example, the following question was set in a yearly written examination: 'What experiment in social psychology seems to you to have the most important implications for mankind? Briefly describe the experiment and give reasons for your choice.'

This question was thought by the teacher to offer about as much freedom for making a coherent well-argued personal statement as it was possible to give. Answers varied enormously in the variety of experiments selected and in the 'quality' of the explanations and justifications that were offered, although in fact clusters of similar answers did appear, showing the impact of the teacher's beliefs and values on the student's offerings. However, a certain student's answer started:

'One day a Zen master was approached by two of his apprentices who had been squabbling for some time about the ownership of a young kitten which they had found. The master offered them opportunity after opportunity to resolve the problem for themselves, but they could not come to terms. So he finally took the kitten and cut it in half, giving one half to each.' This is the most significant social psychological experiment that ever took place. My reasons for choosing this experiment are, like the kitten, implicit in the experiment itself.

The teacher marking the script did not feel able to award any marks for this 'Wisdom of Solomon' answer. The Zen example was outside the universe of discourse (range of convenience) of his construing of experiments in social psychology. But a subsequent private tutorial session in which the student was encouraged to uncover and explore how social psychology related to Zen philosophy proved a significant event in the academic lives of both student and teacher alike. The student went on to a very successful career in clinical psychology. The same zero mark coupled with uncomprehending disapproval might have produced quite different results.

Such opportunities to exchange and explore mutually incompatible construings proliferate within the educational system. Much of the alienation to science, mathematics and technological subjects can be seen to arise within the context of the teacher knowing the 'right answer' and being unable or unwilling to construe the learner's personal meanings in any terms other than 'right v. wrong'. On the other hand, the humanities can too easily slip into an over-valuing of style and attractive verbal forms which conceal serious mismatches between the patterns of personal meaning of the learner and the examiner. The intuitively good teacher can negotiate such mis-construing and mismatches; he or she can work them through into new and more viable systems of personal meaning. More rigorous methods for separating 'form' from 'content' might help less-skilled teachers to improve the quality of teaching in some of these subjects.

Examination performance and the examiner's and the learner's grids

After a mock 'O' level English essay examination, the students and the teacher/examiner were asked to 'do a grid' using the essays as elements. Each student grid was then PAIRed with the teacher's grid, i.e.

	E1 – – – – – – – – – – – – – – – – – E20	
C1 C11	Student's constructs	C1 C11
C12 C21	Examiner's constructs	C12 C21

Figure 10.8 Raw grids to be PAIRed

The composite grids were each FOCUSed in the usual way. No attempt will be made here to present the results in detail. But two composite grids were of particular interest. For the purpose of clarity only the clusterings of constructs are presented.

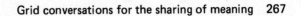

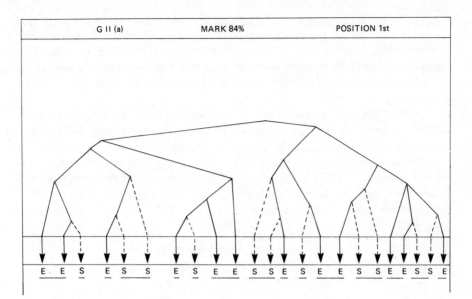

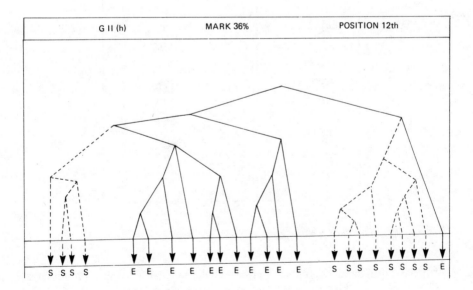

Figure 10.9 The clustering of constructs in two PAIRed grids

In the diagrams the Ss denote student constructs and the Es denote examiner's constructs. PAIRed grid 1 shows much intermingling of the two construct systems. This can be taken to imply that student G11(a) and the examiner shared much the same descriptive and evaluative system when they construed the English essays. Student G11(a) scored 84 per cent for his mock 'O' level essay.

PAIRed grid 2 shows a contrasting situation. The hierarchical cluster analysis separates the Ss from the Es. Student G11(h) and the examiner shared no common view of the essays. Student G11(h) scored 36 per cent.

The study shows that for the twelve students who volunteered grids, there was a correlation of Spearman's Rho − 0.83 (i.e. sig. at .01 per cent) level between the measures of overlap between student and examiner grids and the mark awarded in the mock examination.

'O' Level English mark	Student/examiner grid overlap
84	68%
81	58%
76	54%
70	63%
68	45%
66	52%
60	37%
58	37%
54	58%
48	24%
38	18%
36	24%

Figure 10.10 The marking and construing of 'O' level essays

Being both an undergraduate project and our first venture into this area of investigation, this study suffers from a number of methodological weaknesses. But the trend was clear both for English essays and in the pilot work which was done on the marking of laboratory reports.

e.g.

Laboratory report mark	Student/examiner grid overlap
75	58%
55	43%
50	47%
42	40%
32	32%

and

Laboratory report mark	Student/examiner grid overlap
72	62%
55	54%
52	57%
50	49%
40	32%

Figure 10.11 The marking and construing of laboratory reports

The implications to be drawn from experiments of this type are quite far-reaching. First, it would appear that the students whose work received low marks were not only unable to write an essay which the examiner could value, but more importantly they were unable to construe essays in ways that related to the examiner's evaluative system. This might indicate that they had two equally viable, but incompatible, systems of personal meaning. If this were so, negotiation through the medium of EXCHANGE grids might prove an effective way of opening up the educational conversation. The negotiation of teaching/learning contracts, discussed in chapter 12, confronts some of these issues.

The evidence of this grid study of examining shows that some low marks did accrue from a clash of values between students and examiner, but most of the low marks arose among those students who were unable to differentiate very well between essays. This indicates that a limited amount of time spent negotiating a more sensitive and differentiated system for attributing personal meaning to essays might pay enormous dividends compared to merely endlessly writing more and more poor essays from within a totally inadequate scheme of appreciation. Perhaps some exercises in the construing of English essays would benefit poor 'O' level students rather more than endless repetition of writing essays from within their inadequate but unconscious and unreviewed construing systems. The EVALUATION grids introduced in chapters 8 and 9 might serve as a vehicle for reflectively learning how better to appreciate essays.

Reflecting upon the issues raised by those simple investigations highlights many of the questions inherent in examining and assessing. Is it the purpose of an examiner to assess the extent to which the student 'thinks and feels like me'? If it is, then what is it that the student and examiner should think and feel similarly about? Is it simply a matter of agreeing about content? Is it the style of the display and presentation that matters? Is it the quality of the thought processes that is important? Or is the most significant overlap to be found in the areas of value and beliefs? These questions are open to investigation by grid methods, but they have not to our knowledge been investigated in this way.

But the conversational use of grids offers a much more radical approach. The ability to appreciate the quality of one's own products can be seen as the mechanism by which a learner can control the development of their own skills and knowledge. External assessment and examinations merely serve as a means for expanding and calibrating the evaluative system of the self-organised learner. If this is accepted, then practice in the marking and evaluation of one's own work and the work of peers becomes a central educational activity. Learning how to make informed evaluative judgments is crucial to improving one's capacity for learning.

On the meaning of the mathematics exam questions

One more grid study does have implications for examinations, although it was not actually conducted under examination conditions. Eighteen mathematics students took part. They were each asked to rank the questions in a series of examination papers in terms of the likelihood that they would choose to tackle them under exam conditions. They then did grids. The results show how their construing of the questions might influence their examination behaviour. This description of the study has been extracted and simplified from a much larger PhD study. The Raiffa Technique for ascribing weightings to constructs, in terms of how much they contribute to a decision, was used. This technique was described in chapter 9.

In a first session the students, each individually, were asked to rank the questions in a series of exam papers. These rankings were used to calculate a preference order for the command words that 'define the problem' in the question.

One illustrative student gave the following rankings:

Most prefer: 1 Calculate
                  2 Find
                  3 Show
                  4 Explain
                  5 Prove
Least prefer: 6 Define

Figure 10.12 Preferences for mathematics command words

Then they were conversationally introduced to the grid technique and a grid using the six words was elicited. (For ease of explanation the number of command words is reduced to six and the 'preferred' pole of each construct is shown on the left, although it was not necessarily the 'pair' pole in the original raw grid.)

Our illustrative student developed the following grid:

```
                              RAW GRID


                             ELEMENTS
CONSTRUCT POLE RATED - 1 -                        CONSTRUCT POLE RATED - 5 -
                         E1  E2  E3  E4  E5  E6
                        **************************
                         *                    *
        INTERESTING  C1 *  5   5   3   2   3   2 *  C1  NOT COMMITTING
                         *                    *
               EASY  C2 *  4   5   3   1   3   1 *  C2  DIFFICULT
                         *                    *
           COHERENT  C3 *  2   1   3   3   2   3 *  C3  LESS COHERENT
                         *                    *
REQUIRES ROUTINE WORKING C4 *  3   5   2   2   4   3 *  C4  REQUIRES IRREGULAR WORKING
                         *                    *
   I AM CURIOUS ABOUT C5 *  2   3   1   3   3   4 *  C5  I AM BORED BY
                         *                    *
            PRECISE  C6 *  2   1   3   3   2   1 *  C6  VAGUE
                        **************************
                         *   *   *   *   *   *
                         *   *   *   *   *  *CALCULATE
                         *   *   *   *   *
                         *   *   *   *  *EXPLAIN
                         *   *   *   *
                         *   *   *  *SHOW
                         *   *   *
                         *   *  *FIND
                         *   *
                         *  *DEFINE
                         *
                        *PROVE
```

Figure 10.13 'Fred's' grid of command words

this gave the following cluster of constructs:

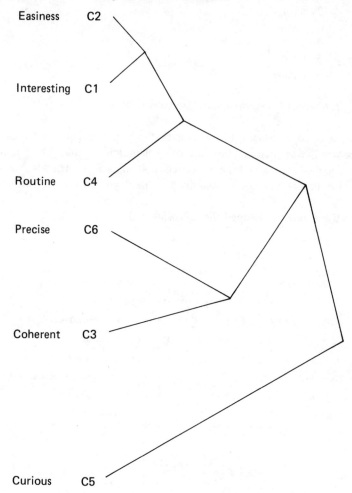

Figure 10.14 Cluster hierarchy of constructs

This tree diagram is another form of display offered by the FOCUS program. C_2 and C_1 are highly related and are joined by C_4 into one 'branch' of the tree. C_6 and C_3 are less closely related but come together before joining with the C_2, C_1, C_4 cluster. C_5 is more isolated and is the last branch of the tree. Thus the tree diagram may be read as a summary of the process of FOCUSing.

A new technique was introduced in the second session. The Raiffa Technique is an elegant method for getting the participant to reveal the importance which he attaches to each construct.

This is achieved without reference back to the elements. The weightings of constructs assigned by our illustrative student were:

Construct	Weighting
He is curious about	30
Allows precise answer	28
Easy to do	22
Interesting	09
Coherent	07
Routine	04

Figure 10.15 Construct weightings

Multiplying each construct by its weighting yielded the following weighted grid:

```
                              WEIGHTED CONSTRUCT GRID

        PREFERRED POLE                 ELEMENTS              NON-PREFERRED POLE


                              E    E    E    E    E    E
                              0    0    0    0    0    0
                              1    2    3    4    5    6
                           ******************************
          INTERESTING  C1 *  45   45   27   18   27   18  * C1   NOT COMMITTING
                 EASY  C2 *  88   10   66   22   66   22  * C2   DIFFICULT
              COHERENT C3 *  14    7   21   21   14   21  * C3   LESS COHERENT
REQUIRES ROUTINE WORKING C4 * 12   20    8    8   16   12  * C4   REQUIRES IRREGULAR WORK
          I AM CURIOUS C5 *  60   90   30   90   90  120  * C5   I AM BORED BY
              PRECISE  C6 *  56   28   84   84   56   28  * C6   VAGUE
                           ******************************
  SUM OF WEIGHTED RATINGS    275  300  236  243  269  221
        PREDICTED RANKING      5    6    2    3    4    1
                              *    *    *    *    *    *
                              *    *    *    *    *    * E6 CALCULATE
                              *    *    *    *    *
                              *    *    *    *    * E5 EXPLAIN
                              *    *    *    *
                              *    *    *  * E4 SHOW
                              *    *    *
                              *    *  * E3 FIND
                              *    *
                              *  * E2 DEFINE
                              *
                              * E1 PROVE
```

Figure 10.16 'Fred's' grid showing weighted construct responses

Thus our illustrative student shows a Spearman's Rho correlation of 1.00.

	Preference for exam question (Ranking)	Weighted grid (Ranking)
Calculate	1	1
Find	2	2
Show	3	3
Explain	4	4
Prove	5	5
Define	6	6

Figure 10.17 'Fred's' rankings of command words compared with the results from the weighted grid

This means that for our specially selected illustrative student 'Fred', we have discovered a way of exploring not only the terms in which he construes maths exam problems, but we can also say how important each construct will be in contributing to his decisions.

These results show that the correlation coefficients of the eighteen students were distributed as shown in Fig. 10.18.

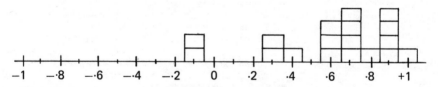

Figure 10.18 Distribution of Spearman's Rho for 18 students

The predictive power of the 'weighted grid' is amazingly good when one realises that what is being attempted is the prediction of the specific actions of individuals under real learning conditions, not the general trend among a group. Follow-up work showed that the five 'low correlation' students were not doing very well in exams. They improved considerably after learning conversations based on these grids (see chapter 12).

Thus what this study has shown is that the grid plus a technique for weighting constructs can offer considerable insight into the decision processes of an individual in an examination situation.

As always the content of all eighteen student grids was fascinating, but too space-consuming to present here. The constructs elicited in another part of this study were presented in chapter 7.

In 'learning-to-learn' courses in schools, colleges and universities the authors often get students to sift through exam papers for the command words used in their subject areas. Grids, EXCHANGE or STRUCTURES OF MEANING exercises using these words can make a considerable impact on exam perform-ance. EXCHANGE between examiners can be embarrassing by revealing serious disagreements about the type of answer demanded by different command words.

The monitoring of tutor-marked assignments

Among the many different ways in which grids can help to improve the quality of the conversation between learner and T-C practitioner we have selected an action research study carried out by one of the authors whilst she was work-ing for the Open University. One of her roles (see 'The Seven Faces of Teaching/ Learning', chapter 12) was to 'monitor' the tutors' marking of students' written assignments on two courses.

During the first stage of the study the written comments made by individual tutors on the assignments before they returned them to the students were collected. Individually the tutors were then taken through a complete grid conversation with talkback and the completion of a revised grid. This awareness-raising exercise was valued highly.

After some six months had elapsed this exercise was repeated using the CHANGE grid technique. Again tutors found this to be a very useful exercise in opening their eyes to their own processes in learning to mark the assign-ments. The tutors then met as a group and EXCHANGEd elements and con-structs. They gradually sorted out some 60 elements and 45 constructs which they together felt fully represented all the 'types of written comments we make on assignments' and all the 'ways of thinking and feeling' about such comments which existed among this group of tutors. These were used to con-struct a CONSENSUS FRAME grid (described more fully in chapter 11). DIF-FERENCE grids and CORE grids were used to reveal the areas of agreement and disagreement among the groups.

This investigation based on the 'conversational science' paradigm yielded a number of interesting results:
1 There was a clear difference in the emphasis given to 'marking' and to 'feed-back' by different tutors. Only one of them had an equal mix of both, and clearly separated the two functions.
2 The FOCUS and CHANGE grid conversations led to a considerable improve-ment in the quality of individual marking both in consistency and in the students' views of the usefulness of the comments.
3 The tutors were very enthusiastic about the sessions in which they POOLed their elements and constructs and arrived at the CONSENSUS FRAME grid. The comparison between CONSENSUS FRAME grids filled in by different tutors clearly revealed why students sometimes raised complaints about 'tight' or 'unfair' marking by some of them, and why the monitor viewed others as

'too soft'. The quality of the discussion and negotiation which took place around these CONSENSUS FRAME grids was very productive and amazingly free from acrimony. This was because difficulties were clearly identified and immediately referable to differences between the personal evaluative meaning systems of the tutors concerned.

Finally, the CONSENSUS FRAME grids clearly separated out three levels of 'feedback' comment which could be written on the assignment. There were those comments that related directly to short items within the student's work. There were those that related to the structure or quality of the assignment treated as a whole. And there were those comments that related to a student's progress (or otherwise) over a sequence of assignments. Tutors varied considerably in the frequency with which they offered these different types of comment. They also differed in the constructs which they found useful in differentiating between comments at each of the three different levels.

Whilst this particular study was only 'fed back' informally to the students there was very clear evidence that one side-effect was a considerable improvement in the conversation which these tutors were later able to sustain with their students. Three of them felt, and went out of their way to tell us, that this exercise was the most significant event they had experienced in influencing their skill and competence as teachers.

The authors have used similar techniques in less well-documented work with tutors and students in a number of different topic (academic subject) areas. One of our current postgraduate students, who is the headmaster of a primary school, has over a period of five years generated analogous conversations between children, staff and parents about alternative perspectives on the quality of written work and of projects. This is part of the systematic introduction into the school curriculum of learning conversations designed to encourage self-organised learning among these children.

Activity 10.4 Revealing an 'examiners' construct system

Readers who as T-C practitioners have access to a representative sample of:
   (1) Examination scripts
   (2) Laboratory reports
   (3) Athletic performances
   (4) Projects
   (5) Attempted works of art
   (6) Manufactured products
or (7) Any other products of learning
or who can collect a sample of 'products of learning' from their peers may find it quite revealing to elicit a straightforward grid using the products as elements. FOCUS it and reflect on the results.

Assign 'marks' to each element and proportionally reduce these marks down to the same rating scale as you have used in the grid. Now FOCUS the marks into the grids. To which constructs do they most relate? Try weighting the constructs so that the weighted scores of the elements align with the marks.

Activity 10.5 Comparing assessors

For those readers who are members of an examining board, a taste panel, a selection committee, a wine tasting club, etc. it is very revealing to get all the members of your group to do activity 10.4.

Now use the PAIRS technique to enable participants to compare with each other. Do the distribution of their constructs in the PAIRed comparisons reveal any of the reasons for inconsistency among the group?

Activity 10.6 Exchanging evaluative systems

Use the EXCHANGE grid technique:

(1) To explore your understanding of the evaluative system used by one of your colleagues or peers.
(2) To explore the areas of agreement and disagreement.

Do the constructs used reveal the evaluative basis of any disagreement in 'marking'?

Activity 10.7 Improving performance by knowing how to evaluate it

As a learner, does a grid on products of learning, i.e. lecture notes, performance, essay, reveal any reasons why you have not been scoring as highly as you might wish? Physical or manual performances can be video-recorded and then used as elements if you keep a record of the tape counter reading at the beginning of each separate performance.

Do EXCHANGE grids with other learners. Does this add to your understanding of the characteristics of a good performance?

The implications of EXCHANGE of meaning

EXCHANGE grids are a powerful addition to the reflective learning tool-bag and they have particular significance in the area of self-assessment and examinations.

Firstly, at the content-level of conversation the whole tool-set of FOCUS, TRIGRID, REFLECT, PERCEIVE, EVALUATE, etc. can be used by each participant separately to enhance their understanding of the subject matter or topic of the conversation. When the sensory, descriptive and inferential classification of constructs in the perceptual grid is replaced by the factual, instructional, explanatory, constructional and creative categories of the content of conversation, we open up possibilities for illuminating differences between the systems of personal meaning from which the T-C content contributions are sent and personal meaning systems into which they are received and vice versa. Using the EXCHANGE and COMBINE techniques allows us:

(a) To make any asymmetry in conversation explicit to both learners and practitioners of T-C.

(b) To combine different versions of the topic in shared, agreed and mutually more constructive and creative terms, thus redefining it.

(c) To externalise and elaborate content construing and thus improve the quality of the teaching/learning conversation.

As the participants become familiar with elicitation, hand-FOCUSing, and EXCHANGE, these techniques can be fully recruited into the conversation; being used when and where, but only to the extent that they serve its immediate ongoing purposes. Gradually the constructions of the mind induced by such grid conversations become second nature to their users and many of the results can be achieved without the explicit use of externalised grid techniques at all. This is a significant move in the direction of self-organisation.

Great though the gains from grid illumination of the *content* of a conversation may be, they pall into insignificance when compared with the consequences of using grids to illuminate the conversational *process*.

Again, the early contributions of grid techniques to the process level of the conversation recruit the individual techniques described in earlier chapters of the book. Thus each participant may explore their view of themselves as conversationalists by doing a 'people I know well as participants in this kind of conversation' grid in which the classic 'me as I am' and 'me as I would like to be' are introduced as additional elements. Comparing, exchanging and combining constructs can add a sharing component to this activity.

Similarly, but more intensively, each participant can do a grid in which conversations are the elements: more intensively still the elements can be representative samples of events within a teaching/learning conversation. These two types of grid about conversation begin to illuminate the system of personal meaning which the participant has about the conversational process. Scrutiny of the levels of construct (i.e. ritualistic, instructional or explanatory) which each person uses again indicates any potentially disabling asymmetry between them.

Finally, participants in a serious ongoing conversational process (i.e. a long-term tutoring, coaching, training, counselling, teaching, consulting, therapeutic or custodial relationship) are well advised to take time out after a few sessions and use the experience of those shared sessions as a source of 'items of significant conversational experience'. These can then be used to transact a fully fledged EXCHANGE and COMBINE exercise.

Thus, in outline, we see how these techniques can contribute to the power of a mind to develop patterns of personal meaning about itself, about other minds with which it converses, and about the process of conversation itself. It is in this context that an exchange about referents and standards can produce the conditions in which both self-evaluation and public assessment can both thrive and serve their differently useful purposes.

This exploration brings us to one final important characteristic of conversation. Some conversations are intended to achieve as much understanding as possible, some even strive for large areas of agreement but neither of these purposes is necessary for certain types of conversation. If the aim of self-organised learning is to produce systems of personally relevant and viable meaning in the individual, and if personal meaning is always self-constructed, then we can begin to envisage conversations designed to optimise this process in each participant separately. The use of understanding and agreement is merely a means to this end. Nobody need understand everything that is going on so long as it enriches the personal meaning systems of the participants.

The general observation has been made that in education the learner and the teacher too often live in their own private worlds, making only minimal contact. This leads the teacher to see the learners as 'ruffians' or 'barbarians' who are incapable of appreciating the pearls he or she has to offer, or it leads to the teacher devaluing themselves first as a professional and eventually as a person. Given the intention, this inability to communicate arises from a combination of attitude, experience and lack of technique. Given the technique, the attitude and intentionality may change and develop, gradually building up experience of successful interactions which feed back positively into the personal myths about the teaching/learning situation.

The repertory grid is obviously only one of many methods that can be used to generate more effective communication. Essays, discussions, interactive lessons or seminars, role-playing, educational games and many other devices can be used. The grid has the advantage of starting from scratch with no givens and therefore provides an arena for the negotiation of understanding out of a situation in which very little exists.

In summary, there are four different approaches to the exchange of meaning. In the first method, person A sets out to enter B's world in B's terms. By attempting to use B's elements and B's constructs as he feels B would himself use them, A suspends his own system and attempts to see the topic area through B's eyes. The 'DIFFERENCE grid' measures A's success and by defining those elements and constructs on which there is most difference diagnoses the area of least communication. The ensuing conversation can lead A step by step to B's point of view. This 'see it through my eyes' is the epitome of the 'interpreter of knowledge' approach to education.

The second method is in some ways only an extension of the first, since B attempts to enter A's world whilst A enters B's. However, the reciprocality of this approach usually leads to an extension of the EXCHANGE situation. Having each entered the other's world, the participants usually begin to compare and contrast their points of view. This process is made explicit in the third and fourth methods.

In method three the participants have already agreed a mutually acceptable set of elements so their grids cannot only be EXCHANGEd, their constructs and the associated ratings can be pooled into a common grid where FOCUSing with PAIRS highlights the degree of overlap between the two ways of construing the same elements.

The fourth method extends the negotiation still further. Starting only with a common topic in mind the participants are taken step by step through the whole process of generating 'real' conversation. The two participants each generate their own elements and elicit their own grids. This takes them into their own worlds. They then EXCHANGE each, trying to rate the other's elements on the other's constructs. When A's view of B's grid is compared to B's original form the extent of one half of the communication problem is revealed. When B does A's grid the other side of the coin appears. This simple EXCHANGE process can proceed reiteratively until understanding is achieved on both sides, but the two worlds still remain separate. As A's elements are introduced into B's grid and vice versa the meanings begin to be shared. As they also try to use each other's constructs the area of shared meaning extends. If the EXCHANGE is continued until each can reproduce the other's combined grid understanding has been achieved. To the extent that the two combined grids map on to each other agreement has also been reached. When A looks at B's grid in the context of his own, he is assessing it and vice versa. If two participants can complete this total sequence of exchange a 'good' conversation will have occurred.

If three people A, B, and C participate in exchange activities, three potential pairs appear. A with B, B with C and C with A. As the size of group increases, the measures of relatedness or overlap become quite complex. When two grids are FOCUSed together a measure of the relationship can be obtained using the PAIRS technique. This method was used in the English essays example earlier. Other measures of overlap can be obtained as will be seen in the next chapter, but the principle remains the same. Overlap is a measure of the degree to which the two sets of constructs order the shared elements in the same way. Now, reverting to our three participants, the three pairings yield three measures of relatedness. Thus, the participants can be represented in a triangle in which distance indicates lack of relatedness. A and C are more like each other than either of them is to B.

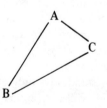

Figure 10.19 Network of three grids

As more participants attempt to exchange meanings, the pairings multiply. The whole matrix of 'relatedness measures' highlights the expected areas of communication difficulty within the group. This approach is the POOL, RE-FINE, SOCIO-GRID, CONSENSUS FRAME and THESAURUS techniques described in the next chapter.

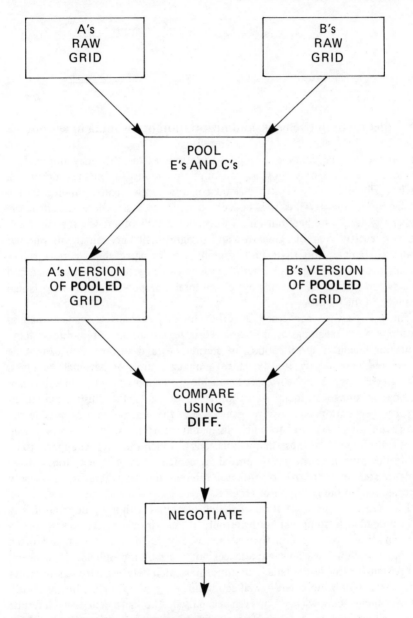

Figure 10.20 POOL and EXCHANGE: an algorithm

Chapter 11

Groups and institutions as personal learning systems

The construction, exchange and negotiation of meaning in a group

The theme of this chapter is not so ambitious as the title may imply. It is intended to explore only those aspects of group and institutional learning which can be easily and clearly identified as the construction, exchange and negotiation of shared meanings. Thus it is concerned with those situations in which the primary issue is whether individuals understand each other, whether they can validly identify areas of agreement and disagreement between them, whether groups of people who share understanding and/or agree about certain topics can discover each other and whether groups can negotiate new extended and valid systems of shared meaning out of the total mindpool of individual personal meanings in the groups.

The book is not concerned directly with de-personalised, institutionalised meanings. Such meanings as are expressed in legal contracts, in auditors' documents, in technical specifications, in dictionaries and so on, often cannot be shared and clarified by the exchange and negotiation of personal meanings. The agreed referent in such cases is outside the group who may directly share personal meaning. As many of us know, to our cost, the illusion that interpersonal negotiation can resolve issues where the real referent is outside the negotiating group can lead to much dissipated effort and wasted emotion. Even more troublesome are those many situations in which the referent appears to be within the control of the group, until disagreement or interference from outside demonstrates that control of the real referent lies elsewhere and had only appeared within the group on sufferance.

The idea that the negotiation of shared meanings within a group can in any sense be called learning will surprise only those who have never taken part in such an enterprise. Such activities are usually highly significant and often traumatic personal learning experiences for most of the individuals involved. The reason for this is the large amount of mismatch between personal meanings which exist within apparently well-communicating groups or institutions without ever being acknowledged or even recognised. The inefficiency which results from such inadequate personal communication is often misconstrued as resulting from a lack of motivation or incompetence. The increase in group efficiency which can be achieved by creating a system of shared meanings is analogous to personal learning by the individual. It is this that has made T-groups, encounter groups, TA and social skills active areas of industrial and commercial training. It is the inability to identify and pin down the real issues in this area that has made it a victim of fashion and the latest well-publicised training method.

Whilst totally valid, the previous paragraph may have been misleading. The idea of a group as a learning system can have two interpretations. The first interpretation implies that the group is the locus for much individual personal learning. This is usually so and chapters 9 and 10 have explored this. But can a group be said to learn? And if so how? By analogy to the individual a group might be said to learn if:

(a) its behaviour changes in valued ways;
(b) its capacity to attribute meaning to people, things, or events changes in valued ways.

If we take our personal learning analogy further, for the change to be 'group learning' it must be valued by the group itself.

Within the terms of reference of this book the emphasis is on the second of these definitions. The previous chapter has shown us how two people can increase their capacity to converse by using EXCHANGE grids as aids to conversation. Here we are concerned to extend this usage.

SOCIO-GRIDS: in which elements are shared and constructs are personal

Phase 1

In chapter 4 Mr Donaldson was introduced and his grid was offered as an example of how to explore issues of staff appraisal by increasing the individuals' awareness of the personal meanings which are applied. Seven managers in the Management Services Department elicited grids using their subordinates (i.e. the people answering directly to them) as elements. In some cases the number of elements was augmented by including other employees who were well known to them. Using the PEGASUS Interactive Grid Elicitation Program each manager was encouraged to examine the basic dimensions of his own thoughts and feelings about his subordinates as he felt they contributed to the work of the department. Immediately they had completed the PEGASUS run, each of them was talked back through their FOCUSed grid, thus enabling them to achieve a greater explicit awareness of their own 'natural' processes of judging and appraising.

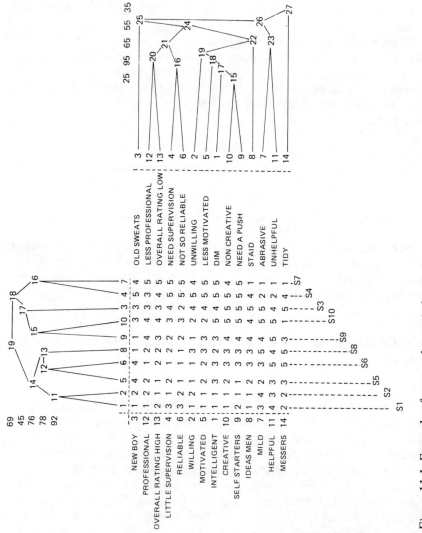

Figure 11.1 Example of a second appraisal grid

Phase 2

During the period in which these initial grids were elicited, the group had identified twelve of the people working for them who were well known to all of them.
These twelve were chosen as representing the full range and variety of employees
in the department. Each manager privately considered their 'shared elements' in
the light of his 'dimensions of judgment' as revealed in the FOCUSed grid from
the first PEGASUS run. A week or ten days later they each elicited another grid
on PEGASUS. Each of them used the set of shared 'people' elements. Again,
each manager was immediately talked back through his FOCUSed grid. An
example of their second FOCUSed grid is shown in Fig. 11.1.

Phase 3

The results from Phase 2 were analysed. The SOCIO-GRID package allows one
repertory grid to be compared with another. This is only possible when the users
have agreed a set of shared elements. The program numerically identifies the
degree to which each construct (dimension of judgment) used by one person is
shared by the others. By comparing each of the seven managers with each of
his colleagues a matrix of similarity scores is calculated.

Thus the five constructs which matched highest among the whole group were:

planning/creative ability	v.	poor planning/problem analysis
persistence	v.	lack of determination
works independently	v.	needs supervision
communicator	v.	dumb
intelligent	v.	unintelligent

In this project the results obtained by comparing grids was used as a spur to
further negotiation among the client group. For example, the implications of the
construct ordering is illustrated by constructing a 'MODE grid' in which the
fifteen most shared constructs with the responses assigned by the manager using
them are reconstituted. A version of the MODE grid is shown in Fig. 11.2.

Each grid is compared with each other grid with respect to the degree to
which one person's constructs are shared by the other. A matrix showing the
similarity between all possible pairs among the seven managers is computed.
From this a series of sociometric diagrams is constructed showing which managers
most share their construing. These SOCIO-NETS are shown in Figure 11.3. The
numbers in the diagrams represent the seven managers; the lines show who is
thinking and feeling most like whom; the dotted lines in each diagram indicates
the last relationship to be added. Thus link 1 shows that managers 4 and 5 have
the greatest degree of similarity in their construing of the twelve shared elements. (The direction of the arrow indicates that 5 has a wider range of construing than 4 and therefore shares less of his constructs with 4 than 4 does
with 5.) Link 2 shows that managers 5 and 3 also have much in common. Link 3
shows that manager 6 next joins 4 and so on.

ELEMENTS

Construct (–)	E12	E9	E10	E4	E8	E1	E3	E7	E5	E6	E2	E11	Construct (+)	Contributed by Manager
Juniors	x	x	x	x	x	x	o		o	o	o	o	Seniors	6
Needs supervision	x	x	x	x			o		o	o	o	o	Works independently	2
Less professional	x	x	x	x	x		o	o		o	o	o	Professional	6
Intelligent	x	x	x	x	x		o	o		o	o	o	Intelligent	6
Dislike pressure	x	x	x	x	x		o	o		o	o	o	Accept pressure	4
Needs supervision	x	x	x	x	x	x	x		x	o	o	o	Unsupervised	4
Lacks judgment	x	x	x	x	x					o	o	o	Has good judgment	5
Poor communication	x	x	x	x	x			o	o	o	o		Good communication	3
Follow	x	x	x	x	x			o	o	o	o		Lead	7
Oral communication poor	x	x	x				o	o	o	o	o	x	Oral communication good	4
Dumb	x	x	x	x		x	o	o	o	o	o	o	Communicator	1
Lack of determination	x	x	x	x		x	o	o	o	o	o		Persistence	3
Poor planning/ Problem analysis	x	x	x		x		o		o	o	o		Planning/ creative ability	3
Narrow view	x	x	x	o			o	o	o	o	o	o	Wider view	4
No staff responsibilities	x	x		o			o	o	o	o	o	o	Has/had staff responsibilities	5

o = ratings 1 or 2   x = ratings 4 or 5   blank = rating 3

Figure 11.2 Simplified mode grid showing which managers contributed which constructs

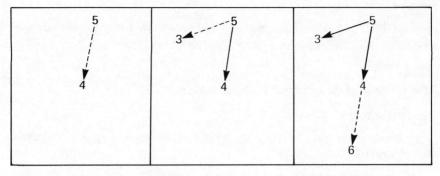

LINK 1   LINK 2   LINK 3

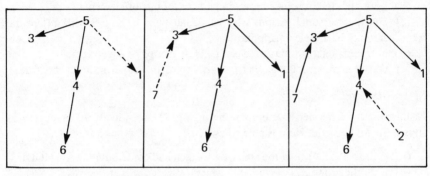

LINK 4   LINK 5   LINK 6

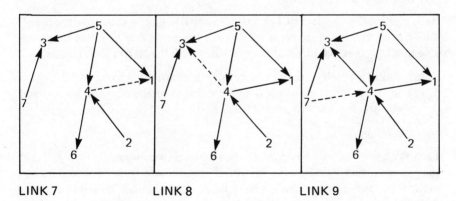

LINK 7   LINK 8   LINK 9

Figure 11.3 SOCIO-NETS

Phase 4

The results of the Phase 3 analysis were fed back individually to each manager. These feedback sessions took about an hour to an hour and a half.

The structure of the individual feedback session*

(i) PEGASUS 2

Each manager was asked to reflect on the analysis of his second run on PEGASUS in order to:

- (a) refresh his memory of the personal constructs he used when considering the shared set of 12 individuals (elements);
- (b) note high relationships between pairs or groups of elements;
- (c) consider personal reasons why particular pairs or groups within the total set may be alike or dissimilar;
- (d) note high relationships between pairs or groups of constructs;
- (e) consider construct clusters to ascertain possible superordinate constructs.

(ii) MODE grid

Having discussed his personal construing of the 12 individuals, the manager was shown the MODE grid. He was able to:

- (a) explore the nature of the constructs which had contributed to the MODE;
- (b) note the groupings of elements which reflected this consensus.

(iii) Individual with the MODE

Each individual grid was FOCUSed with the MODE grid to show how the individual related to the central construing of the group. At this point the client was able to see his personal PEGASUS 2 compared with the MODE grid. He could:

- (a) consider which (if any) of his constructs contributed to the MODE;
- (b) note the extent to which both his ordering of elements and his personal constructs related to the MODE analysis.

(iv) 'Grid mix' similarity measures

Each manager was able to examine the relationship between his own grid and that of any other member. He was encouraged to note those to whom he was most alike and also members who differed from himself in terms of their appraisal of the shared set of individuals.

(v) SOCIO-NET

Having explored the relationships between his own grid and those of other members of the exercise, the client was now shown the inter-linkage within the group. He could note:

---

* Each particular session may have deviated slightly from this outline at the discretion of the consultants.

    (a) the most highly matched pair within the group;

    (b) the order in which individual members were drawn into the SOCIO-NET;

    (c) where he himself was placed within this overall pattern;

    (d) which individual or individuals were least like other members;

    (e) which individual member had the most inter-link with the others within the group.

(vi) Element tree diagram

The manager was asked to reflect on the similarities and differences between his own element tree diagram and those of the other group members. Particular areas of disagreement were commented on. The manager was encouraged to consider whether any particular different ordering of elements could 'make sense' to him.

(vii) List of constructs

This list was provided for each manager so that he could note the range of constructs used by the group. It was suggested that he considered these in terms of how easily he felt he might identify with and use constructs which he had omitted from his personal grid.

The feedback sessions revealed the extent to which individual managers were aware of the structure of construing about appraisal that existed within the group and where they stood within this. Discussion of the position of the person in the group was often very intense.

Phase 5

PEGASUS 1 repeated.

Each manager was later asked to reflect on his original PEGASUS 1 grid (using his own subordinates) and to fill in this grid again. He was also asked to complete appraisal forms for each person. This data was then used to measure changes over the duration of the study.

Results and conclusions

The managers all reported that they enjoyed the PEGASUS elicitation sessions on the computer. They appeared to be deeply involved in the interaction and felt that the feedback comments generated by the computer were often quite revealing and pushed them to explore what they thought and felt more exactly than they otherwise would. The fact that the whole elicitation was carried on in the user's own terms maintained the reality of the conversation throughout. The talkback sessions with the FOCUSed grid also seemed to involve each of the seven managers quite deeply, although they varied in terms of how much it revealed something new to them and how much it seemed to be merely confirming and making explicit something which they already felt. The most general finding was that all seven managers had quite a clear pattern of construing of subordinates but varied considerably in the verbal labels used to describe their constructs.

When the grids of shared elements were analysed the results again showed that the words used to differentiate among subordinates were much more varied than the basic structure and pattern of construing. Thus much of the apparent elaboration of construing is more verbal than operational. The MODE grid illustrates this; the fifteen constructs which were most representative of the group's construing were all quite alike in the way in which they sorted the elements.

One measure of the impact of the PEGASUS program is to compare the constructs elicited during the two PEGASUS interactions. Some managers changed their constructs considerably whilst others preserved the terms of their construing. The authors also classified all the constructs produced during the PEGASUS 2 runs using the nine major categories of the appraisal form. This is shown in Fig. 11.4. It is interesting to note that the authors were unable to assign almost half of the personal constructs used by the managers to the appraisal form categories.

The empirical study finished with a brief EXCHANGE session with all the managers. Whilst a number of interesting EXCHANGES took place, the level of interaction was quite superficial. The study included negotiation and evaluation of the existing appraisal system. The information in Fig. 11.4 was used as the basis for a more prolonged discussion. The participants did not always agree with the consultants' classification of their constructs and the evidence was re-assessed to encompass the consensus classification produced by the group.

In order to appreciate the quality of this interaction, the reader is invited to produce his own category system of the participants' constructs and to map this on to the categories in the existing appraisal form.

Follow-up

The follow-up data consisted of the original PEGASUS 1 grids compared with the same elements and constructs re-rated one month after the study, and it also included a comparison of the ratings given on the appraisal form before the study was completed. The comparison of the before and after PEGASUS runs was made using the CORE program described in chapter 9. This program shows the degree to which elements and constructs change between the two elicitations.

Negotiating shared elements and shared constructs for a group topic

The repertory grid is a method for enabling individuals to explore their own experience. It allows them to inquire into their intuitive understanding of a topic or an area of mutual concern. It helps each of them to become more aware of how they perceive, think and feel about events and it encourages them to express this increased understanding in their own personal terms.

	G2	G1	G5	G4	G7	G6	G3
3 Communication skills	C2	C11	C7	C3, C10	C8		C6, C2
7 Motivation	C3, C8	C4, C9	C10, C14, C1	C8		C8	
6 Technical skills	C4, C13	C12	C5	C4	C4		
8 Effectiveness	C9	C7		C9, C11		C1	C7, C5
1 Managerial and supervisory skills		C8, C2	C9, C4		C5, C11	C6	
9 Creativity	C1, C11				C9, C1	C13	C4
5 Contribution to work activity outside remit	C10	C13					
4 Knowledge of division			C8				
2 Relationships				C12			
Not accounted for	C5, C6, C7, C12	C1, C3, C5, C6, C10, C14	C2, C3, C6, C11, C12, C13, C15	C1, C2, C5, C6, C7, C13, C14, C15	C2, C3, C6, C7, C10	C2, C3, C4, C5, C7, C9, C10, C11, C12	C1, C3

Figure 11.4 Personal constructs categorised according to items on appraisal form

The core of this 'soft technology' consists in the series of well-defined, content-free conversational procedures which have been developed in earlier chapters. These regulate quite exactly the process by which the conversation is generated, but they leave the participants completely free to contribute their own content in their own terms.

Although the units of personal meanings elicited in such regulated conversations are unique to the individual, they are expressed in a form which can be analysed using various computer programs, e.g. FOCUS. These programs identify the underlying pattern of personal meaning which can then be offered back to the individual, for him (or her) to 'REFLECT' upon. The 'REFLECT' procedure, whereby the FOCUSed results are offered back and talked through, is itself another well-defined content-free conversational procedure.

The conversational procedures and computer programs of the CSHL communication technology combine to offer a powerful resource for breaking through the partial understanding and misunderstanding of conventional unregulated conversation.

This is achieved by enabling each individual to explore their own experiences and to:

1 Identify the personal meaning of an area of mutual concern (e.g. the quality of product x).
2 Analyse, systematise and display the patterns of personal meaning so that individuals may reflect upon them and increase their awareness of their own perceptions, thoughts and feelings about the topic (e.g. the FOCUSed grid).
3 Identify areas of shared experience and recognise those areas in which experience is not shared (e.g. manufacturing processes and marketing influences).
4 Identify a shared terminology which arises out of individual usage and represents all the significant nuances of meaning expressed by each and every participant.
5 Enable each participant to express their own experience and personal meanings in this shared two-dimensional terminology of the group (e.g. quality 'faults' and 'ways of thinking and feeling about quality').
6 Compare and contrast individual expressions of personal experience to identify patterns of agreement and disagreement between participants.
7 Use the techniques in cascade to negotiate a better understanding and more agreement about the area of mutual concern.

POOL, REFINE and CONSENSUS FRAME

The following account summarises the variety of personal meaning attributed by managers to the same topic, i.e. the quality of a product.

The 129 descriptions of 'faults' used in the eleven individual grids were reproduced as sets of 129 cards. There was naturally considerable overlap both in the actual verbal labels used to describe faults, e.g. fines, over toast, etc. and in ideas behind the terminology, i.e. dusty, powdery, double berries, married berries, etc.

However, *it is an important part of the 'POOL' procedure that the consultants do not allow their judgments, understanding or prejudice to intrude into the process of generating the CONSENSUS FRAME language.*

This is the crucial aspect of the content-free procedures. The consultants do not interfere with the content of the conversation, they merely regulate the procedures by which the conversation is generated. Thus, in spite of the apparent overlap and repetition, all 129 cards were used in POOL conversation.

The results from these POOL conversations were then processed using the CSHL THESAURUS computer program. This program compares and contrasts the ways in which each item is valued and categorised by the individuals in the group. It downgrades items which are consistently viewed as ambiguous and/or unimportant by most of the group. These items can, however, be recycled, clarified, refined, dropped or reintroduced back into the THESAURUS analysis later. By a method of reiterative multiple clustering, the program identifies patterns of coherent meaning from the consistency of individual usage.

The output from the THESAURUS program was discussed with Mr X and Mr Y using the 'REFINE' procedure. This discussion produced a non-redundant set of 50 elements. In other studies this REFINE activity has involved more (or even all) members of the participating group. In this study the results were unambiguous enough not to require more widespread discussion.

Similarly the POOL, THESAURUS and REFINE processes were carried out using the 230 pole descriptions of 'ways of thinking and feeling about quality' which emerged from the 11 individual repertory grids. This eventually produced a non-redundant set of 30 'ways of thinking and feeling about quality' (constructs).

Together these two conversationally negotiated sets of 'faults' and 'ways of thinking and feeling about quality' constitute the common CONSENSUS FRAME of an apparently shared, two-dimensional language which includes every personal meaning offered by any member of the group.

Personal interpretations of the shared language: individual CONSENSUS FRAME grids

The CONSENSUS FRAME procedure is similar to CONSTRUCT except that the CF elements (faults) and CF constructs (ways of thinking and feeling about quality) are already defined and were therefore available on sets of pre-prepared cards. Each participant was asked to rate all the CF elements on all the CF constructs.

Fig. 11.5 shows Mr Production's CONSENSUS FRAME grid after it had been through the FOCUS computer analysis and display.

The REFLECT 'B' conversational procedure (Fig. 11.10) uses the CONSENSUS FRAME grid to talk the individual manager back through his

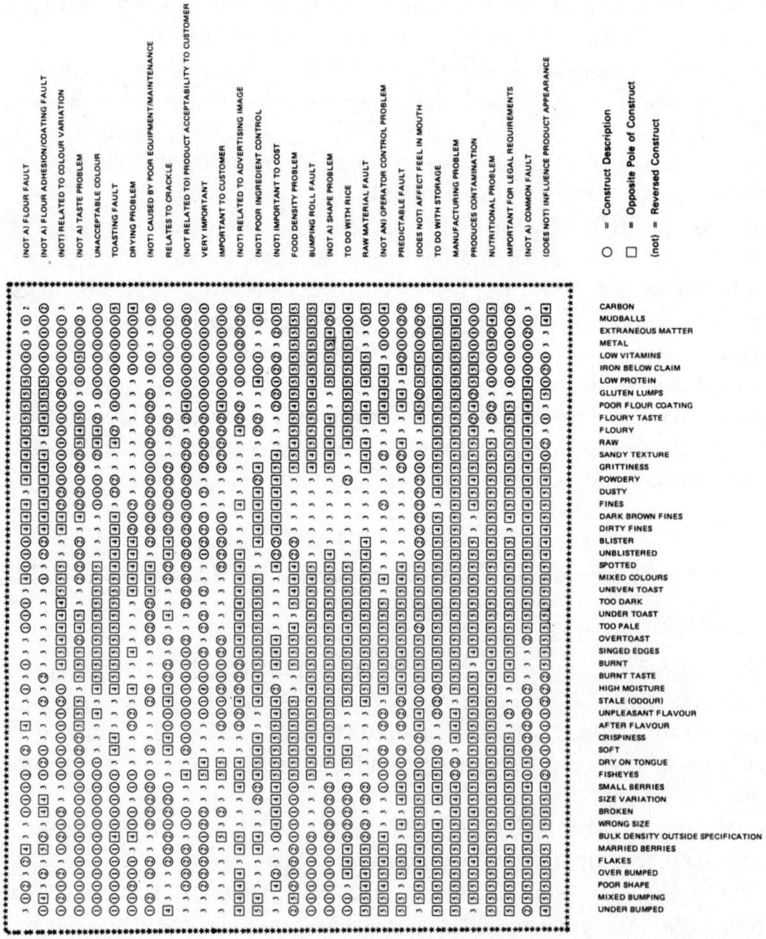

Figure 11.5 Mr Production's CONSENSUS FRAME grid

the CONSENSUS FRAME grid to talk the individual manager back through his views of quality to raise awareness and encourage reflection about the personal inferences which he draws from the evidence of faults on the product. This also serves as preparation for the EXCHANGE and CONVERSE procedures in which personal views are shared, compared and negotiated with others in the Management Group. Extracts from a transcript of a REFLECT 'B' conversation was presented in chapter 5.

Exploring and comparing the views of the management group

Comparing two managers' usage of the shared language

Each manager has rated each CF (consensus frame) element (fault) on every CF construct (ways of thinking and feeling about quality). It is therefore possible to examine in detail how any two managers differ in their experience and use of the shared language.

As Mr Production and Mr Marketing have both used exactly the same set of CF elements and CF constructs it follows that a complete analysis of areas of agreement and disagreement between them can be calculated.

By computing the difference in each cell, an elaborate map of the pattern of agreement and disagreement is obtained. But 1500 separate differences are difficult to assimilate. By summing the total differences in each column, it is possible to compare elements (faults) for the amount of agreement and disagreement they evoke.

E.g. Mr Production and Mr Marketing

agree most about:	*disagree most about*:
Grittiness	Mud balls
Sandy texture	Low protein
Too dark	Bulky density outside spec.
Powdery	High moisture

When the total differences across rows in the CONSENSUS FRAME grids are computed we see the amount of agreement or disagreement about constructs (ways of thinking and feeling about quality).

E.g. Mr Production and Mr Marketing

agree most about:	*disagree most about*:
Manufacturing problem	Relates to advertising image
Nutritional problem	Caused by poor equipment/ maintenance
Importance for legal requirements	Important for cost
To do with storage	Common fault

MR PRODUCTION and MR MARKETING	MR PRODUCTION and MR QUALITY	MR QUALITY and MR MARKETING
Grittiness MOST AGREEMENT	METAL MOST AGREEMENT	Under toast
Sandy texture	Too dark	Burnt taste
Too dark	Low protein	After flavour
Powdery	Mud balls	Low vitamins
Floury	High moisture	Uneven toast
Under toast	Extraneous matter	Too dark
Over toast	Too pale	Over toast
Metal	Iron below claim	Floury
Under bumped	Small berries	Size variation
Singed edges	Fisheyes	Blister
Iron below claim	Under toast	Burnt
Raw	Unpleasant flavour	Singed edges
Extraneous matter	Broken	Soft
Stale	Over bumped	Fines
After flavour	Floury	Small berries
Small berries	Size variation	Floury taste
Uneven toast	Mixed colours	Wrong size
Burnt	Uneven toast	Gluten lumps
Mixed bumping	Burnt	Mixed colours
Gluten lumps	Soft	Metal
Flakes	Dirty fines	Under bumped
Floury taste	Spotted	Iron below claim
Soft	Dry on tongue	Stale
Fines	Floury taste	Too pale
Unpleasant flavour	Fines	Extraneous matter
Size variation	Low vitamins	Dusty
Broken	Poor shape	Poor shape
Spotted	Wrong size	Broken
Dusty	Under bumped	Unpleasant flavour
Poor shape	Sandy texture	Grittiness
Fisheyes	Singed edges	Raw
Burnt taste	Raw	Fisheyes
Low vitamins	Burnt taste	Spotted
Mixed colours	Dusty	Carbon
Dirty fines	Unblistered	Sandy texture
Crispiness	Over toast	High moisture
Married berries	Bulk density outside spec.	Low protein
Wrong size	Crispiness	Dry on tongue
Too pale	Dark brown fines	Poor flour coating
Poor flour coating	Carbon	Crispiness
Over bumped	After flavour	Married berries
Unblistered	Flakes	Flakes
Dark brown fines	Blister	Over bumped
Carbon	Stale	Dark brown fines
Blister	Grittiness	Bulk density outside spec.
Dry on tongue	Gluten lumps	Dirty fines
High moisture	Mixed bumping	Unblistered
Bulk density outside spec.	Powdery	Mixed bumping
Low protein	Married berries	Powdery
Mud balls LEAST AGREEMENT	Poor flour coating LEAST AGREEMENT	Mud balls

Figure 11.6 Agreement and disagreement on Es

MR PRODUCTION and MR MARKETING	MR PRODUCTION and MR QUALITY	MR QUALITY and MR MARKETING
MOST AGREEMENT	**MOST AGREEMENT**	
Manufacturing problem	Nutritional problems	Nutritional problem
Nutritional problem	Manufacturing problem	Manufacturing problem
Important for legal requirements	Toasting fault	To do with storage
To do with storage	Influences product appearance	Important for legal requirements
Related to colour variation	To do with storage	Related to colour variation
Influences product appearance	Importance for legal requirements	Produces contamination
Predictable fault	Produces contamination	Influences product appearance
Toasting fault	Bumping roll fault	Bumping roll fault
Produces contamination	Shape problem	Taste problem
Unacceptable colour	Related to colour variation	Drying problem
- - - - - - - - - - - - - -	- - - - - - - - - - - - - -	- - - - - - - - - - - - - -
Relates to crackle	Food density problem	Raw material fault
Taste problem	Product acceptability to customer	Unacceptable colour
Bumping roll fault	Taste problem	Toasting fault
Shape fault	To do with rice	Shape problem
Operator control problem	Operator control problem	Very important
Flour fault	Unacceptable colour	Caused by poor equipment/maintenance
Raw material fault	Raw material fault	Relates to crackle
Very important	Poor ingredient control	To do with rice
To do with rice	Relates to advertising image	Affects feel in mouth
Important to customer	Very important	Flour fault
- - - - - - - - - - - - - -	- - - - - - - - - - - - - -	- - - - - - - - - - - - - -
Product acceptability to customer	Common fault	Product acceptability to customer
Poor ingredient control	Relates to crackle	Important to customer
Drying problem	Drying problem	Important for cost
Food density problem	Affects feel in mouth	Flour adhesion/coating problem
Flour adhesion/coating fault	Flour fault	Food density problem
Affects feel in mouth	Important to customer	Operator control problem
Common fault	Caused by poor equipment/maintenance	Common fault
Important for cost	Predictable fault	Predictable fault
Caused by poor equipment/maintenance	Important for cost	Poor ingredient control
Relates to advertising image	Flour adhesion/coating fault	Relates to advertising image
LEAST AGREEMENT	**LEAST AGREEMENT**	

Figure 11.7 Agreement and disagreement on Cs

The full computations of the areas of agreement and disagreement between Mr Production, Mr Quality and Mr Marketing are shown in Figures 11.6 and 11.7.

SOCIO-NETS in which elements and constructs are shared

When the ratings on any two CONSENSUS FRAME grids are compared, it is possible to compute a 'total difference score' between them. Of the ten managers who completed the CONSENSUS FRAME grids, four were in quality assurance, three were in production and three in marketing. Thus, there are forty-five pairs for whom a total difference score can be calculated. It is possible to express this visually by constructing a sequence of diagrams starting with the pair who agree most with each other and gradually introducing additional pairings on the basis of decreasing degrees of agreement. This is illustrated in the SOCIO-NET display, Fig. 11.8.

Inspection of Item 1 in this display shows that the pair who agree most are Q1 and P2. The next pair are Q2 and Q1 (Item 2). In Item 3, Q3 pairs with P2. The first seventeen items show the four quality managers and the three production managers gradually coming together into a network of agreement. It is only at Item 18 that the first marketing manager (M2) joins this group. M3 joins at Item 22 and at Item 26. This visually illustrates that there is a greater consensus of agreement about quality among the Qs and Ps than there is between this whole group and the Ms. Reference to the detailed DIFF. grids showed that this relative agreement between Qs and Ps conceals a wealth of individual differences. The SOCIO-NET display shows that the Ms not only disagree with the Qs and Ps but also disagree with each other.

This account shows how negotiation about a topic among a Management Group can start by eliciting repertory grids. The topic could be research policy, views of the potential market, identifying high-flyers, new product, quality (as in this example) or any other issue of importance to the company. It goes on to demonstrate how personal 'items of experience' and 'ways of thinking and feeling about these items' as elicited in the individual grids can be POOLed and sifted to construct a two-dimensional CONSENSUS FRAME language out of the group's own real experience. Individual managers can then use this shared natural language to explore and exhibit their own attitudes, understanding and prejudices about the topic. Comparison between individual CONSENSUS FRAME grids reveals in great detail the anatomy of agreement and disagreement between managers.

The SOCIO-NET technique visually summarises the patterns of agreement and disagreement among the group. The group FOCUSed grids (p. 306, Fig. 11.10) summarises the views of the topic which are common to the group. These evidences can serve as guides in further negotiations; adding rigour and precision to decision-making about policy and day-to-day practice.

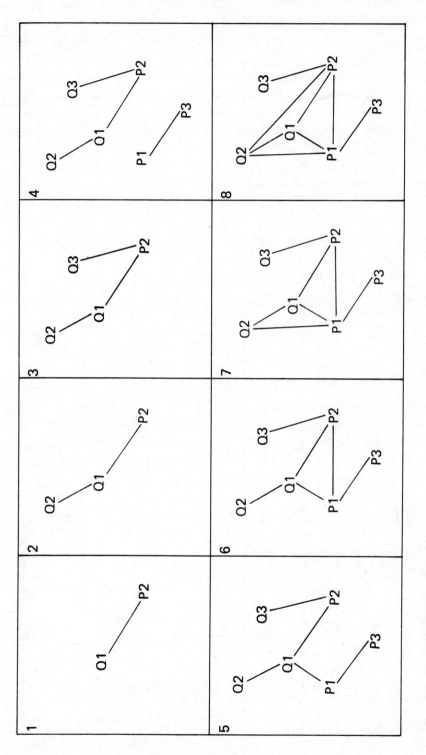

Figure 11.8 SOCIO-NET items (1-8)

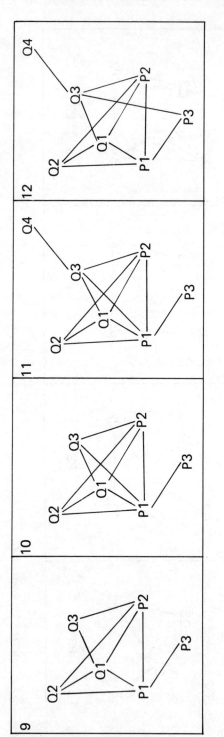

Figure 11.8 SOCIO-NET items (9-12)

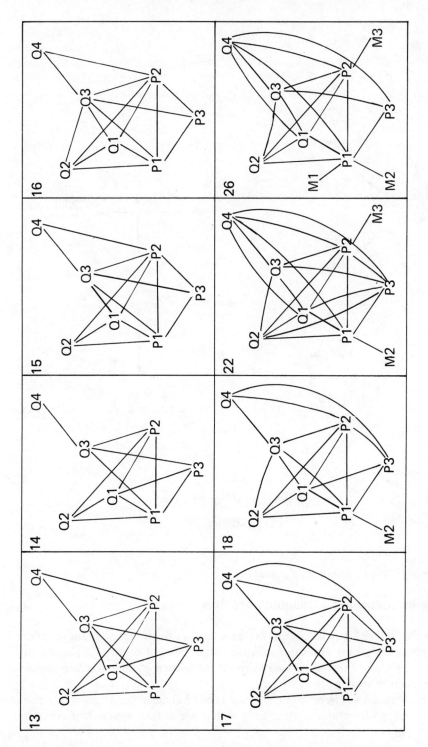

Figure 11.8 SOCIO-NET items (13-18, 22, 26)

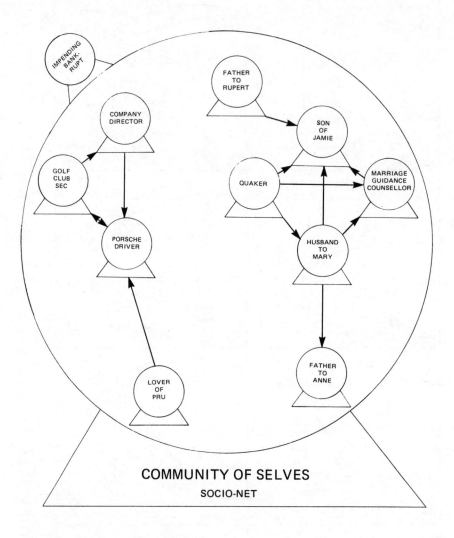

Figure 11.9(i) Community of selves

The individual as a community of selves

The SOCIO-NET has been shown to be a method for comparing each member of the group's view of a topic with each other member of the group's view of the same topic. This can be used to reveal the pattern of understanding and/or agreement in a group.

Each person will have different thoughts and feelings about a topic depending upon the position and context-from within which they approach it. Thus if

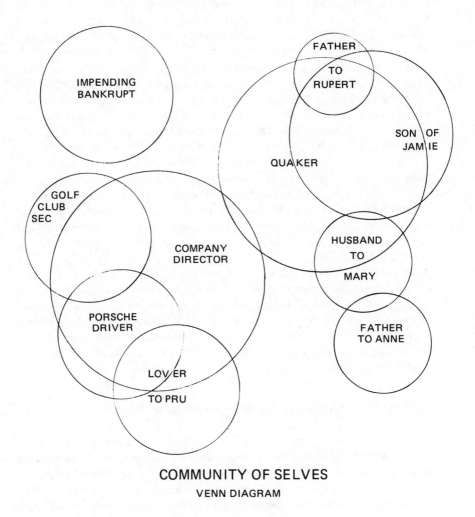

COMMUNITY OF SELVES
VENN DIAGRAM

Figure 11.9(ii) Community of selves

'significant others' are identified, it is possible to use any or all grid group techniques to clarify and reflect on one person's views. In chapter 10 it was explained how ARGUS could be used to initiate this.

The process consists of identifying a complete set of 'significant others' in a person's life. These will include relatives, colleagues, friends, enemies, lovers, teachers, and so on. Having elicited as complete a list of significant others as possible, these can be used as elements in a grid. The FOCUSed grid is used for REFELCTion and review until, say, four to eight clusters of elements are identified. If too many clusters appear the criteria can be lowered for defining the clusters. If too few clusters appear one can try to find more relevant constructs, thus providing further differentiation. The most significant others in each cluster can now be identified.

When we have identified a group of 'significant others' and a topic which relates to their significance, a set of elements which serve to define this topic can be gradually clarified. Now one can try to complete a grid, using this set of elements as one of the chosen 'significant others' would construe it. Using the same set of elements, but not necessarily the same constructs, a series of different grids can be completed for each 'significant others'' thoughts, and feelings about the topic. Now using the SOCIO-GRID technique one can map 'significant others'' grids one on to the other.

What are the areas of agreement and disagreement, understanding and misunderstanding which emerge? One can confront these and reflect upon them. Are they related to your objective understanding of each of these 'significant others' in your life? Or are they more related to your own thoughts and feelings about them?

To some extent and to different degrees the 'significant others' in a person's life are 'people within you' as well as people in the external real world. The family, social and professional roles one occupies also identify different personal perspectives. These may be construed as a community of semi-distinct selves residing within the same body. The ability of these selves to relate and communicate can be construed in terms of inner harmony or strife. Fig. 11.9 illustrates this.

Activity 11.1 Exploring the different selves within

More significant are the different or partly different selves within each of us. Do you think and feel about things in the same way when in your job role or in your spouse or in your parent role, and so on? Explore your different selves.

One easy way to start this is to list the different groups or individuals with whom you have significant experiences. Extend this by adding different situations, e.g. at home, on holiday, on business trips, or preparing for exams, writing lab reports, tutorials and so on.

Use the various grid techniques explained earlier to try to identify, say five to eight significantly different selves. Choose an important topic and identify a set of elements to represent this topic. Now elicit grids from the point of view of each self in turn. Map these grids one on to another and begin to explore how your community of selves relate one to another.

The whole power of the exchange grids and conversational techniques can now be used selectively to explore:
(1) 'blank' areas between different selves;
(2) areas of misunderstanding between different selves;
(3) areas of agreement and disagreement between different selves.

Now, having familiarised yourself with this community of 'significant others' and community of selves techniques, seek ways in which they can expand your capacity for learning.

Activity 11.2 Exploring topics from different points of view

Take some topic areas in which you feel your restricted capacity for learning is particularly irksome to you. This may be because you feel that you have little talent in the area or because you have particularly great needs, ambitions or demands upon you. Either way, *what* you learn and *how* you learn the topic is causing you particular problems.

Now, from each point of view elicit as many elements (significant items of experience) related to the topic as you can. POOL all these elements and elicit as many constructs as you can from each point of view. POOL all your constructs, REFINE the elements and constructs to produce a CONSENSUS FRAME grid. Fill this in from each point of view in turn. Spend some time placing yourself and talking yourself into each point of view. Fill in the grid from that point of view. Allow some time (a day or two) to elapse before putting yourself into another way of thinking and feeling about the topic.

Use all the DIFF., CORE, and SOCIO-NET techniques to explore how your various selves stand one in relation to another. Prepare a Venn diagram of your community of selves (Fig. 11.9).

The choice of the appropriate selves or 'significant others' and a thorough-going attempt to become aware of their relationships can have a very startling effect on freeing yourself internally to become a more self-organised learner. The community of selves is another way of thinking about the possibility of internal conversation. Conversation between identical selves will create nothing new. Conversations between totally alien selves cannot take place. The recognition of too much internal consistency as a lack of personal development, and the identification of selves that seem unable to converse, are both useful starting points for growth.

Another way of approaching this issue is to take bodies of alienated or public knowledge which seem important but are somehow boring or uninteresting. Put yourself into the position of 'significant others' in this area. Try to identify different theoretical positions, different value systems, different areas of application, and so on.

The algorithm shown in Fig. 11.10 summarises the series of techniques which were used in two industrial studies. These can be recruited for exploring the community of selves within.

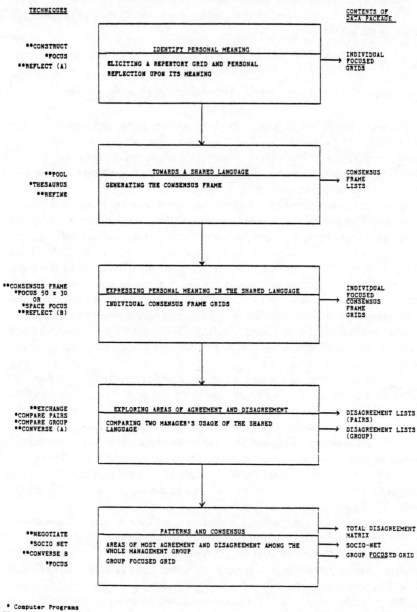

Figure 11.10 The CSHL repertory grid communication technology

The theory and practice of conversational science: tools for the T-C practitioner

The related questions of how learning can be made personal, how learners can become more self-organised and how people can significantly increase their capacity for learning were first raised in the General Introduction. These issues have been developed and commented upon throughout the book. In the central chapters the repertory grid has been used to illustrate and explain the principles out of which a technology for constructing, eliciting, reflecting upon, exchanging, negotiating and reconstructing personal meaning, may be built. The aim has been to offer an outline plan of action and some of the tools with which the rather scarce skills of good teaching, tutoring, training, therapy, counselling, coaching, custodianship and consulting can be developed and distributed more widely among practitioners and learners. Good teachers are not born. They learn how to become good teachers by becoming self-organised learners, reflecting upon their own processes of learning and using the resulting insights to inform their teaching. This last chapter leaves the repertory grid and returns to these more comprehensive issues. It introduces some ideas intended to enrich the theoretical context within which CSHL Reflective Learning Technology may be applied.

Learning as an inference from behaviour and experience

Some of the most profound ideas are either unappreciated or they appear obvious. Their implications are therefore often ignored.

'Learning' does not exist in its own right any more than do 'mass', 'entropy' or 'gravity'. It is, like them, a concept invented by mankind. It cannot be directly observed. It can only be inferred from evidence which is evaluated from within a particular theory or model of reality. Physicists have found it convenient to create, test and carefully develop models of reality which, for many purposes, they can all accept. This is because these models not only meet the scientists' very rigorous criteria of a valid theory, but they also enable the achievement of practical objectives to which physicists and others wish to direct themselves.

Unfortunately, no model of psychological or pedagogical reality yet attracts such universal allegiance: nor is there much sign of any one model of the process of learning which can yet produce consistent repeatable or outstanding results in the realm of practical affairs. If learning is an inference, what is the evidence from which it can be inferred? Many trainers have been trained to believe that only changes in the behaviour of their trainees can offer valid evidence that learning has occurred. Other members of the T-C fraternity would argue that only a change in personal understanding, or the structure of experience, is truly valid evidence in learning. The art student who learns to perceive Picasso's three clowns with new insight, the Hell's Angel who can listen to his motorbike and identify the need to adjust the idling jet of the carburettor, the cricketer who 'instinctively' knows where the ball is going even before the batsman has hit it, have all been through profound changes since their original experience of similar events. The repertory grid is demonstrably a technique with which such changes in one's perceiving, thinking and feeling about events can be systematically examined. Performance, be it that of a juggler, a Shakespearean actor or computer programmer, is behavioural evidence of learning. Video-tape or more specialist records can capture such behaviour for systematic analysis.

Changes in behaviour and changes in experience can both be valid indicators of learning. If you are a teacher the problem with relying on the learner's experience as evidence is that such evidence is not directly available to you. As a learner, the trouble with relying solely on the teacher's inferences from observing your behaviour is that the inferences which the teacher makes about your learning may not feel right.

The learner alone has direct access to his or her *experience*; but only an observer can describe the learner's *behaviour* with accuracy and precision. The learner and the observer must share this evidence. This is another cogent reason for insisting that teaching/learning must always be a conversational process. Once this is recognised, the techniques for improving the quality of the conversation introduced in chapters 9, 10 and 11 can be recruited into the sharing and evaluation of the evidence of learning.

Appreciative perspectives on learning

Each learner is an independent node of personally viable understanding. To fully accept that learners will be having their own thoughts and feelings, whilst the teachers are thinking and feeling about their learning, defines or perhaps re-defines the whole nature of the organised learning enterprise. It implies that there are at least two quite different but equally legitimate perspectives from which to view and evaluate any learning event. The teacher continues to have his or her view of what learning is being achieved. This will be assessed using criteria that arise out of the teacher's intentions. This is as it should be, since someone, the learner, the local education authority, the company, other psychoanalysts or the MCC has chosen the teacher for his knowledge and teaching ability. But the learner may operate from a separate and independent focus of evaluation. For example, learners may feel that they have not learned anything even though their behaviour has changed in ways valued by their teachers. On the other hand, a learner may feel that he or she has had a really significant learning experience even though his or her behaviour shows no sign of meeting the teacher's pre-conceived criteria for evaluating change.

Teacher and learner do not necessarily share the same purpose. The view of the 'evidence of learning' from the position of the learner is not the same as the view of the 'evidence of learning' available to the teacher. Learner and teacher therefore differ in defining the criteria for evaluating whatever evidence is available to them. Thus, if they do not negotiate a shared purpose, the learner and the teacher are each likely to draw different inferences about the learning that has, or has not, been achieved. To explore the implications of these different perspectives on learning is another direction from which the question of enhancing a person's capacity for learning may be approached.

Three paradigm situations, those of teaching, training and counselling, will each in turn serve to elaborate, analyse and clarify the implications of this relativity in the evaluation of learning.

The public stereotype of the teaching situation is that of one staff member 'privately' facing a class of learners. In a whole series of studies the authors have shown that what each learner can be enabled to identify as his or her own personal learning in such a situation may be both more and different from what is revealed by staff observations, questions or written tests. Similarly, what the teacher infers as learning may be more and different from that felt and identified by the learner. The situation is similar in the reading of a text. The pattern of personal meaning attributed to the lecture/lesson/text is constructed out of items of experience which come from within the listener or reader. It is the lack of such structures of experience which prevents people from making sense of areas of specialist knowledge not familiar to them. The problem lies not in the words or technical jargon but in the lack of such items and structures of experience with which to construct significant meanings to associate with them. A fuller and more useful understanding of the nature of personal learning is achieved once the implications of this are more fully explored. The levels of construing articulated by the PERCEPTUAL grids (chapter 8) introduce a powerful technology for exploring this issue.

Again, only by accepting and recognising that teaching/learning is a conversational process can personal meanings of teachers and learners be mapped one on to the other. First the experiential and behavioural evidence of learning must be pooled and then the purposes of the learner and the purposes of the teacher must be clarified, shared and negotiated.

Step 1

In illuminating the nature of learning in the teaching situation allow for at least two perspectives or points of view.

The teacher	The learner
T	L

Fig. 12.1 Two perspectives of learning

A point of view in this instance implies more than merely a different skin from within which to observe events. Both the teacher and the learner bring their own purposes and past experience to the situation. These selectively focus and colour their perceptions of what goes on. The consequences of this are more than just a recognition of the need for the learner to align his purposes to those of the teacher. It is an inevitable characteristic of every teaching/learning event that the learner will have experience, needs and purposes which differ from those of the teacher. To accept both perspectives enriches our understanding of the nature of learning. To dismiss either perspective as illegitimate or irrelevant is to diminish our understanding. But learners' views in the light of their purposes and the teacher's view in the light of her purpose are not a sufficient taxonomy of the perspectives from which to illuminate the nature of learning.

As was reported in chapter 2, asking people about significant learning events which have befallen them reveals that the event was very often not pre-planned. Even if the event was planned, almost without exception the significant learning was unexpected. It could only be fully appreciated in retrospect after the learner had had time to reflect; after he or she had taken time to identify and construct the system of values within which the learning acquired its significance. This system of values is not that which the teacher used in planning the event. This throws a new light on much of the psychological and educational research into learning. For the research to be orthodoxly respectable, the conditions and criteria of the scientific experiment must be pre-planned, thus excluding just those psychological circumstances in which significant learning takes place.

This is yet another reason why a conversational research paradigm is necessary for the study of human learning. Only thus can we explore the changing perspectives from within which learning is appreciated.

Step 2

In illuminating the nature of learning add 'retrospectively defined evaluative systems' to those which were prospectively defined.

The teacher	The learner	Evaluation system
Tp	Lp	Prospectively defined
Tr	Lr	Retrospectively defined

Figure 12.2 The four perspectives of teaching/learning

These four perspectives are the minimum viewpoints from within which a teaching/learning situation can be adequately described.

But if we increase the time-span of the events these four are scarcely adequate. The inference systems directly impinging on the situation are only restricted to those of the teacher and learner during the period in which their teaching/learning events remain private to them. The restriction to four perspectives remains valid over longer periods of time only if the relevant context does not expand beyond these face-to-face events (e.g. these conditions may remain true over a period of six months when a disciple visits his guru or when a child has a private tutor). More normally, e.g. in a typical school situation, the school organisation and the learner's home circumstances influence what goes on. The headteacher and the parent can be expected to be drawing inferences about the learning which is taking place.

School and curriculum	Teacher	Learner	Home and parents	Evaluative system
Sp	Tp	Lp	Pp	Prospectively defined
Sr	Tr	Lr	Pr	Retrospectively defined

Figure 12.3 The eight perspectives of teaching/learning

Step 3

For most non-trivial purposes a proper understanding of the teaching/learning process requires at least eight perspectives from which to view the evidence and evaluate the learning. This does not mean that nothing can be understood unless all eight are explicit but it does mean that if any one of these perspectives is ignored and then takes on an unexpected complexion, the learning process may begin to exhibit unexplainable variety. This is because each perspective not only contains its own evaluation of the learning but also acts as a source of feedback and comment into the conversational learning activity.

Step 4

Learning at work, learning in industrial, commercial and governmental training, also has its important vantage points. Trainers and their learners will differ in both their prospective and retrospective value systems. But, training, in addition to any contribution to personal development, usually has a fairly immediate work purpose. The learner's manager, supervisor and/or colleagues form a powerful reference system from within which the sources of his or her learning and training will be evaluated.

T	L	*Ws	Evaluative system
Tp	Lp	Wsp	Prospectively defined
Tr	Lr	Wsr	Retrospectively defined

*Ws = Work situation

Figure 12.4 The work perspective of teaching/learning

Introducing the learner's working environment as a further perspective raises other, time-related, issues. Is the training expected to show immediate dividends; what if its effects wear off after two or three months? The time-span of evaluation is important. We will value the 'same' learning differently depending upon whether we take a short-, medium- or long-term view. Thus, as we try to confront the nature of learning in education, work, and life, the variety of perspectives from which to infer and value it multiplies. This reveals a whole new area of application for the pair and group technology culminating in chapter 11.

The POOL, REFINE and CONSENSUS FRAME techniques used for negotiating subjective standards in the quality of a product (from exam answers to paint finishes on a prestige car), can be applied to reveal the total structure of personal meanings within which learning is to be evaluated. The measured areas of agreement and disagreement, of understanding and misunderstanding, serve to define the crucial items to be negotiated conversationally.

Step 5

Finally, how does contemplation of the counselling situation add to an understanding of the perspectives which illuminate learning? Client-centred tutors and counsellors will suggest that all questions of purpose and time perspective are the responsibility of the client/learner. In the context of a prevalent behaviourist preoccupation with observed performance, this emphasis provides a necessary theoretical counter-balance. But once the existence of multiple perspectives is acknowledged, a little probing soon reveals that a totally client-centred view of counselling is more apparent than real. In its more extreme forms this view may also severely reduce the effectiveness of therapy. To the extent that counsellors acknowledge their own perspectives, they either approximate to the descriptions of the teaching or training described previously or they must make their perspectives explicit and be prepared to negotiate about which value system best represents the learner's interests. This is one contribution which tutoring and counselling makes to understanding the nature of organised learning. It is a responsibility of the teacher to negotiate with the learner about the nature of the evaluative systems which will be applied to the evidences of learning.

This may lead to:

(1) learners recognising and accepting the teacher and the institutional and social values which are operating within the learning opportunities to which they are exposed (or choose for them);

(2) recognition of this evaluative system may lead them to opt out of that learning opportunity and seek another;

or

(3) it may result in their choosing, creatively, to maintain and develop their own values whilst recognising, coping with, and even exploiting, the values of the teacher, the institution and the society within which they operate.

A greater understanding of the issues crucial to the counselling/tutoring role may also help to bring the development of the individual back as an important consideration into all types of learning.

The idea of a more fully rounded learning conversation now emerges. The values by which learning is to be selected, defined and judged are a necessary issue to be negotiated in any conversational learning.

Finally, the idea of counselling/tutoring sometimes carries connotations of referral, for example, the child who is sent to the educational psychologist, the manager who has a breakdown or the undergraduate who is referred to the student counselling service. Referral often implies that it is the person who is being judged and devalued rather than just his or her performance. It is you and not just your essay or your work which is being rejected. This tendency to equate learning performance with the value of the person can produce deep and enduring wounds. The technology of personal learning requires methods which offer Carl Rogers's interpersonal conditions of *unconditional positive regard*, *empathy* and *congruence* to the person operating evaluatively with the evidence of learning (chapter 10). Thus perhaps an adequate summary of the relevant minimal perspectives on learning might be as follows:

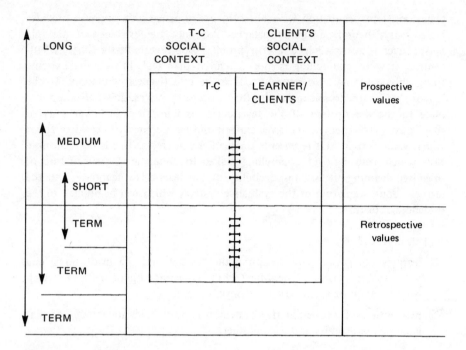

Figure 12.5 (i) Perspectives on learning

In the short term the crucial perspectives are those of the T-C and the learner/client as they conceive their purposes in advance of the learning event and as they evaluate the learning in retrospect. For many short-term considerations these are sufficient. But in the medium term the T-C cannot ignore the institutional value within which they are operating; and the learner/client cannot ignore the context of home, work or peer group which may have their own different views about the value of the learning. Many difficulties and frustrations arise when T-C, learner/client or the institution are not prepared for the differences in perspective which exist; or when one or other is not able or prepared to negotiate about these differences. As will be demonstrated later, the CSHL developments of repertory grid technology can facilitate such negotiations by clarifying and articulating the dimensions of understanding, misunderstanding, agreements and disagreements.

Finally, the society or community within which the system of short- and medium-term perspectives exists is itself a further long-term perspective within which social, political, economic and technical changes will throw a hopefully evolving evaluative light on the learning that can be achieved. It is a purpose of the authors to contribute to this evolution by contributing to a change in the social norms about both the quantity and quality of learning which can be expected from the multitudinous events that constitute the complexity of all T-C learning situations.

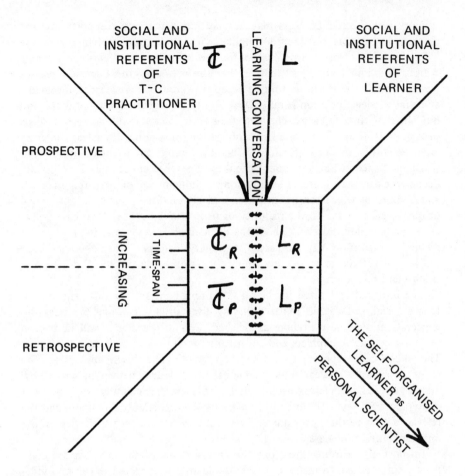

Figure 12.5 (ii) Perspectives on learning

The teaching/learning contract

There are many organised learning events in which the teacher/trainer and the learner do not begin with a clearly agreed contract. The child on first entering school is one extreme example of the state of affairs. It may take months before even a minimal agreement is reached, and then all too often there is a large component of 'live and let live'. Similarly, many people sent on courses by their employers do not really accept that they need to learn about 'supervisory skills', 'financial control', 'safety regulations', 'report writing', 'motivation', 'repertory grids' or whatever it is that has currently caught the Personnel Department's attention.

In every teaching, training, tutoring, therapy, coaching and counselling, custodial and consulting situation there is an implicit contract. The teachers and their institutions offer some type of course, workshop, instructional package, support system, etc. Learners may or may not pay for this opportunity and associated amenities, but they do implicitly undertake to play their part in the T-C learning enterprise. One reason for the infrequency of personal learning within organised learning systems is that the nature of this contract remains un-negotiated. The institution might argue that contracts are legal arrangements and that the legal position is quite clear if only the learner would bother to find out about it. Indeed, when challenged, in such events as the Hornsey College of Art affair, in questions of a firm's obligation for offering day release, in grant arrangements of the Youth Training Scheme initiatives and in the confrontations which have occurred in and about various local government schools, it eventually becomes clear that there is usually some minimum set of legal requirements and obligations which can be identified and then enforced through some actual or quasi-legal system. To the majority of people in T-C, those legal base points are seldom visible. Publicity about the difficulties of colleagues in another not dissimilar institution may raise some temporary feelings of unease but generally the basic legal contract does not appear to impinge on the actual day-to-day, face-to-face relationships.

The informal and often implicit T-C learning contract is a different matter. It is a social, not a legal, contract. In any given situation various practices and expectations will have become established. Certain precedents will have been set. Prospectuses, pamphlets and advertising literature will have been published. This superficially appears to define the contract, but this is misleading. The expectations of first-year undergraduates differ widely depending upon how much past experience has been available to them from family, slightly older contemporaries, etc. The use they make of this experience of others and the relevance of it to their own university situation will influence their view of the implicit contract they are entering.

In most T-C learning situations the crucial items of the contract are completely unspecified. In many contracts the learner is expected to suspend judgment and go along with everything that happens because the government, the local authority, the company, some charity or the parents are footing the bill and anyway those that know best guarantee that the eventual pay-off will be disproportionately great. This offered pay-off may be in career prospects, in improved social acceptability, in health, in fame, in the capacity for living, etc. This imbalance between the long-term pay-off and the short-term dependence disturbs some of the basic conditions for the development of self-organisation and personal learning. One has only to organise and run economically viable and competitive short courses, attended by people who have themselves made the positive decision to attend and who are paying for the privileges (not financed by their organisation or obliquely subsidised by the T-C institution itself), to realise just what a difference an equitable contract would make in most other T-C learning situations.

We are not here concerned with political, social or economic solutions, particularly since such solutions usually tackle problems which are either illusory or so misconceived that the consequence of the 'solution' turn out to be worse than the symptoms of the original problem. The purpose here is to try for a realistic and not consciously prejudiced analysis of what it is about many situations which prevents personal learning and the development of self-organised learning capacity.

One qualification for claiming to be able to make a contribution to this analysis is to have sat through some thirty three-hour sessions with a group of students who had opted for a self-organised psychology of education course. The mutual layers of habit, assumption, self-fulfilling prophesies, misunderstanding, hurt, pride, shame and incredible depths of good will which were uncovered as we together sought to design, run and assess the results of the course were indeed an education in the psychology of education.

Most teachers and trainers intend to bring about pre-conceived changes in the behaviour and/or experience of their clients. They are employed to help people acquire certain attitudes, knowledge and skills. Sometimes the nature of these intended changes is very well defined. Sometimes they are precisely specified. But even when vague, the purpose of the proposed learning will almost always have been pre-conceived by the teachers/trainers and their institutions. Indeed most T-Cs would feel that they were failing in their duty to the learner if they had not researched the learning needs of their clients and pre-empted most of the decisions about the content to be learned. They will also have very carefully planned and prepared the process of T-C by which the learning is to be provoked, guided and achieved. When, rather late in the day, the learners join the learning enterprise, they are inevitably entering into a rather unbalanced contract.

The first dimension of imbalance in the T-C learning contract is usually in the amount and clarity of information which is possessed about the nature of coming events by the staff and the clients. What may be well defined is the syllabus (i.e. the content of the public knowledge to be on offer) and the timetable. What makes the situation more difficult is quite often that both parties do not know what it is that they do not know. The institution is quite likely to arbitrarily but completely change the nature of the contract by moving staff around and replacing them with similarly qualified (and therefore apparently the same) people who actually have quite different assumptions about the nature of learning. They therefore 'cover the same content' but offer a completely different learning experience. It is this which makes free, compulsory education such a lottery and therefore such a hot but unresolvable political issue. The learner does not enter the contract 'tabula-rasa'. Their previous learning experiences have set deep, well-defined, but unexpressed and invisible expectations. These expectations can be very varied among any group of learners. Most people cannot talk about their expectations in sensible terms because they know of no alternatives. One has only to attempt to run, quite explicitly, an experiental learning course for mechanical engineering managers and be faced with outraged demands for lecture notes or to run a structured learning course for client-centred psychotherapists and be faced with a revolt and an implacable demand for experiential learning to realise how deeply emotional, restricted and inflexible most people's learning skills really are.

One basic requirement of a technology for personal learning is a series of methods, procedures and techniques for making the nature of the T-C learning contract explicit and for negotiating sensibly about it. It may be useful to indicate three typical resolutions of the teaching/training/learning contract:

1 The person who has made an unconventional and deliberate choice to attend a course which is particularly well defined and attractive to them. They know of the staff who will be running it, they know what it will be about and they know the philosophy on which it is based and the methods which will be used. This may be a primary school, a postgraduate course, a crash language course or a distance-learning book.
2 The person who is taking what is for them the traditional and socially expected next step, who believes that society knows best and that if he or she merely goes along the usual path and does his or her best then they will learn all that it is necessary to know. This may be a school, a postgraduate course, a short course 'everyone goes on' or a conventional textbook.
3 The person who does not believe in what they are doing but who sees it as a socially acceptable means to a personally desirable end.

The seven faces of teaching and learning

Learners' freedom to negotiate equally in the formulation of the teaching/ learning contract depends not only upon their appreciation of a variety of perspectives but also upon how they construe teaching/learning events. Their earlier, more naive, personal myths about the nature of learning (chapter 1) need to be superseded by developing more personally viable assumptions. Here a simple classification is proposed, merely to challenge the more familiar categories of thought on this topic and so provoke the reader into working out some more viable model for themselves.

For purposes of analysis, the T-C learning process may be conceived as involving three components:

(i)   T = The teacher(s), tutors(s), coach(es) or counsellor(s)
(ii) L = The learner(s)
(iii) R = The resource(s)

The most traditional relationship between these three might be designated 'Teacher interpreting the resource' and represented as in Fig. 12.6.

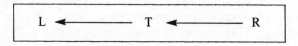

Figure 12.6 The teacher interpreting the resource

The prototype of this relationship is the type of lecture where the T carefully researches the 'public knowledge of the topic' and presents his/her 'objective' view of it in a logical and well-organised form. This example might be a certain type of secondary school 'lesson', or a specialist talk to a commercial or industrial audience. A more universal form of this relationship might be represented as in Fig. 12.7.

Figure 12.7 The teacher interpreting the resource and the learner questioning

where the learner can question the teacher who may need to re-consult the resources as the learning proceeds. Other versions of this relationship are:

(a) a certain form of seminar where T is merely presenting a review of the literature; or

(b) a practical demonstration by, say, a catering school chef of how to make an omelette; or

(c) learning a production skill from sitting by Nellie (who in her time learned it from someone else).

A technology of personal learning needs to offer ways of enabling learners to reconstruct the public knowledge on offer into forms which are more immediately relevant and amenable to their own situations. These should probably take the form of techniques for exercising, listening, reading, looking, touching, smelling, and tasting as active rather than passive learning skills.

But the more effective lectures, demonstrations and seminars usually shade into a different relationship. That of 'T as resource'.

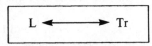

Figure 12.8 The teacher as resource

This represents any situation where what Ts are presenting is not merely an impersonal interpretation of public knowledge but they are offering their own experiences or personal knowledge which has been digested, tested and reconstructed into something unique to the T. Tutors and counsellors may operate in this mode. Significant 'T-C learning events' that make a lasting impact are often of this kind. This is because they are a living demonstration of the effectiveness of personal learning.

Another type of relationship can vary from reading someone's lecture notes to exploiting the possibilities of a lavishly stocked resource centre, and from learning to manoeuvre a submarine by operating a computer-driven simulator to carrying out an experiment according to well-constructed laboratory instructions. Such relationships might be represented as in Fig. 12.9.

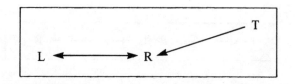

Figure 12.9 The teacher as resource organiser/designer/minder

But these three relationships of T as resource organiser, T as resource interpreter and T as resource can all be seen to be concerned with R. They emphasise the content of the public knowledge and the nature of the environment to which skill or competence must be applied. The technology of learning should offer techniques for enabling people to participate in a mentally and emotionally active way in exploiting their resources. This does not exhaust the possibilities of relationship between T, R and L. These are at least four others and it is these that hark back more clearly, more directly to the concept of personal learning introduced throughout the book. They may also be seen as crossing the traditional boundaries.

The pure counselling role, of which there is some component in almost all effective teaching, training or coaching, might be represented as in Fig. 12.10.

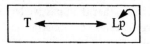

Figure 12.10 The teacher helping the learner to reflect on self as person

where the P is intended to indicate that both T and L are concerned with L as a person and not merely as a receptacle of knowledge. Again most people remember certain key events in their education (whether they occurred within T-C or not) in which they were helped significantly when someone offered this type of counsel. It is one component of effective tutoring and of coaching as that term is used both in sport and in management development. The reader will almost certainly be able to recall occasions when they were either L or T in such an event. Involving oneself with learners as people has its dangers and raises certain professional issues about the role of the T. Repertory grid techniques can be used not only to make this relationship more effective but also to define and thus professionalise it.

Another relationship which is often overlooked is that in which T enables L to reflect on him/herself as a resource, as shown in Fig. 12.11.

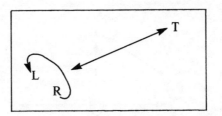

Figure 12.11 The teacher helping the learner to reflect using personal experience as resource

This is another important aspect of the process of tutoring. It is the situation in which learners are enabled to access their own experience as a significant source of knowledge in the topic area. Another version of this, of which certain counselling techniques, social skills, training and discovery learning techniques might serve as examplars, is what might be called 'exploring' and 'experimenting'. This is where the learner does not already have the relevant experience but is encouraged and enabled to explore and experiment to generate new experiences for themselves. For this type of relationship to be effective it must escape the feeling by the learner that the event is being stage-managed so that he or she gets 'the right results'. The natural curiosity of learners leads them to invent their own questions. The nature of the exploration or experimentation is also invented by the learner who is seeking personally satisfying results. T merely facilitates the process of curiosity, invention and testing out. This relationship might be represented as in Fig. 12.12.

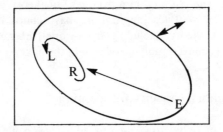

Figure 12.12 The teacher helping the learner to explore and experiment

Here E represents some part of the (social or physical) environment.

The personal learning technology requires a battery of techniques for enabling learners to reflect upon their own experience, use others as additional sources of experience, and explore and question their environment to enlarge, elaborate and refine their fund of personal experience.

Finally, a rather different type of relationship might be represented as in Fig. 12.13.

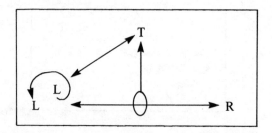

Figure 12.13 Learning-to-learn reflecting on the learning process

Here the emphasis is on the relationship between learner and resource. The focus is on learning skill. T monitors the learning and by illuminating it enables learners to reflect upon the nature of the process of learning rather than the content or product.

Again this might form part of effective tutoring or counselling. The process reflected upon might be anything from encouraging seven-year-olds to explain how they do a two-digit subtraction sum to helping undergraduates to improve their use of reading as a learning skill, to helping fighter pilots reflect on how they are evolving intercept tactics, to helping a deaf person develop lip-reading skills. This aspect of the 'T-C-L' relationship is very under-represented in most education training and counselling. This is another reason why institutional T-C often does not produce personal learners.

Having offered them as a resource to the reader, these seven faces of teaching, training, tutoring, coaching and counselling can themselves be reflected upon. It is suggested that readers reconstruct this explanatory model to serve their own T-C purposes. The last section introduces our theory of learning conversations. The seven faces of teaching/learning have contributed to the various components of this theory, including the tutorial, life, and learning-to-learn levels of the learning conversation introduced in the next section.

Increasing the human capacity for learning

Self-organisation can only arise and properly develop within the appropriate psychological conditions. Some of these have been defined in the last three sections.

Some of the fundamental requirements for becoming a self-organised learner run counter to the prevalent myths of Western society. Self-organisation is not primarily a question of logic and doing the right things at the right time. Rogers defines the fully functioning person as one who can rely on his or her own organism. For this to be facilitated, he defines three necessary conditions

(General Introduction). We have argued that creating the right conditions, including those described in this chapter, is not sufficient. A conversational paradigm within which an awareness-raising technology is recruited becomes necessary for an enhancement of the capacity to learn.

Learners who can explore themselves and recognise the relevant perspectives from which learning may be usefully assessed, who have clearly negotiated the nature of the teaching/learning contract, and who construe teaching/learning events according to their 'seven faces' or in other ways which are useful to them, are already well on the road to self-organisation. Without these psychological conditions, there is a real danger that attempts at self-organisation degenerate into a series of clever but empty tricks. Given these conditions, the processes of self-organisation can be discussed. The learner who has challenged his or her own personal myths and who has acquired the knack of making all learning personal is ready to increase his or her capacity for learning. By this we mean a permanent increase in learning competence. This is more than the skills that accrue from learning a topic or solving a problem. It is the ability to continue improving one's learning skills by reflection on the processes of learning. Fig. 12.14 illustrates this.

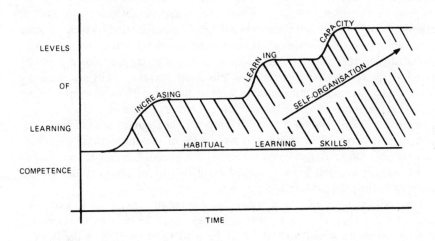

Figure 12.14 The capacity for learning

Accepting responsibility for developing one's own learning requires a 'problem identifying, formulating and solving' mode of operation. The identification of what should be learned, and the formulation of a clear learning purpose, is often the crucial part of self-organisation. This process is iterative. The original purpose is necessary to formulate some strategies and tactics for proceeding. But as learning occurs, the purpose must be reviewed and revised. New strategy and tactics lead to more learning which makes it easier to formulate a worthwhile but achievable purpose. Only when the learning out-come meets criteria arising out of the well-formulated purpose does the learning task become fully formulated and by then it is achieved. Recognition of the iterative nature of learning allows the learner to avoid many of the pitfalls associated with learning difficulties and loss of motivation.

Thus, the self-organised learner is able to identify and formulate a purpose, devise strategy and tactics for achieving it, and define criteria by which to recognise or measure the successful outcome. Formulating such a 'personal learning contract' is part of what we designate the 'tutorial level' of a *Learning Conversation*. The ability to guide this process whilst leaving learners free to construct their own purpose, strategy and criteria for assessing outcome is one part of the skill of the T-C in conducting a learning conversation with their clients.

It is useful to identify two other levels in the learning conversation. A learner's attempt to carry out the personal learning contract can fail in two very different ways. The contract may be fulfilled, but, despite meeting the criteria set by the purpose, the learner may find the outcome unsatisfactory. This state of affairs is reflected throughout education and in much training and therapy. 'I'm good at chemistry but I do not really like it' or 'I can do second order differential equations but I do not really see the point of them' are comments which indicate the need for what we designate the 'life' or 'relevance' level of the learning conversation. This is a mode in which personal needs are explored and identified. Long-term aims are translated into more immediate learning purposes. The content of the learning is explored to reveal its relevance (or irrelevance). In this 'life' level personal needs are gradually identified and translated into feasible learning purposes. This conversation deals with what are often called the 'motivation' problems of learning.

When the learner values his or her purposes, but cannot achieve them, the problem is different. The 'learning-to-learn' level of the conversation deals with such lack of skill or competence. We will elaborate this 'learning-to-learn' mode in the last section, but before proceeding to this let us return to the tutorial level and to the personal learning contract.

Learners must be able to monitor the process of attempting to carry out their personal contract. To achieve this they must be able to represent the personal meanings which they attribute both to the topic and to the learning process.

In chapter 1 it was suggested that learning could be viewed as the construc-tion, reconstruction, exchange and negotiation of personally relevant and viable meaning. In chapter 7 considerable space was given to a discussion of the meaning of meaning. Throughout this book we have taken the repertory grid to be the form in which such meaning can be represented. This has proved useful for two reasons. Firstly, the repertory grid is an unfamiliar form in which to represent meaning. It is therefore perfect for awareness-raising since no habitual modes of thought, feeling and action can slip into a repertory grid without reflection. Secondly, it is a form with fairly minimal constraints. It requires only the appreciation of similarities and differences between items of personal experience. But the grid as we shall see, is only one of an infinite set of methods.

Beyond the grid

The conversational grid techniques described throughout this book probably take the grid as far as possible as a device for raising awareness.

Despite its proven advantages, the grid is limited in terms of its sensitivity in eliciting and exhibiting meaning. It fails to capture the nature of the relationships between items. Neither the level nor the hierarchical structure of a construct system can be represented in its two-dimensional format. It has no power to represent intentionality unless the elements themselves are purposive, or to make a person's predictions and anticipations explicit. Furthermore, it restricts both the number and nature of items that can be represented within the range of convenience of a topic or problem. The only way in which items acquire meaning is by their positions on bi-polar constructs, which are restricted by scaling procedures. The requirement to place each element on each construct demands tight differentiation, which may prevent a rich and open exploration of the topic. Since the relationships between elements and between constructs are correlational, the grid cannot indicate directional, temporal or cause-and-effect relationships, or any of the other associative mechanisms by which meaning is structured.

The T-C practitioner needs a whole library of additional 'beyond the grid' aids, each with its own characteristics for contributing to the learning conversation. As we pointed out in the last section, in order to raise awareness of learning within the personal learning contract, it is necessary to represent the personal meaning of a topic or problem. We also pointed out that the process of constructing meaning must also be represented and reflected upon. Minimally, the characteristics of awareness-raising tools for representing and reflecting upon systems of personal meaning include:

1 Descriptions of experiential and/or behavioural evidences of learning.

2 A display and procedure for 'talkback' which is detailed and specific enough to enable individuals to validly reconstruct the experience.

3 This should facilitate 'talkback' between levels in the hierarchy of the process of learning (for example, purpose-sub-purposes, strategy-tactics) and to relate and integrate different aspects of the process at any one given level (for example, relating purpose-outcome, or purpose-strategy-outcome).

4 A language in which the description of inner experience and behaviour can be articulated in sufficient detail and accuracy to create a new level of awareness of one's own processes. This language should be capable of:

(i) exhibiting meaning as part of a hierarchically organised system;
(ii) tapping personal meaning in all its fullest aspects, as experienced by the individual;

(iii) enabling the individual to become aware of the intentionality which influences thought, feeling and action;

(iv) allowing the exploration of meaning in its most bizarre or idiosyncratic form.

5   The device must be capable of expressing thought and feeling as a pattern in time. Causal models, from repetitive cycles, probabilistic, as well as those from the physical science paradigm and general systems theory, need to be explored and displayed.

6   The incorporation of this new awareness into an integrated personal 'theory' so that effective alternatives can be constructed.

7   The testing out of alternatives in real situations.

8   A system of personal evaluation which:

 (i) indicates the merits and demerits of each alternative;

(ii) throws up indications of the conceptual directions in which more adequate alternatives might be sought.

9   A system of support which enables an individual to intensely explore the awareness and review process.

10   A procedure for weaning the learner away from the tool, replacing it with an enhanced perception and language through which the learner can achieve the same effects, unsupported from the outside.

Provided such characteristics are met, T-C practitioners can invent their own personally relevant tools as aids for managing effective learning conversations. The conversational technology which we have developed within our action research projects goes well beyond the repertory grid. Records of learning behaviour as well as a whole range of devices for representing personal meaning have been developed. For instance, behavioural records of reading can be effectively recruited to help people explore, review and develop their self-organised capacity to read-for-learning. Similarly the interactive use of video records of any learning performance can be used to raise awareness of learning skills. Here, we aim to outline those 'beyond the grid' techniques which overcome some of the limitations of the grid outlines earlier.

STRUCTURES OF MEANING

The STRUCTURES OF MEANING procedures offer flexibility in:

(a) the elicitation of items of meaning;

(b) the sorting of their relationships;

(c) the display of a final pattern.

Items of meaning can represent any aspect of a topic, problem or event. None of the restriction of type, range or number that apply to elements need be considered. This provides a much freer elicitation procedure and ensures a much richer exemplification of the topic. Many different methods can be applied to facilitate this elicitation. Brainstorming techniques, and content-free techniques for enabling different types of associations, including qualifications, refinements, chronological, logical, temporal, analogy, opposite and similar, metaphor, inference, lateral, bizarre, emotive, visual, analytical, causal, intuitive, or pure free association and so forth are recruited to release suppressed or tacit feelings and ideas. The aim at this stage is to minimise internal monitoring and the tightly evaluative processes which often inhibit the potentially creative meaning-generating process.

At any stage in the elicitation, items can be sorted using iterative procedures into clusters of items, which are noted and then the items are returned to the population before selecting a new cluster. Gradually a pattern emerges and stabilises. During this procedure many other items are elicited and these are added to the developing structure of meaning. This stage is analogous to the bi-polar scaling procedure but is much freer, less formal, and more intuitive. An alternative, more formal procedure is to compare each item with every other item attributing a similar score to each dyad. It is also sometimes useful to classify the nature of the relationship between items and to link this to the order of item elicitation. The learner can thus become more aware of the underlying mechanisms which influence memory and the retrieval of meaning.

As the number of items expand and begin to pattern into a structure, less relevant items can be deleted. At this stage, the topic or problem is continuously monitored, reconsidered and evaluated. Gradually, a more evaluative, content-free procedure is introduced which encourages the stabilisation of a pattern of meaning which embodies greater relevance to 'purpose' and the topic. By shifting the focus of attention to a more general or more detailed level, a hierarchically organised structure begins to emerge.

A final stage in the STRUCTURE OF MEANING procedure involves selection of an optimal mode of display to hold and exhibit the system of personal meaning. Networks, hierarchies, heterarchies, entailment structures, cluster diagrams, and Venn diagrams are some examples. Many techniques used in other fields have potential use here; mathematical forms such as Q-analysis, graph theory, data structures, and developments in computer graphics are some examples. But other cultures have arrived at other techniques for displaying meaning. The tantric model of 'all thought and time' represents one such display. Again, Joycean prose, Bardic stances, Haiku poems or sonnets, Zen calligraphy, sculpture and architecture are only a few selections of forms for representing personal meaning. The problem with these culture-bound displays is that because of familiarity and highly developed associations with publicly accepted meaning, learners are often incapable of transcending this to construct a meta-awareness of the process involved in constructing personal meaning within these forms. This is why unfamiliar forms such as the repertory grid and STRUCTURES OF MEANING are well suited as aids within the learning conversation. But obviously unfamiliarity is only one prerequisite. In this section we have tried to highlight some of the others. Within the 'conversational science paradigm', such displays become tools for the articulation of experience and for reflection upon personal meaning.

The STRUCTURES OF MEANING procedures have been developed into a suite of interactive computer programs which can display 2-, 3- or more-dimensional representations of personal meanings. An n-dimensional display is represented in 3-dimensional projections. By offering dynamic displays, the computer can be recruited to explore the intentionality and anticipatory aspects of meaning, thus offering a vehicle for exploring alternate futures. In another culture the Shri-Yantra has been used for similar ends.

Having explored a wide variety of alternate methods for eliciting and representing meaning to be used as awareness-raising tools within the learning conversation, we can now point towards one other dimension of the self-organised learner. He or she can either select or invent appropriate structures for holding and exhibiting aspects of personal meaning in order to explore learning. The self-organised learner is also free to recruit not only those specialist psychic mirrors of process we have described but also appropriate culture-bound devices. These chosen forms of representing meaning must be brought under review within certain time-spans of learning, otherwise habitual mechanisms take over and the reflective device loses its potency.

Not only does the 'conversational science paradigm' (General Introduction) need to be internalised, but it must also be extended outwards into the self-organised learner's life space from learning-to-learn to personal learning contracts and to learning conversations in life. The Zen archer, the theoretical physicist, and the budding Brittens, de Vincis, Oliviers, Gerald Manley Hopkinses, or Keyneseans within our society are demonstrating their abilities to create rich and powerful personal systems of meaning. In our action research projects we have demonstrated that a conversation technology can be used to aid everyone who so chooses to develop their potential. Managers, students, naval officers, trainers, and eight-year-olds have been enabled to significantly develop this capacity. People who learn to achieve this value the process. Each of us can identify our own events in which this rare experience occurred. It can be recognised by the experience of constructing, exchanging and negotiating personally relevant and viable meanings which become the source of effective and creative action. Once the means for representing meaning is recognised as a tool, any forms of representation can be used as aids for achieving awareness. Indeed, readers will recognise that each was invented to serve this very purpose.

Conducting Learning Conversations

As the series of specialist awareness-raising devices is developed, T-C practitioners can recruit them into the learning conversation. At the *life level*, needs and purposes can become the topic for reflection and review so that viable purposes which relate to the personal learning contract can be identified. It is this level of the conversation that can save days, months or even years of alienation, misery and mis-spent effort. This life conversation can identify the personal structure of a topic, problem or job situation and thus help learners to chart their own paths of involvement in it. At the *tutorial level* the content of learning is reflected upon, reviewed, and developed within the personal learning contracts. Resources are identified, specific purposes articulated and strategies put into action. The deployment of basic learning skills is also here put into action; note-making, reading, practicals, project work, revision and essays form part of this process. When issues of lack of competence emerge, the tutorial level refers to the *learning-to-learn* level of the Learning Conversation. It is here that the robotish skills of learning are challenged. The detailed interaction by which habits can be broken, reviewed and rebuilt becomes the focus of attention.

Challenging the robot

Achieving new levels in learning performance usually involves serious personal change. It involves the disruption and breaking of existing skills and the establishment of new attitudes and personally strange ways of thinking, feeling and behaving. Many of the special techniques used in the learning conversation have been specially recruited and developed for such controlled interventions. But however carefully the conversation is developed, the process of significant 'learning-to-learn' will always involve a 'learning trough' in which anxiety and feelings of inadequacy combine to push the person.

We have found it useful to talk of each learner as having a set of personal learning robots: (chapter 8) the learning-by-reading robot; the learning-by-discussion robot; the learning-by-doing robot; the learning-by-listening robot, etc. Each of us has been so habituated in our own ways that we are completely unaware that each of these modes of learning is itself a learned skill. Each learning skill has become so automatic that it is no longer under conscious control. Special techniques are required to challenge the robot, bringing the skill back into awareness and thus available for revision and development. But the disruption of existing skills produces a drop in effective performance. The learner feels that he is getting nowhere and becomes frustrated and anxious. Part of every learning conversation is concerned with offering the learner support through this learning trough.

The need for three related dialogues

The change conversation can be seen to contain three entwining dialogues. The first dialogue serves the purpose of raising awareness of the learning process. The second dialogue offers personal support to the learner, particularly when he is experimenting with new methods of learning and feels vulnerable after having abandoned his habitually safe technique. The third dialogue helps the learner to identify standards: in himself, in other people, and in the situation, which can serve as referents for the quality of the learning which he is attempting to achieve.

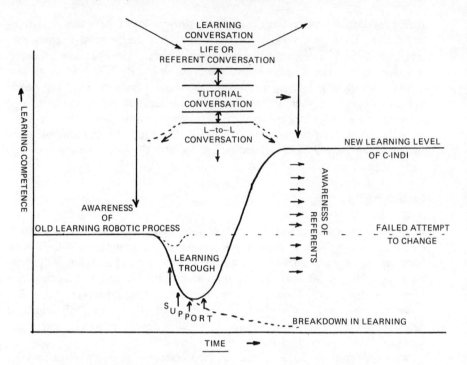

Figure 12.15 The learning trough

The first 'process' dialogue taps unconscious habits and helps the student to become aware of his own learning style. In most areas of activity, for example in manual skills, social skills, reading skills and management skills, people have little or no understanding of their own learning processes. Records of learning behaviour can be used to talk the learner back through his experience. These can be as elaborate or as informal as the situation demands. Careful reconstruction of the experience serves to raise awareness on subsequent occasions. Gradually a personal language for describing learning develops. We have found that the repertory grid can serve as an awareness-raising device for many different tasks from interviewing to industrial inspection, in which perception, judgment, thought and feeling are of central importance.

The second dialogue 'supports' the learner through this process of change. It is as yet largely a matter of sensitivity and intuitive understanding on the part of the manager of learning. However, the work of Carl Rogers and B.F. Skinner together offer some indicators of the ways in which this personal support should be offered. Rogers's technique is to create a very attentive but relaxed and accepting atmosphere in which there is no evaluative comment. His studies show that this frees individuals to experiment and explore their own processes in ways that are normally too threatening for them to attempt alone. Skinner's behavioural reinforcement techniques enable a person to define new patterns of behaviour which they can then be carefully guided into achieving. Some of the 'precision teaching' techniques in which learners observe themselves and provide their own systematic reinforcement seem to be bridging the gap between experiential and behavioural techniques. These two seemingly disparate approaches can be variously adapted and combined to produce a powerful range of methodologies by which the individual can be freed, supported and guided into new ways of behaving. But teachers must explore their own resources and develop those 'mixes' of methods which are most effective in enabling them to support change in others.

The third 'referent' dialogue aims to enable learners to appraise their own performance, but to do so they need to identify examples or referents which they can use as a basis for comparison. The manager helps the learners to identify such examples either in outstanding performers of the skill which they wish to acquire or as measures of quality and/or speed which they can apply to their own activities. Whatever examples learners identify in their own environments they must remain free to use them for their own purposes. In the end, the learner comes to use his or her own previous performances as the basis for evaluating their improvement and should be encouraged not to restrict themselves to the existing norms nor to be discouraged by the outstanding performances of more experienced people.

The management of learning

If we are to encourage people to learn from experience, to think about their needs and purposes, to plan their strategies, to evaluate their success, and to review, revise and improve their methods of learning, then inevitably we are emphasising self-organisation. Self-organised learners expect to go on learning, to make independent judgments and to question. This makes them potentially more useful and productive. Everyone can learn to adapt and develop. This depends on the recruitment of procedures which facilitate personal growth.

An emphasis on the 'process' of learning rather than the 'products' of learning enables the development of a 'language' for negotiating changes in learning capacity. This language is itself content-free and once acquired enables individuals, often for the first time, to take control of the ways they learn from experience. In the crisis-ridden conditions which prevail in much of contemporary society, where 'the valued learning products' of today can easily become the chains restricting tomorrow's growth, the development of a language which enables a way of thinking about personal learning processes becomes an important selective factor in the struggle for personal and industrial survival.

The specialist tools for challenging the robot contribute to the development of this language in which these dialogues can be conducted. The dialogues signpost separate roles for the manager of learning as an agent for change (the Seven Faces). People do not necessarily learn from experience, it depends on the meaning they attribute to their experience and on their capacity to reflect and review it. Much organised learning has tended to disable us as learners and the onus is clearly on teachers and trainers alike to provide a context within which learning conversations can be nourished and sustained.

Learning managers

The emphasis on self-organisation and the practice of Learning Conversations has serious implications. Who are to be the managers of learning? Is it the T-C? Or is it also the job of every manager, parent or social worker to see that his department, family or remand home becomes a more effective learning system?

'Managers of learning' can play a key role in any organisation. They can become the catalysts for change at all levels. Such managers will need guidance in their own development and will also need encouragement and assistance in providing an organisational context for all participants to grow and change. To act as 'managers of learning', people will require new skills, sensitivity, a wide knowledge of learning methods and considerable resources, and above all, they will need to be self-organised learners themselves. Industrial, commercial and educational organisations must meet the challenge involved in enabling staff to adapt themselves to the changing scene. For an organisation to achieve creative growth and change it must work as a system of corporate, self-organised learners. The techniques and philosophy described in this book can be recruited to achieve this. A fully participative corpus, made up of supportive self-organised groups, *is* feasible. To meet the demands of today's society and the challenges of the micro-processor revolution which is already on us, the trajectory to growth must involve the management of people as self-organised learners and fully functioning beings. Only by moving into this unexplored terrain can industrial society survive and grow.

Dear learner,

Allow us to emerge, one last time, from behind the curtain of the third person prose. Do you feel that you have successfully conversed with us on this marathon journey and shared with us the challenges and excitement on route? Will this prove to be a significant and enduring experience? Our approach has been to offer you snippets of our experiences, philosophy, and psychological tools, which you may use to converse more effectively with yourself and others about learning. Having stayed with us this far, in the true spirit of self-organised learning, you will surely no longer need us, as you go on to invent your own approach. We now elect to submerge again, but unlike liquid nitrogen which disappears when exposed to air, we hope that together we have created a conversational encounter, some traces of which will remain.

Good luck with your future learning conversations.

Sheila + Laurie

Grid tricks: an accessing system to the CSHL reflective learning technology

Introduction

The majority of the ideas and methods presented in this book are original, having been developed by the authors with assistance from their postgraduate students. But for completeness some ideas from the clinical grid literature which have influenced us have been included. Where the sources are known to the authors they are acknowledged in the Bibliography.

Section I: On the nature of construing systems

George Kelly's basic idea of a construing system was that items of experience could be thought to derive their meaning from their assignings to a system of bi-polar constructs, and from their non-assigning to other bi-polar constructs. He invented the repertory grid as a method especially designed to elicit and represent meaning in this way. However, he also believed that constructs were hierarchically organised. Some (more specific and restricted) constructs have only a limited range of convenience, and are subordinated to others having a wider range of convenience. Hinkle invented the method of laddering to enable a client to move up and down between subordinate and superordinate constructs. In chapter 9 we introduced the idea of the three-level grid with content grid, main grid and component grid. Thus we can conceive of each part of a construing system as a sub-system of constructs which gives meaning to a set of related items of experience. Each sub-system takes its place in a larger system through the relationships of its constructions to the superordinate constructs of the larger system.

The bi-polarity of a construct is in almost all grid analysis methods assumed to be symmetrical. This enables people to use the traditional statistics of correlation. But the idea of an emergent pole and a submerged pole raises the question of whether assigning an element to the submerged pole is equivalent to assigning it to an emergent pole. In the authors' experience this is often not so. The emergent pole can be imagined as a point in the person's system of meaning whereas the submerged pole is often merely a direction away from that point. Kelly and subsequent adherents to PCP are right to emphasise the need to understand what is *not* being said as a context for understanding *what is said*. But bi-polarity is only one of a number of ways of capturing this crucial characteristic of meaning. Some of the analysis methods in chapter 7 and in the 'Beyond the Grid' section of chapter 12 indicate alternatives to bi-polarity.

Kelly sees the hierarchical system of personal constructs as basically predictive, anticipating events by identifying replications of experience. But one of the inadequacies of the grid is that it does not offer a method for representing a working model which can be cranked backwards or forwards in time to show how the client is anticipating events. The charting techniques for representing perceptual and non-verbal languages introduced in chapters 7 and 8 are an attempt to compensate for this. The CHANGE grid technique described in chapter 9 is another attempt to trace out changes in individual construing over time. Again, dynamic computer graphic displays outlined in chapter 12 offer opportunities for exploring the time dimension of meaning.

Another aspect of meaning which remains implicit in the grid is intentionality. In chapters 3-6 we have shown how systematic conversational procedures involving topic and purposes can regulate intentionality in the grid. The Raiffa technique outlined in chapter 10 shows how personal preference can be weighted in the grid and thus used to explore aspects of personal purposiveness.

Since the meaning represented in each grid is unique, it is inadmissible to compare numbers of grids by traditional statistical analysis. In chapters 9, 10 and 11 we have shown how by conversational elicitation of shared elements and by PAIRed comparisons and conversational exchange procedures, it becomes possible to evaluate 'who thinks and feels like who' and to represent them as a SOCIO-GRID display. These conversational techniques shift the grid away from its exclusive use as a tool for illuminating individual personal meaning towards its application for highlighting the construction and negotiation of shared meaning. Social meanings can be systematically displayed whilst preserving the richness of individual meaning systems, rather than imposing authoritative, statistically averaged methods.

The traditional factor analytical methods for analysing grids, i.e. principal component analysis, suffers from two disadvantages. Firstly, practitioners are tempted to apply their own descriptions to the factors and secondly the computational techniques conceal the process of the pattern-making from the client. The method of cluster analysis used in this book is transparent since it merely groups the client's own descriptions, on the basis of immediately visible similarities. The simplicity of the FOCUS technique results from some fifteen years of testing and refinement of various cluster analysis techniques. TRIGRID, (chapter 7) is the culmination of our attempt to produce the most immediately understandable pattern of similarities.

Section II: The grid as a conversational tool

It is not the purpose of this appendix to repeat the contents of the book. The idea is to pull together into a meta-commentary all the different aspects of the tools and procedures so that the reader may appreciate each chapter in the context of the whole conversational technology. In this section the technology is divided into two parts.

Section IIA describes those techniques and procedures which apply to individual construing, i.e. conversational grids for self-awareness.

Section IIB describes those that apply to groups and institutions as learning systems, i.e. conversational grids for conviviality.

Section IIA: Conversational grids for self-awareness

The grid technology consists in both the process of conversation and the specific grid-based tools that can be used to enable and enhance such conversation. The overall purpose of a grid conversation is to identify, make explicit and develop an area of personal meaning (construing). This involves the following:

(1) Negotiating needs and defining a purpose.

(2) Designing a grid conversation.

(3) Deciding upon the type of grid.

(4) Eliciting the grid.

(5) Choosing the method of analysis and display.

(6) Articulating the talkback.

(7) Using a sequence of grid conversation.

The grid conversation should always be seen in the context of the T-C activity. It is therefore always part of a larger, longer-term process.

(1) Negotiating needs and defining a purpose

The purpose for which a grid conversation (chapter 6) is to be conducted itself depends upon an understanding of:

(a) the types of grids and grid conversations that exist and what they can achieve;

(b) the personal taxonomy of purposes which the client currently acknowledges;

(c) the situational opportunities and constraints within which the T-C and the clients are operating.

The *needs and purposes grid* (chapters 4, 6 and 9) is a useful tool to raise the client's awareness.

(2) Designing a grid conversation

Having identified the purpose, the T-C should design the grid conversation with this purpose in mind. The grid conversation can make an area of personal meaning explicit to the client and can help the client to develop his or her construing in selected ways.

Whilst perceiving, thinking and feeling are all interrelated, the conversation can be designed to emphasise any one of these. Perceptual grids (chapter 8), conceptual grids (chapters 2 and 7) and attitudinal grids (chapters 8 and 9) are merely three of the many forms of grid that can be used.

Similarly the structure and context grids (chapter 9) can be used to give depth to the conversation by making explicit the process whereby meaning is constructed and acquires relevance.

(3) Deciding upon the type of grid

There are many different ways of categorising grids. Some of these are:

(a) the topic (see chapters 2, 9, 6 and Appendix A);

(b) the type of element (see chapter 6 and Appendix A)
     e.g. people, organisms, objects, events, activities, ideas, etc.;

(c) the types of construct (see chapters 8 and 9)
     e.g. verbal, non-verbal, descriptive, sensory, inferential, feelings, evalution, etc.;

(d) the level of construct (see chapters 7 and 9)
     e.g. structure, main, content, etc.;

(e) the method of assigning elements to constructs (see chapter 7)
     e.g. bi-polar, ratings, rankings, 'Not Applicables', measures of certainty.

(4) Eliciting a grid (chapters 2 and 3)

Grids can be elicited:

(a) singly or in groups;

(b) by the T-C working with client(s) or by client(s) themselves;

(c) paper and pencil methods, or in computer-aided conversations;

(d) either to elicit the existing state of personal meaning or to encourage and enable the development of construing. The hand-FOCUSing technique (chapter 4) can be used to build analysis into the elicitation conversation itself.

(5) Choosing the method of analysis and display (see chapters 4 and 7)

Grids can be FOCUSed either by computer or by hand. They can be displayed in the SPACEd or TRIGRID layout. The categories of construct can be identified and indicated (chapters 4 and 7). POLE-MAPS can show relationships between construct poles (chapter 7), the Not Applicable maps can be used to identify operational topics and levels of construing (chapters 6 and 7). The measures of uncertainty (chapter 6) can be superimposed on any of the above to indicate states of provisionality and decisiveness in personal meaning.

(6) Articulating the talkback (chapters 5 and 6)

The talkback conversation can raise awareness by merely REFLECTing on the displays of the analysed grid: or it can be used to develop existing states of personal meaning. The talkback procedure can be designed to encourage the development of construing in many different ways. Elements can be added, eliminated, re-defined, split or combined to extend, elaborate or refine the topic (chapters 5 and 6).

Constructs can be added, eliminated, re-defined, split, or combined (chapters 5 and 6). They can be laddered up or down (chapter 6). They can be categorised and categories related one to another (chapters 8 and 9).

The POLE-MAP, Not Applicable map, structure and content grids can all be used in the DEVELOP mode by encouraging the client to challenge, change and review them (chapter 7).

(7) Using a sequence of grid conversations (chapter 9)

A sequence of grid conversations allow the T-Cs to really incorporate the grid into their armoury of methods.

Conversations can:

(a) use grids on the same topic to monitor, explore and encourage valued change (chapter 9);

(b) use grids on related or sequential issues to enable the client to develop their personal learning (chapter 9).

Section IIB: Grids for conviviality

The grid can be used to encourage and enable conversation among a group who have an area of shared interest, purpose and experience.

The technology of grids as they can be used with a group is usefully divided up as follows:

(1) comparing two grids;

(2) EXCHANGE;

(3) creative encounters: combining two grids;

(4) SOCIO-GRIDS;

(5) POOLING and REFINING;

(6) using a CONSENSUS FRAME language;

(7) groups as learning systems.

(1) Comparing two grids (chapters 9 and 10)

Grids can be compared:

(a) Holistically, i.e. merely by visually comparing elements and constructs.

(b) PAIRS (chapter 9), i.e. where elements are shared and both sets of constructs are FOCUSed together.

(c) DIFF. (chapter 9), i.e. where elements and constructs are superimposed, to identify areas of agreement and difference.

(d) CORE (chapter 9), i.e. where elements and constructs are shared and the iterative process is used to identify the unchanging core of the two grids.

(2) EXCHANGE (chapter 10)

EXCHANGE is the process whereby one person attempts to enter into and use another person's elements and constructs. The resulting 'A' by 'B' grid is then compared with 'A' by 'A' grid.

The 'A' by 'B' grid can be produced as:

(a) 'A' believes B *would* have produced it. This measures understanding.

(b) 'A' believes B *should* have produced it. This measures agreement/disagreement.

(c) 'A' evaluates B's construing. This exercises judgment.

(3) Creative encounters: combining two grids (chapter 10)

Where two people have each produced a separate grid on the same topic, they can go on to produce a grid from attempting to construe both sets of elements with both sets of constructs. The elements are changed and developed and the constructs are changed and developed until one coherent combined grid is achieved.

(4) SOCIO-GRID (chapters 10 and 11)

Where a group of people have explored a topic and have sufficient shared experience they can identify a set of shared elements that define a topic of mutual interest. They each produce a grid using their own repertoire of constructs.

The PAIRS technique is then used to compare the grids from everybody in the group with those from everybody else. This yields:

(a)   measures of total 'similarity − dissimilarity';

(b)   a SOCIO-NET based on (a);

(c)   a MODE grid;

(d)   sub-groups of similar construing.

(5) POOLING and REFINING (chapter 11)

Where a group with shared experience have each produced grids having personal elements and personal constructs, the elements from all the grids and the constructs from all the grids can be POOLed and REFINEd to produce a CONSENSUS FRAME grid (chapter 11).

The CONSENSUS FRAME elements represent every item of experience in the group with redundancy removed. The CONSENSUS FRAME constructs represent all ways of perceiving, thinking and feeling about the topic with redundancy removed. Thus the CONSENSUS FRAME grid presents a two-dimensional language in which members of the group can exchange and negotiate perceptions, thoughts and feelings.

(6) Using a CONSENSUS FRAME language (chapter 11)

The CONSENSUS FRAME grid can be used with a group in much the same way as the repertory grid is used with the individual. It can be used to raise awareness and to develop construing.

The DIFF. and CORE techniques can be used to identify areas of understanding and misunderstanding, agreement and disagreement by comparing one person's grid with another.

(7) Groups as learning systems (chapter 11)

The methods introduced in (1) to (6) can be articulated into a conversational technology for enhancing a group's capacity to function as a learning system.

The group can produce a shared system of meaning which is greater than the sum of its parts. It can recognise the specialist areas of perceptions, thinking and feeling, judging and deciding that exist amongst its members. It can become more aware and thus function more effectively.

Section III: Beyond the grid (chapters 11 and 12)

The directions in which the technology has been further developed are:

(1) alternative ways of representing personal meaning;

(2) ways of more fully relating meaning and behaving;

(3) a more fully developed schema of learning conversations.

(1) Alternative ways of representing personal meaning (chapter 12)

The grid is restrictive in attempting to contain all meaning within a construct/ element space. Alternative methods for representing personal meaning are:

(a) STRUCTURES OF MEANING (chapter 12);

(b) the CHART techniques (chapters 8 and 12);

(c) any and all of the verbal and non-verbal languages ever devised and used by man. These can be re-captured as means for representing personal meaning once the client (and the T-C) has fully appreciated personal meaning as elicited and represented in grid conversations (chapters 8 and 12).

(2) Ways of more fully relating meaning and behaving (chapter 11)

A serious deficiency in grid technology is its incapacity to show exactly how a system of personal meaning leads to a set of behaviours or how a way of behaving can lead to a system of meaning.

There are various ways in which this issue can be approached.

(a) The grid technology has been extended into:
   (i) techniques which attempt to 'weight' constructs in terms of their importance in certain decision-making (chapter 10);
   (ii) alternative behaviours or options which can be used as elements in a grid to discover what types of constructs are applied to the options (chapter 10).

(b) Alternative means of representing meaning can be used which model the system of meaning in more dynamic or causal terms (chapter 12).

(c) Meaning can be seen as analogous to computer programs and so represented. When 'run' against certain situational datas the program predicts behaviours (chapter 12).

(3) A more fully developed schema of LEARNING CONVERSATIONS (chapter 12)

An outline theory of learning conversations is suggested. This requires three levels in the conversation:

(a) life or context;

(b) tutorial or learning contract;

(c) learning-to-learn;

and three types of dialogue:

(a) process – purpose – strategy – outcome – review;

(b) support – challenging the robot;

(c) referent – the self as the primary source of evaluation.

The LEARNING CONVERSATION ascends and descends around the 'double helix' of learning. One helix deals with content, and its complement deals with process. The controlling 'code' is explicitly negotiated and agreed by the T-C practitioner and the learner. One outstanding characteristic of the self-organised learner is that the capacity for conducting such LEARNING CONVERSATIONS with oneself has been internalised.

Section IV: The CSHL computer programs

Associated with this conversational technology is an integrated system of computer programs. These perform three functions. As aids, they provide a back-up resource for those who prefer to use the technology in its face-to-face paper-and-pencil forms. They provide interactive computer-aided conversations which duplicate each and every part of the face-to-face paper-and-pencil technology. They also provide a series of experiential learning events which use the power of the micro to go beyond the paper-and-pencil procedures.

The CSHL BASIC INTERACTIVE COMPUTER PROGRAMS provide CONTENT-FREE TECHNIQUES for eliciting PERSONAL MODELS OF THE WORLD and for BECOMING A PERSONAL SCIENTIST. This CSHL REPERTORY GRID SOFTWARE supersedes all other versions. A shared system of

DATA FILES links all the programs together and allows grids and verbal labels to be transferred from one program to another. The programs are linked through a system of well-tried MENUS. The complete package of REFLECTIVE LEARN-ING GRID PROGRAMS embodies all the techniques described in this book from FOCUS to SOCIO-GRID and POOL, REFINE and CONSENSUS FRAME. Each of these is now fully interactive and elaborated to include the CONVER-SATIONAL SEQUENCES illustrated in the ALGORITHMS in each chapter. In addition the ELEMENT and CONSTRUCT data can be interchanged with the STRUCTURE OF MEANING suite of PROGRAMS and the other BEYOND THE GRID PROGRAMS. The CSHL programs are summarised in APPENDIX B.

A summary list of these programs

Column 1	Column 2	Column 3
NON-INTERACTIVE	INTERACTIVE	INTERACTIVE
GRID-BASED PROGRAMS	GRID-BASED PROGRAMS	BEYOND THE GRID PROGRAMS
McQUITTY AND FOCUS	INTERACTIVE FOCUS	INTERACTIVE AGREE-DISAGREE
HIERARCHY, SPACE and TRIGRID	INTERACTIVE SPACE	INTERACTIVE UNDER-STAND
PAIRS, DIFF. and CORE	INTERACTIVE TRIGRID	INTERACTIVE CREATIVE ENCOUNTER
CHANGE GRID	INTERACTIVE REFLECT	INTERACTIVE COM-MUNITY OF SELVES
NOT APPLICABLE	INTERACTIVE EXCHANGE	INTERACTIVE STRUC-TURES OF MEANING
POLE-MAP	INTERACTIVE PAIRS	INTERACTIVE PERSONAL THESAURUS
EXACT	INTERACTIVE DIFF.	INTERACTIVE CHART
REFLECT	INTERACTIVE CORE	INTERACTIVE READING FOR LEARNING
ARGUS	INTERACTIVE PERCEPTUAL GRIDS	INTERACTIVE VIDEO TALKBACK

SOCIO-GRID	INTERACTIVE DEMON/ PEGASUS/ICARUS	INTERACTIVE LEARNING-TO-LEARN
POOL and REFINE	INTERACTIVE DOUBLE DEMON/PEGASUS BANK	
CONSENSUS FRAME	INTERACTIVE ARGUS	

Applications of the repertory grid

A1.1 A classification of items of personal experience

(PE) Physical Entities
(LT) Living Things
(TE) Temporal Events
(SE) Social Entities
(BA) Behaviours and Activities
(AE) Abstractions and Evaluations
(ES) Emotions and Sensations

It is useful to classify the items of experience used as elements in a repertory grid, since this provides some stimulus for thinking of appropriate elements. The classification system offered has been used to annotate the following elements. However, most of the elements can be construed as members of more than one category, for example, maths exam questions may be viewed as Physical Entities, PE, or as Abstractions, AE. 'Scent' may be viewed as Physical Entity, PE, or Sensations, ES. The category system serves the additional purpose of clarifying the centre of the grid conversation. A conversation about exam questions as Physical Entities will produce a different construct system from one about the same exam questions as Abstractions. The choice of category will depend upon the purpose of the grid conversation. An illustrative list of purposes for grid conversations is presented in Appendix A1.2. Obviously, this can be expanded upon in infinite ways and it is offered solely as a guide to stimulate reflection upon the choice of appropriate purposes.

'Items of personal experience' which have been used by CSHL members as 'elements' in the elicitation of a repertory grid

PE   1   Common Items of Office Stationery
AE   2   Types of Reading Comprehension
PE   3   Pieces of Sculpture

TE	4	Learning Experiences
SE	5	Personal Relationships i.e. How Bill is with Fred
TE	6	Man-Management Events
AE	7	Examination Questions
LT	8	Authority Figures and Peers
LT	9	Colleagues
LT	10	Learners
LT	11	Teachers
TE	12	Creative Events
LT	13	Well-known Psychologists
LT	14	Well-known Architects
AE	15	Spaces in Buildings
ES	16	Drug Experiences
AE	17	Mathematical Command Words, i.e. calculate, solve, prove, discover, etc.
AE	18	Command Words in Exam Papers, i.e. discuss, compare and contrast, write a short essay, explain, etc.
PE	19	Faults or Defects in a Manufactured Product
ES	20	Personal Descriptions in Wine Tasting
PE	21	Blends of Whisky
LT	22	Pupils in a Nursery School
LT	23	Students
TE	24	Events in a Problem-Solving Discussion
AE	25	Topics to be Learned
SE	26	T-C Institutions
LT	27	Well-known Politicians
AE	28	Learning Strategies
AE	29	Purposes to be Achieved by Reading
AE	30	Training Methods and Techniques
BA	31	Events in a Classroom
LT	32	Clients of Marriage Guidance Counsellor
SE	33	Pedagogic Authorities
PE	34	Geological Specimens
AE	35	Personal Myths of Learning
AE	36	Subjects in a School Curriculum
BA	37	Possible New Projects in a Research and Development Department
PE	38	Competitors' Products
LT	39	Subordinates
AE	40	Possible Relationships between Teacher/Trainer, Learner and Resources
LT	41	Green Vegetables
PE	42	Indian Spices
PE	43	Ciders
PE	44	Continental Cakes
BA	45	Events in a Restaurant

BA 46   Events in a Party
LT 47   Clients
LT 48   Delinquents in a Remand Home
PE 49   Weapons
AE 50   National Stereotypes
PE 51   Dutch Oil Paintings
AE 52   Aspects of a Painting
BA 53   Items in an Indian Miniature
LT 54   Footballers
SE 55   Football Teams
PE 56   Photographs
PE 57   Pieces of Graphic Art
AE 58   Items to be Remembered
TE 59   Events that Happened during an Encounter Group
LT 60   'High Flying' Managers
BA 61   Teaching Methods
PE 62   Love Poems
PE 63   Novels by Female Writers
TE 64   Plays of the British Theatres
TE 65   TV Broadcasts for Schools
TE 66   Group Crises during Laboratory Experiments
PE 67   Naval Simulators
ES 68   Sonar Responses
BA 69   EEG Records
AE 70   Teaching Styles
LT 71   Industrial Trainers
ES 72   Human Diseases
LT 73   Wild Flowers
LT 74   Birds' Eggs
PE 75   Bones
LT 76   Extinct Animals
TE 77   Events in a Doctor's Consulting Room
LT 78   Customers
TE 79   Video Sequences of 'Sales' Events
BA 80   'Aspects' of a Foreman's Job
PE 81   Examination Scripts
BA 82   Psychological Methods and Techniques
TE 83   Computer Programs
AE 84   Computer Languages
AE 85   Terms in a Foreign Language
AE 86   Phrases with Varying Syntactic Structures
AE 87   Staff Comments on Student Essays
PE 88   Soldered Joints
PE 89   Decorations on Manufactured Chocolates
TE 90   Events in a Language Class

PE 91   Fashion Clothes
TE 92   Ingenious Mechanisms (Engineering)
PE 93   Precision Tools
TE 94   Sub-Routines
BA 95   Work Study Charting Techniques
PE 96   Chemical Elements
AE 97   Architectural Drawings
BA 98   Laboratory Reports
AE 99   Science Textbooks
AE 100 Journal Articles
TE 101 Events in a Forward Command Post
AE 102 Alternative Futures
TE 103 Recordings of Classical Music
ES 104 Aquatic Sounds
ES 105 Cooking Smells
ES 106 Textures
BA 107 Project Work Events
TE 108 Phases in Consultancy Work
LT 109 'Managers I Know'
BA 110 Events in an Appraisal Interview
PE 111 Items in a Folk Museum
LT 112 Botanical Specimens Collected during a Field Trip
SE 113 Jazz Groups
ES 114 Yoga Breathing Exercises
SE 115 Communes
ES 116 Emotions Provoked by Intense Inter-Personal Events
SE 117 Working Parties
BA 118 Cases in Magistrate's Court
BA 119 Primitive Technologies
SE 120 Project Teams
ES 121 Emotions Tested by an Initiation Rite
BA 122 Items in a Child's Story
PE 123 Pebbles
PE 124 Pieces of Physical Education Apparatus
AE 125 Pathologists
AE 126 Concepts in Physics
AE 127 Mathematical Operations
AE 128 Statistical Concepts
BA 129 Management Activities
BA 130 Equipment Problems
AE 131 Cladistics Techniques
BA 132 Job Descriptions
SE 133 Roles in an Institution
BA 134 Learning Skills
PE 135 Learning Resources

ES 136 Experiences during Pregnancy
TE 137 Events Occurring in Teaching the Educationally Subnormal
AE 138 Problem solving algorithms
TE 139 Ways of 'Using my Time Productively whilst Unemployed'
PE 140 Cheeses (in cheese grading)
PE 141 Polished Surfaces
BA 142 Outcomes of Listening to a Lecture
ES 143 Pieces of Prose
ES 144 'Places I Know'
AE 145 Alternative Designs
AE 146 Forms of Representation
ES 147 Responses to Floral Scents
BA 148 Opening Moves in Chess
BA 149 Psychological Tests
PE 150 Balance Sheets
AE 151 Topics in Accountancy
BA 152 Events in a Selection Interview
BA 153 Indoor Games
BA 154 Safety Measures at Work
TE 155 Video Selections of own Athletic Performance
BA 156 Ice Skating Performances
AE 157 Consumers' Views of Positive Attributes of Products
TE 158 Events in the Work of a Shop Assistant
AE 159 Photographs as Artworks
LT 160 Biological Specimens – Seaweeds
TE 161 Events During an Education Student's First Teaching Practice
LT 162 Boys in a Borstal Institution
PE 163 Faults on Breakfast Cereals
BA 164 Training/Learning Situations
TE 165 Radio Programmes
LT 166 Trees and Shrubs
LT 167 Parasites
PE 168 Postage Stamps
PE 169 Antique Chairs
PE 170 Ikons
ES 171 'Families I Know'
ES 172 Folk Songs
PE 173 Japanese Vases
PE 174 Wallpapers
BA 175 'Methods I found Successful in Breaking Habits'
PE 176 Musical Instruments
AE 177 Chemical Bonds
BA 178 Methods for Bread-making
AE 179 'Good Events' in a Seminar
PE 180 Lenses

TE 181 Syntheses of Organic Compounds
BA 182 Applications of Biotechnology
AE 183 Egyptian Hieroglyphics
TE 184 Bird Songs
TE 185 Events in Omelette-making
BA 186 Thai Dance Sequences
BA 187 Reading Strategies
BA 188 Listening Strategies
BA 189 Mating Behaviours
AE 190 Religions
TE 191 'Negotiating Events' during a Strike
BA 192 Funeral Rites
ES 193 Effects of Hormones
BA 194 Immunological Responses
PE 195 Diamonds
PE 196 Car Paint Finishes
LT 197 Musical Performers
SE 198 Orchestras of the World
AE 199 Criteria for Grading Student Essays
BA 200 'Jobs I'd Like to Do'
BA 201 Decisions Involved in Firing an Industrial Executive
BA 202 Naval Task Books
BA 203 Machine Maintenance Manuals
BA 204 Operating Instructions for Domestic Appliances
AE 205 Repertory Grid Analysis Procedures
BA 206 Learning Events 'On the Job'
BA 207 Origami Techniques
BA 208 Learning-by-Discussion Techniques
BA 209 Non-Verbal Communication Techniques
PE 210 Plastic Finishes
TE 211 'Sticky' Events at Work
TE 212 Personally Significant Events in Language Learning
AE 213 Properties of Intelligent Computer-Aided Learning
BA 214 Characteristics of Food Packaging which Influence Marketing
AE 215 Positive and Negative Attributes of a Brand of Chocolates
SE 216 Ministry of Defence Training Establishments
PE 217 Faults in Underwear Garments
TE 218 Student Counselling Situations
ES 219 Awareness-Raising Techniques
ES 220 Panic-engendering Situations
BA 221 Debrief Procedures in Training for Intercept Control
AE 222 Items of Meta-language
AE 223 Subjective Judgments in Tea Blending
TE 224 Events in Chairing a Meeting
AE 225 Strategies for Learning from Work Placements

AE 226 Metaphors
SE 227 Change Agents
BA 228 Aspects of a Successful Training Enterprise
BA 229 Maths in Educational Research
AE 230 Differences between Real and Simulated Tasks
BA 231 Activities whilst Unemployed
ES 232 Responses to Personal Crises
BA 233 Events Calling for Value Judgment
TE 234 Alternate Systems for Providing Energy
ES 235 Alternate Medicines
TE 236 Occult Phenomena
SE 237 Small Business Enterprises
AE 238 Jargon and Specialist Terminology
SE 239 Playgroups
SE 240 Prayer Meetings
BA 241 Results of a Social Experiment
SE 242 Health Farms
SE 243 Restaurants in the *Good Food Guide*
ES 244 Events in a Japanese Tea Ceremony
BA 245 War Games
ES 246 Soft Fabrics
ES 247 Dreams
SE 248 Board Meetings
BA 249 Robots
ES 250 Asthma Drugs
SE 251 Team of Research Chemists
SE 252 Packaging Line
PE 253 Silicone Chips
ES 254 Descriptions of Pain
BA 255 Table Manners
PE 256 Floor Coverings
PE 257 Household Gadgets
SE 258 Welsh Choirs
PE 259 Love Spoons

A1.2 Purposes for which grids have been elicited

Introducing the Repertory Grid
To Appreciate Different Types of Comprehension
To Develop Students' Appreciation of Sculpture
To Expand the Variety of Learning Experiences
To Improve One's Relationships with People
To Become a More Effective Manager
To Obtain Higher Exam Results
For a Delinquent to Come to Terms with Society

To Improve One's Teaching Performance
To Make Better Use of Staff as Learning Resources
To Develop Strategies for Creativity
To Explore Career Opportunities
Training in Quality Control
To Explore Customers' Views
To Change Personal Preferences in Clothes
To Structure One's Subject
To Negotiate a Learning Contract
To Explore Personal Change
To Develop a Taxonomy of Learning Purposes
To Construct a Personal Thesaurus of Meanings in a Foreign Language
To Explore Personal Learning Task Analysis
To Develop a Problem-solving Algorithm
To Identify the Rules of Dance
To Challenge the Status Quo in an Industrial Dispute
To Identify Categories in Literary Criticism
To Explore Attitudes towards Work
To Identify Functions in a Language
To Generate Alternate Futures in a Forward Planning Exercise
To Compare Views on a Topic of Group Interest
To Evaluate the Effects of a One-year Course
To Identify Attitudes towards Mathematics
To Develop a Scheme for Marking Exam Questions
To Systematise Subjective Comments in Clinical Trials
To Identify Criteria for Subjective Judgment in Quality Control
To Encourage a Shared Understanding of a Business Enterprise
To Categorise Dialogues in a Learning Conversation
To Evaluate a Research Project
To Explore the Context of Learning at Sea
To Analyse a Manual Skill
To Develop a Self-help Diagnosis Chart for Middle-age Illnesses
To Identify the Attributes of Awareness-raising Tools
To Accept a Modus Vivendi in an Industrial Organisation
To Categorise Evidence in a Copyright Case
To Re-structure the Learning Resources in a School
To Refine a Flow Chart of a Manufacturing Process
To Identify Personal Needs in a Marital Relationship
To Devise a New Symbol System for Chemical Compounds
To Identify Strategies in Writing Computer Programs
To Develop an Appraisal Scheme for Middle-Management
To Enhance the Quality of a 'Think Tank'
To Specify Characteristics of an Artificial Intelligence System
To Diagnose Learning Difficulties in a Given Task
To Identify Learning Problems of a University Undergraduate

To Develop Personal Skills in 'Chairmanship'

To Enhance Personal Pleasure in Reading-for-Learning

To Enrich the Working Relationships in a Project Team

To Become a More Effective Salesman

To Improve Classroom Transactions

To Plan a Design for a Town Garden

To Develop a Better Understanding of Grammatical Structures

To Explore the Relationship between Semantic Form and Personal Meaning

To Identify Reasons for Changing One's Job

To Build a Flexible System for Assessing University Staff Teaching Performance

To Develop More Effective Leadership Qualities

To Help a Therapist to Identify Criteria by which She Judges Improvement in
    a Client

To Evaluate Alternate Therapies

To Enhance the Sensitivity of a Psychiatrist to Events in a Therapeutic Rela-
    tionship

To Compare Psychiatrists' Views of Mental Illness Designations

To Expand the Range of Ideas about a Topic

To Enhance an Artist's Non-verbal Appreciation of Pictures

The Centre for the Study of Human Learning

The Centre

Consultants, postgraduates and members of the CSHL form a network of professional people concerned with human learning in all its aspects and who are involved in helping others to become more competent and self-organised learners. They work in education, commerce, health service, industry and various government agencies.

The Centre for the Study of Human Learning has existed as a partially self-financing Research Institute in Brunel University since 1967. Constitutionally it has its own governing board which advises on policy and future planning. It is responsible directly to Senate. Within the university the Centre offers: a postgraduate programme, 'learning-to-learn' opportunities for undergraduates, and staff development seminars with academic colleagues. However the self-financing requirement ensures that many of its activities are directed outside the university. It has run courses, workshops, and conferences for educational, governmental, industrial and commercial organisations in Britain and in the USA, Canada, Australia and Mexico, as well as a number of European countries.

Research is mainly directly towards the study of human learning in its natural habitats. This has led to the creation of a theory of learning conversations and a continually expanding range of awareness-raising techniques. These combine to enable individuals and groups to personally research their skills as learners, so that they may more effectively control the direction, quality and content of their learning. This action-research has been and is funded from a variety of sources including the Nuffield Foundation, the Department of Education and Science, the Social Science Research Council, the Welsh Office and the Ministry of Defence as well as industrial and commercial organisations. The Centre also offers consultancy services and receives people on short secondments to familiarise themselves with its approach and to help them to make practical use of its conversational methods and reflective learning technology.

Aims

1 To research personal learning processes and to invent new tools, procedures and techniques for enabling people to become more aware of, reflect upon and review their learning competence.

2 To develop a systematic methodology of learning conversations for enabling individuals to become more skilled and autonomous learners.

3 To work with educational, commercial and government establishments to maximise the advantages of self-organised learning for the individual, small groups, the institution and society.

The CSHL reflective learning technology and methodology

CSHL interactive computer programs

These programs are designed, primarily, as aids to be used in raising awareness of learning processes, but each of them can also be used as a tool for more general research and investigation. Ten of the programs are based on the repertory grid which was originally invented by George Kelly and has been used and elaborated upon to develop a personal learning technology within which individuals, pairs and groups can be enabled to increase their capacity for personal understanding, communication and learning. For those unfamiliar with repertory grid techniques, lists of publications on this topic are available from CSHL.

FOCUS, TRIGRID, REFLECT and PERCEIVE AND EVALUATE are all concerned with the analysis and reflective display of individual grids.

PEGASUS DOUBLE-DEMON uses the computer to conversationally elicit a grid with simultaneous analysis and comment back to the user.

CHANGE GRID calculates and displays the differences between a series of grids elicited from one person over a period of time.

INTERACTIVE PAIRS and EXCHANGE AND CONVERSE compare grids on the same topic from two people; they are designed to articulate conversational understanding.

SOCIO-GRIDS AND SOCIO-NET and POOL, REFINE AND CONSENSUS FRAME are ways of moving from individual understanding to the personal understandings of a group, reflecting areas of shared understanding and misunderstanding.

In addition to the micro-computer programs above there are a number of programs which do not involve the repertory grid, these include:

READING-FOR-LEARNING, an interactive analysis of how people read, and conversational exercises to improve the use of reading as a learning skill.

CHART is a conversational method of eliciting a person's view of the cause and effect structure of an area of their experience.

effectiveness of an Open University course.

(j) The learning-to-learn materials have been used by self-help groups of industrial trainers to acquaint them with the concept of self-organised learning.

(k) A complete system for the personal development of 'reading as a learning skill' includes methods for eliciting a personal purpose taxonomy, a recorder of reading behaviour, flow diagram analysis of texts and structured network descriptions for evaluating reading outcomes. It has been used with students in colleges of higher education. It had a very significant long-term (two-year follow-up) positive influence on their academic performance.

(l) A workbook of 'learning-to-learn' materials, *The Art and Science of Getting a Degree* has been developed and evaluated with groups of undergraduates, teaching staff and industrial trainers.

(m) Conversational computer-based repertory grid techniques developed by the director, in addition to those already mentioned, include: FOCUS, PEGASUS, TRIGRID, READREC, PERSONAL THESAURUS, STRUCTURES OF MEANING, etc. These have been used in a wide variety of courses and personal learning events including man-management courses, social skills training, quality control training and primary schools.

(n) These techniques have also been applied to enable marketing managers learn to appreciate the personal meanings attributed to products by consumers.

Workshops and courses

The learning-to-learn courses offered by the Centre have aroused widespread interest. They focus on a range of learning skills, for example, discussion, reading, writing, listening, thinking and feeling (construing), decision-making, and subjective judgment.

The courses vary in time, structure and scope but always introduce the concept of LEARNING CONVERSATIONS. These centre on the idea of a learning contract (either implicit or explicit), which can be negotiated in 'tutorial conversations'. The quality of the learning contract and the processes of carrying it out are explored in the 'learning-to-learn conversation'. Alienation or lack of interest in learning arises from either a perceived or real lack of relevance to the individual learner. The personal needs and purposes served by learning are explored in the 'life conversation'. Thus the learning conversation is itself hierarchical, and movement within it depends on the needs, competency and experiences of the learner.

The personal skills, methodology, procedures and tools required to develop and sustain these three learning conversations as a highly articulate systematic continuing awareness-raising experience form the main theme of each course.

Direct experience in the use of listening, discussion, reading, writing, thinking, etc., and the carrying out of relevant manual operations (e.g. soldering, origami, judging the quality of toffee, or assembling toys) is always offered in a context which raises awareness of the processes of learning. The nature of the course and the interests of the participants determine the depth and intensity with which the skills are explored.

The Brunel Reading Recorder and associated paper-and-pencil techniques, the FLOW DIAGRAM technique for exploring the meaning in a text, heuristics for eliciting and displaying the STRUCTURES OF MEANING, algorithms for developing personally meaningful taxonomies of purposes, Kelly repertory grid techniques, interactive computer programs for structuring learning conversations with oneself, are some of the techniques used to articulate, intensify and control these learning-to-learn experiences.

Whilst the exploration of any one or more of the skills may be treated as a serious habit-changing and competence-acquiring exercise in its own right, the courses always include some experience, at least, of three different skills. This allows comparison to be made and analogies to be drawn which focus attention back on to the main integrative theme. Self-organised learning is seen as internalising the learning conversations so that the learner becomes his own tutor.

Workshops and courses are offered to educational, commercial and industrial enterprises. Some of these are available as 'in-company' courses. Recent in-company courses have included:

Learning-to-Learn for Managers; The Development of Learning Contracts for Trainers; Subjective Judgment in Quality Control; Creativity for R&D Staff; Social Skills for Bankers; Learning Conversations for Teachers; and the Self-Organised Learning of Languages.

CSHL publications

Some 100 or more papers and reports describing the research projects, techniques and methodology are available directly from the CSHL.

Enquiries, Please write to:

The Secretary,
Centre for the Study of Human Learning,
Brunel University,
Kingston Lane,
UXBRIDGE,
Middlesex, UB8 3PH.

The personal structure of meaning of the authors

Glossary

This glossary is presented in a rather unusual form. The alphabetical list of special terms used in this book does not have definitions attached to each word or phrase. The authors' views of the nature of meaning precludes this. HERE THE WORDS AND PHRASES ARE REFERENCED IN SHORT PASSAGES IN WHICH A SET OF RELATED TERMS ARE USED TO MAKE A STATE-MENT ABOUT ONE OF TWELVE OF THE MAJOR THEMES OR TOPICS WITH WHICH THIS BOOK IS CONCERNED. Since the authors believe in patterns of meaning, in which the relationship between the parts construct a pattern which has more meaning than they can contain and express separately, this approach seemed both logical and inevitable. The same idea applies across the twelve themes which not only liberally overlap, but also comprise the major items of meaning out of which the glossary summary is composed. THUS MEANING IS DERIVED FROM BOTH CONTEXT AND STRUCTURE. It is hoped that the book provides a context in which personal learning with the repertory grid acquires meaning. It is also hoped that the structure of the book makes this meaning more than just the sum of its parts.

Major themes

  1 Awareness-raising
  2 Content v. process
  3 CSHL conversational technology
  4 Personal meaning and the form of the repertory grid
  5 Learning
  6 Meaning
  7 The repertory grid and its derivatives
  8 Scaling techniques
  9 Specialist terms
  10 Systems of internal representation
  11 Techniques for analysing the grid
  12 T-C

Glossary

Specialist terms	*Themes*
agreement	6
algorithm	9
ARGUS	11
attributes personal meanings	4
attitudes	5
auditory	10
awareness	1
awareness-raising	1,4,5
behaviour	5
bi-polar	4
bi-polar sort	8
capacity for learning	5
categorise	5
Centre for the Study of Human Learning	3
challenging the robot	1
C-indi	3
client	12,5
clinician	12
cluster	11
coach	12
coaching	12
CONSENSUS FRAME grid	7
consciousness	1
construct	4
construction of experience	4,5
construct pole	4
construe	6,3
consultant	12
consulting	12
content and process	2,3
content	2
content-free	2
control	2
conversation	3
conversation entity	3
conversational technology	3
C1P1, C1P2	4
CORE	11
counselling	12
counsellor	12

creative conversation   3
CSHL   3
custodian   12
custody   12

delinquent   12
descriptive grid   7
DIFF.   11
dimension   4
disabled learner   5
dogleg scale   8

element   4
emergent pole   8,4
employee   12
events grid   7
EXCHANGE   3,11,5,6
experience   5,6

FOCUS   11
FOCUSed grid   7
the form of the repertory grid   4,3

grid games/tricks   7,3
guided conversation   1

habitual activity   1
heterarchy   9
hierarchical structures   9,4
how people learn   2

imagination   10
impersonal learning   5
implications grid   7
inferential grid   7
items of meaning   4
items of personal experience   4

kinaesthetic   10
knowledge   5

laddering   11,4
learning activities   2
learning   5
learning competencies   2

learning contract 5
LEARNING CONVERSATION 3,5
learning process 2,5
learning skills 2
learning-to-learn 5

management of learning 5
meaning 6,5
minimum context 4
mirroring 1

negotiate 5,6
nodes of control 3
non-verbal grid 7

objects grid 7
order of agreement 11
organised learning 2
own personal terms 6

pair 4
PAIRS 11
patient 12
pattern of meaning 4,6
PEGASUS 11
perceptions, thoughts and feelings 4
perceptual grid 7
personal assumptions 1
personal constructions 4
personal construct system 4
personal construct psychology 4
personal evaluation 2
personal learning 5
personal meaning 6,3
personal myths 1
personal perspective 6
personal scientist 4
practitioner 12,1,5
prisoner 12
process 2
product 2
PSOR 5
psychiatrist 12
psychic mirror 1
psychic space 4

public evaluation	2
public knowledge	2
pupil	12
ranking	8
rating	8
raw grid	7
records and referents	6
reflect	1
reflecting	1
reflective learning	5
reflective processes	5
relationships grid	7
relevant and viable	2,5
repertory grid	7,1,2,4
resources	2
reversed construct	11
robot	1
role grid	7
scaling techniques	8
science of learning conversations	3
self-organised learning	5,2
sensory grid	7
significant learning event	5
'singleton'	4
SOCIO-GRID	11
space	11
SPACEd FOCUSed grid	7
special terms	9
special versions of the repertory grid	7
staff member	12
strategy	2
structure of meaning	6
student	12
subject matter	2
submerged pole	8,4
sub-ordinate construct	4
sub-vocalisers	10
super-ordinate construct	4
symbolic	10
systems of internal representation	10
structure	3
skills	5

tactics	2
talkback	1
TC	12,5
teacher	12
teaching	12
techniques for analysing the grid	11
technology	3
therapist	12
therapy	12
'three-card trick'	4
tool	3
topic	2
trainee	12
trainer	12
training	12
triad	4
TRIGRID	11
tutor	12
tutoring	12
understanding	6
values grid	7
verbal labels	4
visualisers	10
warder	12

Major themes

1 Awareness-raising

The terms *awareness* and *consciousness* are here used to describe psychological states which contain the property of 'looking at yourself' or describing yourself to yourself. They involve the idea of metaphorically dividing into two entities, one of which observes the other. *Awareness* is here used to indicate a general or diffuse state of observation, whereas *consciousness* is used to imply that the observation has more of the property of paying attention.

The terms *mirroring, reflecting* and *talkback* are used to indicate techniques analogous to 'looking in a mirror' to become more conscious or aware. The *psychic 'mirror'* is here usually the *repertory grid* in one or other of its forms.

Thus the analogy is being made between the experience of looking at one's appearance in a mirror and looking at some representation of your perceptions, thoughts and feelings in the repertory grid. *Mirroring* is used when the process of reflection is passive. *Reflecting* is used to imply a more active thinking and imagining process. *Talkback* is used where emphasis is being placed on the guided conversational nature of the mirroring or reflecting activity. The term *robot* has been taken from an article by Colin Wilson in which he discusses the opposite of awareness. He describes the automatic non-conscious nature of much habitual activity and suggests that in over-familiar or over-learned activities, from typing to making love, we may feel as if some robot was operating our body without any consciousness or participation from us. The process of *challenging the robot* consists in using the *mirroring*, *reflecting* and *talkback* techniques for awareness-raising.

2 Content v. process

A fundamental issue to which lip service is paid by most practitioners of organised learning is that of how much education should be concerned with the *content* and *products* of learning, and how much it should be concerned with its *processes*. Unfortunately this acknowledgment remains only skin or mouth deep. Educational practice only rarely illuminates *how people learn* or *raises their awareness of their own learning processes* to a level at which they can begin to experiment and take conscious control of how they exploit their resources, thus becoming more self-organised in their learning activities.

An overwearing concern with the content of public knowledge (such as is emphasised and publicised by the radio programme *Brain of Britain*) keeps the emphasis in learning away from any concern with the *strategies* and *tactics of learning*, or with the idea of improving on *learning skill* or *learning competencies*.

Here the terms *topic*, *subject matter* and *public knowledge*, are used perhaps with a doubly negative connotation. They are *content*-orientated rather than *process*-orientated and they are placing organisational, social or public evaluation of what is worth knowing above any individual's personal evaluation of what is *relevant* and *viable* for them.

The idea of techniques which are *content-free* has been introduced in an attempt to change this imbalance between content and process. The repertory grid is a content-free technique. It cannot be used without content but the types of content with which it can be used are myriad. Appendix A.1.1 illustrates the universality which accrues from this content-free property.

3 CSHL conversational technology

The CSHL is the Centre for the Study of Human Learning at Brunel University. Here the term *conversational technology* is deliberately used to challenge the assumptions of both artists and scientists, to give food for thought to both those who espouse the humanities and those who owe allegiance to technology. The basic terms are *conversation* and *technology*. By conversation we do not mean chit-chat, nor the ritual or frozen *exchanges* of much human socialising. Conversation is organised but unpredictable because it involves two or more separate nodes of control in the interchange of *construing*. The value of *creative* conversation is that it can produce something which is significantly more than any of the participants could have produced alone. The idea of a conversational entity or C-indi is rooted in the idea that the conversational process is more than the sum of its parts. Metaphorically, but powerfully, it has a life of its own. *Technology* carries the connotation of tools, methods, procedures and operating processes which add power and flexible repetition to the one-off achievements of the artist. It may also carry the idea of loss of uniqueness and individuality, but that is not intended in this context.

The idea of a *learning conversation* is introduced and a science of learning conversations is indicated which gives form and theoretical underpinning to the learning technology.

The detailed structure and content of this learning technology are summarised in Grid tricks: an accessing system to the CSHL reflective learning technology.

4 Personal meaning and the form of the repertory grid

The *repertory grid* is a technique devised by George Kelly to give one operational form to his *personal construct psychology*. He suggested that it is useful to construe Man (by which he meant all human beings) as mediated through a personal construct system. This system is unique to the person and is that through which he or she attributes personal meaning to everything which they experience. Kelly suggests that we each place *personal constructions* upon our experience, thus giving meaning to it.

The repertory grid is the first tool in a technology symbiotic to this PCP theory which construes each individual as their own personal scientist: constructing meanings and validating them through cumulative experience.

The repertory grid is explained in detail and at length (if not ad nauseam) in this book. It is both a procedure and a systematic method of recording a person's *perceptions*, *thoughts* and *feelings* (their construing) of a topic in their own uniquely personal terms. It consists of *elements* which are *items of personal experience* assigned to a series of *personal constructs*. Each construct is bi-polar representing a dimension within the psychic space or personal construct system of that individual. The bi-polarity of a construct embodies an assumption about meaning. For an item of *experience* to become an item of *meaning* it must minimally stand in relationship to two other items being similar to one and different from the other. This is the minimum context in which meaning can exist. The grid represents a personal *pattern of meaning*, being a systematic form for containing the complex set of relationships between those items of meaning which together define a topic.

The *poles* of a *construct* (e.g. C1P1 and C1P2) often carry verbal labels which may merely serve as a private shorthand in which the client can be enabled to converse with himself or herself, thus raising awareness. When using the triadic (or three-card trick) method for eliciting constructs the *pair* identifies the *emergent pole* defined by the similarity between two elements. The *singleton* defines the submerged pole by being different from the other two.

In the process of *laddering*, a construct moves up or down through the hierarchical structure of the construct system, identifying super-ordinate constructs in one direction and sub-ordinate constructs in the other.

5 Learning

The emphasis throughout this book is on *personal learning*. This is contrasted with the impersonal learning produced by much organised T-C. Learning has been defined as: the acquisition of appropriate *knowledge*, *skills* and *attitudes* to be measured according to publicly acknowledged standards, or as the achievement and valued changes in behaviour or experience. But the authors have found it operationally more useful and personally more satisfying to define learning as the *construction* and *reconstruction*, *exhange* and *negotiation* of personally relevant and viable meanings.

This emphasis on personal learning and on the achievement of personally useable meaning has meant the reflective processes are seen to play a central role in the learning process. Reflective learning raises awareness of the whole process of learning, allowing experiment and the achievement of control which enhances self-organised learning. The uncommitted acceptance of instruction in pre-digested packages of public knowledge is believed by the authors to produce impersonal learning which is often associated with boredom and disinterest. This in turn leads to the disabled learner, unwilling and unable to learn. The process of the *learning conversation* is seen as a technique for enabling T-Cs to re-construe what they do as the management of learning. Based on the idea of the *learning contract* and the PSOR (Purpose, Strategy, Outcome, Review) paradigm of the learning conversation, it provides a powerful and systematic method for helping clients to increase their capacity for learning.

6 Meaning

The idea of *meaning* is central to this book. The introduction to this glossary has discussed it. It appears in most of the other sections of the glossary and runs constantly through the book.

Here the term *personal meaning* is used to emphasise that for the authors, in this context, all meaning starts and finishes as being personal. This is a serious and important departure from any view of meaning as being socially defined.

Personal meaning can be exchanged and negotiated, i.e. it can be mediated through conversation. But this requires skill and patience and it often cannot be achieved without recruiting special tools and techniques such as those described in this book. Records of the results of creative conversation, and referents which have been the source of shared experience, may be preserved, but newcomers will have to negotiate new personal meanings out of them and the likelihood is that the newly achieved personal meanings will differ significantly from those they were intended to signpost. Thus Shakespeare is re-interpreted by each generation and the term 'phlogiston' triggers off a completely different pattern of meaning in the author than it did in Lord Kelvin. Each personal perspective produces its own pattern of meaning. We each *construe* our experience differently in our own personal terms.

7 The repertory grid and its derivatives

The *repertory grid* is a technique invented by George Kelly for use by clinical psychologists in their application of his personal construct psychology to therapy. The technique has been developed into a conversational technology by the authors and postgraduate members of the CSHL, together with many other people. The conversational derivatives of the repertory grid are mapped out in detail in the 'Grid tricks' Appendix.

Raw grid

The form of repertory grid which merely records the results of the *elicitation phase* of the repertory grid conversation.

FOCUSed grid

The form of the repertory grid which is specially designed for *talkback* and *reflection*, it results from *two-way cluster analysis* of the raw grid.

SPACEd FOCUSed grid

An additional visual layout of the FOCUSed grid, which emphasises the *clusters of elements* and *clusters of constructs*, and the relationships between them.

Special versions of the repertory grid (see 'grid tricks')

    Perceptual grid, to include:
      Sensory grid
      Descriptive grid
      Inferential grid

    Role grid

    Implications grid

    CONSENSUS FRAME grid

8 Scaling techniques

Here the term *scaling techniques* relates to the various methods used to assign the *elements* to *constructs* in a repertory grid. This is of major concern to GRID USERS and is spelled out in some detail in the 'Grid tricks' Appendix.

There are three major types of scale used: 1 *Bi-polar*; 2 *Rating*; 3 *Ranking*.

The shape of a scale leads to the discussion of such items as 'Dog-leg scale', 'Non-Applicable responses', 'Emergent', and 'Submerged poles', and 'Skewness'.

9 Specialist terms

Scientific or technological terms have only been used where the term adds significantly to possible meanings, for example, throughout the book summary diagrams which are provided as memory aids to the major procedures, contain such terms as eliciting a grid, FOCUSing or EXCHANGE grids. In these diagrams:

The term *'algorithm'* is used to designate an unambiguous specification of a procedure.

The term *'hierarchy'* originally derives from the church where the SUPER-ORDINATE/SUB-ORDINATE relationships were authoritatively defined. This terminology has been taken into organisational theory to indicate any pyramidal system of organisation. A *'heterarchy'* is an organisation in which the same, lower order, items can be brought together into a number of alternate pyramids.

Thus one could have an *algorithm* for boiling an egg. The process of making an omelette might be described *hierarchically*, whereas the skill of making egg dishes would be best represented as a *heterarchy* of lower-order skills such as breaking an egg, beating it, adding ingredients and combining in different dishes.

This glossary attempts to provide a structure and context for an appreciation of how the specialist terms used within the book take on a pattern of meaning which is particular to it.

10 Systems of internal representation

Personal construct psychology suggests that it is not the events experienced by a person that influence their behaviour, but the personal meaning of those events.

Thus if it were possible for two people to construe, (*attribute meaning to*) the same event in the same way, they would behave similarily. However, no two people have the same system of personal constructs and therefore no two people will attribute the same pattern of meaning to an event. This general assumption leads to the identification of items of experience as the basic unit of psychological explanation. Meaning consists in the relationship between items of experience. When such items exist in relationship to each other, they become items of meaning, which combine into patterns of meaning.

However, such general descriptions avoid the basic question of how meaning is represented inside a person. Some experts have equated meaning with language, but even the most superfical consideration of music, art or gardening reveals that much personal experience is not expressed in any form which we would normally call verbal language.

In the body of the text the analogy has been drawn between the *sensorily* disabled (e.g. deaf, blind, dumb) and the *imaginatively* disabled (i.e. those who do not experience visual, auditory or other sensory images).

It is suggested that techniques deriving from the repertory grid can and should be used to enable people to develop the powers of their imagination and to extend the variety of modes in which they construct and represent their experience.

Thus the ability to create visual, auditory and tactile images, and to think and remember smells and tastes adds powerfully to the learner's powers of self-organisation.

T-C pays much less attention to this type of personal development than it warrants. Similarly the power of a whole variety of non-verbal languages from mathematics to ASME symbols, and from musical notation to engineering drawing, is under-used.

More attention is given by professional institutions to standardisation than to creative exploitation and imaginative development of these languages.

Finally, the idea that learning can be increased many-fold by the invention of non-verbal shorthands which are uniquely matched to personal needs and developments finds almost no expression or encouragement within the traditional form of T-C.

11 Techniques for analysing the grid

For a detailed description of different techniques used for analysing the grid the reader should refer to the 'Grid tricks' Appendix, and thence to the body of the book.

In summary, individual grids are cluster analysed using FOCUS, SPACE and TRIGRID, or one can use the various methods of multi-dimensional scaling, including principal component analysis.

Two grids can be compared using 'PAIRS', 'DIFF.' 'CORE', and the hierarchical nature of a construct system can be explored using laddering or subgrid and context methods. Personal meaning can be EXCHANGEd using the 'EXCHANGE and CONVERSE' techniques to combine and expand two grids into one new one.

Groups of grids can be analysed and compared one with another using 'POOL, REFINE and CONSENSUS FRAME', 'THESAURUS' and 'SOCIO-GRID and

SOCIO-NET'.

A series of computer programs including FOCUS, PEGASUS, THESAURUS, CORE, SOCIO-GRID, and ARGUS are available from CSHL to do most of these analytical chores.

12 T-C

The audience at which this book is aimed is anybody whose activities can be construed as the encouragement of learning, the enabling of learning or the management of learning. This cuts across an apparently widely differing set of professions, activities, jobs and voluntary services.

These have been summarised in the body of the book by the abbreviation T-C. Specifically this stands for teaching, training, tutoring, therapy, counselling, coaching, custody and consulting. More generally these were chosen mainly to indicate the apparent diversity of interests. This diversity poses a dilemma in the choice of terminology since each profession or trade has its own specialist terms. Thus teachers, trainers, tutors, therapists, counsellors, coaches, custodians and consultants have been labelled *practitioners*. The general term chosen to designate those being taught, trained, tutored, treated, counselled, coached, restrained or consulted with, is *client*. The following list indicates the relationships between these general terms and the specialist terms in each area.

Teaching practitioner	Teacher/Staff Member/Don
Client	Pupil/Student/Course Member/Kid/Schoolchild
Training practitioner	Trainer/Training Officer/Course Leader
Client	Trainee/Employee/Participant
Tutoring practitioner	Tutor
Client	Student/Pupil
Therapy practitioner	Clinician/Therapist/Psychologist/Doctor
Client	Patient/Client
Counselling practitioner	Counsellor/Samaritan/Clergy
Client	Client/Student/Sufferer
Coaching practitioner	Coach/Professional
Client	Trainee/Player/Manager/Amateur
Custody practitioner	Custodian/Warder/Staff Member
Client	Delinquent/Prisoner/Resident/Inmate/Borstal Boy
Consulting practitioner	Consultant
Client	Client

Bibliography

Chapter 1 The personal nature of self-organised learning

Bach, R. (1979), *Illusions: The Adventures of a Reluctant Messiah*, Pan Books, London.

Bruner, J.S. (1968), *Toward a Theory of Instruction*, Norton, New York.

Chang Chung-Yuan (1971), *Original Teachings of Ch'an Buddhism*, Vintage, New York.

Ferguson, J. (1970), *Socrates*, Open University Press, Milton Keynes.

Herriegel, G. (1974), *Zen in the Art of Flower Arrangement*, Routledge & Kegan Paul, London.

Hilgard, E.R. and Bower, G.H. (1975), *Theories of Learning*, Prentice Hall, Englewood Cliffs, N.J.

Illich, I. (1971), *Celebration of Awareness*, Penguin, Harmondsworth.

Jahoda, M. and Thomas, L.F. (1965), 'A Search for Optimal Conditions of Learning Intellectually Complex Subject Matter', 3rd Progress Report, DES and Centre for the Study of Human Learning Publication, Brunel University, Uxbridge, Middlesex.

Lorenz, K. (1977), *Behind the Mirror*, Methuen, London.

Ouspensky, P.D. (1972), *The Fourth Way*, Routledge & Kegan Paul, London.

Pask, G. (1975), *The Cybernetics of Human Learning and Performance*, Hutchinson, London.

Reason, J. and James, C. (1979), *World of Rugby*, BBC Publications, London.

Rogers, C.R. (1969), *Freedom to Learn*, Charles E. Merrill, Columbia, Ohio.

Shah, I. (1966), *The Exploits of the Incomparable Mulla Nasrudin*, Pan, London.

Skinner, B.F. (1971), *Beyond Freedom and Dignity*, Alfred A. Knopf, New York.

Sutherland, G. (ed.) (1973), *Arnold on Education*, Penguin, Harmondsworth.

School of Barbiana (1970), *Letter to a Teacher*, Penguin, Harmondsworth.

Thomas, L.F. and Jahoda, M. (1966), 'The Mechanics of Learning', *New Scientist*, no. 14, April, and Centre for the Study of Human Learning Publication, Brunel University, Uxbridge, Middlesex.

Thomas, L.F. (1976), 'The Self-Organised Learner at Work', *Personnel Manage-*

ment, vol. 8, no. 6, June, and Centre for the Study of Human Learning Publication, Brunel University, Uxbridge, Middlesex.

Chapter 2 Introducing the repertory grid: elements and constructs

Bannister, D. and Fransella, F. (1971, 1982), *Inquiring Man*, Penguin, Harmondsworth.

Bannister, D. and Mair J.M.M. (1968), *The Evaluation of Personal Constructs*, Academic Press, London.

Gauld, A. and Shotter, J. (1977), *Human Action and its Psychological Investigation*, Routledge & Kegan Paul, London.

Harri-Augstein, E.S. and Thomas, L.F. (1979), 'Self-Organised Learning and the Relativity of Knowing', in *Constructs of Individuality and Sociality*, Bannister, D. and Stringer, P. (eds), Academic Press, London.

Hilgard, E.R. and Bower, G.H. (1975), *Theories of Learning*, Prentice Hall, Englewood Cliffs, New Jersey.

Illich, I. (1975), *Medical Nemesis*, Calder & Boyars, London.

Landfield, A.W. (1971), *Personal Construct Systems in Psychotherapy*, Rand McNally, Chicago.

Mair, M. (1979), 'The Personal Venture', in *Constructs of Individuality and Sociality*, Bannister, D. and Stringer, P. (eds), Academic Press, London.

Mancuso, J.C. and Adams-Webber, J.R. (eds) (1982), *The Construing Person*, Praeger, New York.

Ogden, C.K. and Richards, I.A. (1923), *The Meaning of Meaning*, Harcourt, New York.

Pask, G. (1975), *The Cybernetics of Human Learning and Performance*, Hutchinson, London.

Pirsig, R.M. (1976), *Zen and the Art of Motorcycle Maintenance*, Corgi Books, London.

Polyani, M. (1958), *Personal Knowledge*, Routledge & Kegan Paul, London.

Rosenthal, R. (1966), *Experimental Effects on Behavioural Research*, Appleton-Century Crofts, New York.

Russell, B. (1968), *The Autobiography of Bertrand Russell*, 3 vols, Allen & Unwin, London.

Salmon, P. (ed.) (1980), *Coming to Know*, Routledge & Kegan Paul, London.

Shotter, J. (1975), *Images of Man in Psychological Research*, Methuen, London.

Thomas, L.F. (1976), 'Education and the Negotiation of Meaning', Centre for the Study of Human Learning Publication, Brunel University, Uxbridge, Middlesex.

Thomas, L.F., and Harri-Augstein, E.S. (1974), 'Learing-to-Learn: The Personal Construction and Exchange of Meaning', in *Adult Learning*, Howe, M. (ed.), Wiley, London, and Centre for the Study of Human Learning Publication, Brunel University, Uxbridge, Middlesex.

Todd, R. (1982), 'Exploring Learning Processes in Tactics Training: a Preliminary

Study', paper read at CSHL Symposium – British Conference on PCP, Manchester, and Centre for the Study of Human Learning Publication, Brunel University, Uxbridge, Middlesex.

Warnock, M. (1976), *Imagination*, Faber & Faber, London.

Weinberg, C. (ed.) (1972), *Humanistic Foundations of Education*, Prentice Hall, Englewood Cliffs, New Jersey.

Chapter 3 The construction of personal meaning

Adams-Webber, J.R. (eds) (1983), *Applications in PCP*, Academic Press, London and New York.

Butler, J.A.V. (1970), *The Life Process*, Allen & Unwin, London.

Fransella, F. and Bannister, D. (1977), *A Manual for Repertory Grid Technique*, Academic Press, London.

Kelly, G.A. (1966), 'Humanistic Methodology', in *Clinical Psychology and Personality*, Maher, B. (ed.) (1969), Wiley, New York.

Kelly, G.A. (1963), 'The Autobiography of a Theory', in *Clinical Psychology and Personality*, Maher, B. (ed.) (1969), Wiley, New York.

Laing, R.D. (1970), *Knots*, Penguin, Harmondsworth.

Popper, K. (1972), *Objective Knowledge, An Evolutionary Approach*, Clarendon Press, Oxford.

Rogers, C.R. (1971), *On Becoming a Person*, Constable, London.

Thomas, L.F. (1976), *Eliciting a Repertory Grid*, Centre for the Study of Human Learning Publication, Brunel University, Uxbridge, Middlesex.

Chapter 4 FOCUSing: the emergent pattern

Adams-Webber, J.R. (1978), *Personal Construct Theory: Concepts and Applications*, Wiley, New York.

Fransella, F. (ed.) (1978), *Personal Construct Psychology 1977*, Academic Press, London.

Jankowitz, D. and Thomas, L.F. (1982), 'An Algorithm for the Cluster Analysis of Repertory Grids in Human Resource Development', *Personnel Review*, vol. 1 , no. 4, and Centre for the Study of Human Learning Publication, Brunel University, Uxbridge, Middlesex.

Thomas, L.F. (1974), 'FOCUSing: Exhibiting the Meaning in a Grid', Centre for the Study of Human Learning Publication, Brunel University, Uxbridge, Middlesex.

Thomas, L.F. (1976), 'Exploring Learning with the Grid', Centre for the Study of Human Learning Publication, Brunel University, Uxbridge, Middlesex.

Thomas, L.F., and Harri-Augstein, E.S. (1976), 'Self-Organised Learner and the Printed Word', Final Progress Report, SSRC, and Centre for the Study of Human Learning Publication, Brunel University, Uxbridge, Middlesex.

Thomas, L.F. and Harri Augstein, E.S. (1978), 'The Kelly Repertory Grid as a Vehicle for Eliciting a Personal Taxonomy of Purposes for Reading', *Journal of Research in Reading*, vol. no. 1, Feb., and Centre for the Study of Human Learning Publication, Brunel University, Uxbridge, Middlesex.

Thomas, L.F. and Shaw, M.L.G. (1976), 'FOCUS: A Manual', Centre for the Study of Human Learning Publication, Brunel University, Uxbridge, Middlesex.

Chapter 5 Talkback through a FOCUSed grid

Bannister, D. (ed.) (1970), *Perspectives in Personal Construct Theory*, Academic Press, London.

Bannister, D. (ed.) (1977), *New Perspectives in Personal Construct Theory*, Academic Press, London.

Barrett, P.C. In Aymer, T. *Innovation and Change in Reading Instruction*, University of Chicago Press, 1968.

Jankowicz, A.D. (1982), 'Grid Techniques and the Counselling Dialogue: Avoiding the Tramlines', paper read at CSHL Symposium, British Conference on PCP, Manchester, and Centre for the Study of Human Learning Publication, Brunel University, Uxbridge, Middlesex.

Kelly, G.A. (1955), *The Psychology of Personal Constructs*, vols I and II, Norton, New York.

Kelly, G.A. (1969), 'Clinical Psychology and Personality', in *The Selected Papers of George Kelly*, Maher, B.A. (ed.), Wiley, New York.

Landfield, A.W. (1971), *Personal Construct Systems in Psychotherapy*, Rand McNally, Chicago.

Lorenz, K. (1974), *Behind the Mirror*, Methuen, London.

Thomas, L.F. and Shaw, M.L.G. (1977), 'PEGASUS: A Manual for Program Elicits A Grid and Sorts Using Similarities', Centre for the Study of Human Learning Publication, Brunel University, Uxbridge, Middlesex.

Chapter 6 Grid conversations for achieving self-awareness

Bates, W.N. (1930), *Euripides: A Student of Human Nature*, University of Pennsylvania Press.

Chell, N. (1982), 'Decisions in Man-Management: Mapping Individual Construing onto Behaviour and Conversational Exchange', paper read at a CSHL Symposium on the theme of: The Self-Organised Learner and Personal Construct Psychology: the CSHL Reflective Learning Technology and Conversational Methodology for Teachers, Trainers and Counsellors, presented to the British Conference on Personal Construct Psychology, University of Manchester Institute of Science and Technology, September, and Centre for the Study of Human Learning Publication, Brunel University, Uxbridge, Middlesex.

Harri-Augstein, E.S. and Thomas, L.F. (1982), 'Learning Conversations: Reflective Technology for Learning-to-learn' in Quarterly Source Book, *Helping People Learn How to Learn*, Jossey-Bass, San Francisco and Centre for the Study of Human Learning Publication, Brunel University, Uxbridge, Middlesex.

Hodgkin, R.A. (1976), *Born Curious, New Perspectives in Educational Theory*, Wiley, Chichester.

Reid, F.J.M. (1975), 'A Note on Measures of Similarity and Scaling Metrics for Users of the Repertory Grid', Centre for the Study of Human Learning Publication, Brunel University, Uxbridge, Middlesex.

Richards, I.A. (1974), *Beyond*, Harcourt Brace, New York.

Shaw, M.L.G. and Thomas, L.F. (1978), 'FOCUS on Education – An Interactive Computer System For the Development and Analysis of Repertory Grids', *Int. Journal of Man-Machine Studies*, vol. 10, pp. 139-73, and Centre for the Study of Human Learning Publication, Brunel University, Uxbridge, Middlesex.

Stevens, J.O. (1973), *Awareness: Exploring, Experimenting, Experiencing*, Bantam Books, New York.

Thomas, L.F. (1971), 'Interactive Method of Eliciting Kelly Repertory Grids: Real Time Data Processing', paper presented to the Occupational Section of the BPS Annual Conference, and Centre for the Study of Human Learning Publication, Brunel University, Uxbridge, Middlesex.

Thomas, L.F. (1975), 'Demon and Double Demon: Computer Aided Conversations with Yourself', paper presented at the BPS Annual Conference, and Centre for the Study of Human Learning Publication, Brunel University, Uxbridge, Middlesex.

Chapter 7 The space within which personal meaning may be represented

Atkin, R.H. (1974), *Mathematical Structure in Human Affairs*, Heinemann, London.

Bateson, G. (1972), 'Steps to an Ecology of Mind', Chandler Publishing Company, San Francisco.

Bertalanffy, L.V. (1973), *General Systems Theory*, Penguin Books, Harmondsworth.

Chomsky, N. (1968), *Language and Mind*, Harcourt, Brace & World, New York.

Grene, M. (1975), *The Knower and the Known*, Faber & Faber, London.

Hinkle, D.N. (1965), 'The Change of Personal Constructs from the Viewpoint of a Theory of Implications', unpublished PhD thesis, Ohio State University.

Jankowitz, D., and Thomas, L.F. (1982), 'An Algorithm for the Cluster Analysis of Repertory Grids in Human Resource Management', *Personnel Review*, vol. II, no. 4, and Centre for the Study of Human Learning Publications, Brunel University, Uxbridge, Middlesex.

Kendall, M.G. (1975), 'Multivariate Analysis', Griffin Books, London.

Kruskall, J.B. and Wish, M. (1971), *Multidimensional Scaling*, Sage, London.

Maslow, A.H. (1975), *The Farther Reaches of Human Nature*, Viking Press, New York.

Neisser, V. (1967), *Cognitive Psychology*, Appleton, Century-Croft, New York.

Osgood, C.E., Suci, G.J. and Tannenbaurn, P.H. (1957), *The Measurement of Meaning*, University of Illinois Press, Ilobana, Illinois.

Plackett, R.L. (1981), *The Analysis of Categorical Data*, Griffin Books, High Wycombe.

Sartre, J.P. (1976), *Worlds*, Penguin, Harmondsworth.

Sharma, J.S. (1978), *Knowledge: Its Origin and Growth from the Earliest Times to the Present*, Sterling, New Delhi.

Slater, P. (1965), *The Principal Components of a Repertory Grid*, Andrews, London.

Slater, P. (ed.) (1976), *Explorations of Intrapersonal Space*, Wiley, Chichester.

Slater, P. (ed.) (1977), *Dimensions of Intrapersonal Space*, Wiley, Chichester.

Sneath, P.H.A. and Sokal, R.P. (1973), *Numerical Taxonomy*, W.H. Freeman, Reading, Berks.

Thomas, L.F. (1974), 'FOCUSing: Exhibiting the Meaning in a Grid', Centre for the Study of Human Learning Publication, Brunel University, Uxbridge, Middlesex.

Thomas, L.F. and Harri-Augstein, E.S. (1981, 1983), 'The Personal Scientist as Self-Organised Learner: A Conversational Technology for Reflecting on Behaviour and Experience', in *Applications of P.C.P.*, Adams-Webber, J.R. (ed.) (1983), Academic Press, London.

Ushenko, A.P. (1958), *The Theory of Meaning*, University of Michigan Press, Ann Arbor.

Zadeh, L.A. (1971), 'Towards a Theory of Fuzzy Sets', in *Aspects of Network and System Theory*, Kalam, R.E. and Declares, N. (eds), Holt Rinehart & Winston, New York.

Zadeh, L.A. (1976), 'Fuzzy Sets', *Journal of Information Control*, vol. 8, pp. 338-53.

Chapter 8 A PCP approach to perception

Abercrombie, J.M.L. (1960), *The Anatomy of Judgement*, Hutchinson, London.

Ghiselin, B. (1952), *The Creative Process*, Mentor, New York.

Gregory, R.L. (1966), *Eye and Brain: The Psychology of Seeing*, World University Press, London.

Heston, J.M. (1968), *The Eye: Phenomenology and Psychology of Function and Disorder*, Tavistock, London.

Koestler, A. (1964), *The Act of Creation*, Hutchinson, London.

Koestler, A. (1967), 'The Three Domains of Creativity', in Bugental, J. (ed.), *Challenges of Humanistic Psychology*, McGraw Hill, New York, London, Toronto.

Mendoza, S. and Thomas, L.F. (1972), 'The Individual's Construction of his

Visual World as Projected by the Repertory Grid', paper presented at the BPS Annual Conference, Nottingham, and Centre for the Study of Human Learning Publication, Brunel University, Uxbridge, Middlesex.

Menuhin, Y. (1977), *Unfinished Journey*, Futura, London.

Merleau-Ponty, M. (1962), *The Phenomenology of Perception*, trans. by Colin Smith, Humanities Press, New York.

Miller, G.A., Galanter, E. and Pribram, K.H. (1960), *Plans and the Structure of Behaviour*, Holt Rinehart & Winston, New York.

Moncrieff, M.M. (1921), *The Clairvoyant Theory of Prescription*, Faber & Faber, London.

Oatley, K. (1978), *Perception and Representation*, Methuen, London.

Piaget, J. (1969), *The Mechanisms of Perception*, Routledge & Kegan Paul, London.

Polyani, M. (1966), *The Tacit Dimension*, Routledge & Kegan Paul, London.

Rampa, T.L. (1973), *The Third Eye*, Corgi, London.

Sharp, A. (1979), *Bicycles and Tricycles*, MIT Press, Cambridge, Massachusets.

Vernon, M.D. (1962), *The Psychology of Perception*, Penguin, Harmondsworth.

Welford, A.T. (1968), *Fundamentals of Skill*, Methuen, London.

Wiener, N. (1950), *The Human Use of Human Beings: Cybernetics and Society*, Houghton Mifflin, Boston.

Chapter 9 The critical self: conversational self-assessment

Bamborough, J.B. (1952), *The Little World of Man*, Longmans Green, London.

Berne, E. (1975), *Language and Mind*, Harcourt Brace & World, New York.

Boud, D. (1981), *Developing Student Anatomy in Learning*, Kogan Page, London.

Bruner, J.S. (1972), *The Relevance of Education*, Allen & Unwin, London.

De Bono, E. (1972), *About Think*, Cape, London.

Fingarette, H. (1969), *Self-Deception*, Routledge & Kegan Paul, London.

Fransella, F. (1975), *Need to Change*, Methuen, London.

Freud, S. (1937), *The Ego and the Mechanisms of Defence*, Hogarth, London.

Goffman, E. (1971), *The Presentation of Self in Everyday Life*, Penguin, Harmondsworth.

Harri-Augstein, E.S. (1979), 'The CHANGE Grid: A Conversational Heuristic for Self Development', in *Proceedings of the 3rd Congress on Personal Construct Psychology*, Centre for the Study of Human Learning Publication, Brunel University, Uxbridge, Middlesex.

Harri-Augstein, E.S., Smith, M. and Thomas, L.F. (1982), *Reading-to-Learn*, Methuen, London, New York.

Jung, C.G. (1963), *Memories, Dreams, Reflections*, Routledge & Kegan Paul, London.

Karlins, M. and Andrews, L.M. (1973), *Biofeedback*, Garnstone Press, London.

Laing, R.D. (1960), *The Divided Self*, Tavistock, London.

Laing, R.D. (1961), *Self and Others*, Tavistock, London.

Maslow, A.H. (1962), 'Notes on Being – Psychology', *J. Humanistic Psychology*, vol. 1, pp. 47-71.

Nietsche, F. (1961), *Thus Spoke Zarathustra*, trans. by R.J. Hollingdale, Penguin, Harmondsworth.

Percival, F. and Ellington, H. (1981), *Distance Learning and Evaluation*, Kogan Page, London.

Rogers, R. and Coulson, W.R. (1968), *Man and the Science of Man*, Charles E. Merrill, Columbus, Ohio.

Sartre, J.P. (1957), *Being and Nothingness*, Methuen, London.

Schultz, D. (1977), *Growth Psychology. Models of the Healthy Personality*, Van Nostrand, New York.

Sheehy, G. (1974, 1976), *Passages: Predictable Crises of Adult Life*, Dutton, New York.

Smail, D.J. (1978), *Psychotherapy: A Personal Approach*, Dent, London.

Thomas, L.F. (1978), 'Human Judgement and Perceiving the Complexity of Quality', *Journal of the Institute of Quality Assurance*, vol. 4, no. 4, December, and Centre for the Study of Human Learning Publication, Brunel University, Uxbridge, Middlesex.

Thomas, L.F. and Snapes, A.W. (1969), *Research into Training for Skills in the Hotel and Catering Industry*, Final Report, H.C.I.T.B., and Centre for the Study of Human Learning Publication, Brunel University, Uxbridge, Middlesex.

Thomas, L.F. and Courtney, A.J. (1972), *The Development and Field Testing of an Industrial Training Device*, Final Report, D.E.P., and Centre for the Study of Human Learning Publication, Brunel University, Uxbridge, Middlesex.

Welwood, J. (1979), *The Meeting of the Ways – Explorations in East/West Psychology*, Shocken Books, New York.

Whipple, K. (1975), *Psychotherapy versus Behavioural Therapy*, Harvard University Press, Cambridge, Massachussets.

Wilson, C. (1967), 'Existential Psychology: A Novelist's Approach', in Bugental, J. (ed.), *Challenges of Humanistic Psychology*, McGraw Hill, New York, London, Toronto.

Zurcher, L.A. Jr. (1977), *The Mutable Self: A Self-Concept for Social Change*, Sage, London.

Chapter 10 Grid conversations for the sharing of meaning

Bateson, G. (1980), *Mind and Nature: A Necessary Unit*, Bantam, New York.

Blakemore, C. (1977), *Mechanisms of the Mind*, Cambridge University Press, New York, Cambridge.

Chomsky, N. (1971), *Chomsky: Selected Readings*, Allen, J., Van Bunen, P., (eds), Oxford University Press, London.

Duck, S.W. (1973), *Personal Relationships and Personal Constructs: A Study of Friendship Formation*, Wiley, New York.

Duck, S.W. (1977), 'Inquiry, Hypnosis and the Quest for Validation', in *Theory and Practise of Interpersonal Attraction*, Duck, S.W. (ed.), Academic Press, London and New York.

Fareira, A.J. (1969), 'Interpersonal Perceptivity among Family Members', in Winter, D. and Fereira, A.J. (eds), *Research in Family Interaction*, Palo Alto: Science and Behaviour Books.

Harri Augstein, E.S. (1976), 'Monitoring Tutor Marked Assignments: What are the Criteria? How Does it Relate to the Self-Organised Learner?', Part 1, A paper to the Monitoring Committee; The Open University, and Centre for the Study of Human Learning Publication, Brunel University, Uxbridge, Middlesex.

Illich, I. (1973), *Tools for Conviviality*, Harper & Row, London.

Jung, C.G. (1972), *Synchronicity: An Acausal Connecting Principle*, Routledge & Kegan Paul, London.

Luria, A.R. (1973), *The Working Brain*, Penguin, Harmondsworth.

McCulloch, W.S. (1965), *Embodiments of Mind*, MIT Press, Cambridge, Massachussets.

Mendoza, S. (1982), 'The Exchange Grid: Reality testing and Identification', Centre for the Study of Human Learning Publication, Brunel University, Uxbridge, Middlesex.

Radley, A. (1977), 'Living on the Horizon', in *New Perspectives in Personal Construct Psychology*, Bannister, D. (ed.), Academic Press, London.

Thomas, L.F. (1982), 'Learning Conversations: The Skill of Managing Personal and Inter-Personal Learning', in *Social Skills*, Singleton, W.T. (ed.), MIT Press, and Centre for the Study of Human Learning Publication, Brunel University, Uxbridge, Middlesex.

Thomas, L.F. and Harri-Augstein, E.S. (1977), 'Learning-to-Learn: The Personal Construction and Exchange of Meaning', in *Adult Learning*, Howe, M. (ed.), Wiley, Chichester, and Centre for the Study of Human Learning Publication, Brunel University, Uxbridge, Middlesex.

Chapter 11 Groups and institutions as personal learning systems

Arendt, H. (1978), *The Life of the Mind*, 2 vols, Secker & Warburg, London.

Bartlett, F.C. (1932), *Remembering*, Cambridge University Press, Cambridge.

Berger, P.L. and Luckman, T. (1966), *The Social Construction of Reality*, Penguin, Harmondsworth.

Harne, R. and Second, P.F. (1972), *The Explanation of Social Behaviour*, Blackwell, Oxford.

Kolb, D., Rubin, I. and McIntyre, J. (1971), *Organisational Psychology: An Experiential Approach*, Prentiče Hall, Englewood Cliffs, N.J.

Leinhart, S. (1977), *Social Networks: A Developing Paradigm*, Academic Press, London, New York.

Mair, M. (1977), 'The Community of Self', in *New Perspectives in Personal Construct Theory*, Bannister, D. (ed.), Academic Press, London, New York.

McCormick, E.J. and Tiffin, J. (1975), *Industrial Psychology*, Prentice Hall, Englewood Cliffs, New Jersey.

Meltzer, B.N., Petras, J.W. and Reynolds, L.T. (1975), *Symbolic Interactionism: Genesis, Varieties and Criticism*, Routledge & Kegan Paul, London.

Reid, F. (1979), 'Personal Constructs and Social Competence', in *Constructs of Sociality and Individuality*, Stringer, P. and Bannister, D. (eds), Academic Press, London, New York.

Reid, F. (1982), 'Group Belonging, Social Identity and Inter-group Construing', Centre for the Study of Human Learning Publication, Brunel University, Uxbridge, Middlesex.

Revans, R.W. (1971), *Developing Effective Managers – A New Approach to Business Education*, Praeger, New York.

Schutz, A.(1967), *The Phenomenology of the Social World*, trans. by Walsh, G. and Lehnert, F., North Western University Press, Evanston, Illinois.

Sperry, L., Michelson, D.J. and Hunsaker, P.L. (1977), *You Can Make it Happen. A Guide to Self-Actualisation and Organisational Change*, Addison Wesley, Reading, Mass.

Tinbergen, N. (1953), *Social Behaviour in Animals*, Methuen, London.

Thomas, L.F. (1975), 'Areas in Industry where the Application of the Expertise of the C.S.H.L may be Appropriate', Centre for the Study of Human Learning Publication, Brunel University, Uxbridge, Middlesex.

Thomas, L.F. and Harri-Augstein, E.S. (1981), 'The Dynamics of Learning Conversations: A Self-Organised Approach to Management Development', in *Handbook of Management Self Development*, Boydell, T. (ed.), Gower Press, Farnborough, Hants, and Centre for the Study of Human Learning Publication, Brunel University, Uxbridge, Middlesex.

Thomas, L.F., McKnight, C. and Shaw, M.L.G. (1976), 'Grids and Group Structures', paper presented to the Social Psychology Section of the BPS, University of Surrey, and Centre for the Study of Human Learning Publication, Brunel University, Uxbridge, Middlesex.

Chapter 12 The theory and practice of conversational science

Bendix, R. (1971), 'Man, Freedom and the Future', in *The Twentieth Century*, Bullock, A. (ed.), Thames & Hudson, London.

Entwistle, N.J. and Nisbert, J.D. (1972), *Educational Research in Action*, University of London Press, London.

Farreira, A.J. (1968), 'Family Myth and Homeostasis', in *A Modern Introduction to the Family*, Bell, N.W. and Vogel, E.F. (eds), Free Press, New York.

Freire, P. (1972), *Pedagogy of the Oppressed*, Penguin, Harmondsworth.

Freud, S. (1913), *The Interpretation of Dreams*, Macmillan, London.

Harri-Augstein, E.S. (1976), 'How to Become a Self-Organised Learner: A Conversational Methodology for Learning to Learn in Action', Part II, paper presented to a Research Committee, Open University, and Centre for the Study of Human Learning Publication, Brunel University, Uxbridge, Middlesex.

Harri-Augstein, E.S. (1978), 'Reflecting on Structures of Meaning: A Process of Learning to Learn', in *Personal Construct Psychology 77*, Fransella, F. (ed.), Academic Press, London.

Harri-Augstein, E.S., Smith, M. and Thomas, L.F. (1982), *Reading-to-Learn*, Methuen, London, New York.

Harri-Augstein, E.S. and Thomas, L.F. (1976), 'Tools for Raising Awareness of the Learning Process', Centre for the Study of Human Learning Publication, Brunel University, Uxbridge, Middlesex.

Harri-Augstein, E.S. and Thomas, L.F. (1977), *The Art and Science of Getting a Degree*, A Learning to Learn Workbook for Students, Centre for the Study of Human Learning Publication, Brunel University, Uxbridge, Middlesex.

Harri-Augstein, E.S. and Thomas, L.F. (1978), 'Learning Conversations: A Person Centred Approach to Self-Organised Learning', *British Journal of Guidance and Counselling*, July, and Centre for the Study of Human Learning Publication, Brunel University, Uxbridge, Middlesex.

Harri-Augstein, E.S. and Thomas, L.F. (1979), 'Comprehending Reading: The Dynamics of Learning Conversations', in *Growth in Reading*, Ward Lock, London, and Centre for the Study of Human Learning Publication, Brunel University, Uxbridge, Middlesex.

Heilbroner, R.L. (1974), *The Human Prospect*, Norton, New York.

Hofstadter, D.R. (1979), *Godel, Escher, Bach: An External Golden Braid*, Penguin, Harmondsworth.

James, C. (1983), *The Rugby Coach*, BBC Publication, London.

James, C. (1972), 'Coaching', in *Lions Speak*, Reason, J. (ed.), Rugby Books, London.

Kuhn, T.S. (1962), *The Structure of Scientific Revolution*, Chicago Press, Chicago.

Lévi-Strauss, C. (1966), *The Savage Mind*, Weidenfeld & Nicholson, London.

Newell, A. and Simon, H.A. (1972), *Human Problem Solving*, Prentice Hall, Englewood Cliffs, New Jersey.

Ortega y Gasset, J. (1958), *Man and Crisis*, Allen & Unwin, London.

Thomas, L.F. and Harri-Augstein, E.S. (1975), 'Towards a Theory of Learning Conversation and a Paradigm for Conversational Research', paper read at BPS Annual Conference, Nottingham and Centre for the Study of Human Learning Publication, Brunel University, Uxbridge, Middlesex.

Thomas, L.F. et al., (1978), 'A Personal Construct Approach to Learning in Education, Training and Therapy', in *Personal Construct Psychology 1977*, Fransella, F. (ed.), Academic Press, London, New York, and Centre for the Study of Human Learning Publication, Brunel University, Uxbridge, Middlesex.

Thomas, L.F. and Harri-Augstein, E.S. (1981), 'The Personal Scientist as Self-Organised Learner: A Conversational Technology for Reflecting on Behaviour and Experience', invited paper to the Fourth International Conference on Personal Construct Psychology, Brock University, St Catherines, Ontario, and in *Applications of P.C.P.*, Adams-Webber, J.R. (ed.) (1983), Academic Press, London, New York.

Wittgenstein, L. (1953), *Philosophical Investigations*, Macmillan, New York.

List of relevant CSHL projects for B.Tech, MSc and PhD

Mendoza, S. (1970), 'Personal Construction of the World and its Control and Development by the Individual', Project for B.Tech., supervised by L.F. Thomas, Centre for the Study of Human Learning, Brunel University.

Harri-Augstein, E.S. (1971), 'Reading Strategies and Learning Outcomes', PhD thesis, supervised by L.F. Thomas, Centre for the Study of Human Learning, Brunel University.

De Mille, P. (1971), 'A Study of the Reichian Concept that Sexual Activity is Viewed in Culturally Perverse Terms, using the Repertory Grid test of G.A. Kelly; and the Examination of the Rationale Behind the Two Ideologies', project for B.Tech., supervised by L.F. Thomas, Centre for the Study of Human Learning, Brunel University.

Hastings, M. (1971), 'Some Comments on the Phenomenal World of 25 Delinquent Boys', project for B.Tech., supervised by L.F. Thomas, Centre for the Study of Human Learning, Brunel University.

Blewitt, S. (1972), 'An Investigation, using the Repertory Grid Technique, to Study the Thought Processes of Examination Scripts', project for B.Tech., supervised by L.F. Thomas, Centre for the Study of Human Learning, Brunel University.

Bodlakova, V. (1972), 'An Investigation of the Clinical Condition of Affective Fattening in Relation to Personal Constructs and Other Variables', project for B. Tech., supervised by L.F. Thomas, Centre for the Study of Human Learning, Brunel University.

George, R.E. (1972), 'A Repertory Grid Analysis of Psychotherapy Group Interaction', project for B.Tech., supervised by L.F. Thomas, Centre for the Study of Human Learning, Brunel University.

Kovaly, O. (1972), 'Some Aspects of Self-Reflective Construing in Psychiatric Patients', project for B.Tech., supervised by L.F. Thomas, Centre for the Study of Human Learning, Brunel University.

Lipshitz, S. (1972), 'An Exploration of some Girl School Leavers' Expectations of Their Lives using the Kelly Grid', M. Phil. thesis, supervised by L.F. Thomas, Centre for the Study of Human Learning, Brunel University.

McKnight, C. (1972), 'Structuring the Future: the Psychological Process of Planning', project for B.Tech., supervised by L.F. Thomas, Centre for the Study of Human Learning, Brunel University.

Pope, M.L. (1973), 'Kelly and Education', project for B.Tech., supervised by L.F. Thomas, Centre for the Study of Human Learning, Brunel University.

Robertson-Pirie, P. (1973), 'A Longitudinal Pilot Study of the Drug Dependence Unit at Holloway Prison', project for B.Tech., supervised by L.F. Thomas, Centre for the Study of Human Learning, Brunel University.

Summerfield, A. (1973), 'Inside the Scrubs: An Investigation into the Lives of Long-Term Prison Inmates', project for B.Tech., supervised by L.F. Thomas, Centre for the Study of Human Learning, Brunel University.

Chapman, L.R. (1974), 'An Exploration of a Mathematical Command System', PhD thesis, supervised by L.F. Thomas, Centre for the Study of Human Learning, Brunel University.

Hastings, N. (1974), 'Educational Assessment and Construct Compatibility', MSc thesis, Institute of Education, University of London, Centre for the Study of Human Learning, Brunel University.

McKnight, C. (1976), 'Purposive Preferences for Multi-attributed Alternatives: A Study of Choice Behaviour using Personal Construct Theory in Conjunction with Decision Theory', PhD thesis, supervised by L.F. Thomas, Centre for the Study of Human Learning, Brunel University.

Reid, F.J.M. (1976), 'A Conversational Skills Approach to Personal Reconstruction: Longitudinal Studies using the Repertory Grid', PhD thesis, supervised by L.F. Thomas, Centre for the Study of Human Learning, Brunel University.

Shaw, M.L.G. (1978), 'On Becoming a Personal Scientist: Interactive Computer Elicitation of Personal Models of the World', PhD thesis, supervised by L.F. Thomas, Centre for the Study of Human Learning, Brunel University.

Pope, M.L. (1978), 'Constructive Alternatives in Education', PhD thesis, supervised by L.F. Thomas, Centre for the Study of Human Learning, Brunel University.

Beard, R. (1982), 'Course Evaluation and the Repertory Grid', PhD thesis, supervised by L.F. Thomas, Centre for the Study of Human Learning, Brunel University.

Index

agreement, 243-6, 295-8, 367-8; order of, 370-1
algorithms, 369; introducing a topic, 36-7; eliciting a grid, 50; FOCUSing a grid, 74; SPACEing a FOCUSed grid, 75; talkback, 83; grid conversations, 94, 115; TRIGRID, 141; perceptual grid, 184; evaluative grid, 195; PAIRS, 201-2; DIFF., 211; CORE, 212; CHANGE, 215-17; EXCHANGE, 259; creative encounter, 263. 281, 306, 358
alienation, 16, 190
analysis: of conversation, 237-43; of grids, 139-42, 333-43; 370-1; see also cluster analysis; FOCUS; SPACE; TRIGRID
ARGUS, 227, 303, 342-3, 356, 370-1
assessment: learning, 264-77; self, 187-236
attitudes, 10-11, 100, 367
attribution of meaning, xxvii-xxix, 2, 160-1, 366-7
auditory system, 12, 162, 369-70
awareness-raising, 77-9, 92-116, 224-6, 323, 324-6, 328-30, 364-5
awareness-raising tools, see tools

Bannister, D., xix-xx, 373, 375
Bartlett, F., xix, 380
behaviour, 307-8, 367
Berne, E., 110, 378
beyond grids, 325-8, 340-1
bi-polarity, 104-7, 149, 333-4, 366-9
Brunel Reading Recorder, 195, 358
Bruner, J.S., 175, 372, 378

C1P1, C1P2, see poles of a construct
capacity for learning, xxii-xxiv, 322-5, 367
categorisation, 28-33, 150-5, 177-9, 219, 367
Centre for the Study of Human Learning, xxxiii-xxxiv, 18-19, 213, 306, 353-8, 365-6; see also computer programs; grid tricks
challenging the robot, 329, 364-5; see also awareness-raising

CHANGE grid, 213-24, 342, 355
CHART, 342-3, 354-6
Chomsky, N., 240, 243, 376, 379
C-indi, xxviii, 365-6
classification, 28-33, 150-5, 344, 367
clients, 8, 92-116, 367, 371
clinicians, see T-C
cluster analysis, 57, 81-2, 368; see also FOCUS; SPACE; TRIGRID
clustering, 58-62, 113-14, 117, 132-5, 148, 368, 370-1
coaches and coaching, xxiv-xxv, 4-5, 371; see also T-C
COMBINE, 278
communication technology, 306; see also conversational technology
community of selves, 149, 191, 301-5
competence, see skill
computer programs, 73, 81, 93, 139, 149, 227, 341-3, 354-6, 358, 371
consciousness, see awareness raising
CONSENSUS FRAME grid, 275-6, 292-5, 298, 312, 339, 343, 354-5, 368
construct poles, 22-7, 39-42, 142-5, 148-9, 333-4, 366-7, 369
constructions: of experience, 77-9; of meaning, xxvii-xxix, 2, 38-56
constructs, personal, 366-7; assigning elements to, 107-9; eliciting, 21-7, 39-42, 45-9, 102-7; offering, 93-6; and socio-grids, 283-90; see also personal meaning; repertory grid
constructs, shared, 290-2, 298-301
construing, 102-4, 333-4, 365-8
consultants, xxiv-xxv, 4-5, 371; see also T-C
content and process, 92-3, 237-43, 278, 329-30, 365-6
content-free techniques, 4, 17, 23, 365
contract, teaching/learning, 315-18
control, 92-3, 365; see also content and process
conversation, 92-3, 365-6; and CHANGE grid, 218-24; creative, 97-8, 238; eliciting

constructs, 104-7; eliciting a perceptual
grid, 164-8; levels of, 237-43; and self-
assessment, 187-236; talkback with
FOCUSed grid, 81-90; guided, 165,
364-5; *see also* grid conversation
conversational methodology, xxv-xxix
conversational paradigm, xxiii, xxiv, 324,
328
conversational science, xxvi-xxvii, 110-11,
307-32
conversational technology, xxviii, 38-9,
325-6, 335-40, 365-6
CORE, 201-12, 231, 275, 338, 370-1
counselling, xxiv-xxv, 4-5, 371; perspectives
of, 312-13; *see also* T-C
creative conversation, 97-8, 238, 365-6
creative encounter, 260-3
creativity, 16, 163, 173-4
criticism: external, 189-91; self-, 187-236
CSHL, *see* Centre for the Study of Human
Learning
custodians/custody, xxiv-xxv, 4-5, 371;
see also T-C

delinquency, 16, 371; *see also* T-C
DEMON, 97, 148, 227, 342-3, 355
DIFF., 201-12, 338, 370-1
difference: grid, 201-12, 251-2, 275, 279;
matrix, 132, 136-9, 203; triangle of,
123-7
dimension, 366-7; *see also* personal meaning
disabled learner, 12, 14-16, 367
dogleg scale, 369

elements, 6-7, 23-7, 39-40, 43, 344, 366-7;
assigning to constructs, 107-9; choice of,
98-102; eliciting, 43-5; offering, 93-6;
paired, 253; shared, 283-92, 298-301;
see also repertory grid
elicitation: of constructs, 21-7, 102-7; of
perceptual grid, 164-68; of repertory grid,
42-56, 336-7
Ellis, A., 110
emergent pole, 148-9, 333-4, 366-7, 369
employee, 371; *see also* management; T-C
evaluation, 14-15; public, 199-200, 365;
self, 189-92
EVALUATIVE grid, 189, 194, 270, 354-6
examinations, 264-77
exchange: grid, 246-60, 269, 275; levels of,
237-8; mutual, 253; and shared meaning,
243-6, 277-81
EXCHANGE, 277-8, 290, 338, 365-8, 370-1
EXCHANGE and CONVERSE, 295, 355
experience, 5-7, 77-9, 307-8, 366-8; *see
also* learning; meaning

feedback, 192-3
FOCUS, 57-76, 186, 342-3, 353-6, 370-1;
algorithm, 74; FOCUSing constructs,

62-6; FOCUSing elements, 58-62;
by hand, 58-61, 76; of non-verbal
constructs, 163; of ranked or rated grid,
127-35
FOCUSed grid, 66-8, 70-3, 77-9, 117-23,
368
Freud, S., 111, 175, 191, 193-4, 378, 382
FULLER CONTEXT, 109

grid, *see* personal construct psychology;
repertory grid
grid conversations, 92-8; CHANGE grid,
218-24; FOCUSed grid, 81-90; and
perception, 164-8; and self-assessment,
187-236; and self-awareness, 92-116,
224-6, 335-7; and shared meaning,
237-81
grid tricks, 333-40, 365-6, 368
groups, 282-306, 338-40
guided conversation, 165, 364-5; *see also*
awareness-raising

Harri-Augstein, E.S., xix-xx, 373-5, 377-8,
380-3
heterarchies, 148-50, 369
hierarchies, 148-50, 176-7, 193-4, 272,
333-4, 369; *see also* personal meaning;
repertory grid
Hinkle, D.N., 333, 376

ICARUS, 97, 227, 343-3, 355
impersonal learning, 14-15, 367
individual, as community of selves, 149,
302-5
inferential grid, 182-6, 368
institutions, 8-9, 282-306; *see also* T-C
INTERACTIVE PAIRS, 200-1, 342-3,
354-5
items, *see* elements; experience; meaning

judgment, 243-6

Kelly, G., xix-xx, xxvii, 333-4, 354, 366,
368, 374-5
kinaesthetic sense, 192-3, 369-70
Klein, M., 175
knots, 191-3
knowledge, *see* learning

labels, verbal, 178-9, 366-7; *see also*
personal meaning
laddering, 105-7, 147-8, 333-4, 366-7,
370-1
Laing, R.D., 110, 192-4, 374, 379
language, shared, 293-8
learning, xxii, 1-3, 365-7; capacity,
xxiii-xxiv, 322-5; conditions of, 246;
contract, 315-18; conversations,
328-32, 341, 358; disabled, 12, 14-16;
events, 23-7; and groups, 282-306;

impersonal, 14-15; images of, 6; inferred, 307-8; learning managers, 332; management of, 4-5, 331-2; and perception, 156-74; personal, 14-15, 22-4; personal myths of, 10-14; perspectives on, 308-15; process, 92-3; resources, 5-7, 318-22; self-organised, 4-5, 16-17, 324; -to-learn, xxvii-xxix, 322, 329
Lorenz, K., 174, 180, 243, 372, 375

McQuitty, L.L., 142
Mager, R., xxiv-xxvi
management: of learning, 4-5, 331-2, 367; of people, 28-33, 295-8
Maslow, A.H., 260, 262, 377, 379
matrix: difference, 132, 136-9, 203; similarity, 117-23, 285
meaning, 367-8; construction of, xxvii-xxix, 2, 38-56; exchange of, 243-6, 277-81; and groups, 282-306; identified from grid, 49-53, 79-81; meaning of, 19-20; pattern of, 193-4, 366-8; and perception, 174-6; 'spaces for', 145-50; structures of, 326-8; see also personal meaning; shared meaning
methodology, see conversational technology; grid tricks
Miller, N., 193
mindpool, xxi
mirroring, see awareness-raising
MODE grid, 285-6, 288, 339
model, 261, 326, 327, 334; see also personal model
multiple imagery, 12, 369-70
mutual exchange, 253
myths: of learning, 10-14; of self, 224-6, 364-5; of skill, 183-4

'NAs', see 'Not Applicables'
negotiation, 96-8, 282-3, 290-2, 367-8
nodes of control, 92-3, 365-6; see also conversational technology
'Not Applicables' ('NAs'), 108-9, 146-7, 232, 336, 342-3
non-verbal constructs/grid, 162-3, 178-9, 232, 236, 368

objects grid, 33-5, 368
order of agreement, 370-1
organised learning, 14-16, 365; see also T-C
overlap grid, 230-2

paired elements, 253; see also repertory grid
PAIRS, 109, 185-6, 338, 370-1; INTERACTIVE, 200-1, 342-3, 354-5
pattern of meaning, 79-81, 193-4, 366-8; see also personal meaning
PCP, see personal construct psychology
PEGASUS, 73, 76, 97, 227, 283-5, 288-90, 342-3, 354-6, 370-1

perception, 366-7; and learning, 156-74; and meaning, 174-6; and personal constructs, 156-86; of self, 187-9, 193-4
perceptual grids, 164-8, 179-80, 184-6, 368
PERCEPTUAL GRIDS, 185, 194, 342-3, 354-6
Perls, F., 110, 194
person-centred learning, xxv-xxvii; see also impersonal learning; personal learning
personal construct psychology, xxvii, 18-37, 366-7; and perception, 156-86
personal constructs, 366-7; assigning elements to, 107-9; eliciting, 21-7, 39-42, 45-9, 102-7; offering, 93-6; and socio-grids, 283-90; system of, 39; see also personal meaning; repertory grid
personal learning, 14-15, 224, 367; and groups, 282-306
personal meaning, 365-8; attribution of, xxviii-xxix, 160-1, 366-7; construction of, 38-56; representation of, 117-55, 340; and self-organised learning, xxiii-xxiv
'personal science' paradigm, xxvi, 110-11, 366-7
perspectives on learning, 308-15
'physical science' paradigm, xxvi, 110-11, 366-7
Piaget, J., 175, 378
POLE MAP, 142-5, 186, 342-3
poles, construct, 22-7, 39-42, 142-5, 366-7; emergent and submerged, 148-9, 333-4, 369
POOL, 275, 292-5, 312, 339, 342-3, 354-6
Postman, L., 175
practitioner, see awareness-raising; grid conversations; learning; T-C
principal component analysis, 139-42
prisoner, see T-C
process v. content, 92-3, 237-43, 278, 365-6
PSOR (Purpose, Strategy, Outcome, Review), 367; see also learning; personal construct psychology
psychiatry, see T-C
psychology, xxiv-xxvii, 371; of personal constructs, 18-37, 156-86, 366-7; see also T-C
public evaluation, 199-200, 365
public knowledge, xxix, 365; see also shared meaning
public perception grid, 181-6
pupil, see T-C

Raiffa techniques, 229-30, 270-2
ranked/rated responses, 127-31, 135-6, 369
raw grid, see repertory grid
reading, 195-9
READING-FOR-LEARNING, 195, 354-5

'Real Me' grid, 228-9
records of learning behaviour, 326, 363
referents, 189-91, 315, 367-8; see also meaning
REFINE, 292-5, 312, 339, 342-3, 354-6
REFLECT, 81, 292-3, 342-3, 354-6
reflecting, see awareness-raising
reflective learning, 277, 307, 320-1, 367; technology, 307, 342-3, 354-8
Reich, W., 192
repertory grid, xxvii, 6-7, 18-37, 39, 324, 327, 354, 364-8; analysis of, 333-43, 370-1; applications of, 335-41, 344-52; beyond, 325-41; and communication, 304-6; eliciting, 42-56, 336-7; and meaning, 49-53; and robots, 176-7; and self-awareness, 92-116; see also FOCUSed grid; perceptual grid, etc.
resources, learning, 5-7, 318-22, 365
robot, 176-7, 188, 329, 364-5; see also awareness-raising
Rogers, C., xxv-xxvi, 110, 246, 313, 330-1, 372, 374
role grid, 226-8, 368
Russell, B., 243, 373

Sartre, J.-P., 243, 377, 379
scaling techniques, 127-31, 135-6, 369
science: conversational, xxvi-xxvii, 110-11, 307-32, 365-6; personal v. physical, xxvi, 110-11, 366-7
self-assessment, 187-236; and CHANGE grid, 213-24; and feedback, 192-3; other grids, 226-36; as perceptual process, 193-4
self-awareness, 91-116, 224-6, 335-7, 364-5
self-organised learning, xxiii-xxiv, 4-5, 16-17, 324, 331, 332, 365, 367
self-perception, 187-9, 193-4
sense-datum grid, 180-6
senses, 11-12, 162, 192-3, 369-70
sensory grid, 180-6, 368
shared meaning, xxvii; and grid conversations, 237-81; and groups, 282-306
Shaw, M.L.G., 356, 384
signficant learning events, 23-7, 367
similarity matrix, 117-23, 285
singleton, 22, 366-7; see also constructs; elements; repertory grid; triads
situation grid, 226-8
skill: mythology of, 183-4; and perception, 168-74; social, 28-33
Skinner, B.F., xxv-xxvi, 111, 330, 372
Slater, P., 141-2, 377
SOCIO-GRIDS, 283-5, 304, 339, 342-3, 354-6, 370-1

SOCIO-NETS, 285, 287-8, 298-302, 339, 354-6
software, 139, 149, 227, 341-3, 354-6, 371
SPACE, 68-9, 75-6, 135-6, 186, 370-1
SPACEd FOCUSed grid, 68-9, 117-23, 136, 140, 368
'spaces for meaning', 145-50
strategies, xxii-xxiii, 160-1, 365
STRUCTURES OF MEANING, 326-8, 342-3, 354-6, 359, 367-8
sub-grids, 147-8, 232
submerged pole, 148-9, 333-4, 366-7, 369
sub-vocalising, 12, 369-70
super-grids, 147-8

talkback, 70-3, 77-91, 163-8, 217-24, 325, 364-5; see also awareness-raising
talkdown, 226-7
task grid, 226-8
T-C, xxiv-xxv, 4-6, 14-16, 20-1, 110-11, 168-70, 307-32, 367, 371
teaching, xxiv-xxv, 4-5, 307-12, 315-22, 371; see also T-C
technology, conversational, xxviii, 38-9, 325-6, 335-40, 365-6
therapy, xxiv-xxvii, 4-5, 18-19, 371; see also T-C
THESAURUS, 293, 342-3, 354-6, 370-1
Thomas, L.F., xix-xx, 372-83
'three-card trick', 21-3, 106-7, 366-7; see also personal meaning; repertory grid
Tinbergen, N., 174, 381
tools, xxvi; awareness-raising, 325-6, 328, 334, 353
topics: for grids, 28-37; influence on learning, 7-8, 365
training, xxiv-xxv, 4-5, 307-12, 315-22, 371; see also T-C
TRIAD, 109
triads, 29, 106-7, 366-7; see also elements; repertory grid
triangle of differences, 123-7
TRIGRID, 123-7, 136-41, 186, 342-3, 354-6, 370-1
tutoring, see T-C

understanding, 100, 243-6, 367-8; see also meaning

verbal labels, 178-9, 366-7; see also personal meaning
visualisers, 11-12, 369-70

Wilson, C., 177, 379